Religion and
Politics in America

EXPLORATIONS
Contemporary Perspectives on Religion

*Lynn Davidman, Gillian Lindt, Charles H. Long,
John P. Reeder Jr., Ninian Smart, John F. Wilson,
and Robert Wuthnow,* Advisory Board

Religion and Politics in America: Faith, Culture,
and Strategic Choices, Second Edition, *Robert Booth Fowler,
Allen D. Hertzke, and Laura R. Olson*

Transformations of the Confucian Way, *John Berthrong*

Recognizing the Latino Resurgence in U.S. Religion: The Emmaus
Paradigm, *Ana María Díaz-Stevens and Anthony M. Stevens-Arroyo*

The Culture of Religious Pluralism, *Richard E. Wentz*

New Religions as Global Cultures: Making the Human Sacred,
Irving Hexham and Karla Poewe

Church, Book, and Bishop: Conflict and Authority in Early Latin
Christianity, *Peter Iver Kaufman*

Birth of a Worldview: Early Christianity in Its Jewish and Pagan
Context, *Robert Doran*

FORTHCOMING

Images of Jesus, *L. Michael White*
Ancient Israelite Religion, *Saul M. Olyan*

Religion and Politics in America

FAITH, CULTURE, AND STRATEGIC CHOICES

Second Edition

Robert Booth Fowler
University of Wisconsin–Madison

Allen D. Hertzke
University of Oklahoma

Laura R. Olson
Clemson University

Westview Press
A Member of the Perseus Books Group

Explorations: Contemporary Perspectives on Religion

Copyright © 1995, 1999 by Westview Press, A Member of the Perseus Books Group

Published in 1999 in the United States of America by Westview Press, 5500 Central Avenue, Boulder, Colorado 80301-2877, and in the United Kingdom by Westview Press, 12 Hid's Copse Road, Cumnor Hill, Oxford OX2 9JJ

Library of Congress Cataloging-in-Publication Data
Fowler, Robert Booth, 1940–
  Religion and politics in America : faith, culture, and strategic
choices / Robert Booth Fowler, Allen D. Hertzke, Laura R. Olson. —
2nd ed.
    p.   cm. — (Explorations)
  Includes bibliographical references and index.
  ISBN 0-8133-3490-X (pbk.)
    1. Religion and politics—United States.   2. United States—
Religion.   3. United States—Politics and government.   I. Hertzke,
Allen D., 1950–   .   II. Olson, Laura R., 1967–   .   III. Title.
IV. Series: Explorations (Boulder, Colo.)
BL2525.F677   1999
322'.1'0973—dc21   98-42302
                                                                                          CIP

The paper used in this publication meets the requirements of the American National Standard for Permanence of Paper for Printed Library Materials Z39.48-1984.

10   9   8   7   6   5   4   3   2

To Leon Epstein,
mentor and friend

Contents

Tables and Boxes

Introduction

$\mathcal{R}$eligion and politics and the dynamic interactions between them are visible everywhere in the United States—and they are the focus of this book. Eminently evident is the vigorous presence of the conservative religious movement, which concerns itself with abortion, pornography, sex education, prayer in public schools, and family breakdown. We also see the growing assertiveness of the Catholic Church, which allies itself with evangelical Protestants on abortion and educational choice and with liberal Protestants on foreign policy and social welfare issues. We note the increasing politicization of African American religion and the lasting impact of the two presidential campaigns of one of its most prominent clergy, Rev. Jesse Jackson. We continue to observe vigorous lobbying efforts by liberal religious groups, both Protestant and Catholic. We consider the prominent role played by Jewish groups in American politics, especially regarding support for Israel; their involvement contrasts sharply with the fitful efforts of the growing Muslim population to gain a modicum of political influence. We watch the rising flood of cases in the American judicial system, especially cases brought by religious minority groups. Everywhere one looks, religion and politics appear to be intertwined in American public life.

The aim of this book is to understand the politics of religion in the United States and to appreciate the strategic choices that politicians and religious participants make when they participate in politics. We try to make sense of how religion and politics come together in the voting booth, Congress and the state legislatures, the executive branch, the courts, the interest group system, and the larger culture of the United States. The subject is large and complex, and it features fascinating and often contradictory currents. It is a topic of great importance, since we believe one can understand American politics and society today only with an appreciation of religion's role in them.

We have attempted to make this book accessible. Our goal was to produce a readable and informative text, not a scholarly tome. We have updated the content of the first edition to reflect current trends and important changes in the relationship between religion and politics. One of the chal-

1

Religion and Political Culture in America: The Historical Legacy

$\mathcal{I}$t would be hard to understand American politics today without understanding American religion. And it would be equally difficult to understand either without a sense of history, a sense of how the interplay among religion, politics, and culture has shaped the story of the United States. Since colonial days, religion has played a profound role in molding American culture, directly and indirectly, in ways that no one could have imagined or predicted. In order to sort out the complex history of the relationship among religion, politics, and culture, we have organized this chapter around four themes: the Puritan temper, pluralism, the evangelical dimension, and populism.

The Puritan Temper

The United States was born of religious zeal. Its colonization coincided with, and was fueled by, vast upheavals in Europe that had been unleashed by the Protestant Reformation. None of these was so important as the Puritan revolution, which shook England and inspired many to travel to the New World. Today, of course, the term *puritanical* connotes a narrow-minded, self-righteous rejection of anything pleasurable. But the Puritan legacy is, in fact, a great one; the Puritans bequeathed to Americans strong civic institutions, a sense of national mission, and a reformist zeal that sometimes continues to move American society. Moreover, many contemporary religious people, especially Protestant evangelicals, echo Puritan ideas about human sin and its relation to social organization, politics, and government.

Who were the early Puritans, and how did they contribute to American life and thought? The Puritans earned their name from their desire to "purify" the Church of England and, more broadly, society itself in the late 1500s and early 1600s. Inspired by Calvinist Reformed theology, Puritans reacted vehemently against what they saw as laxity and corruption infecting Christian churches. Infused with a sense of moral urgency, Puritans threatened established political and religious elites, and they suffered persecution wherever they agitated. But if the encrusted Old World of Europe resisted renovation, the American colonies offered a fresh start. Thus the Puritans (along with other religious dissenters) found their way to the American seaboard in the early 1600s.[1]

Though the American colonies had been characterized by religious diversity from the beginning, the Puritans brought with them such a powerful vision that they exercised a disproportionate influence for a century and a half before the Revolutionary War. Perhaps 75 percent or more of the population at the time, regardless of their denominational affiliation, embraced the central tenets of Puritanism. Many of the leading colonial intellectuals were Puritan ministers.[2]

To the Puritans, the new land was not just a place where they could freely exercise their religion. It was literally the New Israel, the promised land on which the faithful could build a holy commonwealth unencumbered by Old World corruption. They called their mission an "Errand in the Wilderness" and saw it as divinely ordained. In the celebrated Puritan phrase that Ronald Reagan often quoted, America was to be "a city upon a hill," a light to the nations. This sense of the nation's providential destiny continues to fascinate, mystify, and sometimes horrify people in other nations. From the "manifest destiny" of westward expansion, to Abraham Lincoln's determination to preserve the Union, to Woodrow Wilson's quest to "make the world safe for democracy," to John Kennedy's Peace Corps, Americans have acted on a sense of special mission and destiny, whether for good or ill. Understanding this legacy is especially important now that the United States, as the only surviving superpower, strives to define its global responsibilities.

Puritan doctrine also helped to nurture self-government. Puritans articulated a "covenant theology" that rejected the idea of the divine right of kings. As the Puritans saw it, political leaders do not derive their authority directly from God; instead they favored government created by a community's covenant with God. Puritan churches were organized on the congregational model, on the basis of an autonomous, self-governing parish. Transmuted into politics, this tradition cultivated an incipient practice of self-governing communities. To be sure, this was not democracy as we know it today. Only the religious "elect," or church members, were allowed to participate. People could become church members only by persuading the church fathers that they were most likely predestined to be saved by God (understood to be only a small percentage of the population). But even if the Puritan colonies were more theocracies than democracies, a form of self-government was fostered from the start. Christian colonists had become outraged by 1775 as England and its established church continued to assert authority over the colonies. The colonists had governed themselves for more than a century, and they believed their religious doctrine gave them the right to do so.[3]

The Puritan emphasis on original sin (or human depravity) also affected American politics, though scholars disagree on the extent. Certainly it contributed to the American fear of concentrated governmental power. If leaders are as tempted by sin as others, then precautions against abuse must be built into the system. Thus some see evidence of the residual cultural influence of Puritan Christian doctrine in James Madison's concern with diffusing and checking power in the national Constitution. Others note that the early Americans largely avoided romantic and utopian thinking of the kind that led to the excesses of the French Revolution. A deeply ingrained understanding of sin thus tempered the practice of popular democracy.[4]

In addition, throughout the nation's history, many Americans have based their social practices on the Puritan understanding of the need to restrain individual sin for the good of the community. As French statesman-author-observer Alexis de Tocqueville noted in the 1830s, the majority of Americans shared the Puritan conviction that freedom did not mean license to do anything one pleased, but rather the ability to do that which is good and right. Tocqueville found Americans remarkably faithful to that idea in their organization of churches, schools, communities, and families. Powerful socialization restrained those human impulses deemed destructive to the community.[5] Thus morally intrusive laws and practices that may seem suffocating today were viewed by most Americans in the past as an aid in liberating the individual from "slavery to sin."[6]

And though one would never guess by watching modern television, many Americans continue to reflect these views. When popular radio commentator and psychologist James Dobson argues that Satan uses human appetites, greed, and lust to destroy us, he is echoing the basic Puritan understanding of the world. The African American leader Rev. Jesse Jackson also shares the Puritan conviction that the moral laws contained in the Ten Commandments protect the individual from self-destructive behavior and are in that sense "liberating."[7]

Puritans emphasized the strong role of the community in nurturing and restraining the individual. This aspect of their outlook is receiving renewed attention today, especially in light of the perceived excesses of individualism. The Puritans and their heirs could be harsh, but in their focus on community they did not leave people in isolation or misery. Women were not abandoned if they became widows; children were cared for; people did not suffer from rootlessness. Religious mores and strong communities restrained the atomizing tendencies unleashed by modern political freedom. Most Americans continue to align themselves at least nominally with religious groups, even if their attendance is sporadic, in part just because they see in churches at least vestiges of this sense of community.[8]

As heirs of the Reformation, the Puritans rejected the view that people need a mediator (or priest) to communicate with God. Thus they placed a great emphasis on education so that people could read and comprehend scripture on their own. Rigorous training in Greek, Latin, and theology, for example, along with the natural sciences, was the heart of the original curriculum of Harvard College, the oldest institution of higher education in the country. Harvard's Puritan charter stated that its purpose was to fight the "Old Deluder," Satan. Most of the nation's older colleges, in fact, were founded by churches, and much of early secondary education was church-based or religiously oriented.

For much of the nation's history Americans lived as "people of the book," familiar with numerous scriptural passages and the rich meaning they evoked. Political leaders from Lincoln to Franklin Roosevelt strengthened their identification with the people through their use of biblical allusions, a tradition carried on by former President Jimmy Carter and Rev. Jesse Jackson, among others, in recent years.

Finally, Puritanism, which has been described as a "vast and extended revival movement," bequeathed to the nation a mighty store of moral zeal that did not often recognize that shades of gray are needed in a political system whose lifeblood is compromise. Critics note how Puritan clergy moved with equal stridency from depicting the French as anti-Christ during the French and Indian War, to viewing the British in similar terms only a decade later during the American Revolution.[9] More sympathetic voices note that sometimes issues cry out for an infusion of religious conviction and fervor. Where would the nation be, they ask, without the uncompromising zeal of the abolitionists in the nineteenth century or the reformist energies of suffragists?

Whether for good or ill, we see evidence of this zeal among religionists across the political spectrum today. When such figures as Rev. Pat Robertson and Rev. Jesse Jackson prophesy against the evils of society and equate their political struggles with God's cause, they are exemplifying the American Puritan tradition.

Religious Freedom and Pluralism

Important as the Puritan legacy was and is, religious pluralism played an equally strong role in shaping the nation's history. The roots of the dominant characteristic of American religion today—its almost bewildering multiplicity of religions, denominations, theologies, and organizational styles—can be traced to early colonial patterns. Moreover, the American break with the 1,500-year European tradition of a state-established church, as well as the eventual constitutional protection for religious freedom, combined to allow religious pluralism to flourish in the New World.

No one planned this turn of events, certainly not the Puritans, who came to the New World to flee persecution of their religion and to create a holy commonwealth in which the most minute details of people's lives were regulated by the community (for their own good, it was believed). Most colonies, in fact, did follow the European practice of establishing a state church, which meant that citizens had to pay a tax to support the colonial church and had to be married by a government-supported minister. Such practices, which seem positively un-American today, were commonplace.[10] In fact, in some states there was often a kind of multiple establishment; different units of local government supported their own chosen churches.[11]

The New England colonies established the Congregational (or Puritan) Church, whereas most southern colonies established the Anglican Church (the Church of England, which later became the Episcopal Church in the United States). But compared with Europe, the degree of religious freedom and experimentation in the colonies was extraordinary. This freedom allowed for the development of a variety of other churches, which evolved into mainstream denominations, as well as a fascination with spiritualism, astrology, and the occult.[12]

Despite the existence of some established churches, dissenting religious people—Jews, Quakers, Baptists, and Catholics from Protestant countries—all found more room to practice their faiths in the New World than they had in Europe. If one found Massachusetts too suffocating, there was always Rhode Island, home to a host of dissenters, or New York, which had Jewish settlers by the late seventeenth century. Then there were the middle colonies, which more than the others provided a model of religious tolerance for the new nation. And there was always the seemingly endless wilderness, which became a haven to nonconformists, ne'er-do-wells, and religious visionaries. So Catholics settled in Maryland and tolerated Protestants; Quakers settled in Pennsylvania and tolerated Lutherans. Baptists agitated for their own freedom in a number of colonies. The idea of the denominational society, in which each faith tolerated the others in order to enjoy its own freedom, began to sprout.[13]

This movement was hastened during the late eighteenth century when the Constitution and the Bill of Rights were drafted and adopted, and the United States was officially formed. The framers of the American Constitution faced an enormous challenge: how to knit together thirteen colonies with different cultures, religions, economies, and climates. The so-lutions, including those relating to religion, were born of necessity and compromise.

Enormous complexities surrounded the founding period, and debates continue among scholars about the motives behind, and meaning of, the religion clauses of the First Amendment to the Constitution. They read: "Congress shall make no law respecting an establishment of religion, or prohibiting the free exercise thereof."

Then as now, the idea of religious freedom meant different things to dif-ferent people. Some of the framers, such as Benjamin Franklin, Thomas Jefferson, and James Madison, hoped to reduce clerical interference with politics, which to them represented a vestige of the corrupt and oppressive European world. Some were Enlightenment deists who believed in a God who had set the universe on course with natural laws and then left it alone. They saw a chance to create an enduring United States free of the intense religious squabbles that infected the Old World.

Jefferson, who had written his own version of the New Testament in which he did not affirm Christ as God, authored the Virginia Statute of Religious Freedom (a precursor of the First Amendment). James Madison shared Jefferson's belief that individual conscience unfettered by the state was the best guide in religion and morality. He therefore fought to dises-tablish the state church in Virginia.

But this is not the full story. Fervent Baptists, along with other religious dissenters, strongly supported constitutional protection of religious free-dom and an end to state support for the established church. Persecuted by Anglican authorities in the southern colonies and Congregational ones in New England, Baptists remembered when they had been jailed for seeking marriages outside the established church or for refusing to pay the church tax. As a result they were natural allies of Jefferson and Madison.

But even for those Christians who initially favored state-established churches, the sheer necessity of protecting their own faiths ultimately led them to support the notion of religious freedom. Given the pluralism among the thirteen colonies, no one could ensure that any particular church would be the one established by the new national government. All believers wanted freedom for themselves, but they concluded that the "only way to get it for themselves was to grant it to all others."[14]

Ambiguity was built into the wording of the First Amendment religion clauses. The language was initially understood to restrict only the federal government's activities, an interpretation that lasted until the 1940s. Moreover, the language on establishment was understood to have a double meaning: It prohibited the national government from establishing a church *and* prohibited it from interfering with established state churches that still existed at the time.[15] But the bold national experiment, as embodied in the

First Amendment, did set the stage for an end to established religion. States acted on their own to end the practice. Massachusetts was the last, disestablishing the Congregational Church in 1833.

This ideal of church-state separation and religious freedom is deeply ingrained in American culture today. It is also one of the central contributions of the United States to the world. To understand the uniqueness of the American experiment, it is only necessary to observe that from the time of the Emperor Constantine in the fourth century to the founding of the colonies in the seventeenth century, European practice and doctrine had been to establish an official religion by state law. So embedded is this practice that state support for religion continues to this day in the largely secular nations of Europe.

By the nineteenth century, state governments continued to help organized religion in a few ways, but it was mostly on its own. Cut off from the paternalistic hand of government and largely freed from persecution, churches became voluntary associations, dependent upon the continued support of their members for survival. And contrary to what some thought might happen, churches thrived. Indeed, in the wake of disestablishment, remarkable religious growth occurred in the nineteenth century, spurred by those denominations—especially Baptists and Methodists—that adapted best to the new conditions. Unsupported by the state and facing the vastness of the frontier, "volunteerist churches" sprang up as circuit-riding ministers traveled to preach the gospel.

A new kind of entrepreneurial climate fostered a multiplicity of worship styles and faith interpretations. If you did not like the local minister or if you held unorthodox views, you could always form a new congregation. Churches blossomed and denominations sprouted as religious entrepreneurs competed with one another for the loyalty of the faithful. Religious practice, in turn, adapted endlessly to changing economic and social circumstances. The peculiar vitality of American religion today (in contrast to the relatively moribund state churches of Europe) owes its origin to this yeasty blend of religious freedom, evangelical fervor, and frontier life.

The fruit of this religious culture was a boom of religious experiments, from utopian communities to the practice of transcendentalism. Another more lasting development was the sprouting of millennial sects. Convinced they could divine the coming of the end times prophesied in scripture, charismatic leaders of the nineteenth century forged new denominations and contributed to the eschatological theology of modern fundamentalism. A host of movements and sects today can trace their lineage to this time, from churches such as the Seventh-Day Adventists to cults such as the Branch Davidians of David Koresh. The popularity of writer Hal Lindsey, whose books on the signs of the imminent second coming of Christ have sold millions, shows the continuing appeal of millennial religion in

America today. It is also noteworthy that a charismatic revival of large proportions began in 1995 in Pensacola, Florida, at Rev. Stephen Hill's Brownsville Assembly of God.[16]

This God-intoxicated culture also produced religious movements in the nineteenth century that the Protestant-dominated society viewed as threats. The most important of these was the Church of Jesus Christ of Latter-day Saints, commonly known as the LDS or Mormon Church. Its story illustrates the limits of tolerance and how religious clashes in America sometimes took violent turns. The Mormon story also illustrates how the American experience gave rise to a popular new faith, one with worldwide membership that is continuing to grow rapidly in the 1990s.

The Mormons trace their origins to the vision of Joseph Smith Jr. of Palmyra, New York, who claimed to have found sacred tablets describing how the lost tribe of Israel migrated to the New World. A farmer's son with limited formal education, in 1830 Smith published his translations of sacred tablets and created what became known as the Book of Mormon. Within a few years of the book's publication, Smith's following became a serious religious movement.[17]

In a sense, Smith was both a product of nineteenth-century American religious culture and a victim of it. He had attended religious revivals, had intense interest in prophecy, and knew the King James Bible well. But the religious sect he fashioned—fervent, disciplined, and situated outside of the mainstream with its practice of polygamy—aroused the enmity of neighbors. Smith's followers were chased successively out of New York, Ohio, Missouri, and Illinois. Smith himself fled a near war in Missouri (where the governor issued an extermination order against Mormons); after founding the city of Nauvoo, Illinois, he was arrested by the Illinois state militia. Before Smith could stand trial, a lynch mob stormed the jail in Carthage, Illinois, and killed him. Smith's successor, Brigham Young, then led the faithful to safety in the Salt Lake Valley, where he founded what amounted to a theocratic nation.[18]

The safe haven was short lived, however, because the territory of Utah came under United States control in 1848, following the Mexican War. To Protestant culture the Mormon practice of polygamy was repugnant, and politicians responded vigorously. President James Buchanan ordered troops to besiege Salt Lake City in 1857, and Congress followed suit by passing a series of laws outlawing polygamy in the territories. Penalties included the confiscation of church property and the loss of citizenship privileges. These actions, which were upheld by the U.S. Supreme Court, ultimately succeeded in forcing the Mormons to conform to the norms of mainstream American culture. The leaders of the LDS Church issued a declaration late in the nineteenth century against plural marriages and pledged loyalty to the laws of the United States. Only then could Utah be admitted to the Union, in 1890.[19]

This story also illustrates how a religious movement can be transformed by its clash with the political mainstream. Today the Mormons claim about 4.7 million members (about 2 percent of the American population),[20] are dominant in Utah and quite influential elsewhere. As one of the fastest growing churches in the nation (which also features a large worldwide missionary program), the LDS Church is widely accepted by most other Americans and is now actively courted by conservative religionists for alliance in political struggles. Still, residual hostility remains; evangelical bookstores continue to feature exposés of the "Mormon cult."

In addition to homegrown pluralism, of course, immigration also fueled religious diversity, and continues to do so. By far the most important legacy of the nineteenth century was the dramatic expansion of the Roman Catholic population. From the mid-1800s on, successive waves of immigrants from Catholic countries such as Ireland, Italy, and Poland poured into the United States. This phenomenon produced the most enduring cultural divide in American history—the Catholic-Protestant split—which shaped partisan political loyalties for over a century and a half. Indeed, one cannot understand the meaning of John Kennedy's election in 1960, or the significance of contemporary alliances between Catholics and evangelical Protestants today, without appreciating how much the divide between Protestants and Catholics has shaped American political history. Though its hegemony has been seriously undercut in recent years,[21] Protestantism was the culturally dominant American religion in the nineteenth century, and Catholicism posed a serious challenge to it.

The Catholic-Protestant split was salient because to the Protestant majority of the nineteenth and early twentieth centuries, Catholics personified the "corrupt" Old World of European kings and papal intrigue. Catholics were derided as "papists" loyal to a Church hierarchy in Rome. Sometimes they also spoke with strange accents or in foreign tongues and had different cultural practices. Thus they were suspect as Americans, and this suspicion did not quickly disappear even as American Catholics adapted to pluralist and democratic norms.

The first large wave of Roman Catholics came in the 1840s and 1850s, as Irish immigrants settled in American cities and built a vigorous and public Catholic Church. A second group came from Germany throughout the second half of the nineteenth century. A third large group came at the turn of the century, this time from southern, central, and eastern Europe. As the Catholic presence grew, some political issues took on overtones reflecting religious division. Temperance was in part a Protestant attempt to discipline Catholic drinkers; campaigns against "corrupt" big city machines also were partly a reaction against the political power of Catholic immigrants and their descendants. Even as early as the Civil War there were occasional Catholic-Protestant skirmishes. Draft riots in New York, in which

Irish Catholics attacked African Americans in protest against military conscription, demonstrated their resistance to the evangelical Protestant tendency to view the Civil War as a holy crusade. Some Catholics, at least, wanted no part of this "Protestant" war.

Political parties, which were much stronger in the late nineteenth century than they are now, naturally channeled this cultural combat, especially in the North. There Protestant voters were disproportionately Republican, whereas most Catholics became loyal Democrats. Something of this division lingers to this day. As we will see in Chapter 4, white Protestants as a group are still more Republican than Catholics.

One of the most graphic examples of the Catholic-Protestant split concerned education. Though church and state institutions were constitutionally separated in nineteenth-century America, Protestant domination of the society produced a kind of cultural Protestant establishment. Public schools frequently used texts—from the Protestant King James Bible to ordinary readers—that to Catholics appeared to promote Protestant values. In defense, Catholics developed their own parochial school system and, where they were strong enough, pushed for state aid for it. Protestants fought against such efforts at the time, just as many do today.

In the wake of the Civil War, Catholics intensified their effort for state support for their church-run schools. Protestant fealty to the Republican party produced its response: the Blaine Amendment, an attempt by the Republican administration of Ulysses S. Grant to amend the U.S. Constitution to prohibit any state governmental aid to parochial schools. Introduced in the House of Representatives by James G. Blaine of Maine in 1875, the amendment became a symbol of anti-Catholic sentiment among the Protestant majority (Blaine, a Republican, became associated with the charge that the Democrats were the party of "Rum, Romanism, and Rebellion"). The proposed constitutional amendment passed the House but fell short of the two-thirds vote needed in the Senate. Republican platforms from 1876 to 1892, however, continued to call for an end to government aid to sectarian schools.

President Grant ignited another church-state controversy when he tried to promote peace among western Native American tribes by allowing churches to operate schools and relief programs on reservations. Sparked by Quaker protests that Indian agencies were corrupt, Grant began appointing Indian agents from lists the Quakers provided, a policy that evolved into formally assigning various churches the responsibility of education and relief on reservations. Roman Catholics were particularly aggressive in meeting this need, supplementing government money with private donations, whereas Protestant groups became skittish about government-supported church schools. By the 1890s, Protestants were agitating increasingly against the program. By 1899 they succeeded in ending it—though not before Catholics had received several million dollars from the federal government to operate Indian schools.[22]

These kinds of battles continued to be fought at the state level. Catholics had to take their case all the way to the U.S. Supreme Court in the 1920s when the state of Oregon decreed that all children had to attend public schools—in effect making parochial systems illegal. Catholics won and the Oregon law was overturned. With that victory, however, the battle shifted once again to state public support, which remains a major issue today.

The Evangelical Dimension

Intimately linked with both the Puritan heritage and the American experiment in religious freedom is the strong evangelical dimension of American religion. We mean "evangelical dimension" in two senses. First, we mean the branch of Protestantism that teaches traditional tenets of Christian faith and stresses the adult conversion experience and aggressive evangelizing (seeking converts). A driving force for much of American history, evangelicalism was the dominant strain of Protestantism in the nineteenth and early twentieth centuries. Its reemergence as a force in the late 1970s brought back a mere portion of its previous influence. Second, the evangelical dimension also refers to the fact that all major churches, to some extent, had to adopt evangelizing strategies to survive in the American religious marketplace. Because evangelical Protestants have been extremely aggressive about seeking converts, evangelical Protestantism has become almost the paradigm of successful church life in America. Whether Protestant or Catholic, Mormon or Muslim, faiths must evangelize to thrive. It can be argued that evangelical Protestants have done so more effectively than any other American religious group. And given the link between culture and politics, the phenomenon of evangelicalism often produces political fallout.

These two senses of the evangelical dimension are intimately related. In a major study of patterns of church growth and decline from the revolutionary era to today, Roger Finke and Rodney Stark show a consistent pattern of evangelical renewal in American religion.[23] Disestablishment, religious freedom, and the frontier combined, they argue, to produce a "religious marketplace." In this marketplace churches thrive or decline on the basis of how well they serve the needs of existing and potential members. And contrary to what we might expect, thriving churches are often more orthodox, more evangelical, and more in tension with the broader mainstream culture than declining churches.[24]

This study confirms what others have argued: Sometimes the overall intensity of the religious experience a church offers wanes; this is usually due to the fact that the church's members have become comfortable and worldly.

Clergy also contribute to this decline in intensity when they grow complacent and accommodating. As a result the church's message becomes watered down and the church itself becomes unable to convey a powerful message about the meaning of life. People yearning for such meaning will therefore leave and seek it in other religious settings. And there is ample evidence that the United States today is a nation of seekers; in fact many people who do not profess any particular faith attend religious services in search of answers to life's questions.[25] As Dean Kelley notes, the "business of religion is meaning," and strict evangelical faiths convey that they really mean what they preach with their often demanding style. Churches that do not convey such conviction cannot expect to flourish.[26] Religious communities must distinguish themselves by conveying clear, consistent, and meaningful messages.

In American history we do see a recurrent pattern of rising sects and declining established churches. For example, Puritan sects of the seventeenth century, which were otherworldly and severe, were eventually transformed into the comfortable Congregational churches of the eighteenth century. When they did become more comfortable, these churches lost a good share of their members to new evangelical congregations born of revivals in the 1730s and 1740s. As these churches in turn became comfortable with the world and less distinct from the mainstream culture, upstart Methodist and Baptist congregations, which had grown dramatically since the founding era, eclipsed them. The cycle continued: As Methodism became the home of an increasingly settled membership and its ministers grew less strict about enforcing traditional rules in the late nineteenth century, a fervent Holiness religious movement drew away a significant portion of its membership.

This dynamic occurs because many people turn to religion in part to get something distinct and different from what can be found in the broader culture. When churches become too worldly, they offer a less unique experience and therefore cease to address this need. Some measure of sectlike tension with the world, along with an evangelical zeal, is necessary for continued church success (Box 1.1).

Consider the experience of the Roman Catholic Church. In America, Catholic priests had to evangelize just like Protestant ministers did. Many "Catholic" immigrants were, in fact, only nominal Catholics, and there were many Protestants reaching out to them in the competitive American religious marketplace. Thus the Catholic Church of the nineteenth century "aggressively marketed a relatively intense, otherworldly religious faith," including devotional activities that produced "its own brand of revivalism."[27] Like Methodist circuit riders, Jesuit missionaries traveled thousands of miles under primitive conditions in order to build their church. The danger for the contemporary Roman Catholic Church is that in becoming "mainstream," it may become too comfortable and accommodating to the world and thus begin to lose its place in the American religious

---

BOX 1.1 ARE HIGHLY PAID MINISTERS THE SIGN OF A DECLINING CHURCH?

Yes, say Roger Finke and Rodney Stark. In their book, *The Churching of America*, Finke and Stark demonstrate that there has been an inverse ratio between clergy salaries and church vitality throughout American history. Upstart churches with few material resources depend on ministers who are willing to make extraordinary sacrifices for their cause.

Low-paid circuit-riding clergy transformed the Methodist Church from a tiny sect in the mid-1700s into the largest denomination in the United States a century later. The Methodist Church grew rapidly in relation to Congregational, Episcopal, and Presbyterian churches, which paid their ministers far more. But as the Methodist Church became more affluent and comfortable with the world—and paid its ministers accordingly—it began to lose its vigor, ceased making high demands on its members, and slipped into decline. Methodism thus lost its "market share" to Baptist and Pentecostal churches, both of which have an abundance of low-paid clergy.

SOURCE: Roger Finke and Rodney Stark, *The Churching of America, 1776–1990: Winners and Losers in Our Religious Economy* (New Brunswick, NJ: Rutgers University Press, 1992), 115.

---

marketplace.[28] Moreover, sociologist Andrew Greeley has recently noted that Hispanic Catholics, who have traditionally constituted an active and vibrant presence in the American Catholic community, are leaving the Church in droves.[29]

The great religious movements in American history have often stimulated significant political upheaval. Consider several major examples of political fallout from Protestant evangelical revivalism, beginning in the eighteenth century and continuing into the twentieth. Religion, for example, played a key role in the events leading up to the Revolutionary War. The religious revival movement of the 1730s and 1740s known as the Great Awakening helped prepare the colonists for the break from England.[30] At this time the educated and upper classes in the cities had largely abandoned Puritan rigors for the more pleasing tenets of Enlightenment rationalism. But the spiritual hungers of the common people could not be satisfied by academic postulates, and they were ready to respond to preaching that touched their emotions and reflected their direct experiences. That is precisely what preachers such as Jonathan Edwards and George Whitefield did as they led a vast revival in the colonies. In the process, they began to transform Puritanism into a less pessimistic and more populist evangelicalism that dominated the culture for more than a century and a half. The Calvinist doctrine of predestination gradually gave way to an emphasis on the conversion experience, which seemed to indicate that one could be born again, or saved, no matter what had gone before. The new worship style emphasized an egalitarian inclusiveness that also served to encourage a more democratic culture.

This religious transformation helped make many common citizens more optimistic and self-confident in their views—and more resistant to religious and political interference from abroad. Protestant evangelical leaders came to view the creation of a new nation as an essential step in God's plan for America, and they mobilized the ordinary people whose support and involvement proved crucial in the war for independence. The seeds of the American Revolution were thus sown two decades earlier, when this change occurred in the minds and hearts of the American people: "a change in their religious sentiments," as John Adams put it.[31]

The evangelical zest for societal transformation continued into the nineteenth century. Led by Baptists, Methodists, and others, church growth ignited broad movements for social and political reform. Believers sought to reduce the distance between their religious visions and the disappointing reality of the world. They established schools, hospitals, and orphanages; reformed prisons; created temperance and abolitionist societies; and passed laws against dueling.

The same energy exists today. For example, evangelist Charles Colson leads the most visible movement for prison reform in the 1990s. Colson is a former "hatchet man" for President Richard Nixon who went to jail for his Watergate crimes. After experiencing a religious conversion, Colson created Prison Fellowship, a worldwide program that not only spreads the Christian gospel among prisoners but fights for reform of inhumane prisons. Lauded by conservatives and liberals alike, Colson's evangelical quest to redeem prisoners and prisons is yet another chapter in a long history of Christian reform efforts.

Habitat for Humanity is another contemporary example. Through this organization, Jimmy Carter and many other Christians imbued with religious faith work to build houses with and for poor people in the United States and abroad. For them, the need to minister to a suffering and limited world is urgent, and their faith provides the reforming energy to make a difference in people's lives.

Special Case: Evangelicals, Slavery, and the Civil War

One of the characteristics of evangelicalism in America has been its Puritan tendency to view politics at times as an unambiguous, cosmic struggle between good and evil. We see this evangelical temper in one of the most momentous, religiously infused movements in the nation's history: the crusade against slavery. No issue so tormented the young nation as slavery, America's "original sin." Black servitude came to the New World with the first colonists. It was a contradiction with both professed political ideals and Christian beliefs from the beginning. Some early leaders such as George Washington and Thomas Jefferson acknowledged this contradiction. Quakers expelled slaveholding Friends in 1776, and antislavery societies sprouted among churchgoing people. But the practice of slavery was so entrenched that the Constitution itself made a "pact with the devil" by accepting servitude and allowing southern states to count, for purposes of allocating members in the House of Representatives, three-fifths of the enslaved population.

A revolution in northern thinking against slavery began in the early 1800s, as antislavery societies sprang up in the wake of religious revivals. These revivals awakened Christian consciences against slavery, and churches increasingly became the fulcrum of antislavery agitation through the decades leading up to the Civil War. Many great revivalists and preachers eventually joined the cause. During debate over the Kansas-Nebraska bill, which allowed the extension of slavery into new territories, Congress was presented with a petition from 3,000 New England ministers who opposed the bill.[32] Some, such as Henry Ward Beecher, went so far as to raise money to buy rifles for the fight over Kansas that preceded the Civil War. The rifles were called "Beecher's Bibles." And, of course, there was Harriet Beecher Stowe, who wrote *Uncle Tom's Cabin*, the religious antislavery novel that was called a "verbal earthquake."[33]

This heightened northern agitation served only to harden southern attitudes. White southern evangelical Protestants came to view the defense of their land and institutions as divinely ordained, and biblical justifications for slavery became common.[34] The evangelical tendency to see political clashes as spiritual struggles between good and evil increasingly characterized both sides. Thus the irreconcilable conflict was, in some sense, a clash of evangelicals.

When war came, preachers in both camps depicted their cause in religious terms. From the pulpits of both the North and South came invocations of God's wrath toward the other side in martial prayers of vivid and bloody mien. Hymns similarly carried an almost apocalyptic message, as this stanza of Julia Ward Howe's "Battle Hymn of the Republic" shows:

> *I have read a fiery gospel, writ in burnished rows of steel.*
> *"As ye deal with my contemners, so with you my grace shall deal";*
> *Let the Hero, born of woman, crush the serpent with his heel,*
> *Since God is marching on.*

But how could both sides invoke God? And how could anyone find God's will in the carnage of the Civil War? These questions deeply vexed Abraham Lincoln, whose story is central to the religious and political history of America. His thinking on the meaning of the Civil War reveals a great deal about the potential of religiously inspired politics.

Lincoln was a product of the pervasively Protestant culture of nineteenth-century America. He memorized passages from the King James Bible and its depiction of the story of God's people, and he filled his speeches with biblical allusions. He shared the Puritan notion that America was the hope of the world, but his vision was tempered by a skepticism about human ability to understand the will of God. Americans might be, in his evocative phrase, "an almost chosen people," but if so, they could also expect to suffer under God's judgment like the ancient Israelites.

The second Inaugural Address (1865) was perhaps Lincoln's greatest speech. Reflecting on the bloodthirsty prayers of partisans, Lincoln observed that "both North and South read the same Bible, and pray to the same God. . . . The prayers of both could not be answered; that of neither has been answered fully. The Almighty has his own purposes." Perhaps, pondered Lincoln, God had prolonged the war as the means to eradicate slavery, something neither side had expected. Perhaps the war was also God's punishment of *both* North and South for the sin of slavery.

Lincoln prayed for a speedy end to the war but accepted that God might will that it last until "every drop of blood drawn with the lash, shall be paid by another drawn with the sword." For Lincoln, this decision was God's. The same God expected him to articulate a forgiving vision of reconstruction and reunification once the war was over: "with malice toward none, with charity for all."

Special Case: Evangelicals and the Crusade Against Alcohol

The crusade against intoxicating drink constitutes another example of evangelical politics, and it provides some important practical lessons for religious partisans today. The crusade, which began in the early 1800s and lasted well into the twentieth century, was one of the landmark efforts by churches to affect American politics. Led by Protestant ministers and laity, it attained a remarkable public following. The temperance movement was in large part rooted in patterns of extraordinary alcohol consumption that had begun in the colonial period and continued long afterward. Alcohol use in the colonies was widespread and included use of hard liquor by youth. Spurred by the hard life on the frontier, consumption rose to extraordinary levels. Alcoholism was a pervasive problem, especially among males. Given the role of the male as breadwinner at the time, this posed an enormous threat to women and children and was debilitating to community life as well.

The early efforts of reformers focused on temperance—to get people to drink in moderation or abstain voluntarily—not prohibition. From the early 1800s to midcentury, temperance societies led by prominent Protestants grew rapidly and became a standard part of the culture. By the 1830s there were more than 5,000 local temperance organizations with more than 1 million members.[35]

The temperance movement belied stereotypes we may have of it today. For example, one key leader was Frances Willard, founder and leader of the Women's Christian Temperance Union. Professor of aesthetics, dean of a women's college, and sympathetic to Christian socialism, she focused on temperance education in the same way that drug education has become a staple in public schools today. As Willard illustrated, liberal reformers frequently led the crusade against drink and were often the very activists who also favored such reforms as child labor laws, health and safety regulations, and women's suffrage. Many women reformers in particular agitated to regulate saloons—which were commonly open twenty-four hours a day and often promoted prostitution—just as they strove to raise the age of sexual consent and to increase prosecutions for rape. They often perceived a need to temper the raw masculinity of frontier America, and it is therefore no surprise that it was in frontier Wyoming where women first obtained the right to vote.

To understand the central role of churches in this movement, it is helpful to trace the history of one of the most effective pressure groups in American political history, the Anti-Saloon League. The League united Protestant pietists across denominational lines in a brilliantly conceived strategic approach that led to political success.

The idea of banning alcohol altogether had simmered for decades before it took root nationally. Neal Dow achieved the first breakthrough by securing the famous Maine Law of 1851, which made the making and selling of alcohol illegal in that state. Later the Prohibition party ran candidates for office, but it faltered because loyalty to the two major parties was too strong. What ultimately did take hold was the formation of a nonpartisan interest group that promoted regulating and closing down saloons. These measures enjoyed broader support than an outright ban on alcohol (some antiabortion activists began to emulate this strategy in the 1990s).

The roots of the movement can be traced to Ohio in 1887, when faculty at Oberlin College joined with local ministers to fight for state legislation granting a "local option" to ban the saloon. Oberlin, which admitted African Americans and women in the 1840s, had been a reform center for antislavery agitation and women's suffrage. It soon became a nerve center for a growing national movement against the saloon. After a vigorous lobbying campaign, local option legislation passed in Ohio and local governments throughout the state began closing down saloons.

In 1895, inspired by this success, Rev. Howard Hyde Russell founded the Anti-Saloon League. Because of its close ties to Protestant churches, which served as the precinct bases for local organization, the League became a formidable national force, able to field 20,000 speakers nationwide for the cause.[36]

What made the Anti-Saloon League successful was its relentless pressure and clear strategic calculation. Knowing that state legislatures would resist, League leaders realized they would win only through ceaseless education, lobbying, and electioneering. The organization overcame the multitude of divisions within Protestantism with a simple message of democratic appeal: Fight for the right of local communities to regulate or close down saloons. League organizers compromised when necessary, formed alliances, flooded wavering legislators with mail, and played hardball with opponents. Where they could expand on Protestant fears of Catholic immigrants, they would. Where they could form alliances with Catholics, they would. State after state fell into line.

Moreover, once local option laws passed, the League moved to get local communities in line. Where they were not powerful enough to close down saloons, they fought to regulate their hours, gambling, and locations. As more and more local communities acted, remaining wet areas became isolated, and most of a state went dry. Then organizers fought to repeal local option laws in favor of stricter statewide prohibition.[37]

The strategy of beginning a political effort in states before acting nationally worked beautifully. In 1900, five states were dry and four held down the amount of drinking by enacting high license fees from sellers. The others had local option, but wet areas still predominated in many of them. The Anti-Saloon League increasingly began to avoid state legislatures, which were often responsive to beer and alcohol interests. They moved instead to get voters to decide about alcohol policy directly through state referenda. State after state enacted prohibition in this manner. Swept by a mood of optimism, the League finally turned to the federal government, where Congress passed the Eighteenth Amendment to the Constitution banning the production and sale of intoxicating beverages. Only the heavily Catholic states of Connecticut and Rhode Island refused to ratify the amendment. Prohibition became the law of the land in 1920.

Though the common understanding today is that this effort to legislate morality failed, evidence suggests that the diverse efforts to curb alcohol consumption—from voluntary temperance to legal prohibition—succeeded in changing drinking habits. One study argues that per capita yearly consumption of alcohol went from an astonishing ten gallons of alcohol in the 1830s to a little over two gallons by 1850. With westward expansion, alcohol consumption went up again. But the prohibition movement succeeded in changing that pattern also. Even after Prohibition was repealed, consumption remained below the 1910 level.[38]

Prohibition represented the high-water mark of the popularity and political clout of pietist (evangelical) Protestantism. But its success helped lead to its downfall. Evangelicals faced increasing opposition throughout the 1920s. One reason is that while Prohibition reduced drinking, it also fueled political corruption and gangsterism and made lawbreakers out of millions of otherwise law-abiding citizens. Moreover, during the Roaring Twenties, the culture itself was changing. Catholics and Jews grew in number and assertiveness, and the religious pluralism of the nation expanded. Evangelical Protestant domination of the culture eroded. The Great Depression was the final straw, making pietist moral concerns far less pressing than economic ones. Though many Protestant churches vigorously fought the repeal of Prohibition, the nation moved on, and Prohibition was repealed in 1933.

Conservative evangelicals responded by retreating into separatist institutions, concerning themselves exclusively with personal salvation. But the patterns of American history would recur—and evangelical politics has reappeared with new energy and new objectives in the 1980s and 1990s.

The Populist Dimension of American Religion

Churches in America, as we have seen, depend upon the voluntary support of the faithful to survive, let alone thrive. But thrive many do. Churches were, and are, the most common means (apart from work and family) by which ordinary Americans get together collectively. To a great extent religion in America is popular religion—and the churches that succeed connect with this reality. Thus popular religion is often a way for people to discover and express their common hopes and concerns. It can be, therefore, a conservative force, helping to preserve traditions people cherish. It can also be a radical force, channeling mass discontent and challenging elites with prophetic denunciations of injustice. Whatever its specific directions, however, popular religion often fosters populist politics focused on mass-based democracy and determined that elites be responsive to the people.

This populist dimension was evident in the religious Great Awakening of the eighteenth century, which fostered grassroots evangelism and prepared colonists for the Revolution. It was present in the crusades against slavery and alcohol. It is alive today in black churches that serve as vital social and political centers for many African Americans, directing both their discontents and their hopes. Rev. Jesse Jackson's religious rhetoric, with its blend of radical economics, traditional morality, and democratic discontent, reflects this distinctive outlook. There is also a kind of populism alive today among Christian conservatives who lash out against the hegemony of "cultural elites." To understand this form of contemporary religious politics it is helpful to note some important chapters in the evolution of popular democracy and populist politics.

As we noted earlier, politics in the early colonies was not fundamentally democratic; citizenship itself was often quite restricted. But in the period leading up to the Revolutionary War and shortly thereafter, evangelical revivals helped foster a more democratic society.[39] After the Revolution, members of churches that had been formed or transformed by the Great Awakening were on the forefront of the movement toward popular democracy.

The drafters of the Constitution did not view direct democracy or majority rule favorably at all. Such figures as James Madison feared popular demagogues and knew that the "demos" could as easily trample on liberty as a single tyrant could. The resulting Constitution, as well as standard suffrage restrictions (the exclusion of women and African Americans, for example) and the lack of strong political parties to mobilize the electorate, ensured that politics in the early nation remained far from fully democratic.

As Nathan Hatch suggests, however, a continuing democratization of Christianity advanced political democracy in the early 1800s. At the forefront of democratized religion were itinerant and often untutored grassroots preachers (especially Baptists and Methodists) who understood the special needs of people on the frontier.[40] Tent revivals, which brought souls to Christ by the thousands, originated in this period (Rev. Billy Graham later updated the setting and technology). Clergy who arose from among the common people dominated this religious life on the frontier because, as George Whitefield has observed, Harvard and Yale divinity schools did not prepare their elite students "to spend half their days in the saddle going from one rural hamlet to another."[41]

Circuit-riding preachers endured real hardships to spread their message to the masses and brought with them a democratic faith that all were equal before God. Many people were profoundly moved by this populist Christianity and began refusing to see themselves as inferior to others. They pushed for elimination of property restrictions on voting and other measures that served to democratize politics. By the late 1820s, mass democracy (among white males only, however) had come to America, propelled in part by Protestant evangelical forces in the young nation.

This link between popular religion and popular democracy emerged again toward the end of the nineteenth century, the era from which the term "populist" derives.[42] This was a time when industrialists garnered wealth while millions of farmers and workers struggled to survive as the nation experienced the development of industrial capitalism. Along with rapid economic growth and ferment came a new set of ideas—especially the gospel of wealth, conspicuous consumption, and social Darwinism. In 1859 biologist Charles Darwin had shocked religious sensibilities with the publication of *The Origin of Species*, with its claim that life-forms developed by a natural process of evolution. Herbert Spencer and William Graham Sumner popularized a social counterpart to this theory, in which competitive "survival of the fittest" was the model of human social evolution. Some saw captains of industry as the "fittest" by virtue of their success and wealth. To critics, this new doctrine provided a suspicious justification for the plunder perpetrated by nineteenth-century robber barons.

This new age and its justifying doctrine clashed sharply with rural Christian life, where more traditional communal norms of barter, shared work, and extended families still operated. This clash of worldviews turned into a fierce political struggle when hard times settled over much of agricultural America for a decade beginning in the 1880s. In both the West and the South overproduction sent commodity prices plummeting. Railroads held a monopoly on freights, and banks' tight money policies forced farmers to pay back loans with deflated money. Then when the weather turned sour, production fell, bank notes came due, foreclosures multiplied, and millions of farmers became impoverished.

From this economic depression arose the populist movement, a political effort by farmers to redress their grievances. Populists formed cooperatives (including African American branches) to avoid creditors, interest groups to lobby, and ultimately a political party that elected a number of governors and members of Congress. Populist organs also fought a war of ideas, linking the plight of the farm community to the rise of exploitative banks, railroads, and robber barons.

For our purposes, what is notable about the populist movement was its religious overtone. Many populists were evangelical Protestants. The crusade took on a distinct revivalist flavor, complete with camp meetings and stirring speeches. The crusade was "a pentecost of politics in which a tongue of flame sat upon every man."[43] Populists sought a series of religiously connected goals aimed at a moral structuring of society, which was also reflected in the Protestant-led temperance movement (many populists were also "temperance men"). They concluded that the threat posed by industrialists required that government act with vigor and authority to protect the people. They proposed some radical ideas, from inflationary monetary policies to outright state ownership of the railroads and the telegraph.

In 1896, Democrats nominated William Jennings Bryan, a fiery speaker who shared the populist repugnance for the emerging industrial society. Bryan could sound like a socialist one minute and a pietist preacher the next. With Bryan, as with many populists, the gospel of the New Testament was the proper basis for a good and caring society.[44]

To be sure, many other pietist Protestants branded the populists and Bryan dangerous radicals. But careful voting studies suggest that Bryan, as a Democrat, did better than expected among pietist Republican voters in the West, although faring relatively poorly among many Democrats (especially Catholics and Lutherans) who were not comfortable with his brand of evangelical politics. Indeed, the two parties, for a time, seemed to have swapped characteristics. Many Republicans shifted from pietist concerns and embraced emergent entrepreneurial capitalism, whereas Bryan Democrats lauded the pietist idea of creating a Bible-based moral social order, insisting like Bryan that "You shall not crucify mankind on a cross of Gold."[45]

Bryan's crusade was inherently limited, however, because it divided rural from urban and undercut traditional Democratic support among Catholics and liturgical Protestants. It could not cut deeply enough into the Protestant loyalty for the Republican party in the Northeast and Midwest. But Bryan's legacy lived on. We even hear echoes of Bryan and populism today—from across the political spectrum—as religious and political leaders denounce "elites" and demand that the "people," in their economic or cultural discontent, be heard.[46]

Conclusion

American religious currents were intimately woven into the social and political development of the United States. In order to provide a road map through this history, we have emphasized the Puritan, pluralist, evangelical, and populist dimensions of American religion. In later chapters we will see how these themes, along with some new ones, help us understand politics and religion today.

Further Reading

Ahlstrom, Sydney. *A Religious History of the American People.* New Haven, CT: Yale University Press, 1972. The standard history of religion in the United States.

Butler, Jon. *Awash in a Sea of Faith: Christianizing the American People.* Cambridge, MA: Harvard University Press, 1990. A bold reinterpretation of the history of Christianity in America.

Clark, Norman H. *Deliver Us from Evil: An Interpretation of American Prohibition.* New York: Norton, 1976. A thoughtful modern history of the Prohibition experience.

Finke, Roger, and Rodney Stark. *The Churching of America, 1776–1990: Winners and Losers in Our Religious Economy.* New Brunswick, NJ: Rutgers University Press, 1992. Pioneering work on a market interpretation of the history of American religion.

Hicks, John D. *The Populist Revolt: A History of the Farmers' Alliance and the People's Party.* Lincoln, NE: University of Nebraska Press, 1961. The classic account of populism.

Kleppner, Paul. *The Cross of Culture: A Social Analysis of Midwestern Politics, 1850–1900,* 2d ed. New York: Free Press, 1970. Fascinating account of the interactions of religion, ethnicity, and politics in nineteenth-century America.

McLoughlin, William. *Revivals, Awakening, and Reform: An Essay on Religion and Social Change in America, 1607–1977*. Chicago: University of Chicago Press, 1978. Especially useful discussion of the Great Awakening.

Marty, Martin E. *Pilgrims in Their Own Land: 500 Years of Religion in America.* Boston: Little, Brown, 1984. Sweeping history by one of the nation's foremost church historians.

Miller, Perry. *Errand into the Wilderness.* Cambridge, MA: Belknap Press of Harvard University Press, 1956. The classic intellectual history of Puritanism.

Morgan, Edmund. *The Puritan Dilemma: The Story of John Winthrop.* Boston: Little, Brown, 1958. A readable introduction to Puritan religion and politics.

Noll, Mark, ed. *One Nation Under God? Christian Faith and Political Action in America.* San Francisco: Harper, 1988. An excellent series of essays on Christianity and American politics.

Reichley, A. James. *Religion in American Public Life.* Washington, DC: Brookings Institution, 1985. A superb introduction to its subject.

2

Contemporary Religion and Political Culture

In this chapter we analyze the status of religion in America and chart its impact on the nation's political culture. At one level there has always been great continuity in religion's vitality in the United States. But the picture is complex. Religious pluralism continues to grow while secular forces, especially at the elite level, also make their mark. To understand the political ramifications of these forces, we must examine the status of religion in contemporary American society.

The Status of Religion in the United States

American religion today is thriving, active, and diverse. Some 94 percent of Americans profess a belief in God or a universal spirit, with well over 80 percent describing God as a heavenly father reachable by prayer.[1] Seventy-one percent of all Americans say they have absolute confidence in God, and 75 percent believe that God can work miracles.[2] Ninety-two percent express a religious preference,[3] and 58 percent say that religion is "very important" in their lives.[4] Nearly six in ten believe that "religion can answer all or most of today's problems."[5] Clearly the United States is a believing society. This is not to say that all Americans are religious, of course. Some scholars point to the existence of a small but growing segment of secular Americans, many of whom have become increasingly politically active in recent years, as evidence of a "culture war" in the United States.[6] Still, the vast majority of Americans make religion an important part of their lives.

One way to understand the dimensions of faith in the United States is to compare Americans with citizens of other nations. On every measure—belief in God and Christ, born-again experiences, church attendance, and daily prayer—Americans consistently express far more religious faith than

British and French people, as well as citizens of most other European nations. While some 70 percent of Americans express belief in life after death, only 66 percent of those in Great Britain, 66 percent in France, and 66 percent in Denmark share this belief.[7] Sixty-five percent of Americans believe in the devil versus 28 percent of those in Great Britain. Over 40 percent of Americans say they pray daily compared with only 18 percent in Great Britain.[8]

Moreover, a recent study has shown that Americans are far more likely than Europeans to believe in the creationist account of the origins of the human species. George Bishop found that 45 percent of all Americans believe that God created humans in their present form; another 40 percent believe that humans developed from less advanced life-forms through God's guidance. Only 7 percent of those surveyed in Great Britain shared the creationist perspective.[9] Finally, when asked how important God is in their lives (on a scale of one to ten with ten being highest), survey respondents in America averaged 8.2, which was the top score among sixteen Western nations surveyed. By comparison, ratings in Italy were near 7; in Great Britain below 6; in France and Japan below 5; and in Sweden below 4.[10] Though some recent indications suggest a revival of faith in Europe, the gap with the United States remains large.

On the other hand, among nations outside Europe and the Pacific Rim, the United States is not so exceptional. We see evidence of religion's continuing strength, and often its resurgence, from the Middle East to Latin America to Africa. This is especially true in the many areas of the world where Islam is influential. From this perspective, the United States is hardly unusual, and it is Western Europe that is the exception.

There are some intriguing differences beneath the overall figures for the United States. Faith is especially important to women and minorities, for example. Two-thirds of women in the United States say religion is very important to them, compared with less than half of men. An amazing 82 percent of African Americans, compared with 55 percent of whites, agree.[11] In fact, African Americans give the highest average responses to the question about the importance of God of any group Gallup has surveyed around the world.[12] This high salience of religion is the basis for the tremendous political role of the black church, which we explore in later chapters.

The U.S. population is decidedly Christian, with 85 percent claiming adherence to some form of Christian faith.[13] As many as eight in ten Americans have some confidence in Jesus' divinity, for example, and six in ten say that the "only assurance of eternal life is personal faith in Jesus Christ."[14] Two-thirds say they have made a "commitment to Jesus Christ."[15] Seven in ten believe in life after death (and most of those believe their chances of getting to heaven are good!), though fewer believe in hell. Most Americans have a high view of scripture as well, with over half saying it is the inerrant (as opposed to just inspired) word of God; only 10 percent explicitly reject any divine connection with scripture.[16]

Many Americans also reject strictly scientific explanations of life on Earth. According to one survey, some 46 percent espouse the creationist view that God created humans basically as they are within the last 10,000 years. Another 40 percent believe that God used evolution to create all forms of life on Earth.[17] Only 9 percent share the view set forth by most prominent biologists that purely material forces govern the evolution of life.[18] Once again, women and African Americans are more likely to embrace traditional religious beliefs. These figures help us understand why doctrinally conservative churches continue to grow while their theologically liberal counterparts struggle to keep their flocks together.

A sizable portion of Americans say they have had extraordinary spiritual experiences. One-third say they have had a powerful religious awakening that changed their lives. Forty-one percent claim to be "born-again" Christians.[19] Experiences with faith healing, hearing God, and being filled with the Holy Spirit are also commonly reported. When sociologist and Catholic priest Andrew Greeley looked at the evidence, he proclaimed the United States a "nation of mystics." This was an exaggeration, but for a notable portion of the population extraordinary experiences are part of life (Box 2.1).[20]

Americans invest considerable trust in their religious institutions and clergy. For years, Americans have expressed confidence in organized religion, more so than other private and public institutions. Moreover, clergy consistently rank highest among sets of social leaders in terms of public regard for their ethics and honesty. Confidence in clergy dropped briefly in the wake of the televangelist scandals of the late 1980s, however, and the church was passed by the military as the most trusted institution in the nation. Still, the public expresses more confidence in organized religion than it does in the U.S. Supreme Court, Congress, banks, public schools, television, organized labor, and big business. Here again, Americans are distinct from those in other Western nations. Whereas Americans express more confidence in churches than they do in the public schools, for example, the figures are reversed in Germany.[21]

Many Americans are also churchgoing people; in fact, 28 percent say they attend weekly, and another 28 percent say they attend at least monthly.[22] Some scholars, however, argue that people are less than truthful in responding to surveys about church attendance.[23] It is quite possible that many Americans have in fact become more secular in their habits but are unwilling to admit it. Even if attendance figures are inflated, the fact remains that church participation is the single most common group activity in America. Among religious groups, evangelical (conservative) Protestants attend services most frequently in America today, followed by Roman

BOX 2.1   MEASURING AMERICAN RELIGION

Afterlife is steady, Hell is down 2 points, and
biblical inerrancy is up after heavy trading.

Reporting on the results of surveys often invokes images of the stock market. This is because polling organizations like Gallup register monthly ups and downs, as well as long-range trends, regarding the American public's religious faith and committment. And though scientific surveys are a reasonably reliable way of gathering information, it is important to be aware that they are not precise.

There is some error involved in all surveys, and sampling techniques and wording changes can have a big impact on results. This is why different surveys produce somewhat different results. Another problem is the trade-off that exists between the survey's length and the detail that respondents are able to provide. A small number of respondents may be asked a large number of questions, or vice-versa. To do both is prohibitively expensive. Thus information on membership in smaller religious groups, which do not register more than a blip in a 2,000-person national sample, is unreliable. Larger surveys provide better raw numbers for small groups but less detailed information generally. Another problem with surveys is that some people are simply harder to reach than others, so there is undercounting here and there.

Catholics (whose weekly attendance has been in decline since the 1960s), with mainline (theologically liberal) Protestants and Jews trailing far behind. As we will see in Chapter 4 when we discuss voting behavior, this pattern has increased the political clout of evangelical voters while reducing that of mainline Protestants.

On balance, the portrait of religious America is one of enduring faith. Whether this makes much difference in the daily lives of Americans, let alone in their politics, is another matter. Critics suggest that religion in America is like the proverbial prairie river, a mile wide and an inch deep. They note an obvious gap between high levels of apparent faith and considerable business dishonesty, tax fraud, sexual promiscuity, marital infidelity, family breakdown, cheating in school, crime, violence, and vulgarity in the popular culture. George Gallup Jr., whose surveys demonstrate the widespread appeal of religion in the United States, has concluded that much of American faith is indeed shallow, biblically illiterate, and marked by a gap between faith and ethics. As evidence of this gap one could consider the continued popularity of President Bill Clinton despite a myriad of widely publicized sex scandals. Gallup finds many teens, for example, who say they are born again but are not more behaviorally conservative than their peers.[24] On the one hand, these findings are not too surprising given the powerful secular forces at play in the popular culture. A society that celebrates the individual pursuit of happiness and unfettered capitalism, some suggest, will produce pervasive hedonism and materialism that compete with religious socialization.[25]

On the other hand, we have evidence that religious belief and practice do make a difference in people's lives. Research suggests that religious conviction and practice are correlated with personal happiness, physical health, and general life stability.[26] But salience and authenticity of religious conviction matters more than nominal affiliation: the greater the faith or practice, the more intense the benefits, irrespective of denomination. Thus strong religious commitment apparently contributes to longer lives, speedier recovery from injuries, greater happiness, fewer psychological disorders, and a lowered risk for depression and suicide.[27] Religious people, moreover, are far more likely to stay married, to express happiness in marriage, and to have extended sex lives within marriage—notable findings given how much family breakdown has hurt children and society at large.[28] On the social and civic level, religious people are more likely than the secular to contribute to charities, vote, and become involved in the community.[29]

Religious institutions also play an important role in helping to sustain a healthy American civic life. In a huge study of civic voluntarism, a distinguished team of scholars headed by Sidney Verba found that churches provide a crucial venue in which people may develop "civic skills." The argument is that people are more likely to participate in politics when they have done things that occur frequently in church settings, such as organizing meetings. People who are deeply involved in churches or synagogues, therefore, may be expected to possess substantial civic skills.[30]

In a slightly different vein, a variety of scholars have argued that places of worship facilitate interactions among people that contribute to what Robert Putnam has termed "social capital."[31] Social capital, which refers to networks of relationships and trust among citizens, has been shown to contribute to the effectiveness of government and even the economy. And social interactions in places of worship help shape political attitudes as well, as both Christopher Gilbert and Kenneth Wald and colleagues have demonstrated.[32]

Religious commitment also translates frequently into activism. This often comes in the form of evangelism: the effort to win converts or bring new members to one's religion. This is a must for churches in the competitive environment of American religion, where some churches grow and others decline. For example, the conservative Assemblies of God grew by some 70 percent in one decade (and continues to grow rapidly, especially among Hispanics[33]), while the liberal United Methodist Church declined by 8 percent. The thriving LDS (Mormon) Church illustrates well the importance of active evangelism. The Mormons send out an estimated 50,000 young missionaries each year worldwide, and the LDS Church's remarkable growth rates and aggressive missionary activity have led some to predict that it could be one of the major world religions by the middle of the twenty-first century. Churches are very active in American society. A large share of the charitable giving in the United States is done by churches. People of modest means are particularly likely to donate almost exclusively through religious outlets. This generosity enables churches to operate an impressive array of social organizations, hospitals, schools, universities, charitable agencies, and international relief organizations. Even small denominations make their presence felt. The Seventh-Day Adventists, with only 791,000 members in the United States,[34] support ten liberal arts colleges, two universities, a seminary, a medical school, and numerous welfare agencies. Private education, of course, is a major activity of many religious groups. The Catholic Church operates the largest religious educational system, with 9,000 elementary and secondary schools attended by 3 million students. Evangelical Protestant schools enroll nearly 1 million children in 11,000 smaller schools, and an additional 5,000 religious schools enroll over 600,000 students.[35]

Social involvement by churches has clear political ramifications. Church-run charities, adoption agencies, and international relief programs operate in a milieu that is heavily influenced by government. Interaction between these institutions and government is inevitable. A large number of the religious charities and hospitals, for example, receive government money to perform their services.[36] Moreover, no major health-care changes can succeed without the participation of religious hospitals. Thus public policy and organized religion frequently meet, and religious institutions fully understand the importance of these inevitable interactions.

A less widespread, but more controversial, activity of religious groups is political activism. Political efforts that grow out of a church's charitable or educational ministries are common. So is public testimony on issues by church leaders, as are ministerial exhortations to vote. It is also common for clergy to speak to social and political issues from the pulpit. Far less common is religion's overt involvement in partisan politics. Most ministers are not comfortable endorsing candidates from the pulpit or raising money for them. Such efforts can be divisive and threaten a church's tax-exempt status.[37] In some cases, however, active lay members (or ministers) use their church as an organizational base for political efforts. In the 1950s and 1960s, the civil rights movement was based in African American churches.[38] Today, the antiabortion movement and the Christian Right depend on such a base of churches.

One reason American religion has so much vitality is its pluralism. In Europe, people who become alienated from the established church simply drift away from it; in America people are more likely to form or join a new church. A bewildering diversity of religious expression continues unabated in the United States and remains its defining characteristic. A constitutional

doctrine that protects religious freedom, a relative openness to immigration, and a tradition of individualism that promotes the continual formation of new sects combine to foster American religious pluralism.

Part of this pluralism, of course, is reflected in the division of people into
the familiar categories of Protestant, Roman Catholic, and Jew. Today one
must add Muslim, Buddhist, and Hindu. Moreover, diversity within these
broad traditions increases the pluralism of American religion. Every
branch of Judaism may be found in the United States, including Reform,
Conservative, Orthodox, and the ultraorthodox Hasidim. The United
States is home to virtually every Protestant denomination or sect in existence, some of which are very diverse of their own right. Consider the
Baptists as one example. There are black Baptist denominations and white
ones, fundamentalists and moderates, northern branches and southern
ones. Indeed, there are several hundred Baptist groupings, a pluralist reality that nonetheless exaggerates Baptist unity because every one of these
groupings considers itself sovereign. There are also a myriad of independent evangelical churches sprouting, some affiliated with national organizations, others entirely separate. Even the Catholic Church with its clear
hierarchy is pluralistic. There are liberal and conservative Catholics, a host
of religious orders from Jesuits to Maryknolls, and numerous religious lay
groups from the most traditional to the decidedly radical. The patchwork
of American pluralism also includes small pacifist churches, such as the
Quakers, Brethren, Mennonites, and Amish, as well as Mormons,
Jehovah's Witnesses, black Muslims, Native American religionists, view-
ers of television ministries, pre- and postmillennial fundamentalists, Pentecostals and charismatics, evangelical Presbyterians, high church
Episcopalians, and members of gay churches[39]—not to mention people
who join the host of small cults that sprout with regularity.

Protestant Christianity remains the faith of a majority of Americans
(around 60 percent or somewhat less), with Catholics accounting for a sizable 23 percent (or more),[40] and the remaining population comprising
Jews, Orthodox Christians, Mormons, Muslims, adherents of other faiths,
the unaffiliated, and those who do not believe at all (Box 2.2).

Getting a good handle on actual church membership is harder than it
might seem. Churches keep their own records and they tend to count *members* according to their own, often differing, methods; independent opinion
surveys of people's *religious preferences* look at another, broader picture
and do not always arrive at the same results. Nonetheless, the general out-
lines of affiliation provide a basic sketch of American religious pluralism.
And religious preferences fluctuate over time, as Table 2.1 illustrates.

The tremendous diversity that characterizes American religion has frequently given rise to intense cultural clashes. Roughly one-fourth of the
American population is Catholic, one-fourth white evangelical Protestant,

BOX 2.2   THE CHANGING PROFILE OF
RELIGIOUS AMERICA

Current Religious Affiliations

Protestant	
Baptist	19 percent
Church of Christ	2 percent
Episcopalian	2 percent
Lutheran	7 percent
Methodist	9 percent
Pentecostal	2 percent
Presbyterian	5 percent
Other Protestant	14 percent
Roman Catholic	23 percent
Jewish	2 percent
Mormon	1 percent
Other	4 percent
None	10 percent

Selected Religious Groups: Membership Change, 1966–1996

Episcopalian	–44 percent
Methodist	–38 percent
Roman Catholic	–3 percent
Southern Baptist	+8 percent
Mormon	+96 percent
Jehovah's Witnesses	+119 percent
Assemblies of God	+211 percent
Church of God in Christ	+863 percent

SOURCES: George Gallup Jr., *The Gallup Poll: Public Opinion 1995* (Wilmington, DE: Scholarly Resources, 1996), 260; Russell Shorto, "Belief by the Numbers," *New York Times Magazine* (December 7, 1997), 60.

less than one-fourth liberal mainline Protestant, and nearly one-tenth African American Protestant.[41] When we categorize people by religious persuasion, evangelicals are the most numerous. It is also noteworthy that there are more conservative members of liberal denominations than there are liberal adherents of conservative denominations.

The political significance of religious pluralism is manifold. Pluralism acts as a check on the political impact of any religious group; no one group dominates, nor can it. Religious pluralism also requires a willingness on the part of activists to overcome theological differences in the interest of coalition building, which is a must for successful political endeavors.

TABLE 2.1 American Religious Preferences, 1992–1996

	Percent Protestant	*Percent Catholic*	*Percent Jew*	*Percent Orthodox*	*Percent Mormon*	*Percent Other*	*Percent None*	*Percent Undecided*
1996	58	25	3	1	1	3	7	2
1995	56	27	2	1	1	5	6	2
1994	60	24	2	1	1	4	6	2
1993	57	26	1	2	1	5	6	2
1992	56	26	2	1	1	4	7	2

SOURCE: http://www.prrc.com/data.html.

Deeply held convictions must sometimes be modified if effective political alliances are to result (Box 2.2).

The Major Religious Traditions and Politics

Discussion of the major religious traditions constitutes much of this book. These broad traditions—evangelical, liberal, and African American Protestants, Catholics, and Jews—often remain distinct in their history, theology, ethnic makeup, and attitudes toward politics. Moreover, these traditions are politically distinct, although, to be sure, the boundaries sometimes become blurry. The theological orientations of many African American Christians, for example, are firmly planted within the evangelical world, yet because of the American legacy of slavery and segregation, black churches developed in directions that diverge from white evangelical churches. We discuss the black church tradition only briefly here, however, because Chapter 7 is devoted entirely to it. In addition to the five major American religious groupings, of course, are the Mormons, who do not fit neatly into any category, along with a host of smaller sects, which we treat more fully in Chapter 9.

Evangelical Protestantism

As we saw in Chapter 1, much of American history has been influenced by evangelical Protestant culture. By the 1920s that evangelical presence seemed to be in retreat, but it reemerged decades later with considerable vigor.

An important watershed for modern evangelicals was the year 1976, when presidential candidate Jimmy Carter said he was a "born-again Christian." It was at that time that evangelicals burst onto the pages of the elite press and into academic consciousness; a bevy of journalists made pilgrimages to the South to discover just what evangelicalism was. Then George Gallup Jr. stunned the literati by announcing that fully one-third of Americans claimed to be born-again evangelicals. Some surveys now put that figure at over 40 percent.[42] Conservative churches were evidently offering precisely what their members found lacking as the society rushed headlong into liberal modernity: strong faith, meaning, and community. One reason for the incredible growth in evangelicalism in the United States has been the presence of active evangelical student organizations on college campuses. InterVarsity Christian Fellowship, founded in 1941, had almost 41,000 members in 1997, and Campus Crusade for Christ, founded in 1951, had close to 24,000.[43]

But this evangelical phenomenon would have remained of limited interest had the religious Right (which is another name for the Christian Right) not burst onto the scene as a political force in the late 1970s. It began with isolated protests by parents against public school texts in the mid-1970s; gained momentum through the movement to defeat the Equal Rights Amendment led by Phyllis Schlafly; and hit stride with the creation of the Moral Majority and other national groups in 1979. Ronald Reagan acknowledged white evangelical voters in the 1980s and embraced their concerns, at least rhetorically.[44] By the end of the 1990s white evangelicals had become one of the most loyal and important Republican constituencies.[45]

What does it mean to be an evangelical? That question may be answered by self-identification or by a statement of beliefs and characteristics. Around 44 percent of the population (including a majority of African Americans) answer "yes" to the question, "Do you consider yourself a born-again or evangelical Christian?"[46] This question taps a central tenet of Protestant evangelical Christianity: the need for an adult conversion, or a "born-again" experience. Evangelicals also hold a highly respectful view of scripture, and for some this means a strictly literal interpretation of the Bible. Evangelicals also accept the orthodox tenets of the Christian faith (Christ's divinity, his atoning death and resurrection, everlasting salvation or damnation) and are committed to the great commission to evangelize others by spreading the good news. At least a third of the American population share most of these beliefs.[47]

Evangelicals also share a common language and basic assumptions. Evangelicals ask others, "Are you saved?" or, "When did you commit your life to Christ?" Though a number of denominations are heavily evangelical (the Southern Baptist Convention [SBC], the Lutheran Church–Missouri Synod, the Church of the Nazarene, the Assemblies of God, and most of the major African American denominations), born-again Christians are scattered throughout the Protestant world. Indeed, there are even evangelical "renewal" groups within liberal mainline denominations and some evangelically oriented local Presbyterian and Methodist congregations.

By far the most important distinction within the evangelical world is a racial one. Normally when scholars and commentators speak of evangelicals, they are referring to *white* evangelicals. Yet many black Baptists and Pentecostals are also fervent evangelicals. Moreover, decreased segregation and increased racial tolerance have brought increased interaction between white and black evangelicals. The Southern Baptist Convention, for example, now trumpets its growing black membership, and many Pentecostal and charismatic congregations are truly interracial. There have even been some modestly successful efforts by Christian Right leaders to build alliances with black clergy on such issues as school prayer, abortion, gay rights, and pornography. The evangelical Christian Coalition, for example, undertook vigorous initiatives to reach out to the African American community in 1996, including its Samaritan Project to assist central city neighborhoods and its Save the Churches Fund to rebuild burned churches.[48] It has since scaled back these efforts, however.

Nonetheless, a considerable gulf remains between black and white evangelicals. African American churches feature a unique blend of theological conservatism and political progressivism; piety is combined with prophetic witness. In black churches one hears the "liberationist" messages of the Bible about God's mercy toward the poor and the captives and His harsh judgment of the rich and powerful. This combination lends itself naturally to political liberalism, at least on economic and civil rights issues. The vast majority of evangelical African Americans are also loyal Democrats, which is just another indication of how they continue to exist in a world apart from their white evangelical brothers and sisters.

Beyond race, a number of theological and cultural divisions also exist within the evangelical world. Here pluralism reigns, just as it does elsewhere in religious America. There are "mainstream" evangelicals who accept the need for humans to interpret scripture and exhibit less hostility toward the broader culture than such Christian Right leaders as Rev. Jerry Falwell and Rev. Pat Robertson. There are fundamentalists who tend to be biblical literalists, militant toward the "fallen" culture around them, and often angry.[49] There are premillennialists who expect certain biblical prophecies to come true before Jesus returns for his thousand-year reign on Earth (the popular writer Hal Lindsey fits this category). And there are postmillennialists who believe a Christian reign will precede Jesus' second coming (the small but influential group of Christian Reconstructionists, who hold that believers should structure society as a theocracy on the basis of Old Testament law, fit here). There are Pentecostals and charismatics who stress the availability of gifts of the spirit—such as speaking in tongues, faith healing, and prophecy.[50] Though Pentecostals and charismatics are fervent believers in traditional values, fundamentalists and other evangelicals remain skeptical of them because of their strong emphasis on personal spiritualism. There are also a variety of television and radio evangelists, some of whom actively compete with one another.

We see this diversity reflected in leading evangelical personalities. Such diverse figures as Rev. Billy Graham, Rev. Jerry Falwell, Rev. Pat Robertson, Charles Colson, and Rev. Bob Jones III are all evangelicals, but so are the African American preacher Rev. E. V. Hill and Mississippi community developer John Perkins. Senator Jesse Helms (R–North Carolina) represents the evangelical world in elective office, but so does Representative Tony Hall (D–Ohio). There are both evangelical Democrats and Republicans serving in Congress and in state governments.

One way to clarify this diversity is to think of the evangelical world as a tree with several main branches and numerous smaller ones. We have already spoken of the African American branch. Another main branch is represented by the National Association of Evangelicals (NAE). This group says it wishes to transform the world spiritually and is generally conservative politically, but not militant. Another branch is fundamentalism, which has historically been separatist, biblically literalist, and more militantly opposed to the secular world.[51] Finally, there is the fast-growing Pentecostal/charismatic branch, whose members share many of the political views of fellow evangelicals, but whose vibrant religious practice and emphasis on spiritual gifts sets them apart. Whereas a fundamentalist church service usually features traditional Bible reading and conventional preaching, charismatic congregations enjoy contemporary music, speaking in tongues, and a free-form worship style.[52] Though some of these distinctions may seem trivial to outsiders, to evangelical leaders they present a very serious challenge to political unity.

A major recent change in the evangelical world involves attitudes about political participation. Evangelicals have long viewed politics with distaste; political activity constituted an engagement with the sinful world God meant them to eschew. To be sure, many evangelical churches have always stressed the civic duty of voting, but beyond occasional local issues like gambling or alcohol, not much effort was expended on politics. That left the political field open for liberal mainline churches, which rode the crest of civil rights and antiwar activism in the 1960s.[53] But by the 1970s all of that began to change. Many evangelical leaders came to believe that the government and the broader culture had become dangerously secular and intrusive, so they felt they had to fight back. Others felt inspired to rekindle the nineteenth-century evangelical commitment to bringing the gospel message to all corners of society. Moreover, evangelical churches were growing. Their members were becoming better educated and more affluent, and their television and radio ministries more popular. They had the motivation to fight and increasing resources to do so.

Not all evangelicals, however, agree with each other politically. Many moderate evangelicals oppose the tactics and even the aims of the religious Right—some vigorously so. Some fundamentalists oppose the recent turn to national politics, because such a turn means engaging with the fallen world. Fundamentalist pastor Bob Jones II once called Jerry Falwell the most dangerous man in America because he thought Falwell's political efforts would undermine the fundamentalist aim of separating from the broader (sinful) society. Television preachers, moreover, are by no means universally popular among the born again. Southern Baptists, for example, voted heavily against Pat Robertson in the 1988 presidential primaries (and at least some voted for fellow Southern Baptist Bill Clinton in 1992 and 1996).

One small evangelical branch provides a kind of left-wing political witness. Represented by sociologist and Baptist pastor Tony Campolo, Jim

Wallis of the radical group Sojourners, and Ronald Sider, founder of Evangelicals for Social Action, this branch exercises some influence in religious circles. Evangelicals for Social Action was founded in 1978 and works for social justice, gender equality, and the preservation of the natural environment. It says it views injustice in all forms as "a personal affront to God."[54]

As a group, evangelicals are more conservative politically than many other religionists, but real fissures belie the depiction of a disciplined army marching to take over America. Still, as we show in Chapter 4, most white evangelical voters have realigned into the Republican party and now constitute a key GOP voting bloc in both national and local politics. Beneath the diversity of theologies and traditions, therefore, lies a broad and growing consensus in support of conservative politics. How political leaders deal with this constituency will determine a key dimension of American politics in the years to come.[55]

Liberal Protestantism

Liberal Protestantism takes its name from theology, not politics. Theological liberals view the Bible as inspired by God but by no means literally true in all ways. They also argue that scripture must be read in the context of history and modern science. This does not mean liberal Protestants somehow abandon the central tenets of Christian faith, but they do place more emphasis on the goal of gradual, reflective spiritual development and less on the "born-again" conversion experience. For liberal Protestants, the "simplistic" literalism of fundamentalists, the "undisciplined" emotionalism of Pentecostals, or the "questionable" claims of faith healing among charismatics can indicate a lack of mature, reasonable faith.

Here, too, considerable variation exists from church to church. Mainline Lutherans (adherents of the Evangelical Lutheran Church in America, or ELCA) maintain their distinct liturgical tradition and ethnic roots; Methodists still stress doing good works in the world as a manifestation of faithfulness; Episcopalians often treasure a formal high mass; and some denominations, such as the United Church of Christ, are far more theologically liberal than most others. Despite these differences, however, liberal Protestants do have a lot in common, not only in theology but in worship style. In liberal Protestant churches one does not hear fiery sermons about sin and damnation. More common are scholarly discussions of the meaning of divine incarnation, the ethical insights of Jesus' teachings, and the like. Services are orderly, with well-prepared choral and organ music. Liberal Protestant churches are also more accepting of skepticism about portions of the Bible than their evangelical counterparts. Bible discussions, therefore, are likely to focus on the profound moral precepts contained in the Bible and to welcome examinations of the context of biblical times. For example, in discussions of the Apostle Paul's statements about wives submitting to husbands, one would likely hear about how Paul was captive to his patriarchal Jewish culture. This is not to say that there are no traditional religionists sitting in the pews of the liberal mainline churches—there are indeed—but most mainline church leaders do not reinforce their outlook.

In many liberal churches, doctrinal orthodoxy has given way to a general call to love one's brother or sister. Moreover, Christian love is often interpreted in collective ways as well as individual ones. Mainline clergy in particular embrace the idea of a "social gospel," in which Christians must address the world's injustices not just by individual charity but by collective efforts to change societal structures. Mainline seminaries, which had been relatively liberal both in theological and political terms since the early twentieth century, became radicalized during the civil rights movement in the 1960s, leading an entire generation of clergy to have some exposure to liberal politics.[56] Indeed, unless one changes such structures, mainline church activists argue, injustice and oppression will continue irrespective of personal acts of mercy and love.

Among mainline clergy and denominational leaders this theological liberalism often correlates with activist liberal politics. Among their parishioners, however, there is usually no clear link between liberal theology and liberal politics, especially on economic issues. This may be particularly true in congregations that do not face great financial challenges.[57] Indeed, the majority of Presbyterians, Methodists, and Episcopalians vote Republican, just as we would expect them to do on the basis of their socioeconomic status. Theological liberalism does correlate, however, with liberal attitudes among parishioners on such issues as abortion and gay rights. Here theological and political beliefs are more consistent.[58] When this liberal theological orientation became the dominant force in the major Protestant seminaries, fundamentalists split off and formed their own churches. Because of this split, liberal Protestantism came to control the so-called mainline denominations that once dominated the Protestant world.

To understand liberal Protestantism, therefore, we need to examine mainline churches. In the 1950s the well-established Protestant denominations could still lay claim to the appellation "mainline." Methodists, Presbyterians, Episcopalians, Congregationalists, many Lutherans, and northern (American) Baptists, as well as their shared organizational arm, the National Council of Churches (NCC), did indeed represent a kind of core culture. From Main Street to Wall Street to Washington, mainline Protestants were well entrenched. And when radical social movements gathered steam in the 1960s, mainline leaders were predisposed to political engagement and sympathetic with the aims of these movements.

The 1960s exercised a strong influence on liberal Protestant leaders. They embraced—and continue to embrace—issues of poverty, racism, sexism, and oppression—and the unjust structures they see as incorporating these evils. If one were to summarize how liberal church leaders view their work, it would be as champions of "peace and justice." By this phrase they mean their mission is to fight for their interpretation of justice, especially for the poor. They support expanded government funding for welfare and economic assistance for developing nations. They also work for world peace, which often translates into frequent criticism of American foreign policy as being too militaristic and too oriented toward gain for the U.S. economy.

Two significant problems confront mainline clergy. First, most lay members do not share the ideological orientations of their national leaders and activist local pastors. Indeed, because of the structure of political decision-making in these large denominations, lay members are not always consulted as political positions are developed.[59] Most Methodists, Lutherans, Episcopalians, Presbyterians, and northern Baptists are moderate to conservative on many political issues. Furthermore, they are either ignorant of their leaders' political activities or simply disagree with them. For example, the majority of mainline Protestants voted for Ronald Reagan, even though many of their leaders frankly despised what he stood for and opposed him at every turn. Critics thus speak of "generals without armies" in liberal churches.[60] Government leaders therefore often discount the pronouncements of mainline clergy because they know few of them have lay support.

A second problem is that mainline Protestantism does not appear to represent the religious wave of the future. Membership declines have been so dramatic that by the 1990s observers began describing mainline churches as "old-line" or even "sideline." Explanations abound, including the assertion that by turning to politics the mainline churches turned off their parishioners.[61] But Dean Kelley offered the most convincing explanation when he argued that because the "business of religion is meaning," stricter and more demanding churches, especially conservative evangelical congregations, offer more of what people desire from religion. As we saw in Chapter 1, this theme echoes throughout American history; whenever churches relax their firm beliefs, they decline in proportion to more demanding churches. Theological liberalism, then, not political activism, may undermine the ability of mainline churches to compete in the religious marketplace.[62]

Despite their decline, however, mainline churches still possess a wealth of inherited capital in the form of buildings, institutions, and endowments, as well as the loyalty of a considerable number of parishioners who remain uncomfortable with evangelical expressions of faith. Local churches continue to operate a host of food banks and day-care centers, and national church organizations operate large hospitals, charitable agencies, and highly respected international development organizations. Thus extensive community involvement continues to thrive in liberal Protestantism. Overt political advocacy, which is pervasive at the national level, is usually more sporadic and cautious at the local level.

Liberal Protestants remain important players in American culture and politics, and they benefit when the winds of political change blow their way. Largely shut out of the White House and executive agencies in the 1980s, the liberal Protestant community found the Clinton administration far more congenial to their goals.[63] But their long-term prospects do not look favorable; unless membership decline can be arrested, the importance of liberal Protestants in American society will diminish.[64]

Roman Catholicism

In Chapter 1 we observed that the Catholic-Protestant split played an important role in shaping American political culture for a century and a half. Catholics were profoundly "other" in American society, living in ethnic neighborhoods and sustaining separate institutions to shield themselves from the dominance of Protestant culture. This cleavage lingers in a few places, but it is mostly a memory. Modern suburban Roman Catholics are hardly outsiders anymore. Indeed, complaints are heard among Catholics themselves that the distinctive Catholic culture has been lost amid a homogenized mass society. Still, Catholics remain theologically distinct, preserving a sacramental approach to the "mysteries" of the faith and a unique intellectual tradition.[65]

Today, Catholics inhabit a strategic place in American politics. Catholics are key swing voters, and both liberal Protestants and conservative evangelicals frequently seek political alliances with Catholic elites. To the envy of liberal Protestant leaders, Catholic bishops make news whenever they speak on political issues. But Catholics, especially at the parish level, do not speak with a single political voice; here pluralism reigns just as it does elsewhere in religious America. This lack of unity hampers Catholic political clout, though the size of the Catholic population, along with the institutional strength of the Church, ensure that Roman Catholics are important players in the American system.

Some historical perspective is helpful in appreciating the place of Catholics in America today. The Catholic Church is literally the oldest institution in the world; it is a truly global church with a distinct hierarchical structure headquartered at the Vatican in Rome. This adds a unique dimension to Catholic politics. One cannot focus merely on the American Church; one must consider the pope and his relationship to Church officials. The structure of the Church hierarchy is rooted in two millennia of history. Priests belong to a diocese or archdiocese (a geographic area) headed by a bishop or archbishop, who receives his appointment from the pope. A few of these archdiocese leaders around the world become cardinals, the top elites of the Church responsible for electing a new pope each time the "bishop of Rome" dies.

At the heart of Church structure is the doctrine of apostolic succession, the idea that the pope is literally the successor of the Apostle Peter. Though hierarchy remains a defining characteristic of the Church, American Catholicism is also characterized by pluralism. Diverse holy orders of monks and nuns, each with a distinct focus and élan, exist alongside the traditional structure. Thus one finds left-wing Jesuits, feminist nuns, and Maryknoll missionaries spreading liberation theology alongside more conservative orders and groups of Catholic fundamentalists (such as Opus Dei) that are fiercely loyal to orthodoxy (and to Rome).

One of the distinctive features of the Catholic Church is its appreciation of politics. Throughout European history, for example, the Roman Catholic Church was deeply enmeshed in statecraft. Politics was not alien to Church leaders then, nor is it today. There has always been intense Catholic political involvement around the globe, from the Philippines to Latin America, from Eastern Europe to the United States. In one sense this political comfort level is an asset: the Church and its activists do not need to overcome as much resistance to politics as do some evangelical Protestants. On the other hand, for much of American history the Catholic Church was seen as a suspect institution because of its political legacy. The Church's roots in the medieval world of kings and princes, along with its skepticism about democracy and religious freedom, placed it at odds with the American liberal tradition. Well into the twentieth century, for example, the Catholic Church resisted many liberal democratic reforms and allied itself with authoritarian governments.

These tendencies created a huge problem for American Catholics, whom many Protestants viewed as lacking a fundamental commitment to American democracy and liberal freedoms. Though Catholics in fact embraced the American creed of democracy and individual liberty, whether or not such an embrace was compatible with their tradition remained in question into the 1950s.[66]

What changed all that was a profound revolution within the Catholic Church itself, a revolution in which the United States and its Church leaders played a pivotal role. In 1961 Pope John XXIII declared that the Church needed to open its windows and get some fresh air. For only the second time in Catholic history he called for a meeting of the world's bishops to modernize the Church. Vatican II, as this meeting came to be called, lasted from 1962 to 1965. It was an earthquake for the Church, and its effects are still being felt. Through it the Church embraced democracy and ordered liberty, and for the first time Protestants were accepted as fellow Christians rather than as apostates. The mass, which had always been said in Latin, would thereafter be in the vernacular of the people. And the bishops' councils in each country were given greater authority to speak on behalf of the Church in their respective lands. One worldwide impact of the Church's change, as Samuel Huntington shows, was to help lead a wave of democratization in formerly authoritarian and largely Catholic nations.[67]

In the United States Vatican II legitimated the Catholic accommodation with liberal democracy and accelerated the mainstreaming process for Catholics. Even before Vatican II leaders of the American Church had begun to assert themselves politically. After Vatican II the bishops were joined by many others in the Catholic Church in political engagement. Nuns and priests marched in civil rights demonstrations, and Philip and Daniel Berrigan, radical antiwar priests, poured blood on the Pentagon to protest U.S. involvement in Vietnam. Catholic charities and the Campaign for Human Development sponsored antipoverty projects in inner cities and rural backwaters. The Catholic Church also lent support to the farmworker movement led by César Chávez.

Ultimately Vatican II led to an increased role for the National Conference of Catholic Bishops (NCCB), which is made up of the approximately 260 leaders of Catholic dioceses in the United States. Headquartered in Washington, D.C., the NCCB and its staff arm, the United States Catholic Conference, now lead the Church's social and political efforts. The politics of the bishops are not easily categorized, which is why they are sought after by conservatives and liberals alike today. On social welfare, labor, civil rights, and military policies the bishops have taken a rather liberal posture. At least some of this agenda stems from the Church's historical concern that untrammeled industrial capitalism exploits workers and undermines the dignity of work and the vitality of community and family. On the other hand, the Church's positions on abortion, sexual ethics, and educational policy are quite conservative.

Liberals celebrated when the bishops drafted their "pastoral letters" on nuclear arms and the economy; conservatives applauded the bishops when they condemned abortion. Similarly, liberal activists welcomed the support of Catholics who lobbied against Reagan's support for the Nicaraguan Contras, and conservative Republicans embraced the cause of Catholics fighting for day-care vouchers and school choice. The Church is thus strategically placed as a sort of bridge between evangelical and liberal Protestants.

Ironically, at the very time that the Catholic Church is so strategically poised to exercise influence in American society and politics, it shows signs of the same malaise found in mainline Protestantism. Since Vatican II Catholic attendance rates at masses have declined and numerous nominal

"Catholics" pay little or no attention to the Church. The post–Vatican II generation of American Catholics practices what might be called "cafeteria-style Catholicism" in that they pick and choose what to take from the faith and what to leave.[68] The number of young people willing to become priests and nuns is very low, and trends suggest a huge shortage in the near future. A variety of explanations account for this apparent stagnation. Conservatives charge that the Church changed too radically after Vatican II in the 1960s, whereas liberals claim that backward policies on birth control, celibacy, and the role of women have alienated some of the faithful. The most penetrating explanations for the loss of vitality, however, point to the evolution of American Catholicism into a mainstream denomination. As we saw in Chapter 1, church growth and decline in the American religious marketplace operate with a seemingly ineluctable logic. To the extent that the Catholic Church becomes a mainstream institution in the United States, it becomes subject to the profound encounter with the outside world that leads to church decline.[69] Many Hispanic Catholics, for example, have been leaving the Church in favor of evangelical Protestantism, particularly in its Pentecostal incarnations. In fact, sociologist Andrew Greeley reports that one in seven Hispanic Catholics left the Church between 1970 and 1995.[70]

This should not surprise us. Catholics today are no longer found disproportionately among the working classes, as was the case at the turn of the century. Now Catholics and white Protestants have equal educational levels and are equally represented in professional and managerial occupations. And herein lies a paradox. When American Catholics resided at the lower end of the socioeconomic scale they represented a distinct and much more unified constituency that tended to accept the authority of the Church. Today many Catholics, especially highly educated ones, do not feel bound by the dictates of the Church, let alone its political efforts. The Catholic Church, as a consequence, does not exercise anywhere near the clout that it might. Nonetheless, it remains a major player, if a somewhat stumbling one (Box 2.3).

Judaism

Jews are the most successful minority group in America by almost any standard. After suffering persecution for centuries throughout the world, Jews have found the United States, with its doctrine of religious tolerance, a remarkably hospitable place. This is not to say that they have not faced discrimination, especially in past years, for they have. But the constitutional protection of religious liberty, combined with a social system that rewards strong families, hard work, and education, has enabled Jews to prosper in the United States. By every measure—education, income, professional status—Jews are disproportionately well off. Jews have moved into

---

BOX 2.3   A TALE OF TWO CARDINALS

Two leading figures in the American Catholic Church in recent years have been the late Joseph Cardinal Bernardin, who was Archbishop of Chicago, and John Cardinal O'Connor, Archbishop of New York. As leaders of the two largest archdioceses in the nation, these cardinals have engaged in highly visible political advocacy on such wide-ranging issues as nuclear arms, abortion, education, and AIDS policy. Though they had much in common, their differences were notable. Cardinal Bernardin, who died in 1996 after a widely publicized battle with cancer, was viewed as the more liberal of the two. He chaired the committee that drafted the so-called Peace Pastoral *(The Challenge of Peace: God's Promise and Our Response)*, which was critical of American nuclear policy during the Reagan years.

While he opposed abortion, Bernardin argued that the Church should not advance a single-issue political agenda. Rather, in a famous metaphor, he argued that the Church's political efforts should form a "seamless garment," representing a consistent ethic of life encompassing opposition to abortion, the death penalty, and weapons escalation, along with public support for the health and welfare of the poor. Cardinal O'Connor, on the other hand, has criticized this implicit deemphasizing of abortion. While he is supportive of public efforts on behalf of the poor, he continues to believe that "destruction of the unborn" is the most important issue facing the nation. O'Connor has also been the subject of much criticism because of his opposition to gay relationships and condom distribution in schools.

SOURCE: Timothy Byrnes, *Catholic Bishops in American Politics* (Princeton, NJ: Princeton University Press, 1991).

---

positions of prominence in business, law, higher education, journalism, and entertainment in which they exercise considerable influence.[71]

However, we need to avoid reinforcing stereotypes of Jewish cabals working to take over the world. The truth is that Jews have played by the rules in the American system and have played very well. Moreover, their influence is sometimes exaggerated. Constituting less than 2 percent of the population,[72] their voting strength makes an impact only in cities and states where their numbers are concentrated. And Jews are influential on some issues—backing for Israel, for example—because they enjoy broad support from Christians.

Though a discussion of Jews obviously makes sense in a text on religion and politics, it must be noted that many, perhaps most, Jews are in fact largely secular. Synagogue attendance rates are low, and many Jews admit to agnostic views about God. Indeed, one of the serious issues in Jewish circles today is the problem of maintaining a Jewish culture without a religious dimension. Intermarriage rates among American Jews are high, and children are often raised with only a vague sense of their Jewish heritage. Calls to reclaim that heritage only confirm the concern. In an effort to reconnect with their heritage, an increasing number of American Jews are embracing new forms of spirituality such as meditation, the renewal movement of Rabbi Zalman Schachter, and the mysticism of kabbalah.[73]

Jews have a well-deserved reputation for political liberalism that derives from a combination of several factors. The majority of American Jews with religious affiliation are adherents of the more theologically liberal branches of Judaism: Conservative and Reform. Reform Jews in particular have roots in the liberal Enlightenment and are assertive champions of civil liberties and church-state separation. Moreover, because of their historical experience of persecution, most Jews believe passionately in the need to maintain a society that tolerates minorities and cares about the disadvantaged. Support for unions, welfare, progressive taxation, civil rights, and other liberal causes often places Jews in the vanguard.

Jews exercise political power through a host of robust organizations, the oldest of which is the American Jewish Committee, which was formed in 1906. These organizations exercise influence because they have thriving local chapters, seasoned leaders, and a clear political agenda. Though that agenda is undeniably liberal, there is some evidence of pluralism in American Jewish politics.[74] Indeed, Orthodox Jews and the Hasidim (ultraorthodox Jews) often oppose abortion; support government aid to religious schools; applaud the enforcement of antipornography laws; back various measures to check the advance of secular culture; and vote Republican. But this is not the extent of Jewish pluralism. A highly influential group of intellectuals, including former liberals Norman Podhoretz and Irving Kristol, were leaders of the neoconservative movement, helping to formulate the reaction against the "excesses" of the 1960s and 1970s. Who was it that wrote Dan Quayle's famous family values speech that blasted Murphy Brown, to the applause of conservative Christians? It was none other than a Jewish man, William Kristol. Kristol is the son of Irving Kristol and historian Gertrude Himmelfarb and now heads the conservative magazine *The Weekly Standard*.

Support for Israel, of course, is a major concern for most American Jews, since the connection between American Jews and Israelis has traditionally been deep. No other nation has as many Jewish citizens as the United States; in fact there are more Jews living in the United States than in Israel. There is a great deal of contact between Jews in both lands. But for American Jews, Israel is more than a familiar land where close friends and relatives often live. It has also been the Jewish homeland and a place of refuge (off and on) for several millennia. This is another reason for the strong commitment to the preservation of Israel, but there is often plenty of disagreement with particular Israeli leaders and policies. Thus many American Jews support Israel both politically and financially. In turn, Israeli leaders keep in close contact with Jewish leaders and organizations in the United States (Box 2.4).

A New Cleavage in American Society?

Now that we have examined the various groups that make up the American religious fabric, it is useful to examine the considerable evidence that a new cleavage is emerging between conservative religionists (both Catholic and Protestant) and liberal religionists (who sometimes ally themselves with secular people).[75] One way to understand this fault line in the American political culture is to recall the pietist versus antipietist split in the nineteenth century. That split has been restructured among today's denominations. Thus pious Catholics in the 1970s and 1980s found themselves increasingly aligned with conservative evangelicals on social and political issues. Both groups opposed abortion, supported public expressions of faith, criticized secular public schools, and decried the effects of the sexual revolution. Theological and cultural differences remain between orthodox Catholics and evangelical Protestants, to be sure, but politically they are forging increasingly strong alliances against what they see as a secular assault on traditional values. In the same way, liberal Protestants find they often have more in common with liberal Catholics, Jews, and secular elites than they do with conservatives in their own denominations.

Thus a kind of pietist cultural alliance is forming between conservative evangelicals, fundamentalists, orthodox Catholics, and a few Jews—in what activists call "an ecumenism of orthodoxy." On the other side are liberal Protestants from the mainline denominations, liberal Catholics, most Jews, and a small but highly influential secular segment of American society. Black religionists often join the liberal alliance—indeed, sometimes they lead it— but they do not fit in perfectly. The majority of black Protestants are born-again evangelicals who blend in liberal stands on civil rights, economics, and foreign policy. The growing Muslim population also presents a mixed case. On some issues (especially U.S. policy toward Israel) they join with liberal Protestants in arguing that the Palestinian people have a right to a homeland, but on abortion, drugs, alcohol, sex education, and state aid for parochial schools they line up with conservative evangelicals and Catholics.

This fault line cuts across gender lines too. Conservative evangelical women and female prolife Catholic activists are often at odds with their liberal sisters in the mainline churches and Jewish temples. Female prolife activists overwhelmingly see feminists (especially secular ones) as their adversaries, despite the fact that feminists generally applaud their style of political assertiveness.

Because this cultural divide between traditional religionists and theological liberals transcends gender, class, region, and even race, it suggests that

BOX 2.4   INCOME RANKING BY RELIGIOUS GROUP
(MEDIAN HOUSEHOLD INCOME, 1991)

Jewish	$37,000
Unitarian Universalist	$35,000
Agnostic	$33,000
Episcopalian	$33,000
Eastern Orthodox	$32,000
United Church of Christ	$30,000
Presbyterian	$29,000
Disciples of Christ	$29,000
Buddhist	$29,000
Hindu	$28,000
Roman Catholic	$28,000
Church of Christ	$27,000
Lutheran	$26,000
Christian Scientist	$26,000
Mormon	$26,000
United Methodist	$25,000
Muslim	$25,000
Seventh-Day Adventist	$23,000
Assemblies of God	$22,000
Church of the Nazarene	$22,000
Jehovah's Witnesses	$21,000
Baptist	$21,000
White Baptist	$23,000
Black Baptist	$17,000
Pentecostal	$19,000
Church of the Brethren	$19,000
Holiness	$14,000

SOURCE: Barry A. Kosmin and Seymour P. Lachman, *One Nation Under God: Religion in Contemporary America* (New York: Harmony Books, 1993), 260–265.

it is a powerful trend in religious politics.[76] But we hasten to add that complexities abound in the fluid religious milieu of the United States, as we will see in later chapters.

Conclusion

Religion in America flourishes with pluralism and vitality, yet it does so amid contrary secular forces. Thus we have something of a paradox. On the one hand, professed faith seems to be strong and churches remain heavily involved in society. On the other hand, moral and ethical problems abound and many powerful institutions—such as the mass media, government, business, public schools, and universities—seem to operate with a secular logic that is relatively independent of religious influence.

One of the perennial questions, therefore, is why such an apparently thriving religious community does not exercise more political influence. A major reason lies in religious pluralism. Because unanimity will never exist on most issues, politicians hear a babel of competing religious voices. When religious groups do form a united front, they can be quite effective. But those instances are rare enough to prove the rule: Pluralism dilutes any group's power.

Religious influence is also checked by the nature of the American system. The framers of the Constitution constructed a political order designed to disperse, fragment, and check power. A large majority, for example, is normally required to pass national legislation, which can then be diluted or nullified by the actions of states, bureaucracies, or the courts. To achieve real clout, therefore, a movement or group must work successfully on a number of fronts—from the states to the national government, from Congress and the president to the courts and bureaucracies, from lobbying and electoral mobilization to the shaping of public opinion through the mass media. The challenge is formidable, and continuing success is rare. Though the American political system cannot be dominated by a single movement, it is open enough to provide access to the smallest group. Thus our political structure, which is one that disperses and checks power, ensures many religious groups the chance to have some political influence and blocks each one from achieving real dominance.

Further Reading

Byrnes, Timothy. *Catholic Bishops in American Politics.* Princeton, NJ: Princeton University Press, 1991. An excellent case study on the political activities of Roman Catholic bishops in the United States.

Corbett, Julia Mitchell. *Religion in America,* 2d ed. Englewood Cliffs, NJ: Prentice-Hall, 1990. A good introduction to the sociology of religion in the context of the United States.

Gallup, George H., Jr., and Jim Castelli. *The People's Religion: American Faith in the 90's.* New York: Macmillan, 1989. A valuable data source on religion in America.

Hammond, Phillip. *The Protestant Presence in Twentieth-Century America: Religion and Political Culture.* Albany, NY: State University of New York Press, 1992. Argues that religious pluralism has cost mainline Protestantism its sovereignty over America.

Kelley, Dean. *Why Conservative Churches Are Growing: A Study in Sociology of Religion.* San Francisco: Harper, 1977. The classic work on the rise of evangelical Protestantism and the decline of the mainline.

Wald, Kenneth D. *Religion and Politics in the United States,* 3d ed. Washington, DC: CQ Press, 1997. An accomplished introduction to religion and politics in the United States.

Wuthnow, Robert. *The Restructuring of American Religion: Society and Faith Since World War Two.* Princeton: Princeton University Press, 1988. A thoughtful book reflecting on the evolution of religion in the United States.

Wuthnow, Robert. *The Crisis in the Churches.* New York: Oxford University Press, 1996. An important argument about the changing fortunes of various American religious groups.

3

The Politics of Organized
Religious Groups

*T*hough Americans love individualism and celebrate the heroic individual in literature and history, political power in the United States flows mostly from collective action. To get what you want out of politics you have to get organized. In this chapter we examine organized religious groups by tracing their roots and exploring their responses to the issues of the day. Religious leaders, of course, do not like the term "lobbying" because of its unsavory overtones of shady dealings and corruption. We use the term neutrally, however, to describe any organized effort to influence the direction of public policy. Our emphasis will be on the key players in the interaction between religion and politics in America and how they play the game. We focus on efforts in Washington, D.C., but we also note that increasing state and local activism often emulates national efforts.

One of our central themes is (again) the diversity of religious groups and its effect of preventing any single group from becoming dominant—despite sometimes overheated claims by one group or another. Up to this point, anyway, no single religious group has proven permanently successful; the fortunes of these groups rise and fall with the times as some play the political game better than others.

The Evolution of National Religious Lobbies

Religious advocacy, as we saw in Chapter 1, is as old as the republic. At first, this advocacy was episodic and restricted largely to state and local government for the very good reason that the federal government's role in the lives of American citizens was limited. Issues important to religious people, such as child welfare, prison reform, education, temperance, and gambling, were strictly state and local matters, and the common pattern was that temporary groups would coalesce when issues arose.

In this century, however, the growing prominence and reach of government, especially at the federal level, has acted as a catalyst in the growth of ongoing church lobbies. In the past fifty years a permanent religious presence has emerged in Washington, D.C.; many religious lobby groups are also linked to state or local affiliates. Though the growth of national lobbies occurred principally after World War II, there were precursors. The Methodist Church established a Washington office in 1916 to promote Prohibition; the National Catholic Welfare Conference set up shop in 1919; and the Quakers, who opened the first full-time registered religious lobby in 1943, worked primarily to protect conscientious objector status. By 1950 there were at least sixteen religious offices in Washington, mostly representing mainline Protestant, Jewish, and Catholic groups.[1]

Since then the number of religious lobbies has grown to over one hundred. Included in this number are different Catholic, liberal Protestant, evangelical, Jewish, and African American interest groups. And the pluralism does not stop there. Smaller lobbies range from Hasidic Jews to Muslims to gay and lesbian Christians.

The question is, why has there been all of this growth in the organized political representation of religious interest groups? After all, as Daniel Hofrenning has observed, many religious interest groups have a more difficult time acclimating themselves to political realities than do their secular counterparts.[2] Part of the answer lies in the flowering of American religious pluralism and the growing sense that such pluralism creates an imperative for religious groups to get organized to protect their collective interests. In the 1950s, Baptists established a lobby to "watch" the Catholics; Arab Americans have coalesced recently to counteract the influence of the Jewish lobby for Israel.

Also, as the federal government has expanded, many groups have arisen to monitor its impact on their religious activities. Since churches operate a host of hospitals, schools, charitable organizations, and development agencies, they are often affected by government policy. Finally, many religious people simply have come to the conclusion that they must be involved in politics to promote or defend the values of their religious traditions. Whatever the reasons, the diversity, scope, and number of religious groups lobbying in Washington has never been greater (Box 3.1).

Strategies for Effective Advocacy

The politics of pressure groups has not changed fundamentally since the nineteenth century.[3] New dimensions have been added to the craft, to be

---

BOX 3.1   MENNONITE CENTRAL COMMITTEE: PACIFIST LOBBY

The story of the Mennonite Central Committee illustrates how the actions of the federal government have spurred the growth of church lobbies. One of the perennial issues for pacifist denominations (like the Mennonites) is how to protect their members from compulsory military service. Thus the Mennonites were shocked in 1967 when they learned that proposed selective service legislation during the Vietnam War would not allow the kind of broad conscientious objector provisions that Mennonites enjoyed during World War II. Church leaders traveled to Washington, testified at congressional hearings, and ultimately brought about changes in the law. In the wake of that battle, the Mennonite Central Committee established a permanent Washington office in 1968. Its first director was Deton Franz, a thirty-six-year-old pastor who directed Mennonite lobbying until his retirement in 1994. Though small by Washington standards, the Mennonite office remains a visible player in the religious community.

SOURCE: Keith Graber Miller, *American Mennonites Engage Washington: Wise as Serpents, Innocent as Doves?* (Knoxville: University of Tennessee Press, 1996).

---

sure, including advanced communication technology and the increased role of the mass media. But effective advocacy is—and has always been—a combination of outside pressure and inside influence coalescing in favorable circumstances.

Outside Pressure

Effective interest groups must have a loyal network of members at the grassroots level who can bring pressure to bear on members of Congress and state legislators. The threat of electoral defeat remains a powerful motivator of modern politicians, and groups with many members or well-heeled contributors can make a difference in a politician's fortunes on election day. The kinds of outside pressure interest groups bring vary tremendously by group and context. Mass mobilization, a technique commonly used by conservative Protestant organizations, represents one approach. Television and radio ministry connections, computer lists of contributors, and affiliated churches can generate a sea of letters to elected officials, which can attract attention and (occasionally) affect policy. In the spring of 1994, a deluge of mail from home schoolers spurred Congress to eliminate a provision in an education bill they felt would seriously threaten home schooling.[4] The latest trend in direct mail among religious lobbies has been the use of the Internet. A variety of religious organizations now support web sites that allow supporters to send e-mail about issues of concern directly to Congress. The Christian Coalition even sells a special software package for those who wish to maintain direct and constant contact.[5]

Mass mobilization is necessary but rarely sufficient for success. Members of Congress often discount "artificially inseminated" constituent letters. Effective supplements include elite mobilization and key contact strategies. Indeed, in some cases a few influential community leaders and party contributors can have greater clout than a million relatively unsophisticated supporters or newcomers to politics.

But money and status, though they magnify political influence, are not everything either. Members of the liberal nuns' lobby, NETWORK, for example, have some influence because their members are well read, knowledgeable about politics, and hooked into informational networks around the globe through their religious orders.

Effective religious organizations commonly develop smaller lists of key contact people who can be reached by fax, e-mail, or phone trees for quick responses. For liberal Christian groups this is a way to overcome their lack of a large grassroots following. For Jewish groups it is a way to magnify the considerable influence they already exercise. Ideally, a key contact is a highly committed, politically sophisticated person who knows a member of Congress personally. Religious interest groups attempt to identify such individuals in every state and congressional district.

The key contact approach represents the perfect marriage of the Washington lobbyist and the grassroots following. To appreciate the effectiveness of this strategy, imagine a member of Congress participating in a hearing. At one point the member expresses skepticism about a bill's provisions. A lobbyist in the room notices this lack of support and immediately communicates with contact people from the member's home district. The contact people receive a fax or call at their workplace asking that they register their concern immediately. They respond by calling or sending a fax or telegram to the member. Stories circulate in Washington about groups that are able to deliver telegrams or faxed protests to members of Congress even before a day's hearing is over. Whether or not that happens, members of Congress know that their moves are being watched and being communicated at the speed of light to influential contributors, community leaders, or even their personal friends back in the district. And because most members of Congress want to be reelected, they have to care deeply about what people in their district think.

Money, of course, speaks loudly in contemporary politics. Most religious groups, however, do not form political action committees (PACs), organizations that donate money to candidates. Nor are clergy normally in the position to make substantial individual contributions. Thus religious groups are not major players in the money game, with a few exceptions. Jewish organizations, especially pro-Israel groups, do support PACs; they constitute important sources of money for both individual members of Congress and political parties. Some Jewish citizens are also major contributors and fund-raisers—particularly for the Democrats—and this buys them access. African American churches, as tax-exempt institutions, cannot form PACs or make direct financial contributions, but they do sometimes allow their property to be used for political fund-raisers. They also frequently invite candidates to speak during services. Since overt political involvement is more accepted in the African American religious community than in the rest of organized religion in the United States, favored candidates are sometimes able to raise money through direct appeals made in churches.

Rev. Jesse Jackson raised healthy sums of money through such church appeals, and other politicians have also done so. Conservative evangelical organizations, such as the Christian Coalition, have raised large amounts of money for registration and voting drives. Such efforts may aid specific candidates supported by the Christian Coalition (or the Republican party generally) just as much as if cash contributions were made directly to candidates.

By and large, however, religious actors are not players in the political money game. Some argue that this protects them from the corrupting influences of fund-raising and allows them to present a clearer moral message to leaders. Sometimes that may be true; religious leaders, at their best, present politicians with visions of the public good undiluted by narrow self-interest. But money does speak, and religious leaders often resign themselves to the fact that they will not have that tool at their disposal.

Finally, outside pressure also involves efforts by religious actors to shape public opinion on key issues of the day. When a religious interest group demonstrates the ability to shape public opinion, they bring indirect pressure on politicians. Strategies and success rates for this activity, however, vary. Events staged for media coverage have become common. Demonstrations, dramatic testimony, publicized fact-finding reports, and statements by bishops are all aimed at the mass media and the broader public. Here it is crucial that the religious group enjoy the sympathies of the elite press. Conservative evangelicals and prolife activists complain bitterly that they are not given a fair hearing in the mass media and that they are either ignored or stereotyped. As surveys of elite journalists show, there is some truth to this analysis.[6] By contrast, some liberal church groups receive publicity that belies their actual grassroots support. Though surveys show that the majority of Americans favor school prayer,[7] the mainline Protestant denominations all oppose it, and they received favorable publicity when they announced this opposition on the steps of the U.S. Capitol.[8]

Inside Influence

No matter how much outside pressure one can mount, it means little if interest-group leaders are not skilled at gaining and keeping elite access. Here, too, not all religious groups are equal. Some enjoy excellent access; others have to fight for every bit of access they get. During the 1980s, for example, when so much was made of the rise of the Christian Right, the Moral Majority in fact suffered because they had poor access. Jewish groups, by contrast, enjoyed excellent access. What mattered was how many congressional offices were open and how many executive officials would listen, not how many millions of citizens heard—or agreed with—political TV evangelists.

The quality of interest-group leadership matters greatly. Some groups have lobbyists with years of experience and strong reputations; others suffer from lack of experience and have no reputation at all. Good leaders have a strong strategic sense: They develop a clear, limited set of attainable objectives on the basis of the current political climate. One of the recurrent problems faced by liberal Protestant lobbies is a lack of sharp focus and a tendency to take on too many issues at the same time. For example, in early 1998 the agenda of the National Council of Churches (NCC) included urban initiatives, racial justice, justice for women, economic and environmental justice, managed health care, the fight against church burning, disaster relief, and the battle against religious persecution.[9]

Political fortunes can also change. Republican control of the White House in the 1990s meant that liberal Protestants were shut out of executive deliberations. That changed with the election of Bill Clinton. Similarly, Democratic dominance of Congress, especially the House, presented a huge impediment to the agenda of conservative evangelicals from the late 1970s through the early 1990s. When the Republicans gained control of Congress in 1994, however, evangelical access rose, in part because evangelicals had aided in the Republican electoral victory.

A national lobby's effectiveness is also governed by the total quality of its operation, its resources, staff, research facilities, and technological ability to reach members. That takes money and institutional support. Jewish organizations are well funded and well staffed, as are such conservative Christian groups as the Christian Coalition, the Family Research Council, Focus on the Family, and Concerned Women for America. Catholic lobbies benefit from the institutional strength of the Church, its schools, hospitals, charities, and universities. In contrast, the liberal Protestant churches have met with declining financial and institutional backing as national denominational offices have cut back on their Washington operations.[10]

In spite of the growing presence and diversity of religious lobbies, most are small affairs compared to such giants as the National Education

Association, the Teamsters Union, or the National Association of Manufacturers. A large religious lobby may have thirty staff people, but a major secular lobby generally has 300 or more. This is part of the reason that religious organizations generally exercise only modest political influence in the grand scheme of Washington, or statehouse, politics.

The Legislative Process and the Imperative of Compromise

At the heart of the legislative process—whether in Congress or statehouses—is compromise. Though compromise is a dirty word to some religious activists, legislators themselves view it as the key to action. They know it is the only way to build the coalitions that are necessary to get things done. In order to understand why compromise is so vital, it is important to recall that the American system of government frustrates swift action. The framers of the Constitution were obsessed with checking power because they feared tyranny. The checks and balances they built into the system are there to delay proposals and allow many groups the chance to block proposed legislation. Political insiders know this, so they work to build the strongest possible coalition of supporters. Indeed, Washington politics is renowned for its frequent "strange bedfellows" alliances. There are no permanent friends or enemies, so the saying goes, just shifting coalitions.

This need to build coalitions is especially pressing for those organizations seeking major change. It is far easier to defend the status quo than to pass major new legislation. Christian conservatives, for example, are often in need of allies because they seek so many major changes in policy. Sometimes they are able to forge some new partnerships but they are rarely able to fashion a majority coalition. Throughout the 1980s and 1990s they failed to enact a school prayer amendment, to change abortion policy, or to alter what they view as a secular atmosphere in public schools. The strategic hurdles conservative Christian political groups face account in part for their limited legislative success to date.

Liberal Protestant and Catholic groups, too, have enjoyed only mixed success in playing the coalition-building game. In the 1980s they built a broad coalition to block aid to the Nicaraguan Contras, to expand food programs and development aid, and to enforce sanctions against South Africa under apartheid. On numerous other issues, however, they have failed to change policy. Much of the religious Left's agenda on health care, taxation, welfare, and international relations has remained at the margins of serious policymaking. For example, efforts by the NCC on behalf of the 1994 health-care reform proposals got them nowhere.

One of the most dramatic examples of a strange bedfellows alliance occurred during the lobbying for the Religious Freedom Restoration Act (RFRA), which was enacted in 1993 based on U.S. Supreme Court Justice Antonin Scalia's reasoning in *Employment Division* v. *Smith* (1990), in which the Court ruled in essence that religious free exercise is less important than the upholding of generally applicable secular laws passed for the protection of the common good. A broad coalition of religious actors sought legislative remedy in the wake of this decision, and legislation was introduced to restore the so-called "compelling state interest" test. Up until the *Smith* case, the Supreme Court had used this test in deciding free exercise cases ever since its 1963 decision in *Sherbert* v. *Verner*. In *Sherbert* the Court declared that any burden on a citizen's right to practice the religion of his or her choice must be justified by a "compelling state interest."[11] RFRA enjoyed support from an unusual coalition of liberal Protestant denominations, conservative evangelical organizations, Jewish and Muslim groups, Native American representatives, and civil liberties advocates. This was a real coalition: Concerned Women for America joined the United Methodist Church, Catholics joined Baptists, and evangelicals joined the American Civil Liberties Union (ACLU). All were united in the desire to protect religious liberty.

One liberal Jewish lobbyist noted with amazement how he found himself making joint lobby appearances with Michael Farris, head of the fundamentalist home-schooling legal defense group in support of RFRA. In signing the new law on November 16, 1993, President Bill Clinton acknowledged the remarkable nature of the coalition by saying that with God's power miracles can happen "even in the legislative process."[12] Their efforts led to victory, albeit a temporary one. The Supreme Court ruled RFRA unconstitutional in 1997 in the case of *City of Boerne* v. *Flores*. (For more on the *Boerne* case, see Chapter 11.)

Before it was ruled unconstitutional, RFRA reflected the fact that in modern pluralist America few religious organizations see themselves representing the majority. Each, however, can conceive of itself as a potentially persecuted minority and desire protection as a result. Thus fundamentalist home schoolers seek grounds to protect themselves from persecution by public school authorities, just as Orthodox Jews or Muslims seek to protect the broadest possible range of religious freedom. Perhaps in that sense the bedfellows were not so strange after all.

A Model of Religious Group Effectiveness

What makes for religious group effectiveness?[13] We suggest five factors that contribute to success:

Traditions and Theological Beliefs

Historical traditions and theological beliefs influence whether a religious group will enter politics at all, and if so, how it will strategically approach that task. Some religions are so otherworldly that they eschew politics altogether; others intervene only when directly threatened. The Jehovah's Witnesses are a sect that generally stays out of politics, with the exception of occasional forays into the courts to protect their religious freedom. Others, such as Lutherans, have a deep tradition of teaching civic responsibility for the individual but resisting corporate political witness by the church, a tendency that frustrates Lutheran activists.[14]

Other religious traditions do lend themselves to political action. The Catholic Church has long been at ease with politics. Many Jewish groups approach public action with a keen strategic sense. More than any other American religious group, African American Protestantism has long been deeply involved in political activism. The civil rights movement was organizationally based in black churches. Many African American clergy say they would not be able to imagine their pastoral role without a political component. These proclivities are not etched in stone, however, and change does occur. For example, for at least a generation conservative Protestant churches taught that politics was not for them; now they have become more politicized. Tradition and theological beliefs also structure the political agendas of religious groups and their clergy; certain theological orientations are associated with different types of issue concerns.[15]

Internal Strength and Unity

No religious group will be able to make much of a political impact without supportive lay members. It is important to have a large and unified membership.[16] At the same time, the existence of internal dissent, disputes among leaders, and resistance from members all detract from political clout. Equally important is the intensity of members' commitment. Are lay members only willing to write an occasional letter to Congress? Or are they ready to sacrifice hours of their time building the organization, participating in phone trees, and attending endless meetings? Are they willing to speak, vote, demonstrate, or even go to jail for their convictions?

Even the most committed participants need effective leaders. Strong leaders must exhibit energy, drive, and conviction. They also must have the ability to think strategically, form alliances, and articulate their messages in an appealing manner—often to elites who do not share their religious values.

Finally, resources, especially financial resources, are an absolute necessity for any political organization. Are members affluent, and are they willing to make financial contributions? Do they have time for politics? Are they well connected already, as contributors to political parties, as personal friends of members of Congress, or as leaders in their communities? Many Jewish groups, for example, combine all of these components of internal strength and unity and are therefore politically effective. Even religious groups without such advantages may stand a good chance to build a reasonable degree of political effectiveness. A recent major study shows that when people are deeply involved in any of a religious group's activities (such as serving on a church council), they learn valuable "civic skills" such as organizing and letter writing. These civic skills make people better equipped and more willing to participate in politics.[17]

Strategic Location

Another factor that is crucial to political success, but often overlooked, is the group's "strategic location." Does the group enjoy natural access to elites in government? Or does it have to beat down the door just to get a hearing? Meaningful access does not just involve securing one meeting with a few members of Congress or their staffs. It means getting serious hearings with congressional leaders and committee chairs, top White House officials, high-ranking bureaucrats and administrators (who formulate much policy), and the courts. Meaningful access also involves working with the assorted network of think tanks, law firms, foundations, and influence peddlers in Washington who know how the game is played. It is useful to have connections to state and local officials, who retain enormous influence over the federal government as well. The best access of all is to the elite national press. In a town where the words of the *Washington Post*—and more recently the conservative *Washington Times*—often seem to matter a good deal more than those of the Bible, the ability to gain favorable media exposure is critical.

Though few religious groups consistently enjoy this kind of access, the best strive for it relentlessly. Here we can see the tremendous problem conservative evangelicals and fundamentalists face. No matter how many followers they may have, or how effective their leadership may become, the fact is that few government elites share pietist religious values; worse yet, the elite national press often expresses a jaundiced view of born-again Christians. It is not surprising, therefore, that evangelical Protestants have put so much of their political energy into electing new political leaders, from the local level on up, who share their view.

Constraints and Opposition

The power, intensity, and access of a group's opponents matter. Some groups, of course, ignite more opposition than others. Some face a tougher struggle against opposition within their own ranks. Such opposition is sometimes based in policy disputes. In other instances, members simply see political involvement of any kind as a divisive diversion from their view of the church's mission: providing meaning, spiritual comfort, forgiveness, or conciliation. Moreover, suspicion of religious activism is endemic in American culture. The tradition of church-state separation in the United States encourages skepticism about church involvement in politics. How effectively a group overcomes these hurdles often determines how far it can go politically.

Interest groups seeking influence in Washington also benefit when they pool their resources. When a group like the Christian Coalition can work productively with Catholic groups, for example, the individual voice of each will be magnified and they will be able to attract more attention than they could have on their own. Some religious groups, however, resist such ecumenical (transreligious) coalitions at all costs. In most instances such groups are not interested in working with people of other religious backgrounds because of theological incompatibility. A willingness to work with other groups rather than labeling them as enemies, then, can translate into substantial political influence. The difficulties inherent in coalition building among religio-political interest groups are exemplified by recent efforts led by former U.S. Senator Paul Simon (D–Illinois) to build an interfaith effort to fight poverty. Various religious groups are simply unable to agree on the causes and effects of poverty, much less about the proper way to ameliorate it.[18]

Zeitgeist: Spirit of the Times

The fortunes of a religious group are governed in part by how well its agenda conforms to the tenor of the times. A spirit of political activism in the 1960s aided liberal Protestant churches, just as a more conservative tone since the 1980s has given a lift to conservative churches. Religious groups cannot often affect the prevailing zeitgeist, but they can recognize it and adapt their strategies accordingly. To show how these factors influence the actions and effectiveness of different American religious groups, we now turn to some examples.

Liberal Protestant Groups

As we noted in Chapter 2, mainline Protestants enjoyed a strategic location in American society in the years immediately following World War II. Moreover, because of the influence of the social gospel movement of the early twentieth century, mainline church leaders shared a liberal theology that was conducive to public action. They were thus receptive to political action and in a position to have some influence.

The movement to end discrimination and segregation that burst on the scene in the late 1950s fired the imaginations of liberal white religious leaders and piqued the consciences of many lay members. Though many had participated in early demonstrations and "freedom rides" in the South, the real opportunity for liberal Christians presented itself when the Civil Rights Act of 1964 was proposed. This was one of the truly landmark pieces of legislation in the nation's history.[19] It passed only after intense and effective lobbying by religious groups, especially by African American and liberal Protestants but also by Jews and Catholics.

Clearly liberal Protestants were marching to the spirit of the times. The national media vividly portrayed the reality of segregation and legal discrimination in the South. In his famous speech at the 1963 March on Washington, Dr. Martin Luther King Jr. cast the struggle for civil rights as one that called upon Americans to live up to their basic religious and political principles.

The strategic location of mainline Protestants in the 1960s was excellent. This was a time just before these churches would see their membership decline: The liberal National Council of Churches represented the majority of American Protestants.[20] Moreover, a unique tactical situation ensured the centrality of mainline churches within the religious alliance fighting for African American civil rights. As congressional supporters and opponents began lining up in early 1964, it was clear that the civil rights bill would be won or lost in the Republican—and mainline Protestant—heartland. Conservative southern Democrats opposed the legislation and northern liberal Democrats supported it. Thus the essential swing votes belonged to those midwestern Republicans who had no overriding political predisposition to vote either way and had thus remained uncommitted. Civil rights tacticians, therefore, designed a church-based "Midwest strategy" that relied heavily on liberal Protestant leaders to hold workshops in churches, meet with Republican representatives and senators, and mobilize letter-writing campaigns to persuade wavering members of Congress.

Meanwhile, ministers flocked to Washington to roam the halls of congressional office buildings. And legislators were not accustomed to being lobbied by ministers. One civil rights veteran, Joe Rauh of Americans for Democratic Action, has noted how powerful this novelty was:

Standing outside the Committee Room was the most beautiful sight I had ever seen—twenty Episcopal priests, fully garbed, all beautiful young WASPS. I used to think that the only two people out in front for civil rights were a Negro and a Jew—Mitchell of the NAACP and myself. But this was something the committee membership had never seen before. I knew then we really were in business.[21]

Summing up the role of churches, Senator Hubert Humphrey (D–Minnesota) wrote that without them "this bill could never have become law."[22]

Here we see a number of factors coming together. Church leaders acted strategically and successfully mobilized their lay members at the grassroots level. Though the churches were by no means unified, there was sufficient lay support that the pro–civil rights message would reach undecided members of Congress. Moreover, the issue was relatively clear-cut, and religious arguments enjoyed a certain logic that was compelling to many. How could one really be a Christian and sanction discriminatory laws? Finally, the greatest opposition came from the South, which still supported a separate religious culture; therefore northern Protestant leaders could come out in favor of the legislation without dividing their own churches.

The mid-1960s represented the high-water mark for liberal Protestant politics in Washington and elsewhere. Weakened by declining church memberships and diminishing financial support from the pews, and criticized for being out of touch with lay members, mainline church lobbies now struggle to maintain even a semblance of their previous clout.[23] Nonetheless, the experience of 1960s political activism led to a proliferation of liberal church groups, some of which have tried to move beyond the shrinking base of the old-line Protestant churches. Liberal Christians remain active players, even if their influence is modest, often allying themselves with Catholics, Jews, and secular liberals.

The main liberal Protestant groups active in Washington today include:

- the political arms of the mainline denominations, such as the United Methodists, Presbyterians (PCUSA), Episcopalians, northern (American) Baptists, Congregationalists (United Church of Christ), and Lutherans (ELCA) (Box 3.2);
- the National Council of Churches, the key coalition of theologically liberal denominations;
- small but active pacifist churches (Quakers, Mennonites, and Brethren), along with Unitarians;
- membership groups, such as Bread for the World, a Christian hunger lobby;
- the Interfaith Alliance, which presents itself as a direct opponent of the religious Right;
- international relief agencies, such as Church World Service and Lutheran World Relief, which lobby on foreign aid, trade, and U.S. international policies;
- coalitions sponsored and funded by liberal churches to lobby on specific issues from U.S. defense policy to abortion rights, the environment, and women's issues, including the Religious Coalition for Abortion

---

**BOX 3.2   THE UNITED METHODIST BUILDING,
100 MARYLAND AVENUE**

The nerve center of liberal Protestantism in Washington is the United Methodist building, situated strategically across the street from the United States Capitol. Ironically, the stately building was literally the "house that Prohibition built." Completed in 1923, it embodied the effort of evangelical Methodists to support the constitutional ban on alcoholic beverages. It now houses a number of denominational lobbies, along with affiliated groups and coalitions.

SOURCE: Allen D. Hertzke, "An Assessment of the Mainline Churches Since 1945," in James E. Wood Jr. and Derek Davis, eds., *The Role of Religion in the Making of Public Policy* (Waco, TX: Dawson Institute for Church-State Studies, 1991).

Rights, the Washington Office on Africa, and the Washington Office on Latin America;

- church groups allied with the major African American denominations (such as the National Baptist Convention, USA, Inc.); and
- allied groups on church-state issues, including the Baptist Joint Committee and Americans United for Separation of Church and State (which arose to combat Catholic influence and continues to lobby for a strict separationist position).

The sheer number of these groups suggests enormous activity and coordinated power, and coalition letters to Congress often contain scores of participating churches. The truth is, however, that many of these groups have overlapping memberships, so their grassroots support is greatly exaggerated. Moreover, many have small staffs by Washington standards and are spread thinly, which undermines their effectiveness.

The political agenda of these Protestants is both wide-ranging and decidedly liberal, though there are differences among the many groups. For the most part, however, liberal Protestant leaders seem to be the quintessential children of the 1960s. The National Council of Churches and many of its congregational leaders, for example, took a rather sharp turn to the left on foreign affairs in the late 1960s and early 1970s, endorsing some Marxist liberation struggles in developing nations, softening objections to the Soviet Union and China, and heaping criticism upon the capitalist economy of the United States. On domestic affairs the liberal Protestant community has embraced the broad agenda of women's equality, generous welfare benefits, environmental protection, affirmative action, and, in some cases, abortion rights.

The biggest problem for most of these liberal Protestant groups, however, is that they have often failed to convince their own lay members of the value of their agenda. In part this reflects an ideological gap between clergy and laity, and in part it demonstrates a lack of effort by some leaders to persuade members. For several decades survey evidence has shown that although these church leaders may be liberal or even radical, their lay members are mostly moderate to conservative. The extent of the gap varies from issue to issue and from church to church, but overall it is a debilitating handicap.[24]

But why have liberal religionists not attempted to remedy this problem? In some cases they have. Bread for the World has built a list of members who do support the organization's advocacy on behalf of the hungry. The Friends Committee on National Legislation and the Mennonite Central Committee have good links with their member churches. And most of the old-line Protestant churches have developed modest lists of contacts in congressional districts across the country. But in many cases grassroots support remains undeveloped because sometimes church leaders do not see themselves as the representatives of their parishioners. This may seem odd, but it is one of the persistent dynamics of the religious world. Religious lobbyists often see themselves representing their vision of biblical imperatives, especially the mandate to speak for the poor, the weak, and the oppressed. In language popular among liberals, the proper role of clergy is to "comfort the afflicted and afflict the comfortable." The problem is that many of the "comfortable" are lay parishioners of the old-line churches.[25]

There is some evidence to suggest that this "clergy-laity gap," which keeps some mainline clergy out of politics, may not be as salient in central city or low-income mainline congregations. Central city clergy are sometimes more able to become politically involved for several important reasons. First, while the social gospel agenda may not be well accepted by the members of affluent mainline churches, it resonates well in lower-income mainline churches, particularly when the congregations are racially diverse. Second, there are more problems stemming from economic hardship that may necessitate immediate political action in central city neighborhoods than there are in outlying areas. Third, mainline laity in affluent areas are often politically active in their communities on their own or through secular organizations. Their clergy may therefore have no real incentive to provide them with a stimulus for political involvement; in central city churches, however, such an incentive may exist. Fourth, there are often more opportunities for clergy political participation available in central city contexts because of intense nonprofit and government attention to socioeconomic problems there.[26]

Changing political times can also bring a change in the fortunes of religious actors. Denied access to the White House during the Reagan-Bush years, liberal church leaders celebrated when the Clinton administration took office. Liberal religious leaders found themselves getting their calls returned and receiving invitations to White House policy task forces and meetings with the president and his top advisers. A good part of the access was not just ideological but religious. A telling sign of the mainline's political difficulties lies in the fact that one of its most visible interest groups' key selling points recently has been that it is the polar opposite of the religious Right. The Interfaith Alliance says it presents "a challenge to those who manipulate religion to promote an extreme political agenda based in a false gospel of irresponsible individualism."[27]

Roman Catholic Groups

Catholic interest groups enjoy an advantageous strategic location in the configuration of American pressure groups. On the one hand, Catholic groups have been allied with the Democratic party throughout much of American history and were strongly supportive of the New Deal. They are generally comfortable with the liberal Democratic agenda on such issues as welfare spending, labor laws, civil rights, and the death penalty. On the other hand, they join with Republican conservatives in opposing both abortion and condom distribution to minors, promoting parental choice options in day care and education, and criticizing some elements of pop culture. Thus religio-political activists from across the spectrum—from conservative evangelicals to ecumenical liberals—view Catholics as vital potential allies. Ironically, the Church may be becoming a less useful ally these days, given serious membership and leadership problems that inevitably affect its political strength.

The U.S. Catholic Church has maintained a Washington presence since just after World War I, when the National Catholic Welfare Conference was established. Its successor is the United States Catholic Conference, which, as the staff arm of the National Conference of Catholic Bishops (NCCB), represents the official political positions of the Church. The clear Catholic organizational structure, along with a strong hierarchical tradition, allows its leaders—some 270 bishops—to speak with authority for the Church. This is a distinct political advantage. Thus, even if lay opinion is divided on an issue, the "official" Church position can be articulated clearly; when the bishops present their views on issues, they are guaranteed extensive, though not always favorable, press coverage.

The Catholic lobby, however, is far from monolithic. It includes a host of associations, religious orders, and membership organizations. In most cases these groups do not oppose the bishops directly, but there are large differences in emphasis and even ideology. On the left we find NETWORK, a membership organization composed mostly of activist nuns; the Maryknoll order, which is known for its support of liberation theology[28]; and Pax Christi, a quasi-pacifist group whose members include 1960s activists Daniel Berrigan and Elizabeth McAlister, writer Henri Nouwen, and

---

**BOX 3.3 THE ROMAN CATHOLIC CHURCH
AND HEALTH-CARE POLICY**

The Roman Catholic Church plays a central role in the crafting of health-care policy. Its concern with this policy area is related to a variety of factors, the most central of which is the fact that the Church operates 11 percent of all community hospitals in the United States. Clarke Cochran has argued, though, that there is more to the Church's involvement in health-care policy than material concern for this network of hospitals. The Church's opposition to managed care, for example, owes much to traditional Catholic concern for the less fortunate; managed care and social justice have little in common. From the pope down, the Church views health care as a right that belongs to all persons, so any system that would deny this right is patently unjust in the eyes of many Catholic leaders. Thus the Catholic Hospital Association (CHA) lobbies not only to protect its network of hospitals—which since the beginning have been open to all persons regardless of religion or ability to pay—but to defend the poor.

SOURCES: Clarke E. Cochran, "Sacrament and Solidarity: Catholic Social Thought and Healthcare Policy Reform" (paper presented at the annual meeting of the Southwestern Political Science Association, Houston, 1996); Clarke E. Cochran, "Catholic Polity and Health Care Policy" (paper presented at the annual meeting of the American Political Science Association, San Francisco, 1996); http://www.chausa.org/chahome.asp.

---

feminist theologian Rosemary Radford Ruether. These groups are decidedly more liberal than the United States Catholic Conference, especially on foreign policy issues. Also quite liberal are Jesuit Social Ministries, Catholic Charities, and the Campaign for Human Development, which lobby on issues of poverty and welfare.

A very different posture emerges, however, from large associations of Catholic hospitals and parochial schools, which have tangible financial interests to protect and are generally treated with some respect by policymakers (Box 3.3).

Hillary Rodham Clinton, needing the support of the nation's largest nonprofit hospital system in the country, courted Catholic hospital leaders in her efforts to craft a national health-care plan. Her support for abortion funding, however, was an insurmountable obstacle to their cooperation.

On church-state issues we find the more conservative Catholic League for Religious Civil Rights, which vigorously combats anti-Catholic portrayals in the news and entertainment media. It also represents a generally "accommodationist" position and is opposed by such groups as the American Civil Liberties Union (ACLU) and Americans United for Separation of Church and State. Finally, there are organizations sustained in part by sizable Catholic memberships, including National Right to Life, the nation's oldest antiabortion group; JustLife, which lobbies for the "seamless garment" agenda articulated by Chicago's late Joseph Cardinal Bernardin (opposing abortion, the death penalty, and nuclear weaponry while supporting liberal positions on social welfare); and, to a lesser extent, Bread for the World, the Christian hunger lobby.

Among the strengths of the Catholic lobby are a theological comfort with politics, a scholastic tradition of serious reflection on issues, clear lines of leadership, and a potentially strategic position in broader political alignments. One of the weaknesses of Catholic political groups is a real diversity of opinion in the pews and among Catholic politicians.[29] Another concern is the existence of concerted, well-placed opposition to Catholic politics. A look at Catholic involvement in several key issues illustrates these attributes.

Abortion

From the moment the U.S. Supreme Court struck down restrictive state abortion statutes in *Roe v. Wade* in 1973, the Catholic Church has been at the center of prolife lobbying, both in Washington and more recently at state houses.[30] This prominent role has led to an unusual alliance between Catholics and conservative evangelical Protestants—historical antagonists of Catholics—and a split within the Church between liberal prochoice advocates and supporters of the Church's traditional prolife position. One of the most visible episodes was sparked by John Cardinal O'Connor, the head of the New York archdiocese. The cardinal made himself a national critic of prochoice Catholic politicians when he said in 1984 that he could not imagine how a good Catholic could vote for a candidate who supported abortion—a thinly veiled attack on Democratic vice presidential nominee Geraldine Ferraro. This intensified attacks on the Church from many feminists, academics, liberal politicians, and abortion rights groups.

No issue so clearly illustrates the constraints the Catholic Church faces as abortion. Though the Church has invested enormous political capital in the issue, its successes have been modest. Abortion law in the United States remains among the more liberal in the Western world, despite two decades of agitation by prolife forces.[31] In part this can be attributed to the powerful role of the courts in the American political system. Even though a more conservative Supreme Court has returned some latitude to the states, the room for variation in abortion policy is still small.

Another constraint prolife Catholics face is the partisan nature of the issue. Prochoice activists have succeeded in identifying the Democratic party with their position. Though some exceptions exist, most Democratic leaders support a solidly prochoice policy. This reality limits the Roman Catholic Church's elite access to the Democratic party, at least on this issue.

The Church has also faced legal battles. In one of the most sobering episodes, Abortion Rights Mobilization (ARM) brought suit, charging that the United States Catholic Conference's antiabortion role constituted illegal political activity from a tax-exempt organization. What shocked the Church most was that a New York federal district court judge demanded that it turn over volumes of sensitive internal records to ARM or face fines of $100,000 per day. Though the case was eventually dismissed, the threat was huge and took more than a decade of litigation to turn back.[32] The lawsuit helped bring about a chilling effect on Church involvement in electoral politics. The Catholic bishops have since developed guidelines that limit statements by Church leaders that others might interpret as candidate endorsements.

Finally, lack of unified lay support has hurt the Church. Though polls on abortion are sometimes ambiguous, there is no question that a sizable number of Catholics support some level of abortion rights, and women who identify themselves as Catholics are just as likely to have abortions as are non-Catholic women. The Church can take heart, however, in the fact that prolife support is strongest among those who faithfully attend mass, suggesting that lapsed Catholics are the most likely to reject the Church's prolife position.[33]

Even in the face of these impediments, the Church has had some success in its efforts to pass antiabortion legislation. Most prominent has been the Hyde Amendment banning federal funding for abortion. Rep. Henry Hyde, a Roman Catholic Republican from Illinois, has attached his amendment to a myriad of federal laws since 1976. One of the most dramatic struggles over the Hyde Amendment occurred in the summer of 1993, when, despite opposition from President Clinton and Democratic congressional leaders, Hyde rallied a surprisingly strong majority to support his amendment.

In the wake of the Supreme Court's 1989 decision in *Webster* v. *Reproductive Health Services*, which upheld a Missouri law restricting late-term abortions and providing for parental notification and a waiting period, the politics of abortion has now largely shifted to the state arena. There Catholic success has been limited to a few states under special circumstances.[34]

The Catholic Church has also mobilized recently against late-term abortions. It has been joined in this effort by a range of evangelical Protestant groups (such as the Christian Coalition and Focus on the Family), which share the Church's deep outrage at the federal government's unwillingness to ban "partial-birth" abortion. President Bill Clinton twice vetoed legislation aiming to ban the procedure.[35] The issue of late-term abortion has provoked many new strategic political calculations. Some conservative states have passed their own legislation outlawing the procedure. At the federal level, some Democrats have used the issue as a strategic opportunity to appear moderate by opposing it. Moreover, a variety of groups and individuals have attempted to use the issue to embarrass Clinton. And the battle over this issue is far from over.

Nuclear Arms and Peace Issues

The Catholic Church achieved more success in its efforts to limit the nuclear arms race. In the early 1980s American Catholic bishops wrote a highly publicized "pastoral letter" on nuclear arms in which they applied just war theory in criticizing key aspects of U.S. nuclear policy.[36] Though few lay Catholics read the document itself, the enormous publicity that surrounded its release and subsequent consideration by active lay members affected the political environment of a number of parishes.

Careful analysis suggests that the bishops achieved something quite rare through this pastoral letter: They actually shifted Catholic lay opinion—in this instance, toward a more dovish, antiwar position.[37] Moreover, this shift could not have been timed more strategically. The pastoral letter gave a boost to the nuclear freeze movement, which was lobbying Congress for a freeze resolution. The pastoral letter, "which sent top Reagan Administration officials to the bunkers, called for a freeze using language nearly identical to the House Resolution."[38] Faced with a popular mass movement and a rebellious Congress, the Reagan administration shifted its own nuclear posture. The bishops made a real difference here, and they gained credibility in Washington as a result, leading some liberal Protestants to acknowledge their "Catholic envy."

Catholic peace networks were also instrumental in challenging President Ronald Reagan's military support for the government of El Salvador and his backing of the Contras, who were attempting to overthrow the Marxist Sandinista government of Nicaragua. One advantage churches have on foreign policy questions is that they are international organizations with counterparts abroad. Many also support missionaries, who bring back information about the impact of U.S. policy abroad. During the long battle over Contra aid, Catholic groups allied with others in the peace network to provide information on Contra "atrocities," which proved to be valuable ammunition for opponents of the Reagan administration. Catholic influence was probably magnified by the fact that the Speaker of the House was the Roman Catholic Tip O'Neill (D–Massachusetts), who responded to White House assertions about Central America with the quip, "That's not what the nuns tell me."[39]

Catholic opinion about the Gulf War of 1991 also provides lessons about the limits of Catholic (or religious) influence—in this case regarding the momentous national decision to go to war. In response to Saddam Hussein's invasion of Kuwait, the Catholic hierarchy offered conditional support for the United States' effort to keep the Iraqis from occupying Saudi Arabia, but it opposed the Bush administration's decision to force them from Kuwait. Daniel Pilarczyk, the president of the NCCB, expressed the Church's preference for allowing economic sanctions more time. Other Catholic peace groups went even further in criticizing American policy. The national media featured Catholics prominently in the debate over the Gulf War, frequently featuring discussions of Catholic just war criteria. When Congress voted to authorize the use of force, allowing President George Bush to begin Operation Desert Storm, Roman Catholic parishioners strongly backed the view that it was a just war, so the reservations of Church leaders were ignored.[40]

Education

Catholics lobby about a host of domestic economic and welfare issues. In educational policy they depart from the liberal coalition in a major way. Since the nineteenth century the American Catholic Church has battled to obtain state support for its parochial school system. In the struggle it has faced vigorous and effective opposition from public school teachers and administrators, civil liberties groups, and Protestant organizations such as the Baptist Joint Committee and Americans United for Separation of Church and State. Though the Church has achieved some successes in a number of states, it has not realized its major educational goal of broadening parental choice through tax credits or vouchers for parochial school attendance.

Other Issues

In a way the 1980s were heady times for the Catholic bishops, who achieved visibility and respect in political circles. But now the bishops face a variety of internal problems that weaken their long-term political effectiveness. Among these are the growing shortage of priests, the disaffection of many lay Catholics with the Church, and tensions with the Vatican over such issues as the role of women in the Church. This last issue erupted when the bishops attempted to draft a statement on the status of women in the Church. The proposed pastoral letter began with a self-conscious openness to women's voices and concerns (it included statements by a number of women whose testimony was solicited), and included a denunciation of sexism as sin and a declaration of the equality of men and women. In part this statement was a reflection of the practical necessity of recognizing the active worship and leadership roles taken on by many lay Catholic women in recent years in the face of the serious priest shortage.[41]

However, conservative American bishops and Vatican officials alike criticized the draft, stressing instead traditional Catholic teachings about the different roles of men and women in the Church and the importance of preserving a male clergy. The drafters of the letter backtracked, only to incur the ire of liberal bishops and women's organizations. Ultimately, the letter was opposed by both liberal and conservative bishops—for different reasons—and was not ratified. The issue of the role of women in and out of the Church remains a divisive one for American Roman Catholics, and it will certainly affect its future political posture and influence.

Jewish Groups

Jews have thrived in the United States, with its protection of religious freedoms, after centuries of persecution elsewhere. Though the Jewish proportion of the population in the United States is small, perhaps less than 2 percent, it is also highly educated, affluent, and politically active. These characteristics translate into significant resources, but there are other factors as well that account for the success of Jewish interest groups, especially in Washington.

Jews have lived in the United States since the seventeenth century, but the first national interest group, the American Jewish Committee (AJC), was not formed until 1906, in response to a Russian pogrom. Since then, the AJC has sought to protect Jews both at home and abroad. Its members today represent the elites of the American Jewish community. In 1913, the Anti-Defamation League of B'nai B'rith was founded to combat domestic anti-Semitism, followed by the American Jewish Congress, which was made up at first of Jews devoted to the creation of a Jewish homeland in Palestine.[42] The Washington offices of these organizations today should not be considered strictly religious lobbies, since a number of their members are not observant; many are highly secular. Still, close ties remain between Jewish congregations and these interest groups.

The three major branches of Judaism—Orthodox, Conservative, and Reform—also have national offices to coordinate political activities. Of these the most assertive in Washington is the Union of American Hebrew Congregations, which represents Reform Judaism (the most theologically liberal branch of American Judaism). Its stately building on Embassy Row houses the American Jewish Committee, the American Jewish Congress, and the Leadership Conference on Civil Rights. Though liberal Jews dominate the political scene, Orthodox Jews have also recently gotten into the act. Ultraorthodox Hasidic Jews, for example, opened up their own Washington office in the early 1990s.

In a class by itself is the America Israel Public Affairs Committee, or AIPAC, one of the most formidable lobbies in Washington. Its sole aim is to coordinate American support for Israel, and it has become a model for many other interest groups wishing to influence U.S. foreign policy. For years it has been respected and even feared in Washington politics. AIPAC has combined excellent research resources in its Washington office, a grassroots network of some 55,000 activist members, and a host of affiliated political action committees that contribute money to pro-Israel candidates for federal office. And there is, in fact, tangible evidence of AIPAC's effectiveness in Congress. Largely because of AIPAC's efforts, the billions in foreign aid the United States sends to Israel no longer comes in the form of loans; it is now given as outright grants.[43]

On most issues Jewish political groups are liberal. Jewish lobbies have championed civil liberties (Jews constitute a sizable percentage of the ACLU's membership). Strong support for labor unions, women's rights, and abortion rights has also come from Jewish groups. On church-state relations Jews work aggressively for strict separation. They have reacted with alarm to the rise of the religious Right, fighting vigorously against such parts of its agenda as school prayer and abortion restriction. Many Jewish groups even view Christian fundamentalists as their mortal adversaries.

In terms of alliances, therefore, Jewish groups often join with liberal Protestants on church-state and social issues such as women's rights and abortion. They join with Catholics in supporting the welfare state. They were key allies of African Americans during the civil rights movement. On many foreign and military issues, too, they have often been in the vanguard of the liberal coalition.

On matters involving Israel, however, Jewish groups often part company with their usual religious allies. For many old-line Protestants and liberal Catholics, not to mention African American Christians and Muslims, justice for the Palestinian people demands more U.S. pressure on Israel. American Jews, in contrast, remain strongly united in their resolve to protect the existence of the Jewish homeland, however pained they may be from time to time about some of Israel's own actions and policies. On this issue liberal politics gives way to hardheaded realism. In one of the great ironies of contemporary politics, Christian fundamentalists have emerged as the single Christian group to support Israel strongly. This support is rooted in the fundamentalist belief that Jews must return to their homeland before Jesus Christ can come again. Some Jewish leaders resist fundamentalist help, but AIPAC has welcomed it.

The growing assertiveness of Orthodox Jews, however, has increased the pluralism of Jewish witness. On such issues as opposition to abortion, gay rights, and support for public recognition of faith, Orthodox and Hasidic Jews often share the perspective of Christian evangelicals and conservative Catholics. The Rabbinical Council—the national organization of Orthodox congregations—is also becoming more politically active on such issues as public support for religious schools. Christian conservatives, of course, have leaped at the chance to build alliances here. Rev. Pat Robertson features Jews at meetings of his Christian Coalition, and a Jewish man now leads the fight against religious persecution in all its vari-

---

BOX 3.4   MICHAEL HOROWITZ: A JEWISH ADVOCATE FOR PERSECUTED CHRISTIANS

Barely a blip on the political screen for much of the 1990s, the persecution of Christians abroad has become a major foreign policy battle. By 1998 the White House, Congress, religious groups, and big business were all deeply involved in this matter. Major credit for forcing this issue onto the national agenda belongs to Michael Horowitz, who attended Yeshiva school as a youth in the Bronx and thought about becoming a rabbi. A Washington think tank lawyer, he became involved in the fight against religious persecution when his Ethiopian housekeeper, who was threatened with deportation, told him of being tortured because of his Christian faith.

Horowitz launched his campaign against religious persecution with a 1995 guest editorial in the *Wall Street Journal*, followed by a letter to some 140 evangelical Christian mission boards. He later drafted a "statement of conscience" that was adopted by the National Association of Evangelicals; worked with members of Congress to write legislation; and assembled a lobby coalition that included evangelical Protestants, the United States Catholic Conference, Jewish organizations, and Tibetan Buddhists. With blunt rhetoric he argued that "Christians are the Jews of the twenty first century" and that they had become the "victims of choice for thug regimes." He also "shamed Christian leaders into action" by asking, "I'm a Jew, I'm interested in this, why aren't you?" Recognition of his central role in the movement came when Charles Colson presented Prison Fellowship's 1997 Wilberforce Award ("for combating injustice") to Michael Horowitz.

SOURCES: Samuel G. Freedman, "Horowitz's List," *New York* (March 31, 1997), 46; "The Jews of the Twenty-First Century?" *Jubilee* (Spring 1997); Jeffrey Goldberg, "Washington Discovers Christian Persecution," *New York Times Magazine* (December 21, 1997), 46.

---

eties around the world (Box 3.4). How far such efforts can go, however, remains to be seen.

Why do Jewish groups enjoy such excellent elite access in Washington and elsewhere? Our model of effectiveness, outlined later, helps to explain the components of their success.

First, Jewish faith and tradition promote political participation. Judaism is not an otherworldly faith; it emphasizes worldly engagement. In Jewish scripture, for example, the ancient Hebrews lived under God's mercy and judgment on the basis of how faithfully they organized their communal affairs. Jewish communities in America also foster a robust public life in which people are at home with the debates and compromises of politics. This ease with the world of politics is a major resource. Jewish leaders do not have to spend time and energy convincing their members that politics is a legitimate activity. Often their members are already politically involved.

Second, we see serious internal resources and unity among Jewish political organizations. This strength has a number of dimensions. At the local level, American Jews operate vibrant community organizations and chapters of national groups. Thus, when national leaders seek to mobilize political pressure, they have real grassroots strength to call upon. More than this, however, is the fact that grassroots members of Jewish organizations are generally well educated, affluent, and politically connected. Thus, even in places with small Jewish populations, there are sometimes prominent Jewish citizens who know their congressional representatives personally. Relative affluence is also a real resource—and one that leaders have no timidity tapping. Jews are major contributors to their own interest groups and to political parties, candidates, and pro-Israel PACs.

Jewish political resources are maximized by a host of strong leaders. Indeed, some of them have been legends in Washington, confidants of presidents, friends of members of Congress, quintessential insiders. One reason is the longevity of senior Jewish leadership, a product of stability in the Washington community. This longevity fosters not only wisdom in the ways of politics but a long view of lobbying strategy. These leaders encourage workshops to train new members and foster college clubs to bring a new generation into the fold. They help build relationships with local politicians, mayors, and state representatives, especially because years later these people may be elected to Congress.

Third, and not surprisingly, Jews enjoy excellent strategic access to political elites. In part their strategic location is a function of the presence of Jews in a variety of elite circles. It is, of course, hard to speak of this fact without promoting stereotypes or feeding conspiracy theories that suggest a vast Jewish ruling cabal. The truth of the matter is that American Jews believe in strong families, education, and a strong tradition of political involvement. This results in overrepresentation of Jews at elite levels of government, media, and the academy. They play by the rules, and they play very well.

Jewish leaders employ resources to cultivate political elites throughout the system. Whether it is a Democratic or Republican White House, a Democratic or Republican Congress, a conservative or liberal Supreme Court, Jewish leaders work to win a serious hearing. And they are serious about political victory, not just flying a flag. They work assiduously with top bureaucrats and cabinet members. They cultivate the media, and they build alliances with the vast network of Washington lobbies and law firms. Moreover, like other interest group elites, many leaders of Jewish organizations are shrewd strategists. Sometimes when they cannot win, they strive to lose in such a way as to do better the next time. Other times they seek compromise. Always they insist on access.

The record is more mixed on our model's fourth factor of effectiveness: the role of opposition. On some issues Jews face strong opponents, and they must adapt accordingly. On church-state relations, especially, they have been fighting increasingly assertive evangelicals and Catholics. On Israel, however, they have faced relatively weak domestic opponents. Israel has enjoyed broad popular support as the only democracy in the region, with an image of David among Arab Goliaths. Moreover, Christian support for Israel includes not only fundamentalists who see its formation as a fulfillment of biblical prophecy but also more mainstream Protestants who identify with the "holy land." Though anti-Semitism certainly lurks in some circles, many American Christians view Jews benignly and with respect.[44] American Jews also benefit from their willingness and ability to form coalitions with a wide variety of political bedfellows.

This picture of robust influence, however, rests on circumstances that can change. Changes in the politics of the Middle East, such as the December, 1987, Intifada uprising of Palestinians and the widely publicized Israeli crackdown, weakened uncritical support for Israel in the United States. Problems within the pro-Israel lobby can hurt, too. For example, in the early 1990s cracks appeared in the armor of AIPAC after several of its leaders were forced to step down after offending fellow Jews and others.[45]

Evangelical Protestant Groups

In the 1980s a few fundamentalist organizations generated a lot of heat and received a huge amount of media attention. Moral Majority leader Rev. Jerry Falwell made frequent television appearances on *Nightline* and *Phil Donahue*, Christian Voice director Gary Jarmin blanketed churches with his "Moral Report Card" of the votes of members of Congress, and Beverly LaHaye's Concerned Women for America (now headed by Carmen Pate) mobilized thousands of women opposed to the feminist agenda. These and other groups reflected the early militancy of the religious Right. As a movement, it succeeded in shaping the Washington agenda and putting adversaries on the defensive, primarily through massive constituent mobilization drives and media splashes. On the matter of school prayer, for example, it buried Capitol Hill in millions of pieces of mail in the mid-1980s. But despite this sound and fury, the religious Right achieved only modest policy success. Lack of elite access hurt tremendously, as did unfavorable press coverage and financial instability. The Moral Majority depended on desperate appeals to keep the organization afloat in the 1980s. And Gary Jarmin was discredited when it was revealed that Christian Voice had been supported by the Unification Church of Rev. Sun Myung Moon. When the Moral Majority closed up shop in 1989 and the Christian Voice receded, obituaries were prematurely written for the Christian conservative movement.[46]

What has happened instead is growth and increasing sophistication. One way to comprehend this movement is to list its various groups and compare their ideological hues and issue concerns. Theologically conservative evangelical groups are a diverse lot, and include the following:

- Organizations that work mostly through the courts, but lobby on such issues as the Equal Access Act and the Religious Freedom Restoration Act. These include the Christian Legal Society, an organization made up of lawyers who take on religious freedom issues; the more conservative Rutherford Institute headed by John Whitehead; and Pat Robertson's American Center for Law and Justice, headed by Jay Sekulow, a constitutional law specialist.

- The National Association of Evangelicals (NAE), the umbrella organization for the evangelical mainstream. In Washington since the early 1940s and analogous to the mainline National Council of Churches, its approach is nonconfrontational, and it has frequently parted company with more militant fundamentalists. It is conservative on social issues but also a strong defender of religious liberty. Its most recent political efforts have focused on putting a stop to late-term abortion. The organization has become more activist in recent years, and its leader, Robert Dugan, has joined with other conservative Christians in a call to arms in the "culture wars."[47] And the NAE wields considerable political clout. During the 1996 presidential campaign, Republican nominee Bob Dole alienated NAE officials by twice failing to appear at scheduled meetings with them.

- Denominational organizations, such as the Christian Life Commission of the Southern Baptist Convention (SBC) and the Lutheran Church–Missouri Synod. Newcomers to Washington, their presence is modest but may grow over the years. One of the advantages they do enjoy is a clear-cut church base. Thus, when the SBC-run Christian Life Commission launched a national campaign to block abortion funding in the Clinton health-care plan, it announced that materials on the issue would be mailed to every one of its member congregations—a powerful statement; with over 15 million members, the SBC is the largest of all American Protestant denominations.

- Single-issue groups, including National Right to Life, which works closely with evangelical and Catholic groups in lobbying against abortion, euthanasia, and medical use of fetal tissue; the Association of Home Schoolers, led by attorney Michael Farris; and Prison Fellowship, created and led by evangelical moderate Charles Colson, the former Nixon aide who went to jail for Watergate crimes. Colson's prison experience and conversion led him to create what has become a worldwide organization focused on prison reform and the spiritual rehabilitation of prisoners.

- Broad-based membership organizations, such as Pat Robertson's Christian Coalition, James Dobson's Focus on the Family, Gary Bauer's Family Research Council, and Beverly LaHaye's Concerned Women for America.

The most important organization to emerge in the 1990s was the Christian Coalition.[48] Formed in the wake of Pat Robertson's 1988 presidential bid, the Christian Coalition has succeeded in channeling the energies of many local conservative Christians in a way that the Moral Majority never achieved. In part this is because activists learned from Jerry Falwell's mistakes, and in part it reflects a changing agenda. Though the Moral Majority enjoyed enormous media exposure in the 1980s, it rested on shaky financial ground, frequently depending on continuous emergency appeals for funds from contributors. Even those who acknowledge Falwell's pioneering role note that the Moral Majority remained largely a "mailing list and a string of *Nightline* appearances by Falwell"—not a sustainable organization. Robertson's presidential campaign and subsequent organizing efforts, in contrast, focused on building a grassroots base of activists. This effort was premised on Robertson's recognition that to achieve its long-range goals the evangelical movement had to shift from a national focus to state and local forums, where much of the battle over American culture was being fought.

Though Robertson has always been president and spiritual leader of the Christian Coalition through his Christian Broadcasting Network (CBN) broadcast empire, it was Ralph Reed who led the organizational effort in the 1990s. Reed combined a highly educated background (a Ph.D. in history) with extensive experience as a campaign consultant. Youthful and smooth with the media, Reed also wrote widely for opinion magazines and newspapers as the Christian Coalition's executive director. By the mid-1990s he had built an organization with over 1 million members, fifty state affiliates, nearly 900 local chapters, an active Washington lobby, and a budget of over $20 million.

One of his key strategies was hosting leadership schools in cities across the country to train local activists to run campaigns and influence public policy. In 1993, seventy-five such "schools" trained an estimated 7,500 activists, some of whom planned to run for school boards, city councils, county councils, and leadership positions in the Republican party. Another major focus of the organization has been identifying sympathetic voters, maintaining computer files organized by various electoral districts, and getting voters to the polls.

Christian conservatives have gained control of Republican party machinery in several states, won majorities on some school boards, and fought against things such as gay rights ordinances at the state and local levels. One of their more controversial strategies is what Reed once described as a "stealth strategy": the quiet mobilization of Christian conservatives to vote in elections where certain candidates do not indicate how closely they are allied with the movement. The press picked up on this theme and began characterizing all Christian conservative efforts as "stealth politics," though most Christian Coalition efforts have been public.

In a way the Christian Coalition came of age in the 1994 election cycle. It recruited and supported sympathetic candidates in primaries, generated enormous publicity, and distributed some 30 million "voter guides" rating the records of congressional incumbents on key conservative positions at churches across the country. This effort coincided with and supported the strong Republican conservative tide in congressional elections, and the Coalition enjoyed a number of successes. In Oklahoma, for example, the Coalition helped change the partisan balance of the congressional delegation from 5–3 Democratic to 7–1 Republican. Though a number of factors contributed to the huge Republican victory nationwide, the Christian Coalition could legitimately claim some credit.

Many changes have come upon the Christian Coalition since 1996. First, Ralph Reed resigned effective June 1997 to found his own political consulting firm. He was replaced by the leadership team of president Donald Hodel (a former Reagan cabinet member) and executive director Randy Tate (a former Republican member of Congress). In the wake of these personnel changes, the organization has suffered from declining financial contributions and visibility. In 1997, the Christian Coalition raised only $17 million, after achieving an all-time fund-raising watermark of $26.4 million just one year before. Since Reed's departure, the organization has also been covered more sporadically in the media, and it has been engaged in a battle with the Internal Revenue Service over its tax-exempt status.[49]

It is also important to keep in mind that the Christian Coalition has never been a political leviathan in every American state. There are states where it has gained a foothold in the Republican party, but in many other states it is simply not an important player.[50] The organization is now reconstituting itself in response to these challenges. It has cut the size of its staff, scaled back its political agenda, and phased out the glossy magazine it once sent to members.[51]

As the Christian Coalition has faded somewhat, a new face has gained prominence in the political movement of evangelical Protestants. He is Gary Bauer, president of the Family Research Council. Since Reed's 1997 departure from the Christian Coalition, Bauer, a former Reagan aide, has become one of the most influential moral conservatives in Washington.

The Family Research Council has become adept at fundraising and supports its own political action committee, the Campaign for Working Families. This group also takes a decidedly different tack than the Christian Coalition. Both Bauer and James Dobson, head of Focus on the Family, favor a more confrontational approach to the Republican party than did Reed.

These groups expressed dissatisfaction with the GOP's commitment to the Christian Right agenda in 1998.[52] They want Christian conservatives to have a stronger voice in the GOP and are willing to reshuffle old alliances to accomplish this goal—even if it means alienating economic conservatives by opposing most favored nation status for China because of human rights abuses. Bauer, who is also considering an eventual run for the presidency, has filled a void created by the decline of the Christian Coalition with his keen focus on issues such as abortion, homosexuality, pornography, and religious freedom.[53]

Conclusion

How effective are religious lobbies? Effectiveness is hard to measure. Most legislation involves broad coalitions of groups and members of Congress, so determining any single group's influence is difficult, if not impossible. But the best evidence we have suggests that most groups enjoy only modest and periodic influence. Jewish groups have clearly made a difference on U.S. foreign aid to Israel. The religious prolife lobby has won on the Hyde Amendment, but not much else. Day-care legislation was amended to accommodate religious actors. Catholic groups have succeeded in securing abortion-neutral language in such legislation as the Civil Rights Restoration Act. Aid to the Contras in the 1980s was cut off after heavy religious lobbying. Sanctions against South Africa were imposed over President Reagan's veto in part because of massive pressure brought by African American churches on members of Congress. Bread for the World and religious relief agencies have increased funding for hunger programs. Conservative groups note congressional passage of antipornography legislation. Though these are serious accomplishments, compared to the vast amount of policymaking and budgeting that goes on in Washington and in each state capitol they are relatively modest. However, when religious groups come together, their impact can be dramatic. But since that is rare indeed, one should be cautious about claiming too much for the religious advocacy community.

As we look to the future a number of trends bear watching. First, rapid technological change has speeded up the lobbying process and made the links between leaders and members more sophisticated. Fax technology, e-mail, satellite hookups, and computer phoning services speed the communication between activist citizens, Washington, and other levels of government. Groups that are able to employ the latest means will have the edge. Some conservative Christian organizations have been quicker than their liberal counterparts to adopt such means. Rapid response may also foster changes in the governing structures of organizations to allow leaders the flexibility to respond to breaking events while providing accountability to members and church bodies.

A second trend is the growing importance of intellectual discourse, including the war of ideas fought out in elite journals and magazines; think tank reports; policy institute advocacy; and academic research. Ideas clearly matter, and so does the marshaling of facts and analysis. Groups cannot depend solely upon high pressure or skilled maneuvering in Washington. They must be a part of the intellectual debate. If the conservative Heritage Foundation or the liberal Brookings Institution publishes research supporting school choice (which both have done), then that research becomes grist for religious activists who have complaints about public schools. Similarly, if the Children's Defense Fund releases a well-publicized study on childhood immunization rates, then the liberal church lobby receives a boost in its efforts to immunize children. Washington today teems with this new brand of advocacy, and it seems that every day some "institute" is releasing a new report, calling for a new program, or presenting new facts to support a particular agenda. Similarly, such magazines as the *New Republic, National Review, Commentary*, the *Atlantic Monthly*, and *First Things* provide venues for intellectuals to present ideas publicly and offer solutions to the problems of the day. Religious groups must be a part of this world or they will see their influence wane.

Another trend is the move toward involvement in state and local politics. Though some liberal Protestant and Catholic groups have operated in state and local politics for some time, the state and local scene has become more of a battleground for religio-political groups. Hotly contested school board elections; clashes over gay rights ordinances; battles over school curricula, home-schooling, and vouchers; and the continuing struggle over abortion constitute the true skirmishes in the "culture wars." Given that so many of these issues are of concern to conservative evangelicals and Catholics, we expect to see even more of their efforts focused at this level. But given the pluralism of American society, strong opposition will also emerge to check such efforts.

Finally, it is clear that the struggle over American culture will produce changes in the relative strength and efficacy of national groups. Such groups, especially when they link with broader efforts, will probably see their influence grow over time. Because they seek sweeping social change, conservative evangelical Christian leaders have been busy founding secondary schools, colleges, and media companies for what they see as a long-term struggle with secular society. One can detect modest fruit of this effort. Wander the offices of Concerned Women for America, the Christian Coalition, or the Family Research Council and you will find recent graduates of such institutions as Regent University (founded by Pat Robertson) and Liberty University (founded by Jerry Falwell), as well as alumni of established evangelical institutions like Wheaton College and Calvin College. Christian broadcasting and a growing Christian arts agenda similarly seem focused on a long-term struggle, and they provide a means for new leaders to learn modern skills. But more important still are the countercultural educational efforts of Christian conservatives, who aim to train a generation of young people to move into government, academic, and media positions and ultimately provide them with the elite access they now lack. Whether or not this long-term struggle over the culture will provide such access remains to be seen, but given the barriers these groups now face, it may be the only way they will ever come to exercise more than a marginal influence in the contemporary polity.

Other groups, too, understand this fact. From Orthodox Jews to Catholics, we see efforts to sustain or expand access to schools, media outlets, and other cultural institutions. Thus, if we wish to know something about the future political efficacy of a religious tradition, we should look to its present culture-building activities. Effective national advocacy ultimately rests on the vitality of the religious organizations and the constituencies they represent.

Further Reading

Adams, James. *The Growing Church Lobby in Washington.* Grand Rapids, MI: Eerdmans, 1970. An important study of mostly mainline religious lobbies before the rise of the Christian Right.

Cromartie, Michael, ed. *No Longer Exiles: The Religious New Right in American Politics.* Washington, DC: Ethics and Public Policy Center, 1993. A series of interesting perspectives on the politics of the religious Right.

Ebersole, Luke E. *Church Lobbying in the Nation's Capital.* New York: Macmillan, 1951. The pioneering study of religious interest groups in the United States.

Findlay, James F., Jr. *Church People in the Struggle: The National Council of Churches and the Black Freedom Movement, 1950–1970.* New York: Oxford University Press, 1993. Mainline religious politics in its heyday.

Hertzke, Allen D. *Representing God in Washington: The Role of Religious Lobbies in the American Polity.* Knoxville, TN: University of Tennessee Press, 1988. The standard guide to religious interest groups today.

Hofrenning, Daniel J. B. *In Washington but Not of It: The Prophetic Politics of Religious Lobbyists.* Philadelphia: Temple University Press, 1995. The most recent treatment of religious lobbies, with a provocative thesis.

Moen, Matthew C. *The Transformation of the Christian Right*. Tuscaloosa, AL: University of Alabama Press, 1992. Interesting, reflective study of the recent directions of the Christian Right.

Wilcox, Clyde. *Onward Christian Soldiers? The Religious Right in American Politics*. Boulder, CO: Westview, 1996. A useful discussion of the identity of the Christian Right and its prospects for future success.

4

Voting and Religion
in American Politics

*T*hroughout American history religious currents have flowed powerfully, defining partisan attachments and shaping voting behavior. In this chapter we chart the voting patterns of the key American religious groups in the electorate—Catholics, evangelical Protestants, mainline Protestants, African American Christians, Jews, and secularists—and offer evidence for the existence of value- and religion-based cleavages in the American electorate. Differences among these groups are as real and politically important now as they ever were in the past. But we caution against exaggerating them. Value conflict does not necessarily make for "culture wars." Some religious activists see themselves engaged in a Kulturkampf against mortal enemies, but most voters do not see things that way. Evangelicals, for example, now align strongly with the Republican party, but many do not sympathize with Rev. Pat Robertson's Manichaean view of modern politics.[1] Our overall analysis of religion and voting behavior suggests some enduring continuities as well as some recently changed alignments.

A Historical Review

Religion has played an important role in competitive national elections in the United States from the beginning. In the first contested presidential campaign (in 1800) Thomas Jefferson's Democratic-Republican party challenged the Federalists under John Adams. Episcopalian and Congregational churches were closely aligned with the Federalists, while Jefferson gained support from Baptists, Methodists, and Presbyterians. Part of this alignment can be traced to the class profiles of these churches: Higher-status churches supported the Federalists, whereas populist upstarts backed Jefferson.

Linked with class, however, was the debate over state establishment of religion. Even though the Constitution prohibited a national religion, several states retained legally established churches. Federalists generally backed this form of establishment, but the Jeffersonians did not. Religious minorities thus aligned with Jefferson, even though he represented the more "secularist" viewpoint of his day. During the campaign, in fact, the Federalists mounted scurrilous attacks accusing Jefferson of being an infidel. But Jefferson's deist beliefs were less important to his supporters than the fact that he was committed to protecting religious minorities and ending government preferences for one faith over the other at all levels. Baptists, with their doctrinal commitment to the separation of church and state, also flocked to Jefferson.

After the demise of the Federalist party, a similar division—between the higher-status churches and the upstarts—persisted, manifesting itself particularly in the two elections of Andrew Jackson (in 1828 and 1832), who gained the support of more populist churches but not established ones. By 1833, however, all states had disestablished their churches, and the "underpinnings for the dominant alliance began to crumble."[2]

Immigration of Catholics, which began in the 1830s and continued until 1920, resulted in the replacement of earlier cleavages between Protestant denominations with something far more durable: a Catholic-Protestant divide. This division profoundly shaped political and voting patterns for more than a century. Catholics became heavily Democratic, so northern Protestants gravitated to their opponents: first the Whigs, then the Republicans. This alignment also shaped partisan positions on important issues. State aid to Catholic parochial schools, a perennial issue in American politics, found its strongest resistance (until recently) among Republicans, who took their cues from Protestant activists. Moreover, the Republican party platforms of the late nineteenth and early twentieth centuries contained "strict separationist" planks designed to block Catholic inroads in the states.[3]

Today residual signs of the Catholic-Protestant division remain. Catholic voters are slightly more Democratic as a group than Protestants, though their loyalty to the Democratic party has eroded. Ironically, the modern Republican party has recently taken up the cause of aid to parochial schools, whereas the Democratic party now endorses "strict separation" and opposes such aid.

The Catholic-Protestant split was not the only way in which religious culture played itself out in nineteenth-century elections and politics. Careful studies by historians suggest that those Protestants least prone to evangelical pietism often joined Catholics in voting Democratic in the nineteenth and early twentieth centuries. Thus one way to understand the division of the electorate was that it pitted pietists against others (sometimes termed ritualists).[4] This religious division, which was often inseparably tied to ethnic differences, drew deep and enduring lines on the American political map. The pietists included evangelical Methodists, Baptists, Congregationalists, Presbyterians, and less ritualistic Lutherans. These groups were almost always overwhelmingly Republican in all regions from California to Rhode Island. The ritualists included Roman Catholics as well as many Lutherans, who usually voted Democratic.

What distinguished pietists from ritualists were their incompatible visions of the "good life" and the role government ought to play in it. As heirs to the Puritan evangelical spirit, pietists were moralistic in their understanding of religion and society. They fashioned themselves reformers and they favored active governmental involvement through laws and policies designed to accomplish their moral ends. Whether the perceived evil was alcoholism, gambling, dueling, or the breaking of the Sabbath, pietists were comfortable bringing their desire to reform society into the public realm (just as modern-day pietists are comfortable with government regulation of abortion, pornography, and television violence).

Ritualists, on the other hand, emphasized church liturgies and sacraments in their conception of religion as more important than moral crusades. Compared to pietists, they were more tolerant regarding personal behavior and less likely to support government regulation of morals. This religious and cultural divide between pietists and ritualists was powerful enough to transcend class and immigrant status. In the North, Catholics were Democrats and Methodists were Republicans regardless of their socioeconomic status.[5]

Different candidates and issues could temporarily cut against these partisan loyalties. When the pietist William Jennings Bryan seized the Democratic nomination in 1896, for example, his candidacy attracted support from some normally Republican pietist voters, but lost the votes of some normally Democratic ritualists. Republican Teddy Roosevelt brought most of the pietists back to the GOP by 1904, but in the midst of the Great Depression in the 1930s, Franklin Roosevelt regained a healthy share of pietist voters for the Democrats. He accomplished this largely on the basis of his economic appeal to poor and working-class people, but perhaps his genuinely religious and moralistic rhetoric appealed to pietists as well.

In the South, of course, religious factors were submerged by the politics of race and regional pride. During Reconstruction (1865–1877) the Republican party represented, literally, a conquering army of occupation. Emancipated black people voted only under the protection of northern troops—and they voted overwhelmingly for Republicans, electing a number of state legislators and members of Congress. To be a loyal white southerner one had to be a Democrat. When southern whites reasserted control of politics in their region, they remained deeply wedded to the Democratic party and used it to disenfranchise and otherwise keep African

Americans subordinate. Thus, despite the fact that the white southern population was heavily Baptist and Methodist, pietists in the region voted Democratic—unlike their northern counterparts.

The contemporary movement of evangelical Protestants into the Republican fold (beginning in the 1960s and continuing through the 1990s) represents a return to nineteenth-century patterns that had been interrupted by other divisions. Modern-day pietists have become heavily Republican again, many within only the last decade.[6] In order to appreciate the significance of this trend, we must examine the religious contours of Roosevelt's New Deal coalition. Its breakup has reconfigured religious alignments in contemporary America.

The Religious Vote and the New Deal

The Great Depression, of course, produced what some scholars term a "critical election," resulting in a partisan realignment of voters and creating a relatively stable majority for the new Democratic coalition. Roosevelt's New Deal coalition rested on three factors: region, class, and religion.[7] A fourth dimension, race, was not a major factor during Roosevelt's time because the northern black electorate, though it became generally Democratic by the mid-1930s, constituted a very small percentage of the total population. Only later did African Americans, securely enfranchised by the Voting Rights Act of 1965, come to represent a major voting bloc.

Roosevelt received his highest vote margins in the solidly Democratic South. The Civil War legacy and the total dominance of the Democratic party played key roles here. But so did Roosevelt's activist government policies regarding the economy; these were popular among white southerners, the majority of whom were poor evangelical Protestants. The kind of sociomoral cleavages we see today were largely absent from national partisan politics at the time and thus presented few cross-pressures for southern Democrats.[8]

In the rest of the country, too, class cleavages were vital to Roosevelt's fortunes. He was popular with many poor and working-class voters, labor union members, and others of modest means. Much of his appeal to northern pietists (both traditional evangelicals and Pentecostals) flowed from the fact that many of them were far less affluent than their mainline Protestant counterparts. This same kind of appeal brought northern black voters into the New Deal coalition despite their previously long-standing loyalty to the party of Lincoln.

But religion did play an independent role in the structuring of the New Deal coalition. Not only did Catholics remain a large and loyal Democratic group, they did so independently of class. Catholics at every socioeconomic level were far more likely to identify themselves as Democrats and vote that way than were similarly situated Protestants. Catholics, indeed, constituted one of the central New Deal constituencies.[9] Today, however, as we will see, they are not so loyal to the Democrats.

Also solidly aligned with the Democrats under Roosevelt were Jewish voters. In earlier years, many Jews had been Republicans because they viewed the GOP as the more liberal party. With the Depression and Roosevelt, though, they gravitated heavily to the Democratic party, where most have stayed ever since.[10]

Who, then, opposed Roosevelt? Northern Protestants (especially those from mainline denominations), wealthier individuals, and traditional Yankee Republicans formed the core of his opposition. These groups were often, but not always, mutually reinforcing. Even many modest-income Protestants in the North remained loyal to the GOP, especially in more traditional rural areas. The problem for the Republicans, of course, was that this base was too narrow to mount a serious challenge to Democratic party hegemony. Republican war hero Dwight Eisenhower interrupted that dominance at the presidential level, but Roosevelt's coalition enabled the Democrats to remain the clear majority party at all levels of government until at least 1968, and in some instances beyond that time.

The point here is that religion played an important and predictable role in structuring voting patterns and political outcomes in the Roosevelt years and for all the years that his coalition remained intact. In contemporary times, though, the New Deal coalition has crumbled, producing new alignments while reinforcing some old ones.

Continuity and Change in the Postindustrial Era

Since the 1960s much about American politics has been fluid and unpredictable. Cross-pressures have strained old loyalties, divisive new cultural issues have fractured the New Deal coalition, and politics itself has alienated an increasing number of American voters. Voting rates are down, partisan loyalties have weakened, and citizen discontent is far greater than in 1960. Some scholars attribute these phenomena to the nature of postindustrial society.[11] Traditional class-based and ethnic differences have given way to lifestyle differences and disputes over moral issues. Lyman Kellstedt and his colleagues have argued that the American electorate is in fact now divided not only along religious lines but also in terms of how voters approach modern society. "Traditionalists" emphasize the importance of religious beliefs in the confrontation with modernity, whereas "modernists" embrace modernity and its attending social changes.[12] Religious currents, not surprisingly, play a large part in shaping these new groupings. In order to understand how this is so, we analyze the evolving political attitudes and voting behavior of the major American religious groups.

In the process we focus on voting patterns in the electorate at large (about 50 to 55 percent of the adult population vote in a presidential election year; less than 40 percent vote in off-year congressional elections). Some differences exist among religious groups in terms of their representation in the voting public. Jews, for example, compose a larger share of the electorate (3 percent) than their share of the overall population (2 percent), so they are somewhat overrepresented. African Americans, on the other hand, compose a smaller share of the electorate (8 percent) than their population (12 percent) would indicate, so they are underrepresented.[13] The typical religious breakdown of the electorate is usually about 25 percent Catholic, 25 percent evangelical Protestant, 20 percent (and perhaps less) mainline Protestant, 15 percent (and probably more) secular, with the remaining 15 percent including black Christians, Jews, Mormons, Muslims, and other small groups.[14]

Roman Catholics

We know that from the middle of the nineteenth century through the 1960s Democrats could normally count on a majority of Catholics to vote for them. Indeed, white Catholics generally provided more than a third of the total Democratic presidential vote during the New Deal and in later eras.[15] The cultural divide between Catholics and Protestants continued to be a strong predictor of partisan voting through the early 1960s, especially when Catholic voters were directly mobilized. This happened most recently when Catholic John Kennedy received the Democratic presidential nomination in 1960. His candidacy electrified the Catholic world, and he received an amazing 80 percent of the votes of declared Roman Catholics. His candidacy also provoked skeptical Protestant rumblings. Both mainline and evangelical leaders expressed fears about having a Catholic in the White House. Would his loyalties be divided? Would he be under pressure to take directions from the Vatican? As a Catholic, how could he serve the entire American population? Anti-Catholic tracts began to appear by the thousands, reminiscent of nineteenth-century broadsides against "Romanism" and "papists."[16]

In spite of Kennedy's adroit handling of the religious issue, his Catholicism nearly cost him the election. Gains among Catholic voters were more than offset by losses among the larger group of Protestant Democrats, particularly in border states, but also in places as different as Pennsylvania, New Mexico, California, and Wisconsin.[17] Kennedy probably lost about 1.5 million votes because of his religion.[18] His razor-thin margin of 100,000 votes could have vanished easily had he not personally blunted at least some anti-Catholic prejudice. In the end, however, Kennedy's presidency and assassination, coupled with changes in the Catholic Church after Vatican II, appear to have put to rest the deep cleavage between Catholics and Protestants that existed for over a century in American politics.

Kennedy's election represented the high-water mark for the loyalty of Catholic voters to the Democratic party. This loyalty has trailed off notably since 1960. Catholics are now less loyal to the Democratic party for many of the same reasons that reduced Catholic-Protestant tension. Catholics today are more educated than their forebears, and most have joined the middle class. Many have moved out of ethnic enclaves to the suburbs, where they have often sent their children to public schools. They are now fully acclimated to the modern post–Vatican II Church, and they have integrated into the larger society. Many are now Republicans. Moreover, cross-cutting issues—such as busing to achieve racial integration, crime, abortion, and school prayer—have chipped away at Catholic support for the Democratic party. In addition, some observers have argued that Catholics slowly began turning away from the Democratic party during the cold war because they "have long harbored an intense antipathy toward anything that smacked of Communism."[19] As the Democratic party became associated in some minds with being soft on crime, weak on national defense, sympathetic to social engineering and abortion rights, and indifferent to religion, Republicans made hay among Catholics. Indeed, this was the prediction of Kevin Phillips in his widely cited 1969 book *The Emerging Republican Majority*. He argued that Catholics were ripe for the picking, politically speaking.[20] Richard Nixon's landslide victory in 1972 seemed to corroborate that thesis, with some 60 percent of Catholics voting for Nixon that year.

Later elections, however, suggested a more complex picture. Catholic support for the Democratic party continued to weaken, to be sure, but Catholics had not rushed en masse into the Republican camp either. On a number of issues Catholics remain more liberal than either old-line Protestants or evangelicals. Still, some Catholic voters are clearly not happy with the direction of either the Democratic party or the GOP. They have become the quintessential swing voters.

An evaluation of Catholic voting patterns over the last three decades confirms that the majority of the Catholic vote is up for grabs in any given election. As we see in Table 4.1, in 1980 and 1984 Ronald Reagan won increasing shares of the white Catholic vote from his Democratic opponents; his 57 percent majority in 1984 led some commentators to believe that a permanent Catholic realignment was occurring.[21] Republican presidential candidates, however, did worse among Catholic voters in 1992 and 1996, when Bill Clinton reversed the slide toward the Republicans. The picture was muddied in 1992 and 1996, however, by the independent candidacy of H. Ross Perot, who attracted 22 percent of the Catholic vote in 1992 and kept Clinton from winning a majority of the popular vote in either election.

Catholic votes in key states helped Clinton win the presidency in both 1992 and 1996, but that support did not approach New Deal levels, and it

TABLE 4.1 Presidential Votes of White Protestants, White Christian Right Supporters, and White Catholics, 1980–1996

	% of 1996 Total	1980			1984		1988		1992			1996		
		Reagan	Carter	Anderson	Reagan	Mondale	Bush	Dukakis	Bush	Clinton	Perot	Dole	Clinton	Perot
White Protestants	43	63	31	6	71	28	66	34	47	33	19	56	37	7
White Evangelical Protestants	24	63	33	3	78	22	81	18	61	23	15	61	31	7
White Catholics	23	51	40	7	57	42	56	43	37	42	22	40	51	9
Total Vote	100	51	41	7	59	40	53	45	38	43	19	41	49	8

SOURCES: Exit polls conducted by CBS News and *The New York Times* (1980, 1984, and 1988); Voter Research Survey and Exit Poll, November 1992 (N=1120); Voter Research Survey and Exit Poll, November 1996 (N=16,627); Survey of Religion and Politics (N=4034), University of Akron; John C. Green, Lyman A. Kellstedt, Corwin E. Smidt, and James L. Guth, principal investigators (via personal communication).

NOTE: The categories "White Protestants" and "White Catholics" exclude not only African Americans but also Hispanics and Asians. The category "White Evangelical Protestants" represents a subset of the broader category "White Protestants."

was complex and conditional. In 1996, Catholic voters were drawn to Clinton's stress on Medicare, Medicaid, education, and the environment, but so was the electorate at large. On the other hand, a majority of "traditionalist" Catholics—those who are most devout and adherent to the teachings of the Vatican—supported Bob Dole. There are also generational cleavages evident among Catholics today that may presage the future of American Catholic voting behavior. Older Catholics are more likely to remain true to the party of Roosevelt, while younger Catholics are more willing to turn with some regularity to Republican candidates.[22] Gender also matters among Catholic voters. Catholic women are more likely than Catholic men to be Democrats, and Bill Clinton received much more support from Catholic women than he did from Catholic men.[23] Clearly, Catholics remain a voting constituency that cannot be taken for granted by either party at the presidential level.

At the congressional level, erosion of Democratic voting loyalty has also been evident. Whereas upwards of 70 percent of Catholics might have cast ballots for Democratic congressional candidates during the Roosevelt years, in recent times this has hardly been the case. In fact, in the historic 1994 congressional elections, in which the Republicans won control of both houses of Congress for the first time in four decades, white Catholics cast 53 percent of their votes for Republican candidates. This marked the first time in American history that the majority of white Catholic congressional voters favored the GOP.[24] In 1996, Catholics returned to the Democratic party's congressional candidates, but only marginally: 55 percent of all Catholics and 51 percent of all white Catholics voted for Democrats in House and Senate races.[25] This suggests that Catholics remain a critical Democratic constituency for members of Congress, as well as for candidates in state and local races.

One of the most important recent trends in Catholic America has been the growth of the nonwhite Catholic population (especially Hispanics, but also African Americans, 9 percent of whom are now Roman Catholic). In 1960 the Catholic electorate was largely white, but by the 1990s nonwhites constituted about one-fifth of all Catholic voters. Nonwhite Catholics (with the exception of Asian Americans) are far more Democratic in their voting loyalties than are their white counterparts. Thus their growing numbers have masked a serious slide in white Catholic support for Democratic presidential and congressional candidates. For example, in 1984 Walter Mondale received 45 percent of the total Catholic vote, but only 42 percent of the white Catholic vote. As we see in Table 4.2, Clinton did comparatively well in 1996 among white Catholics, but he still received less support from them than from Catholics as a group. Black and Hispanic Catholics favored Clinton by an overwhelming margin, but he was unable to secure a majority of the votes of white Catholics. Similar gaps can be found in the congres-

TABLE 4.2   Presidential Votes, Congressional Votes, and Party Identification of
Catholics by Race, 1996

	Total %	Dole	Clinton	Perot	Democratic House Vote	Republican Party ID	Democratic Party ID
All		35	55	9	56	30	46
White	81	39	50	10	52	33	41
Black	6	16	78	6	78	16	68
Hispanic	10	11	84	3	82	14	73
Asian	1	40	55	5	50	20	45

SOURCE: Voter Research Survey and Exit Poll, November 1996 (N=16,627).

sional votes of Catholics. Table 4.2 shows that Catholics' votes in the 1996
congressional races mirrored their presidential votes, with black and
Hispanic Catholics vastly preferring Democratic candidates and the votes of
their white counterparts split between the two parties.

The significance here again is that white Catholics, once a mainstay of
the Democratic party, have become a critical swing constituency. They divide largely as the national population does in any given election. In 1992,
Clinton received 43 percent of the national vote and 42 percent of the
white Catholic vote; in 1996, he earned just under half among both
groups. It is not surprising, therefore, that white Catholics have become
something of a bellwether group in the American electorate. Comprising a
quarter of the electorate, they are sandwiched between white Protestants,
who are disproportionately Republican, and African Americans, Jews, and
secular voters, who are disproportionately Democratic. White Catholics, at
least for now, seem to be the median American voting group.

But race and ethnicity are not the only divisions found within the
Catholic electorate. Table 4.3 illustrates a key generational dimension. The
majority of Roman Catholics over 60, both men and women, still strongly
identify themselves as Democrats. Middle-aged groups lean Democratic but
are more mixed. White Catholics under 30 are now slightly more likely to be
Republican than Democratic in their affiliation, a remarkable departure
from the New Deal pattern. Within this group, men are more likely to be
Republican than are women.[26] Should this pattern continue, we would expect white Catholics to tilt more toward the Republican party as the older
New Deal generation disappears, though at this time neither of the major
parties appears to have a definite edge with Catholics. As David Leege has
succinctly observed, "There is no monolithic 'Catholic vote.'"[27]

Table 4.4 elaborates on the issue positions of Catholics (as well as other
religious groups), giving us a sense of the distinctiveness of the Catholic

TABLE 4.3   Presidential Votes, Congressional Votes, and Party Identification of White Catholics by Age, 1996

	Dole	Clinton	Perot	Democratic House Vote	Republican Party ID	Democratic Party ID
All	44	48	8	49	38	45
18–29	37	53	10	48	46	39
30–44	49	42	9	34	43	41
45–59	44	47	9	58	29	52
60+	39	56	6	59	38	52

SOURCE: 1996 Survey of Religion and Politics (N=4034), University of Akron; John C. Green, Lyman A. Kellstedt, Corwin E. Smidt, and James L. Guth, principal investigators (via personal communication).

electorate. Catholics are fairly liberal on a number of issues, no matter how often they attend church. Regularly attending Catholics, however, are more likely to support government health insurance, environmental protection, women's rights, and gay rights than either old-line or evangelical Protestants. But on abortion, regularly attending Catholics are less liberal than their counterparts in old-line Protestant churches.

One of the reasons for the swing character of the Catholic vote is that many Catholic views do not fit neatly with those of either of the two major American political parties. Thus Roman Catholics are often likely to be affected by the characteristics of particular candidates, issues, or other short-term forces. This tendency presents a challenge for both parties. Republican laissez-faire policies on the economy and health care may alienate just as many Catholics as do liberal Democratic views on abortion.

Evangelical Protestants: A Pietist Revival for the GOP

Two momentous developments in the evangelical world have influenced the voting behavior and party alignment of evangelical Protestants. The first has been the growth of evangelical churches over the past several decades and the corresponding decline of mainline denominations. In 1960, over 40 percent of all white adults claimed membership in mainline denominations, compared with only 27 percent in evangelical churches. Today, however, mainline (now more accurately described as old-line) affiliation is barely equal to an evangelical membership that approaches one-quarter of the population. Moreover, since regular church attendance is much lower in old-line churches than in evangelical ones, this estimate exaggerates the number of people who are actually involved in church life.[28] Mainline denominations

TABLE 4.4   Issue Positions by Religious Tradition and Frequency of Attendance
at Religious Services, 1992

	Prochoice	Pro–Women's Rights	Pro–Gay Rights	Government Health Insurance	Pro-Environ-ment	Cut Defense
White evangelical Protestant						
All	29	64	44	41	53	31
Regular attendees	15	52	32	34	43	29
White mainline Protestant						
All	56	75	59	42	56	50
Regular attendees	49	73	53	38	48	44
White Roman Catholic						
All	43	83	67	55	61	51
Regular attendees	28	81	69	52	57	44
White secular						
All	71	85	69	61	70	53
Black Protestant						
All	46	74	72	61	66	52
Regular attendees	36	62	78	63	60	67
Jewish						
All	93	86	82	56	62	67

(continues)

SOURCE: Adapted from Lyman A. Kellstedt, James L. Guth, John C. Green, and Corwin E. Smidt, "Religious Voting Blocs in the 1992 Election: The Year of the Evangelical?" (paper presented at the annual meeting of the American Political Science Association, Washington, DC, 1993), table 7; additional analysis by Lyman A. Kellstedt. See also John C. Green, James L. Guth, Corwin E. Smidt, and Lyman A. Kellstedt, *Religion and the Culture Wars: Dispatches from the Front* (Lanham, MD: Rowman and Littlefield), chap. 14.

NOTE: This table uses data from the 1992 National Election Study.

Evangelical Protestants are differentiated from mainline Protestants using criteria suggested by Lyman A. Kellstedt, "Religion, the Neglected Variable: An Agenda for Future Research on Religion and Political Behavior," in David C. Leege and Lyman A. Kellstedt, eds., *Rediscovering the Religious Factor in American Politics* (Armonk, NY: M. E. Sharpe, 1993); and Lyman A. Kellstedt and John C. Green, "Knowing God's Many People: Denominational Preference and Political Behavior," in Leege and Kellstedt, *Rediscovering the Religious Factor in American Politics.*

Seculars are those respondents who reported never attending religious services and claimed no religious affiliation. Because of small sample size, regular Jewish attendees could not be separated from other Jewish respondents.

Regular attendees are persons who attend church at least once weekly.

The term "prochoice" reflects agreement with the statement "by law, a woman should always be able to obtain an abortion as a matter of personal choice."

The term "pro–women's rights" reflects responses to the question: "Recently there has been a lot of talk about women's rights. Some feel that women should have an equal role with men in running business, industry, and government. Others feel that women's place is in the home. Where would you place yourself on this [7-point] scale?" Respondents are classified as "pro–women's rights" when they indicate some belief that "women and men should have an equal role."

The term "pro–gay rights" reflects affirmative responses to the question: "Do you favor laws protecting homosexuals against job discrimination strongly or not strongly?"

Those respondents who favor "government health insurance" are identified by the question: "There is much concern about the rapid rise in medical and hospital costs. Some people feel there should be a government insurance plan that would cover all medical and hospital expenses for everyone. Others feel that all medical expenses should be paid by individuals, and through private insurance plans like Blue Cross or other company plans. Where would you place yourself on this scale?" Respondents are classified as favoring government health insurance if they indicate some belief in a "government insurance plan."

"Pro-environment" respondents are those who believe that "federal spending . . . on improving and protecting the environment" should be increased.

Respondents who believe it is important to "cut defense" are identified by the question: "Some people believe that we should spend much less money for defense. Others feel that defense spending should be greatly increased. Where would you place yourself on this [7-point] scale?" Respondents are classified as favoring defense cuts if they indicate some belief that we should "greatly decrease defense spending."

BOX 4.1 SURVEY MEASUREMENT AND THE EVANGELICAL ELECTORATE: A SPECIAL CHALLENGE

Estimates of the size of the evangelical electorate vary. Many of our tables, for example, present data from the huge exit polls conducted by the major news organizations (the Voter Research Survey, or VRS polls), which estimate the white evangelical vote at about 17 percent of the electorate. Yet the evangelical portion of the electorate may be as large as 25 percent. The reason for this disparity lies in how evangelicalism is measured. The VRS asks the respondent if he or she is a born-again or fundamentalist Christian. Given the negative connotations attached to the term "fundamentalist," a number of evangelicals will not identify themselves as such.

More sophisticated surveys ask a battery of faith questions along with denominational affiliation—and they give us a better sense of the size of the evangelical camp. Scholars such as Lyman Kellstedt and David Leege have contributed immensely to the development of more valid measures of evangelicalism in recent years. On the basis of such measures, the evangelical vote has been estimated to account for about 25 percent of the total, which is roughly equal to the size of the Catholic electorate.

So why do we continue to use the VRS? We do so because its sample is much larger than those of other surveys, and because it is an actual election day exit poll.

SOURCES: Lyman A. Kellstedt, "The Meaning and Measurement of Evangelicalism: Problems and Prospects," in Ted G. Jelen, ed., *Religion and Political Behavior in the United States* (New York: Praeger, 1989); David C. Leege, "Toward a Mental Measure of Religiosity in Research on Religion and Politics," in Jelen, *Religion and Political Behavior in the United States*; Geoffrey C. Layman, "Religious Beliefs and Politics: Better Measures are Needed," *Chronicle of Higher Education* (March 13, 1998), B3–B4.

---

are increasingly being sidelined in American society and replaced at the strategic center of Protestantism by evangelical churches[29] (Box 4.1).

The second development has been the growing alignment of evangelical Protestants with the Republican party—a development made all the more significant by the numerical growth of evangelicals. These two developments have altered the dynamics of internal GOP politics dramatically. The old Republican party was an alliance of business interests and mainline Protestants, but the new GOP also relies heavily on evangelicals.[30] As a result, politics in the Democratic party has also changed, particularly by solidifying Jewish and secular support for Democrats.[31]

For much of this century many Baptists, Pentecostals, and other evangelicals were Democrats, in spite of general Protestant loyalty to the Republican party. It may seem strange today to think of theological conservatives as Democrats, but it was true for several reasons. First, many evangelicals, especially conservative Baptists and Methodists, lived in the South, where loyalty to the Democratic party reflected the Civil War legacy of opposition to the party of Lincoln. Second, a class dimension reinforced Democratic tendencies among evangelicals. During the New Deal era, for example, lower-status Protestants (who were usually evangelical) were more likely to vote for Roosevelt than upper-class Protestants, who tended to belong to the theologically liberal mainline denominations. Thus Pentecostals, independent Baptists, and other evangelicals were quite a bit more likely to be Democrats than were Presbyterians, Episcopalians, United Methodists, and Congregationalists. We must also remember that Roosevelt himself was a declared Christian and a loyal Episcopalian. His economic agenda was far less threatening to orthodox religionists than the liberal social agenda of some contemporary Democrats.

Things began to change in the 1960s. White southerners, most of them Protestants, began voting Republican at the presidential level at the same time that the Democratic party was embracing African Americans' goal of securing civil rights and voting rights. But race was not the whole story. The 1960s introduced a new kind of cultural politics, associated with the counterculture, the sexual revolution, liberalized abortion, women's rights, and gay rights. As liberalism—and by extension the Democratic party—became associated in some minds with alternative lifestyles, "loose morality," and indifference to orthodox religion, Republicans made sizable gains among conservative Protestants.

Jimmy Carter, a born-again Baptist from the South, temporarily stalled the transition of evangelical voters into the Republican party with his 1976 presidential victory. Analysts concluded that Carter probably did better at the polls among evangelicals than he did among mainline Protestants.[32] But many evangelicals later felt betrayed by Carter's liberal presidency, and simmering cultural forces combined to bring about the emergence of a militant "New Christian Right" just on the eve of the 1980 presidential election. Ronald Reagan skillfully courted the evangelical constituency, and they in turn proved a major factor in his 1980 victory. In that election, of course, a great many evangelicals abandoned their born-again brother Carter.

The real story is the solidifying Republican alignment of evangelicals, as Table 4.1 dramatically illustrates. Though the born-again vote was indistinguishable from the overall white Protestant vote in 1980, evangelicals have become increasingly more Republican since then. By 1988, George Bush garnered over 80 percent of the evangelical vote. In 1992 and 1996, a Southern Baptist, Bill Clinton, sat atop the Democratic ticket. Though he did better than Michael Dukakis had in 1988, Clinton did not attract much support at the polls from white evangelicals in either of his elections. Table 4.1 illustrates that in both 1992 and 1996, Clinton's Republican opponent carried 61 percent of the votes of Christian Right identifiers. In 1992, Clinton failed to register even a quarter of these voters' support; in

TABLE 4.5   Presidential Votes, Congressional Votes, and Party Identification of White Evangelical Protestants by Age, 1996

	Dole	Clinton	Perot	Democratic House Vote	Republican Party ID	Democratic Party ID
All	61	31	7	32	66	30
18–29	78	15	7	18	58	25
30–44	65	27	8	25	64	26
45–59	59	30	11	35	56	26
60+	53	42	5	42	44	41

SOURCE: 1996 Survey of Religion and Politics (N=4034), University of Akron; John C. Green, Lyman A. Kellstedt, Corwin E. Smidt, and James L. Guth, principal investigators (via personal communication).

1996 he still received less than a third of their votes (and Clinton's gains appear to have been Ross Perot's losses). At this point it is no longer a surprise to find evangelical voters firmly in the Republican fold. For several decades they have been undergoing an electoral realignment of sorts.[33]

Evidence for evangelical realignment can be found in generational trends in voting and party affiliation, as we see in Table 4.5. It is younger evangelical voters who have become the most solidly Republican in their identification. Nearly two-thirds (64 percent) of all evangelical voters between the ages of thirty and forty-four identify with the Republican party, as do an also substantial 58 percent of evangelical voters under thirty. It is particularly noteworthy that only 44 percent of evangelicals over the age of sixty identify themselves as Republicans. Another indication of true realignment is voting behavior in races below the presidential level. In 1994, evangelical groups rightfully claimed credit for the historic election of a Republican majority to both houses of Congress. Fully 75 percent of all congressional votes cast in 1994 by evangelicals went to Republican candidates.[34] In 1996, House Democrats received only 32 percent of the evangelical vote, with younger evangelicals providing only 18 percent and the over-sixty group contributing 42 percent. As the older generation is gradually replaced, therefore, we expect to see even higher levels of Republican identification and voting loyalty among evangelicals.

It is important to note that the term "evangelical" is not synonymous with the "Christian Right." Indeed, many evangelicals do not support the rhetoric or agenda of Rev. Pat Robertson or Gary Bauer, just as many did not align themselves with Rev. Jerry Falwell in the 1980s. A good number of Southern

Baptists, for example, look askance at Pentecostal practices and have not been thrilled to see Robertson's charismatic followers flooding Republican party meetings. Realignment, therefore, has brought a series of different (and sometimes competing) evangelical groups into the Republican fold.

The importance of the evangelical constituency to the Republican party is now well recognized in professional campaign circles. No wonder Republican get-out-the-vote drives target the evangelical constituency. In an analysis of the role of the Christian Right in the 1992 election, John Green found that 54 percent of Bush's evangelical voters had been contacted and urged to vote. Bush's social issue conservatives in the old-line Protestant denominations also reported a 75 percent contact rate. In an atomized mass society, with supposedly weak local party structures, these facts are remarkable. Party organizations and religious groups are playing a crucial role in solidifying the evangelical realignment.[35]

Many contemporary evangelicals are solidly middle class and suburban, so they may vote Republican for economic reasons. But clearly there is a strong element of cultural conservatism behind the evangelical-Republican marriage. Table 4.4 shows, for example, that evangelicals are now among the most conservative of all American voters on a host of issues, from abortion and gay rights to health-care reform and defense. Table 4.6 indicates that, unlike the electorate as a whole, evangelicals rank the social nexus of abortion and family values as more important than economic issues. Moreover, the salience of social issues is even higher for frequent church attendees and among middle-aged groups, who are often involved in raising children—and who are most likely to vote.

Christian Right leaders and Republican operatives are now attempting to merge social conservatism with traditional business opposition to taxes and "big government" (Box 4.2). They aim to increase the tax credit for people with children, remove the "marriage tax" that penalizes some married couples, and provide parental choice in education and health-care matters—all issues that can unite profamily evangelicals with probusiness Republicans.

One year-2000 presidential hopeful who has a great deal of support among evangelicals is John Ashcroft. He has established himself as an economic conservative by supporting, among other things, a flat tax rate. Ashcroft also gained notice among evangelical Protestants in 1996 when he arranged for a provision of the Welfare Reform Act that allows religious groups to be compensated by the government for undertaking social welfare programs.[36] In a presidential straw poll at the 1998 convention of the South Carolina Republican party (in which the Christian Right has a significant voice), Ashcroft defeated all other candidates after a speech criticizing abortion, gambling, and governmental regulation.[37] Similarly situated with the Christian Right is Steve Forbes, who advocates a mix of

TABLE 4.6   Issues Most Important to White Evangelical Protestant Voters by Age
and Frequency of Attendance at Religious Services, 1992

	Abortion/ Family Values	Deficit, Economy, Jobs	Other Domestic Issues
Overall			
All	34	32	14
Regular attendees	39	27	12
18–29			
All	32	39	10
Regular attendees	39	34	8
30–44			
All	39	30	12
Regular attendees	46	26	10
45–59			
All	32	30	15
Regular attendees	38	25	14
60+			
All	24	30	21
Regular attendees	24	31	18

SOURCE: Voter Research Survey and Exit Poll, November 1992 (N=1120).

social and economic conservatism.[38] Such candidates are following the
lead of former Christian Coalition executive director Ralph Reed, who encouraged the Christian Right to embrace economic conservatism in addition to its trademark social conservatism.

Mainline Protestants

Unlike the realigned voting behavior of their evangelical counterparts,
there has been enormous continuity in the voting behavior of white
mainline Protestants. Methodists, Presbyterians, Episcopalians, Congregationalists, and northern Baptists continue to tilt toward the
Republicans, just as they have for more than a century.[39] But this continuity is set in a context of three key changes. First, there has been a real decline in membership and attendance in the mainline denominations. This
decline has dramatically decreased the relative importance of the mainline
to the Republican party.

BOX 4.2   1996 CHRISTIAN COALITION VOTER GUIDE

This is one of the millions of voter guides produced by the Christian Coalition and distributed at churches across the United States immediately before the 1996 election. It is interesting to observe that these guides sidestep the endorsement of candidates, which would threaten the tax-exempt status of the churches where they are distributed. Nonetheless, as we see from this example, the "right choice" for conservative Christians is obvious by the stark way the issues are presented.

Critics argue that these guides are crude and that they reduce complex issues to bumper sticker simplicity. Moreover, the highlighting of such issues as

'96 Christian Coalition VOTER GUIDE

PRESIDENTIAL Election

Bill Clinton (D)	ISSUES	Bob Dole (R)
Opposes	Balanced Budget Amendment	Supports
Opposes	15% Federal Income Tax Cut	Supports
Opposes	Banning Partial Birth Abortion	Supports
Supports	Taxpayer Funding of Abortion	Opposes
Opposes	Voluntary School Prayer Amendment	Supports
Opposes	Public and Private School Choice	Supports
Supports	Goals 2000 / Outcome-Based Education	Opposes
Supports	Homosexuals in the Military	Opposes
Opposes	Term Limits for Congress	Supports
Supports	FDA Regulation of Tobacco	Opposes

*Each candidate was sent a 1996 Federal Issues Survey by certified mail or facsimile machine. When possible, positions of candidates on issues were verified or determined using voting records and/or public statements.

*paid for and authorized by the Christian Coalition, Post Office Box 1990, Chesapeake, Virginia 23327-1990. The Christian Coalition is a pro-family citizen action organization. This voter guide is provided for educational purposes only and is not to be construed as an endorsement of any candidate or political party.

★ **Vote on November 5** ★

term limits and FDA regulation of tobacco would seem to serve clearly strategic purposes. Whatever one's view, Coalition guides represent the most notable effort by the Christian Right to influence the outcome of elections in the 1990s.

Second, the mainline's decline has paralleled an increase in the number of voters who may be considered almost entirely secular—those who seldom attend church but who continue to identify themselves as Methodists, Presbyterians, and Baptists. The politics of such individuals are often different from those of people who are more religiously committed. Recent analysis suggests that, although faithful old-line attendees remain rather strongly Republican, many nominal old-line Protestants have become more like the growing secular segment of the electorate, which leans Democratic.[40]

TABLE 4.7   Frequency of Attendance at Religious Services by Religious
Affiliation, 1992

	Attend at Least Weekly	Do Not Attend at Least Weekly
All	40	60
Evangelical Protestant	74	26
Mainline Protestant	34	66
Roman Catholic	48	52
Black Protestant	46	54
Jewish	22	78

SOURCE: Voter Research Survey and Exit Poll, November 1992 (N=1120).

The third change has been a modest increase in Democratic adherence among faithful mainline Protestants. The explanation for this trend may be that old-line Protestants now are rather liberal on social issues, even as they remain moderately conservative on economic issues. In a sense, like Catholic voters, mainline Protestants have become something of a swing constituency. They are the "traditionalist" mainline adherents, who remain solidly Republican and who cast 63 percent of their votes for Bob Dole in 1996. On the other hand, however, there are the "modernist" mainline Protestants, of whom only 42 percent preferred Dole over Clinton (and Perot) in 1996. This split is evident in congressional voting patterns as well. In 1996, 72 percent of all "traditionalist" mainline Protestants voted for Republican congressional candidates, while the same was true of only 46 percent of their "modernist" counterparts.[41]

The church attendance figures noted in Table 4.7 provide an important piece of evidence. Though self-reporting may inflate actual attendance at religious services, the relative differences among groups are huge. White evangelicals attend services most frequently, with 74 percent reporting attendance at least once a week, followed by white Catholics at 48 percent and African American Christians at 46 percent. Trailing far behind are white old-line Protestants at 34 percent and Jews at 22 percent. Frequent attendees who are white, whether Catholic, old-line Protestant, or evangelical, are more likely to vote Republican than their counterparts who attend religious services less frequently. They are also more likely to call themselves conservative.

Even so, there are still vast attitudinal differences among different religious traditions on key political issues. On abortion, for example, old-line Protestants are most liberal. On the other hand, old-line Protestants take a far more conservative position on universal government health care than do either white Catholics or African American Protestants, and they are only slightly less conservative than evangelicals on the issue. Thus, whereas the Democrats reflect old-line sentiments on abortion, Republicans embrace their position on health care. In short, mainline Protestants are cross-pressured in almost exactly the opposite direction as white Catholics, who are conservative on abortion but rather liberal on health care and the environment.

The Secular Vote

In 1960, Americans were decidedly a society of churchgoers. The Democrats depended on churchgoing Catholics and some evangelicals (especially in the South) to offset Republican strength among most Protestant faithful. Only a small percentage of the population claimed no religious preference, and this group's voting rates were relatively low compared to those of the church-based population. Thus secular citizens had a negligible influence on American elections. By the mid 1990s, however, an increasing number of Americans were listing no religious affiliation. They combined with infrequent attendees to create a sizable secular and near-secular portion of the voting population. Educational and economic elites, heavily concentrated on the coasts—and likely to vote—compose a large portion of the secular segment of the electorate.[42]

The size and nature of this secular group are not entirely clear, though analysts agree that it has grown substantially over the past three decades. Estimates today range from 15 to 30 percent of the electorate; differences are dependent upon how one defines the term "secular." In the past, survey researchers included only the 10 percent of the electorate who indicated they embrace no religion. Yet there are also voters who list a religious affiliation but never attend church and otherwise show little indication of religious commitment; they are only nominally religious. Some scholars, therefore, believe that such people should be counted as part of the secular group along with those who list no religious preference.[43] Others resist conflating weak religionists with nonreligionists. Andrew Greeley, for example, argues that lapsed Catholics retain something of the Catholic culture and are therefore distinct from truly secular voters. Old-line Protestant leaders, similarly, might claim that attendance at early Sunday school classes may continue to influence the values of adults who have nevertheless stopped going to church.

It is not necessary for us to sort all this out. Instead, we can suggest a profile of secular voters, however defined, as socially liberal and economically moderate voters who lean Democratic, but who are also diverse and volatile as a group. Some secularists are libertarian in their political inclinations and would vote for Republican candidates who emphasize limited government, shying away from social conservatism on issues such as abortion. Many other secularists have moved toward the Democrats in the past several years. In 1996, Bill Clinton received 53 percent of the votes of people who claimed no religious affiliation and 58 percent from people who were nominally religious. The 1992 and 1996 presidential candidacies of Ross Perot also appealed to the secularist portion of the electorate. Perot voters have been characterized by most observers as highly disaffected with American politics; part of Perot's allure, of course, was his lack of political experience. But many Perot voters also appear to have shared a disengagement from organized religion as well. In 1996, secularists and the nominally religious accounted for nearly 45 percent of all Perot voters, a percentage that far outstrips even the most generous estimates of their proportion of the overall electorate.[44]

With the apparent growth in its size, the secular portion of the electorate is likely to be courted more assiduously in the future. Unlike any religious group in the United States, however, secularists have no shared institution or tradition tying them together. As such they may be the most difficult portion of the electorate for candidates to reach. Positioned on the opposite side of the cultural divide from evangelicals, this constituency may be a check on the power of the religious Right. As such, their natural allies will be the majority of American Jews.

Jews, Liberalism, and Democratic Loyalty

In one sense American Jews have always been in the vanguard of a secular vision of American politics. The vast majority of Jews in the United States are theological liberals who celebrate the Enlightenment ideal of the nonsectarian state. Thus most of them behave like secular voters, only more so—they are very socially liberal and intensely loyal to the Democratic party. But American Jews, even those who are most secular, have traditions shaping their partisan attachments. Their commitment to liberalism extends beyond the social realm to encompass civil rights, the welfare state, and economic issues.

Jewish voters remain one of the true paradoxes of American politics. It is only a slight exaggeration to say that, although they look like Episcopalian Republicans in socioeconomic status, they vote more like African American Democrats. Here we see the impact of a kind of value-based voting that is independent of social class. And in this case, the values are liberal ones, since, as Lee Sigelman puts it, liberalism constitutes a kind of lay religion among American Jews. As illustrated in Table 4.4, Jews are among the most liberal of all American voting groups.[45] And they are liberal across the board; indeed, they are nearly twice as prochoice on abortion as all other American religious groups and extremely supportive of both women's rights and gay rights. Moreover, Jews are far more likely than other citizens to describe themselves as liberals, despite the fact that the "L-word" has taken on such negative connotations that many Democrats now shun it.

This commitment to liberal ideals helps explain the loyalty of many Jews to the Democratic party, though perhaps their relative prosperity might tend to make them Republicans. This Democratic loyalty solidified during the New Deal (during which Roosevelt received an estimated 85 percent of the Jewish vote),[46] continued through the 1960s (when Kennedy, Johnson, and Humphrey also received over 80 percent), and remains to this day. In 1996, Bill Clinton received 81 percent of the votes of Jewish Americans.[47]

Beginning in the mid-1970s, however, Republicans began to see opportunities for making inroads into the Jewish community and attempted to co-opt some of the Jewish activism and financial support that have been mainstays of the Democratic party. As we see in Table 4.8, these hopes had some basis.

In 1976, for example, Jimmy Carter received 64 percent of the Jewish vote, a solid margin but far less substantial than it had been for previous Democrats, leaving Gerald Ford with a healthy 34 percent. A few influential—and neoconservative—Jewish intellectuals had also begun to chip away at the ideal of the liberal state. Even more important was the issue of American support for Israel. Carter's "relatively even-handed approach to the Middle East discomfited many Jews," and that helped to produce widespread Jewish defection from his 1980 candidacy.[48] Ronald Reagan got 39 percent of the Jewish vote (in 1980's three-way race) while Carter got less than 50 percent. Republican hopes for further gains among Jewish voters in the 1980s were buoyed by Reagan's strong pro-Israel outlook and the rise of Rev. Jesse Jackson in the Democratic party, which produced a good deal of anxiety among Jews who believed him to be hostile to the cause of Jews in Israel and elsewhere.

As we see in Table 4.8, these Republican hopes proved false. One reason was that Jackson did not receive the Democratic nomination in 1984 or 1988, which allayed Jewish fears. Moreover, no clear partisan lines were ever drawn on support for Israel. The Reagan and Bush administrations were not always uncritical of Israel, and many Democratic leaders, in spite of Jackson's efforts, remained steadfast in their support for it. But most important, the increasingly evident Republican tie to evangelical Protestants, combined with the prominence of such figures as Rev. Jerry Falwell and Rev.

TABLE 4.8   Presidential Votes of Jews, 1980–1996

	Republican	Democratic	Independent
1976	34 (Ford)	64 (Carter)	
1980	39 (Reagan)	45 (Carter)	15 (Anderson)
1984	31 (Reagan)	67 (Mondale)	
1988	35 (Bush)	64 (Dukakis)	
1992	12 (Bush)	78 (Clinton)	10 (Perot)
1996	16 (Dole)	78 (Clinton)	3 (Perot)

SOURCES: Exit polls conducted by CBS (1976) and by CBS News and *The New York Times* (1980, 1984, and 1988); Voter Research Survey and Exit Poll, November 1992 (N=1120); Voter Research Survey and Exit Poll, November 1996 (N=16,627).

Pat Robertson, raised the specter of historical anti-Jewish bigotry in the heartland. Even though Robertson is strongly supportive of Israel, Christian Right rhetoric describing America as a "Christian nation" unsettled many Jews. Then, in the 1990s, political commentator Patrick Buchanan reintroduced a strain of nativist politics that many Jews strongly opposed. In short, the two Pats—Robertson and Buchanan—frightened many Jews.

Bill Clinton, on the other hand, skillfully touched on issues that lie close to Jewish concerns—tolerance, civil rights, an activist welfare system—and he did better among Jews than had any Democratic presidential candidate since 1968. Thus, in 1992 and 1996, Jews who had been voting Republican for president in the 1980s abandoned the GOP. In 1992, George Bush won a paltry 12 percent of the Jewish vote, and in 1996 Bob Dole netted 16 percent. Evidence of the continuing Democratic loyalty among Jewish voters was also present in the 1994 congressional elections. Jewish voting in those elections ran strongly against the national Republican tide, with 86 percent of all Jews voting for Democratic candidates.

Though we do not have good data on voting breakdowns within the Jewish community, a good part of the vote Republicans receive from Jews comes from adherents of Orthodox Judaism, who share many of the conservative moral attitudes of traditional Christians and who have been leaning Republican in the past few elections. The Orthodox, however, compose only a small portion of the Jewish population. Nor are all Orthodox Jews Republicans by any means.

In summary, the voting behavior of American Jews presents the flip side of the evangelical alignment in the Republican party. Despite vigorous attempts by Republican leaders to court Jews, and despite a sustained effort by vocal Jewish neoconservatives to dismantle traditional Jewish liberalism, Jewish voters have not abandoned the Democratic party. They remain firmly on one side of the cultural divide.

African American Christians

African Americans in the United States are overwhelmingly Christian and predominantly Protestant. This is true despite the public visibility of Louis Farrakhan's small Nation of Islam and the overall growth of orthodox Islam among African Americans. As is the case with the voting behavior of American Jews, African American voters are paradoxical. Their paradox differs substantively from that of their Jewish counterparts, however. Though a great many African Americans are evangelicals, they are also decidedly Democratic in their voting behavior. Well over half of all African Americans, for example, consider themselves born-again Christians and biblical literalists.[49] Moreover, religious salience is quite high in the African American community. Nine out of ten (more than any other demographic or ethnic group) say that religion is very important in their lives and a majority say they pray several times a day.[50]

Part of this paradox may be explained by the uniquely American tradition of black Christianity, which blended evangelical pietism with prophetic and liberationist messages. African American churches were, and are, infused with a keenly visceral understanding of the biblical narratives of captivity and freedom, of God's judgment on oppressors, and succor for the downtrodden. Many African American Christians, and especially their clergy, see themselves as chosen carriers of God's prophetic message of justice to a troubled land. What this means is that black voters often combine religious and moral traditionalism with economic and political progressivism. Thus black voters surpass white voters in their support for school prayer and are far less liberal than Jews, secularists, and old-line white Protestants on abortion. Yet they are far more liberal than other groups in their support for social welfare policies, government-sponsored jobs programs, government health care, civil rights, and affirmative action.

This fascinating blend of issue positions often receives little attention in voting studies of African Americans because what really seems to matter most is their almost monolithic (90 percent or so) support for the Democratic party. African Americans have been loyal to the Democratic party because of its support for the civil rights revolution of the 1960s and also because it remains, however imperfectly, the carrier of the New Deal creed of activist government and egalitarian economic policy.

Black church life, however, is also important for political behavior in ways that aggregate voting studies cannot capture. First, because the church is the

central social institution in the African American community, it has traditionally been a central focus for political organizing, voter registration drives, and
overt campaigning. Unlike most white clergy, some African American pastors
frequently invite political candidates to speak to their congregations from the
pulpit. Some also formally endorse specific candidates at election time. The
church is, in a sense, the precinct for black politics. Rev. Jesse Jackson's two
presidential drives were church-based, with leadership, mobilization, and
fund-raising centered in church and congregational networks. Other
Democrats now routinely campaign in black churches, most recently Bill
Clinton, who sings gospel music and can speak the language of evangelical
redemption and prophetic justice. In the African American community,
church membership serves powerfully to connect people to politics, and it
also increases voter turnout.[51] Black church members are far more likely to
vote than nonmembers. And contrary to the pattern for whites, higher church
attendance is correlated with increased identification with the Democratic
party. Thus church life is positively linked to Democratic support.

Another important development has been the expansion of the black
portion of the electorate. From the 1970s through the 1990s, African
Americans cast about 90 percent of their ballots for Democratic presidential candidates. But this tells us nothing about the relative size of that portion of the electorate and its impact on national politics. Though the
Voting Rights Act of 1965 officially ended the systematic disenfranchise-
ment of African American voters, its promise was not fully realized until
the mid-1980s, when black registration figures mushroomed, especially in
the South. Though many organizations played a part in the registration effort, African American churches and Rev. Jesse Jackson's campaigns were
central to the galvanizing of the black portion of the electorate. The growing number of African American voters profoundly altered the political
calculi of numerous political figures. It has also enhanced the clout of black
leaders in the Democratic party.[52]

There is a final sense in which African American religious conviction has
implications for politics. Because of their views on certain issues—school
prayer, abortion, gay rights, school vouchers—African American evangelicals
are being courted by white religious conservatives as potential allies in their
culture war against "secular elites." These efforts are based on the premise
that even though African Americans vote for Democrats, alienation from secular trends may lead more African Americans to the Republican party.
Christian Right leaders note that increasing the Republican share of African
Americans' votes from 10 percent to 20 percent would change the fortunes of
many congressional candidates. But Republican inroads have been hampered
by the continued temptation of candidates and consultants from both parties
to activate issues that play on racial fears. Until that ends, Republican hopes
to break the Democratic lock on the black vote will most likely fail.

Conclusion

This analysis helps sort out some of the competing claims about the relationship between religion and voting behavior in the United States. No theory about religion and politics receives more attention today than the culture wars thesis. Its proponents suggest that a deep cultural divide separates religious traditionalists (of whatever denomination) from a progressive coalition of liberal Christians, Jews, and secularists. To these analysts, politics increasingly has been transformed into a war of words over the culture, which is being fought locally on school boards and city councils, and nationally in presidential elections and congressional lobbying.[53] Activists on both sides of the divide have adopted the language of struggle and seek allies in the war. Religious conservatives, for example, speak of building an "ecumenism of orthodoxy" that would unite evangelical Protestants, conservative prolife Catholics, Orthodox Jews, and even Muslims (who tend to be conservative on social issues) in a crusade against "liberal secularists."

Our analysis suggests that, although value conflict clearly exists within the American electorate, it is not always so divisive, nor so neatly defined, as the culture wars thesis would suggest. In the first place, we do not think that many average voters consciously view themselves as combatants in a war over the culture—especially one that implies that some of their neighbors are serious enemies. Second, most voters do not always see the world in ideological terms, nor do they vote that way. Many mainline Protestants still vote Republican, even though they are strongly prochoice on abortion, and many Catholics still vote Democratic, even though they are prolife. And the majority of African Americans are born-again Christians, yet they remain loyal Democrats. The cultural divide is not as neat as some would have it.

We find more support for the existence of a softer version of value conflict in the electorate.[54] Among whites, for example, as church attendance increases, the Republican advantage increases, regardless of tradition (see Table 4.9).

Moreover, orthodox religionists—whether Protestant or Catholic, Jewish or African American—tend to be more conservative on social issues than are their theologically liberal counterparts. And with the notable exception of African Americans, they are more Republican than are their liberal sisters and brothers.

The role of church attendance as a guide to partisan attachments was not apparent even as recently as the mid-1970s. It has led some observers to wonder if a European-style party alignment is emerging in the United States,[55] pitting a Christian conservative party (the Republicans) against a more secular, liberal party (the Democrats). There are some problems, however, with such speculation. Many voters, such as socially liberal old-line Republicans and culturally conservative Catholic Democrats, clearly

TABLE 4.9 Presidential Votes and Congressional Votes by Frequency of Attendance at Religious Services, Whites, 1996

	Dole	Clinton	Perot	Democratic House Vote
Attend at least weekly	58	36	6	35
Do not attend at least weekly	38	50	12	53

SOURCE: 1996 Survey of Religion and Politics (N=4034), University of Akron; John C. Green, Lyman A. Kellstedt, Corwin E. Smidt, and James L. Guth, principal investigators (via personal communication).

do not fit this paradigm. Moreover, the most loyally Democratic constituency, African Americans, is strongly Christian and church-rooted. The same pattern holds for many Hispanic Catholics.

What does emerge from this analysis is that value-based voting does occur in American politics, and religious beliefs play a vital role in producing those values. On the eve of the twenty-first century, there is no doubt that religion remains a defining characteristic of American political life.

Further Reading

Kellstedt, Lyman, John C. Green, James L. Guth, and Corwin Smidt. "It's the Culture, Stupid! 1992 and Our Political Future." *First Things* (April 1994), 28–33. A stimulating reflection on religion and the 1992 presidential elections.

Kellstedt, Lyman, and Mark A. Noll. "Religion, Voting for President, and Party Identification 1948–1984." In Mark Noll, ed., *Religion and American Politics.* New York: Oxford University Press, 1990. A succinct survey of its subject.

Leege, David C., and Lyman A. Kellstedt, eds. *Rediscovering the Religious Factor in American Politics.* Armonk, NY: M. E. Sharpe, 1993. An excellent contemporary consideration of several aspects of its subject.

Menendez, Albert. *Religion at the Polls.* Philadelphia: Westminster, 1977. The classic study of religious voting in American politics.

Reichley, A. James. *Religion in American Public Life.* Washington, DC: Brookings Institution, 1985. In a rich book, a good discussion of the voting behaviors of various religious groupings in historical perspective.

Wilcox, Clyde. *God's Warriors: The Christian Right in Twentieth-Century America.* Baltimore: Johns Hopkins University Press, 1992. Valuable, detailed, empirical and historical consideration of the Christian Right.

5

Religion and Political Elites

*R*eligious activism, as we have seen, can focus on shaping the culture, influencing elections, or lobbying the government. To a large degree, the success or failure of these efforts hinges on the accessibility and responsiveness of the leaders of the U.S. political system. As we explore the connections between religious politics and American political elites, we must ask: To what extent are political elites—that is, political leaders, important government officials and bureaucrats, and other opinion leaders—willing to listen and respond to religious groups and activists? We ask this while understanding that elites are not empty vessels. They bring to their work their own religious backgrounds, worldviews, and biases.

One might think that much is known about elite religious views, but we know less about their religious outlooks than we do about those of the general public. In part this reflects the problem of access: Busy members of Congress, executive branch officials, party leaders, or judges can, and often do, refuse to answer questionnaires. Rarely do they agree to provide more than the most cursory interview. Thus we have little data on elites that can compare to standard national surveys of the religious public, such as those the Gallup organization conducts every month. Still, we do have some information that helps us understand the various barriers religious leaders must overcome to gain real clout in government.

As we chart what we know of the religious perspectives of elites and the broader environment in which they work, we will see that there are important religious differences among political elites, just as there are in the general public. But we also note that the religious views of elites as a group are not necessarily representative of the general public. Some perspectives are overrepresented while others are underrepresented, and this fact has political implications.

Religion and the Presidency

The outcomes of presidential elections clearly matter to religious activists. After all, the president appoints top officials of the executive branch, federal judges, U.S. Supreme Court justices, and diplomats. The president often has great influence over domestic policy and charts the nation's defense and foreign policies. Thus the president matters tremendously and can be a powerful ally or foe for activists who wish to further a political agenda based on religious principles. Presidents, for their part, realize the importance of religious constituencies and religious interest groups, and for many years they have designated White House officials to serve as liaisons to them.[1]

But every president also operates under compelling demands and a pragmatic logic that can easily override the moral pleas of religious petitioners. In the high-stakes world of realpolitik, religious niceties often give way to Machiavellian calculations. Moreover, the presidency is really a pluralistic office in which a host of White House aides jockey for influence, calling on religious leaders when it is expedient but ignoring them when it is not. Charles Colson recalls how he and other Nixon aides consciously used religious figures to lend legitimacy to the president and his views, or awed them with tours of the White House to mute their criticism. Religious figures, he has remarked, are often well-meaning but gullible people who understand little of the cutthroat nature of White House politics.[2] In retrospect, some evangelical leaders now suspect that they were naive about what they could get out of the Reagan White House in the 1980s. They have also raised pointed questions as to whether the Clinton White House has used selected religious leaders for its own political purposes.

The chief executive's response to religious groups is constrained by the unique religious dimension of the office of the president. As head of state the president serves a civil religious function.[3] Part of every president's responsibilities include offering prayers to grieving families of soldiers killed in action, invoking God's blessing on the nation on holidays like Thanksgiving and Memorial Day—or even during the presidential inauguration itself. Because of the nation's religious pluralism, presidents avoid clearly sectarian references on these occasions and employ the broadest, or vaguest, kinds of religious imagery.

The president's need to serve, in an important sense, as pastor of the nation can even lessen the political clout of the president's own religious group. The classic illustration involves John Kennedy. His election to the presidency in 1960 brought enormous legitimacy to the Catholic population, but his presidential decisions did not advance the policy agenda of the Roman Catholic Church (for instance, on such issues as government support for parochial schools). Kennedy bent over backward to avoid the hint of favoritism, but some Catholic critics argued that this made his administration even less hospitable to the Roman Catholic Church than previous Protestant administrations.

What can we make of religion and the presidency? We should note at the outset that almost all U.S. presidents have professed to be Christians. Harry Truman was a Baptist, Eisenhower a Presbyterian, and Kennedy a Catholic. But it has only been in the last two decades or so that the issue of religion in the White House itself has become so visible and important. This is a manifestation of the growing politicization of religion. By contrasting presidents Nixon, Carter, Reagan, Bush, and Clinton, we will see both the scope and the limits of religious influence at 1600 Pennsylvania Avenue.

Richard Nixon offers, perhaps, the easiest case. Though raised a Quaker, Nixon demonstrated little personal connection between his declared Christian faith and his politics. Nixon's approach to politics was strategic, not religious or moralistic. Both his successes and his failures were closely connected to his calculating political personality. His approach produced one of the most enduring cautionary tales for would-be religious activists. That tale involved this century's most celebrated evangelist, Rev. Billy Graham.

Born in 1918, Graham emerged as the premier Protestant evangelist by midcentury, and by virtue of that role he became the unofficial pastor to presidents. Indeed, he has been invited to the White House by every president from Truman to Clinton. It does not take a cynic to see why presidents would welcome Graham's blessing and association. Graham relished his role, especially in the 1950s, 1960s, and early 1970s, playing golf with Ike and spending lots of time with Lyndon Johnson and even more with Nixon.

Graham got to know the future president during the Eisenhower years, when Nixon was vice president. Graham came to count Nixon as a friend. When Kennedy opposed Nixon in the 1960 presidential election, Graham (like many evangelicals) did not support Kennedy for religious reasons, but his sympathies also lay with Nixon as a friend. When Nixon gained the Republican nomination for a second time in 1968, Graham emerged as a visible supporter. He visited the Nixon headquarters at the Republican convention, introduced the candidate at a crusade, and announced five days before the election that he planned to vote for Nixon (a public endorsement he repeated in Nixon's 1972 reelection campaign). After Nixon's 1968 victory, Graham was welcomed in the White House and was often included in the presidential entourage.

We now know, however, that Graham was never a member of Nixon's inner circle, nor was he privy to important decisions or secrets. Neither did Graham, as he now realizes, have a real friendship with Nixon, a man he knew much less well than he thought.[4] The Watergate scandal was the crucial moment in the Nixon-Graham relationship. When the Watergate drama unfolded, Graham initially refused to believe that Nixon had done—or could have done—anything so wrong. But as evidence piled up, and tapes revealed Nixon's personal vulgarity, meanness, and calculating manner, Graham changed his mind. The whole experience tempered Graham, leaving him more cautious about the blandishments of politicians and the temptations of power.[5]

Jimmy Carter's presidency (1977–1981) provided something of a contrast to the Nixon years. Lauded for his strict personal morality, Carter was also criticized for his naïveté and lack of strategic ability. A born-again Southern Baptist, a Sunday school teacher, and by all accounts a devout man, Carter's faith mattered to him, and he appears to have drawn close conscious links between his faith and his politics.[6] This was true in his view of the presidency as a trusteeship, in which he believed he should act in the public interest despite adverse political fallout.[7] It was also true, for example, in his approach to environmental politics in the framework of biblical stewardship of God's creation. But it was most obvious in the realm of foreign affairs, where Carter sought to advance what he viewed as the Christian mandates of human rights and peace. Ironically, many who later rose to prominence in the Reagan White House criticized Carter as naïve and claimed that he failed to provide a robust defense of American national interests. Some critics, such as Jeane Kirkpatrick, associated the weaknesses of Carter's foreign policy with his very Christian moralism. Carter was simply not Machiavellian enough to be a good president, they argued.

Carter's greatest triumph—the Camp David Accords, which sealed the peace between Egypt and Israel—reflected aspects of his faith. His belief in redemption, his stubborn determination to foster reconciliation, and his embrace of both sides as religious kin of the "blood of Abraham" made a real difference in the delicate negotiations. Critics of Carter's international role since his presidency, which has taken him to Bosnia, Korea, and Haiti, among other places, claim that he seeks peace at any price and that he places too much stock in the good faith of dictators. But whatever one's view of his efforts, Jimmy Carter's political endeavors are closely connected to his understanding of Christian faith.

An irony is that the evangelical Carter lost the support of evangelicals during the course of his presidency. In part this was because he interpreted his faith in a more liberal way than many of his fellow Southern Baptists. It was partly because the Democratic coalition he led produced liberal policies that angered and insulted many evangelicals. Carter's opponent in the 1980 election, Ronald Reagan, understood this discontent and played on it. Speaking before a convention of mostly evangelical religious broadcasters in 1980, Reagan acknowledged that as religious leaders they could not endorse him. He assured Christian evangelicals, however, that he supported their policy goals. Reagan made his view clear in one succinct declaration: "I endorse you."

Many evangelicals flocked to Reagan's candidacy in 1980 and 1984, though critics complained that he was not much of a churchgoer, had been divorced, and had risen to political prominence out of Hollywood—hardly an evangelical bastion. They also pointed out that his wife Nancy put some stock in astrology (reminiscent of Mary Lincoln's fascination with the occult), evidently to the point of recommending scheduling alterations on the basis of the stars. Still, Reagan remained popular with many evangelicals because he defended traditional values, families, patriotism, and the faith of the framers—with rhetorical skill and apparent sincerity.

This illustrates a key problem in sorting out the role that faith plays in the life of the occupant of the Oval Office. A president's electoral coalition is often formed more on the basis of his political stands than his personal practices or worldview. This is not to gainsay Reagan's religion; he did affirm orthodox beliefs and even shared in speculation about the end times prophesied in scripture. Moreover, his White House staff paid close attention to evangelicals, as well as to Jews and Catholics, while shunning liberal Protestants. In retrospect, however, questions remain about what, if anything, conservative Christians gained during the Reagan years (1981–1989). To be sure, many applauded Reagan's attack on communism and his reduction of tax rates. And there were new, moderate to conservative justices appointed to the U.S. Supreme Court. But most of the Christian Right agenda went nowhere during the Reagan years. Abortion continued, prayer stayed out of public schools, the entertainment media became more violent, divorce remained common, and the rate of out-of-wedlock births spiraled upward. Some evangelical leaders grumbled that the Reagan administration paid only lip service to their agendas.

Reagan's vigorous denunciation of the Soviet Union—he called it the "Evil Empire"—led him to form ties with Pope John Paul II that had a global impact. Prior to his election as pope, John Paul II had been a Polish bishop and a leader in the opposition to communist rule. Once elected, he set about using his authority and freedom to travel as means of fostering growing opposition to communist regimes in Eastern Europe. The Reagan administration was aware of these efforts and bolstered them with initiatives of its own aimed at destabilizing Soviet rule. Whether or not this alliance was instrumental in causing the breakup of the Soviet Union is debatable. But it is a dramatic example of the power of religious and political authorities who work together. Once again, though, we must ask: Was the alliance rooted in Reagan's faith or in geopolitical realities? Or were the two so intertwined as to be inseparable?

This brings us to George Bush, Connecticut Yankee, blue blood, and president from 1989 to 1993. Here too we encounter ironies of faith versus strategic politics. Bush is a mainline Protestant, an Episcopalian, and, although he is a religious man, he is uncomfortable with pietistic politics. The evangelical world of public witnessing, of stories of sin and redemption, of calls for moral renewal, are as alien to Bush as they are to most mainline Protestants. As one of his own evangelical aides confirmed, Bush did not like talking about faith. His Episcopalian sensibility meant that one should not wear one's religion on one's sleeve.[8] And when Bush tried publicly to affirm his faith, his statements came across as strained, awkward, even humorous. Recounting his experience as a U.S. Navy pilot in World War II, Bush described floating in the Pacific after being shot down: "I thought of my family, my Mom and Dad, and the strength I got from them. I thought of my faith, and the separation of church and state."[9]

In spite of his lack of comfort with public religion, Bush worked hard to gain evangelical votes in the 1988 presidential primaries and the November general election. He succeeded, garnering a greater share of the evangelical vote than Reagan had in 1984. Like his predecessor, however, Bush's record, from the standpoint of conservative evangelicals and Catholics, turned out to be very mixed. He generated considerable anger when he hosted a meeting of gay activists at the White House, and he was criticized more generally for his tepid advocacy of the conservative religious agenda. On the other hand, he worked to block abortion funding and fetal experimentation, and he appointed conservative Clarence Thomas to the U.S. Supreme Court. Even in defeat in 1992, Bush received more support from evangelical Protestants than from any other religious group.

It was never clear how much Bush's political actions derived from his religious beliefs. Nor were the political implications, if any, of his religious beliefs clear. It was clear, however, that he did not garner support from other religious groups equal to that of evangelicals. For example, Bush never seemed to connect with Roman Catholic culture, and he clashed with the leaders of the Church, especially over the Gulf War.

Finally we consider Bill Clinton, who defeated George Bush's 1992 reelection bid and was himself reelected in 1996. Raised in Bible Belt Arkansas, Clinton attended Baptist churches and Pentecostal summer camps as a youngster. As governor he joined a prominent Baptist church in Little Rock. He is fluent in the evangelical language of sin and redemption, and he seems equally comfortable in black and white evangelical congregations (often joining in gospel singing from memory). Clinton has also had some exposure to liberal Catholicism from attending the Jesuit Georgetown University. Furthermore, he is familiar with more secular worlds through his Hollywood and other "cosmopolitan" contacts. His wife, Hillary Rodham Clinton, is an active liberal Protestant: a deeply involved Methodist who is sympathetic to the religious Left.

Not surprisingly, the Clintons' religion has been subject to considerable scrutiny. Many conservative evangelicals, especially those mobilized by the Christian Coalition or Focus on the Family, view the Clinton administration as overtly hostile to their aims. Indeed, his 1994 surgeon general appointee, Joycelyn Elders—who was derided by critics (and later fired) for her enthusiasm for condoms and masturbation—as well as his liberal initiatives on gay rights and abortion, helped rejuvenate the religious Right. Whatever happened, they ask, to the moderate Southern Baptist Democrat? One answer is that Clinton has governed on the basis of his core electoral coalition in the Democratic party, whose agenda stands in sharp conflict with that of religious conservatives.

President Clinton has hosted meetings of evangelical leaders (mostly moderates) at the White House, and he has spoken frequently of the importance of faith in America. He attends church frequently, as does his wife, and he says that he is a regular reader of the Bible and a variety of religious books and articles. Moreover, Clinton backed the Religious Freedom Restoration Act, designed to protect religious liberty, and signed it in 1994 in a Rose Garden ceremony before a broad coalition of religious backers. He also instructed his Justice Department to back off from opposing a church in a celebrated court case, an action that earned him praise from the evangelically oriented Christian Legal Society.[10]

One book in particular that drew Clinton's attention is Stephen Carter's *The Culture of Disbelief: How American Law and Politics Trivialize Religious Devotion.* Conservative evangelicals and Catholics have also praised Carter's work because it criticized elite disparagement of religion in American life, a point they had been making for more than a decade (perhaps, cynics speculated, it took a Yale law professor and black Episcopalian to get publicity for the claim). Not only did Clinton read Carter's book ("keeping it at my bedstand" was how he put it) but he talked about it, endorsed it, and encouraged his aides to read it. Though Stephen Carter's well-written argument would likely have made a splash anyway, it did not hurt that Clinton made the thesis the talk of elite Washington for a brief time in 1994.

Nonetheless, by 1998, Clinton was drawing sharp criticism from leaders of the religious Right because of the many allegations of sexual impropriety being made against him. The Family Research Council's Gary Bauer, for example, devoted his entire March 1998 membership newsletter to the president's scandals. He expressed particular concern about what he saw as Americans' lack of moral outrage over the allegations, saying that the United States may have "slipped another notch down the moral precipice."[11]

The presence of the Clintons in Washington has been a boon to the liberal religious community. From the National Council of Churches to the

United Methodists, religious activists shut out of the White House during the Reagan-Bush years were welcomed back. Hillary Rodham Clinton is especially popular among liberal Christians. Her health-care task force invited liberal Protestant leaders to provide testimony. Invitations to attend White House briefings flowed to leaders at the United Methodist building for the first time in more than a decade. And though Clinton was responding mostly to pressure from African Americans, his restoration by force of the Jean-Bertrand Aristide regime in Haiti was welcomed in liberal Christian circles.

Clinton's posture with Catholics is complex. Catholic leaders have certainly not been shut out of White House councils. Indeed, on health care the president and the first lady consulted with Catholic hospital administrators and Catholic health association directors, as well as with more liberal Catholic groups such as NETWORK. But the Clinton administration's relationship has been rocky with the official Roman Catholic Church, as well as with more conservative Catholic organizations, such as the powerful (and antiabortion) Knights of Columbus. Conservative Catholics and Clinton clashed over abortion funding in proposed health-care reform, reaching an impasse that contributed to the administration's inability to pass reform by 1994. Moreover, Joycelyn Elders was forced to apologize after her criticism of the Catholic Church's views on sexual behavior provoked widespread criticism.

The Clinton administration's push for an abortion rights plank at the UN's population summit in Cairo brought about a serious clash with the Vatican itself in 1994. One incident in particular illustrated the tension between the Catholic Church and the Clinton administration. Frustrated at Vatican efforts to block the administration's proposed abortion plank, a Clinton appointee at the State Department castigated the Roman Catholic Church and claimed that its opposition might reflect the fact that the U.S. plan called for the educational and social advancement of women. This statement sparked a vigorous reaction from Catholic leaders, including a number of prominent Catholic women, who took out a full-page ad in the *New York Times* to defend the Church. The Catholic women reminded the Clinton official that the Church had been a leader in education for girls throughout the world and that it supported the provisions of the U.S. plan calling for women's advancement.

Clinton's sympathies, we conclude, probably reside more with the politics of liberal religionists. But sorting out religious motivation from political calculation is a difficult business. As we have seen, every president's faith matters, on some issues, under some circumstances, but the dynamics of political interest and advantage count for as much, if not more, most of the time. Presidents are, after all, very much political animals, and they are in the business of making political judgments and calculations.

Religion and Congress

Today's congresses reflect the religious pluralism of America much more than, say, the journalistic or Hollywood communities. Yet the membership of Congress does not exactly mirror the population. Some religious groups, such as mainline Protestants and Jews, are overrepresented relative to their proportion of the U.S. population, whereas Baptists and other evangelical and fundamentalist Protestants are underrepresented. Several factors explain these trends, including different religious groups' socioeconomic status, their openness to politics, and their geographic concentration.

One way to assess religion in Congress is to look at the patterns of religious affiliation of members over time. In the 1950s, for example, congressional membership was heavily weighted toward the historically mainline Protestant denominations, with Catholics and evangelicals definitely underrepresented. The first big break in this pattern occurred in 1958, when huge Democratic gains in midterm elections brought an unprecedented number of Catholics to Congress. Indeed, it was this influx of Catholics, coupled with Kennedy's presidential candidacy two years later, that sparked scholars to look seriously at the faith of members of Congress.[12]

Congressional membership since 1960 has become more religiously diverse and thus more representative of the nation (see Table 5.1). One striking example concerns Jewish representation. Only 2 percent of the members of the House and Senate were Jews in 1960, which was less than their share of the total population at the time. In 1996, by contrast, 6 percent of House members and 10 percent of senators were Jewish, which is considerably more than their 2 percent of the U.S. population today. Among the reasons for this change are the rise in acceptance of Jews in the country at large, strong political interest within the Jewish community, and high average Jewish economic and educational standing.

Catholics compose about 25 percent of the U.S. population. Though they were slightly underrepresented in 1960 (19 percent), they had achieved more than parity by 1996, when Catholics accounted for 28 percent of congressional membership. Catholic congressional representation, in fact, has consistently remained at or slightly above its proportion of the population for a number of years.

One of the notable changes in Congress in recent years has been the partisan distribution of Catholic members. In 1960, the Catholic congressional delegation was overwhelmingly Democratic. Since then, however, Republicans have made significant inroads. After the 1970 elections 35 percent of Catholics in Congress were Republicans; by the 1994 midterm elections that figure had grown to 43 percent. Here, at least, we see a reflection of Catholic voting patterns: the Democrats retain a slight edge, but their dominance has been greatly diminished from previous years.

TABLE 5.1   Religious Affiliations of Members of Congress, 1996

	House	Senate	Total	Percent of Congress	Percent Change Since 1960
Roman Catholic	127	24	151	28.2	+48
Jewish	25	10	35	6.5	+192
Mormon	11	4	15	2.8	+114
Protestant (total)	245	57	302	56.4	−28
Baptist	58	9	67	12.5	+5
Episcopalian	31	11	42	7.9	−34
Lutheran	17	5	22	4.1	0
Methodist	46	13	59	11.0	−40
Presbyterian	43	10	53	9.9	−21
Unitarian Universalist	2	1	3	0.6	0
United Church of Christ	4	6	10	1.9	−63
Unspecified Protestant	44	2	46	8.6	+92

SOURCES: *Congressional Quarterly Weekly Report* (January 8, 1960), 6; *Congressional Quarterly Weekly Report* (January 4, 1997), 29.

Old-line Protestant denominations continue to be overrepresented relative to their share of the population. Their congressional numbers have declined somewhat since 1960, paralleling sharp declines in mainline church membership. We see this most clearly among Presbyterians and Episcopalians. Though their membership in Congress is down from 1960 by about one-fourth, they still retain robust representation relative to their modest lay membership. This reflects the continuing role of socioeconomic status. Episcopalians and Presbyterians, as a group, are part of a highly educated socioeconomic elite. Some of their members are well positioned to achieve political leadership.

Of course, congressional representation does not by definition translate into clout for the Episcopal or Presbyterian lobbies in Washington, which tend to be far more liberal than Episcopalian and Presbyterian members in Congress. Members of Congress can disagree with each other on political issues, after all, and they also can disagree about how religious they are and thus how much religion matters in their political lives. And in some instances, it is the religious backgrounds of the constituents, rather than those of the members themselves, that bear a strong relationship to congressional voting behavior.[13] Nonetheless, having members of one's own denomination in Congress may provide at least some access.

We do not have complete data on evangelicals in Congress because they are diffused among many denominations. Their numbers have increased since 1960, and definitely did so in the Republican victories of 1994. Still, they remain underrepresented relative to their share of the population, in part because of the overrepresentation of old-line Protestants. The Baptist contingent in Congress, which contains many traditional evangelicals, illustrates this fact. Baptist representation has increased slightly since 1960, but Baptists remain underrepresented. Despite the fact that they make up 19 percent of the population,[14] Baptists compose only 12.5 percent of congressional membership. This should not surprise us given the modest economic and educational profiles of Baptists as a group. The Baptist congressional delegation is also diverse, containing a healthy share of black Baptists whose politics often diverge from the white conservative evangelical agenda.

The Church of Jesus Christ of Latter-day Saints is notable in that, unlike most small faith groups, Mormons have at least as great a proportion of adherents in Congress as they do in the population at large. Mormons composed 1.5 percent of the Congress in 1960, but this share increased to 3 percent by 1996. This proportion is larger than the Mormon share of the U.S. population, which has been steadily increasing and is now around 2 percent.[15] The best explanation for this phenomenon is that Mormons are concentrated heavily in Utah and a few neighboring western states, the very places from which most Mormons win elections. Also, Mormons are mostly middle-class people with access to the educational and financial resources that matter in politics.

The Senate provides an interesting laboratory for discussing the representation of different religious faiths. It has a decidedly more elite religious profile than the House. The largest religious group in the Senate, comprising slightly less than half of the entire membership, is old-line Protestantism. This is despite the fact that this group constitutes less than a quarter of the U.S. population. Next come Catholics at 24 percent, Jews at 10 percent, and Baptists at 9 percent. Evangelicals are underrepresented relative to their share of the population. Episcopalians historically have been overrepresented in the Senate, and this continues to be true. Eleven senators (11 percent) are Episcopalians, even though this denomination makes up less than 2 percent of the population.

The crucial issue, however, is not about the declared affiliation of members of Congress. What matters is whether Catholic, old-line Protestant, Jewish, or Baptist members of Congress constitute distinct voting blocs. The evidence on this is mixed at best. A study of Catholic legislators in the late 1950s, for example, found some evidence for Catholic solidarity in voting in Congress, but only at the margins of normal party voting.[16] Mary Hanna's study of Catholics in the 1970s showed that Roman Catholic members of Congress were not even aware of their own sizable numbers, so they were definitely not cohesive in their votes.[17] This appears to be true today as well. It is not really surprising, since partisan differences, varying regions, specific constituencies, and personal perspectives diffuse the unity and impact of any religious group in Congress. One of the few exceptions may be unified Jewish support for Israel, but beyond that issue cohesiveness dissolves. With other groups, moreover, it is hard to find even a single unifying issue. Considerable partisan and ideological differences exist even among evangelical Protestant legislators.[18] In short, political diversity reigns within religious traditions.

Even acknowledging this fact, we still must ask if shared religions could make a more subtle kind of impact on congressional politics. Catholics in Congress present one of the most useful groups with which to explore that question. Constituting the largest single religious bloc in Congress, their numbers closely mirror the Catholic proportion of the population. They now include sizable numbers of both Democrats and Republicans, which allows us to test whether religion matters regardless of party. Catholics also come from a distinctive Church with a hierarchy that has spoken decisively on some political issues. Moreover, the hierarchy's stands do not fall along clear liberal-conservative lines. On welfare and defense issues the Church has taken liberal stands, but on abortion it has taken a conservative position. Thus we can test whether or not Catholic legislators reflect this distinctive "seamless garment."

Michele Lindo has investigated this issue with regard to Roman Catholics in Congress in the 1990s. She looked at votes by Catholic members of Congress on issues on which the Catholic bishops had taken clear positions—such as support for a 1993 version of the Hyde Amendment banning abortion funding, and opposition to the January 1991 resolution authorizing force against Iraq in Kuwait. She found that Catholicism did appear to matter on some issues, but only with some legislators. Catholic Republicans, for example, generally supported the Hyde Amendment but were hawkish on the Gulf War. Thus they tended to vote like other Republicans on both matters. This is not to say that religion has not shaped the political behaviors of Catholic Republicans. U.S. Representative Henry Hyde (R–Illinois), author of the famous antiabortion amendment, clearly ties his Roman Catholic faith to his politics on that issue.

Catholic Democrats, however, display a wider ideological range in their votes. As a group Catholic Democrats in the House and Senate were overwhelmingly dovish on the Gulf crisis; they were significantly more likely than other Democrats to support giving economic sanctions more time and to oppose any use of force. Moreover, they took a more conservative posture than other Democrats on the Hyde Amendment. Lindo also found intriguing differences among Catholic Democrats by region and state. California Catholic Democrats were uniformly liberal on abortion votes, reflecting the more libertarian culture of the Democratic party of California. Catholic Democrats from the more traditional Rust Belt—Illinois, Michigan, Pennsylvania—more often tended to vote with their Church against abortion.[19]

What this suggests is that on some issues and among some people in Congress religion may play a role independent of party, but even this finding underlines the modest and contingent nature of religious impact. Like Mary Hanna, Lindo found no "block voting" among Catholics, just some indication that Catholicism is one of many factors that explain some votes on selected issues.

But perhaps there are other ways in which religion influences national legislators. After all, denominational affiliation can be a lot less important than *how* one experiences faith. If only we could get inside the minds of members of Congress, we might see how their religious worldviews (as opposed to their nominal religious affiliations) shape their political behaviors. Surely this would be the best guide of all as to how religion affects politics on Capitol Hill. This was exactly the premise of an ambitious study by Peter Benson and Dorothy Williams entitled *Religion on Capitol Hill*.[20]

The authors conducted in-depth interviews with a large sample of members of Congress in the 1980s. The religious themes explored in the interviews reached beyond denominational categories to personal ones. How did they experience God or religion—as comforting or challenging? As restricting or releasing? As an individual or a member of a community? What is the central demand of their religion—reverence for God or service to fellow humans? How did they view God—as a judge or loving presence?

The authors discovered that members of Congress fell into six religious types, which they labeled legalistic, self-concerned, integrated, people-concerned, nontraditional, and nominal. These categories did not correlate with particular religious denominations or political parties, but they proved widely predictive of voting behaviors. In fact, members' religious attitudes predicted their voting patterns better than did their party affiliations. Religious worldviews clearly structured their value systems and their political behaviors. This is not to say that some members of some faiths do not share common attitudes, as we saw with some Catholics above. But what Benson and Williams help us appreciate is the complexity of religious experience and its relationship with politics. Thus a "legalistic" Catholic may have more in common with a Protestant of the same type than with a fellow Catholic whose faith experience is quite different.

A number of interesting findings emerged from the Benson and Williams study. The most politically liberal members of Congress were those whose faith was very "people-concerned." Such members stated that their religions' goals included promoting justice, helping the less fortunate, and other similar missions. By comparison, "legalistic" and "self-concerned" religionists said their faith suggested a reverence for God and proper personal conduct; they were distinctly more politically conservative. Slightly more than a fifth of the members surveyed were "nominal" religionists; their faith seemed weak and unconnected to politics. Many nominally religious politicians were stymied by such questions as "What is the path to salvation?" Intriguingly, this most secular group was not the most liberal—far from it. They tended to be liberal on social issues and conservative on economic and defense issues. By contrast, "integrated religionists," who combined a concern for what they understood as justice on earth and a reverence for a judging God, reversed that pattern, taking more conservative stands on abortion and more liberal ones on welfare and international relations.

The central finding of the Benson and Williams study remains compelling. Members of Congress are not empty vessels; they bring to their jobs years of socialization and religious experiences that mold their worldviews. Those views, in turn, are likely to contribute, consciously and unconsciously, to their politics.

Another way to look at the study of religion and Congress is to examine particular individuals in Congress for whom religion matters a great deal (Box 5.1). One such person is Senator Jesse Helms (R–North Carolina), a conservative Baptist whose crusades for school prayer and against liberalism, abortion, gay rights, and pornography mark him as one of the most visible symbols of the Christian Right. Another is Senator Orrin Hatch (R–Utah), a Mormon whose values are like those of Helms in many respects, but whose style is distinctly more understated. A third is Rep. Henry Hyde (R–Illinois), a Roman Catholic whose passionate advocacy for the unborn is matched by support for government aid for unwed mothers.

On the more liberal side of things, there was former Rep. Floyd Flake (D–New York), an African Methodist Episcopal (AME) minister from Brooklyn who has been pastor of Allen AME Church since 1976. Flake has consistently argued and worked for programs to help impoverished and disadvantaged Americans, especially African Americans. To him, such activism on behalf of the less fortunate is an essential part of what is required of a committed Christian. The late Rep. Tip O'Neill (D–Massachusetts),

---

BOX 5.1 SORTING OUT RELIGIOUS AND POLITICAL MOTIVES: THE CASE OF DICK ARMEY

House Republican leader Dick Armey of Texas provides a fine example of how difficult it can be to sort out religious and political motives. An economist who has long advocated a flat tax and deregulation, Armey has enjoyed strong support from fiscal conservatives in the business community. In 1998, however, he used his position as majority leader to expedite consideration of the Freedom from Religious Persecution bill, which passed the House on May 14, 1998. The bill, which was designed to impose sanctions against countries that practice religious persecution, was vigorously opposed by big business lobbies. So what explains Armey's seemingly contradictory motivations?

One explanation is his own political ambition. As one Hill staffer observed, "Armey realizes that if he wants to be a major player, a future speaker, he has to show that he is not just a narrow flat tax guy. He has to demonstrate broader substance, a values base."

An alternative explanation is religious conviction. Armey is reported to have experienced a recent religious conversion, and Hill observers have noticed his new tendency to speak in faith-based terms. During the floor debate, for example, he spoke movingly about the priority of religious freedom: "I do not want to stand before my colleagues as an economist and say that monetary systems are not important, that systems of trade are not important. Of course, these things are important. But let me ask my colleagues: If you take away from me the right to my faith, can these other things even matter? Without the right of each and every person on this globe to know they are free to practice their faith, most certainly they will be lost, and in the end so will we."

Readers will have to draw their own conclusions.

SOURCES: Interviews and observation by Allen D. Hertzke, August 1997–May 1998, Washington, D.C.; *Congressional Record* (May 14, 1998).

---

longtime Speaker of the House and Roman Catholic, operated in the same tradition. For him, Christianity required an active and generous government, and for many years O'Neill was in a position to bring this understanding to life as a committed Christian and a New Deal Democrat.

Then there is Senator John Ashcroft (R–Missouri), a devout Pentecostal and the son of a minister. In recent years Ashcroft has emerged as one of the most visible social conservatives in Congress. Active in the Assemblies of God, Ashcroft does not drink, smoke, dance, or gamble. This moral conservatism has led him to take actions such as fighting for the inclusion of a "charitable choice" provision in the 1996 Welfare Reform Act. Today Ashcroft, who is also the former governor of Missouri, is being touted as a serious contender for the Republican presidential nomination in 2000. He is relying on key Ronald Reagan aides to help him prepare for the campaign. Ashcroft has a natural constituency in the religious Right, if he can mobilize them. Gary Bauer of the Family Research Council (who may be considering his own run in 2000) has called Ashcroft "a ray of light in Washington."[21]

Rep. J. C. Watts (R–Oklahoma) provides another fascinating example. Watts first gained fame as quarterback of the University of Oklahoma football team. He was elected to the House of Representatives in the 1994 "Republican revolution." Watts is an outspoken advocate for family values; he also favors balancing the federal budget and strengthening education and the national defense. Since his football days, Watts has been active in the Fellowship of Christian Athletes. Moreover, he is associate pastor of Sunnylane Southern Baptist Church in Oklahoma, and when his schedule permits he travels around the country as a guest preacher. Watts joined with another African American pastor serving in the House, Rep. Floyd Flake in introducing a "Community Renewal Project" that was designed in part to enhance the role of churches in central city development efforts.[22]

Few contemporary members of Congress reflect the connection between faith and politics as intensely as does Rep. Tony Hall (D–Ohio), a born-again Christian. Though not a visible figure to the general public, Hall is well known and respected in a variety of religious circles. First elected to Congress in 1978, the former Peace Corps volunteer represents Dayton, Ohio, a heavily Democratic, union-oriented community, but his own politics defy conventional labels. A devout Christian, he participates in such evangelically oriented activities as the National Prayer Breakfast and a weekly Bible study group on Capitol Hill. Strongly opposed to abortion, Hall used his position as a Democratic leader on the powerful Rules Committee to work against abortion funding in the proposed health-care reform of 1994. When Hall's son was diagnosed with leukemia, the conservative evangelical Christian Coalition sent a memo to members asking them to activate prayer chains for the Hall family and to send cards and letters of support.

Hall is best known, however, as a liberal crusader against world hunger, a cause that he sees as flowing from his Christian calling. As chair of the Select Committee on Hunger, Hall has worked to improve both government aid policies and private relief efforts to fight hunger. When informed in 1993 that his committee was to be abolished, Hall went on a hunger strike in protest. As he related the story, he was inspired and fortified by Isaiah 58: "Is this not the fast I choose . . . to share your bread with the hungry?" At first his unconventional action left his colleagues stymied. But stories of his fast began appearing in religious journals from the liberal *Sojourners* to the conservative *Christianity Today*. Bread for the World sent an Action Alert to its 50,000 members, and other liberal Protestant groups responded as well. Spontaneous fasts sprang up around the country and contributions flowed into hunger organizations. By the third week of the fast the World Bank and the U.S. Department of Agriculture had announced plans for separate conferences on world famine and hunger in the United States, and House Democratic leaders were recommending the creation of a permanent hunger committee. A thinning Tony Hall was called to a meeting of the House Democratic caucus, where he received a standing ovation. In lauding Hall's call to conscience, then House Majority Leader Richard Gephardt (D–Missouri) said, "I feel ashamed. You've embarrassed us in the right way."[23]

The 1994 congressional elections brought to Washington an expanded group of conservative evangelical members of Congress, who also consciously link their faith with their politics. Among them are Rep. Steve Largent (R–Oklahoma), former wide receiver for the National Football League's Seattle Seahawks and activist in the Fellowship of Christian Athletes, as well as Rep. Helen Chenoweth (R–Idaho) and Rep. Linda Smith (R–Washington), activists in the Christian Right movement. Their presence and that of many others illustrates that through specific individuals in Congress, as in other ways, religion is very much a part of politics on Capitol Hill.

What tempers the impact of such individuals is the range of beliefs and experiences they express. Religious conviction takes political leaders in different directions. But a testament to the importance of religion, whatever its guise, is the thriving religious culture on Capitol Hill. Full-time chaplains work for the House and Senate, spending many hours counseling harried politicians. Members of Congress also attend various area churches and religious fellowships, and Bible studies have proliferated. Often these groups cross party lines and allow members of Congress to ease the frustrations and stresses of political life by praying together, sharing their stories, and offering each other solace. To be sure, such activities blend with lives that also contain plenty of strategic calculation and hardball politics. Thus the lesson of religion on Capitol Hill is, like so much else, complex and mixed.

Religion and Other Elites

The American political world involves much more, of course, than Congress and the president. And here, too, we see varying influences of faith in political life. It is important to note that despite the conventional wisdom (which derives in part from the teachings of Karl Marx, who called religion "the opiate of the masses"), the wealthy and powerful in America do not all shun religion. In fact, 44 percent of all Americans who earn more than $75,000 annually report attending religious services in a given week as compared with only 28 percent of those who earn less than $15,000.[24] Americans who earn over $100,000 annually, however, have been found to be significantly less religious than Americans of lower socioeconomic status. One recent survey showed that only 61 percent of the wealthiest Americans report a belief in God.[25]

One of the relative bastions of secularism, as we have noted elsewhere, is the elite press, which has great influence over how political issues are framed for the public. One matter of considerable debate is whether the elite press pays little attention to religion because its reporters and editors know little of it or because they are hostile to it.[26] There are a few journalists who are either religious or serious about studying the world of religion, such as Gustav Niebuhr of the *New York Times*. The *Washington Post*, *Newsweek*, and *Time*, among others, also have serious religion journalists, mostly with liberal political views. Such journalists provide some access to religious activists, sometimes enabling them to articulate their message to a broader public. They are complemented by journalists who work for religious publications and write about politics, but whose work rarely reaches broader media markets. Moreover, coverage of religion in the media is increasing at the present time. The Public Broadcasting Service (PBS) now airs the program *Religion and Ethics Newsweekly*. ABC News has a regular religion reporter, as does National Public Radio. Stories about religion no longer focus exclusively on extremism or hypocrisy. This is why some authorities are now challenging Joan Beck's familiar complaint that "Religion is the most under-reported story of our time."[27]

A similar pattern has come to characterize the entertainment media. An increasing number of television shows and motion pictures feature religion and religious figures; many of these, such as the series *Touched by an Angel*, portray religion in a positive light. Still, most television shows and movies simply ignore religion, and many continue to present religious figures in a hostile light.[28]

And there is another side to the story of religious news coverage. While there are 1,500 daily newspapers in the United States, there are fewer than one hundred full-time religious reporters. The *New York Times*, for example, employs about sixty sports reporters but only one full-time religion reporter. Many newspapers feature weekly religion pages, but additional coverage of religious news is quite rare. Many observers, such as clergy, have expressed dissatisfaction with this lack of coverage—and with the biases inherent in many religion stories.

It is also important to consider the growing field of religious media. Radio, rather than television, is the principal medium today for religious communication. Almost 1,500 radio stations (half of which are regular commercial stations) now feature more than fifteen hours of religious programming each week. In 1974, only 1 percent of all television programs were about religion, but by 1996 the figure had increased to 16 percent.[29] While audience size is frequently in dispute, data show that consumers of religious programming tend to be older Protestant women who are orthodox in their Christian beliefs and supportive of religious involvement in politics.

Also important are the proliferating think tanks and policy institutes that contribute to the war of ideas between partisans in Washington and elsewhere. Here, too, we see evidence of a modest religious presence that has made a difference. Important examples include the Ethics and Public Policy Center and the Institute on Religion and Democracy in Washington, D.C., as well as the Institute on Religion and Public Life in New York. These organizations have high-profile leaders, such as Richard John Neuhaus, George Weigel, and Elliott Abrahms, and receive support from intellectuals of considerable note, including Peter Berger, Irving Kristol, and Jean Bethke Elshtain. These institutes conduct policy seminars and produce a flood of publications, including journals. Aware that religion must make its case to skeptics, these groups make a difference by offering an intellectual basis for an active role for religious faith in modern policy debates. They also provide ideas and intellectual support for political allies.

An arena where religious influence often seems submerged is in the upper echelons of the executive branch of the U.S. government. Despite the appointment of a few high-profile presidential aides in the Reagan-Bush years who were profoundly religious, executive policy and bureaucratic decisions are rarely made in overtly religious contexts. Government administration often does not lend itself easily to applying faith to politics and does not often attract employees who are particularly interested in this goal. In addition, administrative leaders often come from elite educational backgrounds, which we know to be more secular than those of the general population. Thus for every C. Everett Koop, Reagan's surgeon general and a conservative Presbyterian, there are a host of others for whom religion seems irrelevant to political activities.

Another arena where faith seems to take a backseat involves the host of political action committees, party committees, and professional consultants who drive the electoral machinery of the nation. Here, too, the game of politics—the strategies and tactics—seems to overwhelm any concern for the integration of faith and political action. Political consultants take note of religious factors when they are relevant to their political planning and plotting, as do candidates for office. But the approach is entirely strategic. No doubt some professional campaign consultants are religious, but we have no evidence that such convictions play any systematic role in their work.

The courts play an important role in the American policymaking process, far more so than in other nations. Judicial review is a powerful tool, and many judges do not hesitate to use it to advance public policies that suit their values. At this point, however, we have little evidence about whether—or to what extent—religious convictions influence judicial decisions. One might wonder about the powerful Supreme Court and decide to explore the religious affiliations of the nine justices—as well as those of other federal judges or of state judges—to see if they help us explain patterns in their decisions. The few studies that have done so provide only limited evidence of a religious impact.[30] We do find a strong commitment to civil liberties among Jewish justices, a modest "seamless garment" blend among Catholics, and so forth. But as a rule judges are more constrained than legislators, and they often operate with judicial philosophies independent of their personal religious views. The three Roman Catholics on the Supreme Court in the early 1990s, for example, spanned the ideological range. Justice Antonin Scalia was the leader of the conservatives; Justice Anthony Kennedy was a key centrist; and the late Justice William Brennan was a dedicated liberal.

Finally, there are state and local politics, which are arenas of increasing importance. States will likely play larger roles in policymaking as the federal government's role diminishes in this era of budget cutting and opposition to Washington's direction of human affairs. From school board members to governors, state and local elites will increasingly make a difference. Unfortunately, we do not have much systematic information on the religious affiliations and attitudes of governors, state legislators, or local officials, much less on whether their affiliations have mattered in terms of policymaking.

At the state level we do see some evidence that religion plays a role, albeit constrained, in public policymaking. One example of a religious current in state politics involves abortion, the debate over which intensified after a 1989 U.S. Supreme Court decision gave new latitude to the states to regulate abortion. Accounts of those battles reveal the importance of the attitudes of governors and state legislators. When conservative Catholic and evangelical groups lobbied in various states for more restrictive abortion statutes, their success depended in part on the views of elected officials (and the political cultures that produced them). Thus restrictive abortion statutes were passed in Idaho and Utah, where Mormons are concentrated; in Pennsylvania, with its sizable and traditional Catholic population; and in Louisiana, where conservative Catholics and evangelicals joined forces. Legislators in those states were sympathetic to prolife religious activists because they shared similar worldviews. On the other hand, restrictive abortion statutes were struck down in New Jersey, Florida, and Connecticut, and abortion laws remain liberal in a variety of states from New York to Colorado to California. Legislators in these and other states, which support more socially libertarian political cultures, have largely ignored antiabortion lobbying (Box 5.2).

BOX 5.2 A TALE OF TWO FORMER GOVERNORS: ROBERT CASEY AND WILLIAM WELD

Former Pennsylvania governor Robert Casey and former Massachusetts governor William Weld illustrate the complexity of religious values and partisanship. Casey, a Democrat, was both a national spokesperson for the prolife movement and the defendant in the famous 1992 abortion case *Planned Parenthood v. Casey*. Weld, a Republican, lost a bid to become the U.S. ambassador to Mexico in part because he had antagonized conservative Senate Republicans with his vigorous prochoice stand (he believes that abortions should be legal through the ninth month).

What accounts for the fact that these popular governors (both of whom served more than one term) took such opposite positions from their own party platforms? One explanation lies in their contrasting religious and social backgrounds. Casey, an Irish Catholic, traces his roots to ancestors who came to the United States in the 1850s to work in the coal mines. He argues that his defense of the unborn is compatible with that of Catholic Christianity and his party's historic postures of "defending the weak" and "welcoming the stranger." William Weld, an Episcopalian, comes from a blue-blood, prep school tradition with deep roots in the Republican party (his wife's great grandfather was Theodore Roosevelt). Weld's blend of fiscal conservatism and social liberalism (he is also a leading supporter of gay rights) resonates with an Episcopalian style.

SOURCES: Michael Barone and Grant Ujifusa, *The Almanac of American Politics 1994* (Washington, DC: National Journal, 1993); Robert Casey, speech before Christian Coalition conference, reprinted in *Christian American* (October 1994), 16–17.

With the likely devolution of power away from the federal government, issues from crime to welfare, education to divorce policy, and drug-abuse prevention to abortion, will be decided more often in state and local political arenas. The result, of course, will be an increasing focus by religious groups on state and local politics—arenas in which they have the potential to hold substantial sway.

Conclusion

It does matter what religious views politicians bring to office. For some political elites, at least, faith clearly shapes worldviews and orientations to politics. But having a religious faith, much less sharing the same faith, does not necessarily engender similar political views—far from it. Moreover, even those who may belong to the same denomination will not always interpret their faith similarly, whereas people from very different faith backgrounds may share identical positions on public issues.

At the same time, religion does not matter to many political elites; even if it does, many other factors—party, constituency, personal experiences—may play a greater role in directing their political behaviors. The situation is not simple. Yet as the pathways of connection among elites, religion, and politics can be complicated and multidirectional, they are worth exploring.

Further Reading

Benson, Peter L., and Dorothy L. Williams. *Religion on Capitol Hill: Myths and Realities*. New York: Oxford University Press, 1982. A pioneering study of how members of Congress experience their faith and connect it with politics.

Byrnes, Timothy, and Mary Segers, eds. *The Catholic Church and the Politics of Abortion: A View from the States*. Boulder, CO: Westview Press, 1992. An excellent reader that contains articles on the role of the Catholic Church in state legislative battles over abortion.

Hatfield, Mark. *Between a Rock and a Hard Place*. Waco, TX: Word Books, 1976. Veteran Senator Mark Hatfield (R–Oregon) describes the dilemmas of bringing one's faith into the political world.

6

The Christian Right
and American Politics

The intertwining of religion and politics in American society has manifested itself in many ways and in many forms. Yet over the past several decades, it has been the phenomenon of the Christian Right that has excited the most interest and inquiry among political and intellectual observers. Some have sought to understand the Christian Right as a fascinating example of the intersection of religion and politics; others have approached the Christian Right with sympathy for the movement and its goals; still others regard it with fear or antagonism. But whatever the motivations that bring people to study this important movement, investigation of the Christian Right can teach us a lot about religion and politics in the United States.

The Christian Right movement grew up primarily among evangelical and fundamentalist Protestants in the late 1970s and early 1980s. The movement's main goal has always been to take political action in response to what it perceives to be an increasingly immoral environment in the United States, which its members find to be disturbingly hostile to Christianity. Whether their complaint is about secularized public schools, vulgar popular culture, interfering government edicts, or collapsing moral codes, Christian Right supporters perceive an assault on traditional standards and Christianity itself in the United States today.

The movement's leaders argue that they do not want to establish Christianity as the official religion of the United States. Instead they wish to foster an atmosphere in which devoted Christians can practice their religion and see its morality honored in the broader culture. They insist that what they see as a fraying of the cultural fabric in the United States—and its attendant increases in broken families, illegitimacy, sexual exploitation, crime, and drug abuse—can only be reversed through Christian renewal.

Critics of the Christian Right, on the other hand, see this movement as a reactionary attempt to reverse progressive social changes such as the evolution of gender roles and increased tolerance of alternative lifestyles. These critics also deny that Christianity is under fire in American culture; instead they suspect paranoia is rife in the Christian Right.

Exactly who belongs to the Christian Right is a matter of dispute. Membership in particular organizations, whether the Moral Majority in the 1980s or the Christian Coalition in the 1990s, is too narrow a test. First, a wide variety of other Christian Right organizations have received a bit less media attention, such as Religious Roundtable, Focus on the Family, Concerned Women for America, and the Family Research Council. Second, there are many people who sympathize with the Christian Right, especially from within the evangelical, fundamentalist, and Pentecostal traditions of Protestantism, but they do not belong to any of these Christian Right political organizations. Sympathizers may not consciously see themselves as part of the Christian Right, and they may not be counted on to support one or another candidate who claims to speak for it. But because they often share similar moral attitudes with the Christian Right, they are in some sense a part of the movement. Sometimes they are silent allies, but other times they are not so silent. By this definition, perhaps 15 percent of the white population has at least been somewhat supportive of the Christian Right in recent years (Box 6.1).[1]

Even less closely associated with the Christian Right are a number of conservative Roman Catholics, Jews, and others who often share the values and agenda of the Christian Right but are uncomfortable with its distinctively Protestant aura. There are also millions of African American Protestants who share the Christian Right's concern about morals and values—and who also embrace a conservative theological outlook. They have largely remained out of the Christian Right movement, however, because race is often a more salient political variable than religion. African Americans tend to be politically liberal on economic issues, for example, while the Christian Right advocates conservative positions. These facts underline what we will often note about the Christian Right: Religious barriers and tensions have been the biggest hobbling factor for a movement that receives far less political support than public opinion polls would predict.

It is therefore important to bear in mind that the term "Christian Right" does not describe the entire white evangelical population of the United States, which now accounts for about a quarter of the public. At times during the 1980s there was strong agreement among evangelicals about the Christian Right's positions on moral issues and its favored presidential candidates (the Republican nominees). As we observed in Chapter 4, around 80 percent of white Christian Right identifiers supported the Republican nominee for president in 1984 and 1988, as did over 60 per-

---

BOX 6.1   IS CHARLES COLSON
OF THE CHRISTIAN RIGHT?

The life of Charles Colson provides a good illustration of how difficult it can be to know who belongs to the Christian Right. Colson, a former "hatchet man" for Richard Nixon, went to jail for his Watergate crimes. There he had a conversion experience that propelled him into ministry as an evangelist, prolific writer, and leader of Prison Fellowship, a Christian outreach to prisoners around the world. Colson's prison ministry is premised on the redemptive power of Jesus Christ, which clearly places him in the evangelical world. He also shares traditional moral values on family life, sexuality, and abortion with other conservative Christians. His writings describe the United States as a nation on the verge of complete moral breakdown. Many Christian Right activists, not surprisingly, view Colson as a brother.

On the other hand, Colson has cautioned his fellow Christians against politicizing the Gospel, and he has criticized some Christian Right tactics. He fears that preoccupation with politics will dilute the Gospel's message, which he believes to hold the only hope for cultural regeneration. Colson also parts company with Christian Right leaders because of his views about crime and punishment. He is a skeptic of the death penalty, believes that too many people are incarcerated, and has fought worldwide for more humane prison conditions. These views make him sound more liberal than many Democratic politicians who have jumped on the bandwagon of prison construction and mandatory jail terms. Basing his views on a biblical vision of "restorative justice," Colson argues that the imprisonment of nonviolent offenders wastes tax money, promotes more crime, and represents a lost opportunity to provide restitution to crime victims. In many respects, therefore, Colson does not fit clearly into the Christian Right camp.

SOURCES: Colson's views are contained in his regular column in *Christianity Today* as well as in Prison Fellowship's newsletter. See also Charles W. Colson, *Born Again* (Old Tappan, NJ: Chosen Books, 1976).

---

cent in 1992 and 1996 (despite the election of Bill Clinton in each of those instances). This is evidence of a remarkable degree of agreement within Christian Right circles.[2]

Yet the Christian Right was and continues to be more of a self-conscious movement than can be described by lumping all evangelical political conservatives together. Clearly most of those who might be described as members of the Christian Right come from the evangelical side of Protestantism. What is not so clear, however, is how many of these evangelicals—sympathetic though they may be about some issues and candidates—should be considered members of the Christian Right camp.

Most African American Christians, for example, belong to evangelical, fundamentalist, or Pentecostal religious communities, but the Christian

Right has received little support from the African American community. Acknowledging this fact, some Christian Right leaders have actively sought black support and participation. The Christian Coalition, for example, features black speakers at its annual "Road to Victory" conferences and articles on African Americans in its publications. It also commissioned a national survey of blacks, which purported to show their sympathy for some of the Christian Right agenda. In 1996, the Christian Coalition undertook some particularly ambitious efforts to aid African Americans, including the Samaritan Project in support of America's central cities and the Save the Churches Fund for burned churches. The jury is still out, however, on whether these efforts made much of an impact—especially now that they have been curtailed.[3] The Family Research Council has undertaken significant research on African American issues, and a black woman, Kay Coles James, was vice president of the organization for a time. Some black ministers have joined with Christian Right groups in local battles against gay rights ordinances and in support of school prayer. Despite these efforts, however, a large cultural and economic gulf separates most African Americans from the largely white Christian Right.

Even within the white evangelical world, Christian Right support is by no means universal. It has no support, of course, from the small but vigorous liberal wing of white evangelicals. More broadly, the Christian Right has found it difficult to mobilize much of its natural constituency of white, conservative Protestants. In part, this problem stems from the lack of a dominant leader with the ability to unite and rally this constituency. Rev. Billy Graham might have had this potential when he was younger, but Graham has studiously avoided giving the Christian Right his blessing.

The main problem faced by the Christian Right, however, is the pluralism and factionalism that characterizes religiously conservative Protestantism in the United States. Traditional evangelicals often do not welcome Pentecostals, who focus on a spirit-filled form of worship that sometimes involves speaking in tongues. Pentecostals are also sometimes divided among themselves. Meanwhile, evangelicals and fundamentalists are divided over how inerrant (true in every regard) the Bible is and how separatist they should be from the outside world. Almost every conservative Protestant church—even those belonging to organized denominations—reserves the right of religious and political self-determination. Almost every evangelical church claims to be sovereign under God. Meanwhile, entire denominations, including the largest (the Southern Baptist Convention), experience significant religious division and dissent. This long tradition of religious individualism among conservative Protestants haunts and hurts the Christian Right's hopes for political success.[4]

Culture and History

Statistics do not come close to telling the whole story of the Christian Right. It is also essential to explore the culture, organization, and history of this movement. Since the 1980s, the Christian Right has been defined in part by groups such as the Moral Majority, Focus on the Family, Concerned Women for America, the Christian Coalition, and the Family Research Council. It also has been defined by its famous leaders, such as Rev. Jerry Falwell of the Moral Majority, Rev. Pat Robertson and Ralph Reed of the Christian Coalition, Beverly LaHaye of Concerned Women for America, Gary Bauer of the Family Research Council, and James Dobson of Focus on the Family. Its televangelism, Washington rallies, and crusades against such things as abortion, violent and immoral television and movies, and liberal Democrats have also served to define it.

But the Christian Right also has a history that did not just begin in the 1980s. In fact, the contemporary Christian Right is only one example of many conservative Christian movements in the history of American politics. Its concerns have a long history in the republic and are hardly a simple creation of modern times. Indeed, some historians have linked the Christian Right to traditions of dissent and populist protest that began even before the United States existed as a nation.[5]

Perhaps the Christian Right's most direct predecessor was the Christian Anti-Communist Crusade (CACC). This organization was well publicized and controversial, particularly in the 1950s. However, it never achieved the prominence or support of the Moral Majority in the 1980s or the Christian Coalition in the 1990s. Its members were political and religious conservatives whose values drove them to political involvement. They were particularly determined to defeat what they perceived to be atheistic and socialistic communism at home and abroad.[6] The CACC and its supporters, however, played no part in the rise of the Christian Right in the late 1970s and 1980s because by then it was no longer active in American politics. In the 1950s, media, intellectual, and political elites routinely treated the CACC as a radical fringe group. But in hindsight we can see that it was an early sign of the widespread, angry, conservative religious politics that came into prominence in the 1990s.

In its short historical life, the contemporary Christian Right has gone through two distinct phases. The first lasted from the late 1970s until the late 1980s.[7] It might be described as the age of discovery and disappointment. The second phase began after the 1988 election and proved to be the age of realism.

The first phase of Christian Right activism built from steady growth in the numbers of evangelical Protestants in the decades after World War II (coupled with a coincident decline in the membership of mainline denominations such as the Episcopal and Presbyterian churches). The factors responsible for these membership dynamics are varied and controversial, but the objective fact of the growth is neither. Moreover, as many evangelical leaders observed the upswing of their brand of Christianity, their self-confidence rose and so did their willingness to engage in public discourse on their own behalf. At the same time, the economic and educational standing of evangelicals in American society was improving. The typical conservative Protestant today belongs to the middle class.

The political origins of the Christian Right were connected in part with discontent over a series of decisions by the U.S. Supreme Court. The Court's rulings in the 1960s declaring prayer and Bible reading in the schools unconstitutional, followed by the 1973 *Roe* v. *Wade* decision establishing the constitutionality of abortion, led to great dissatisfaction among many conservative Christians. For them, these judgments symbolized America's retreat from Christianity. They were ominous signs that the country had fallen into the hands of secular elites who were hostile to traditional faith and its norms. As Franky Schaeffer suggested in his influential book, this was *Bad News for Modern Man*.[8]

Another factor that stimulated the rise of the Christian Right was widespread evangelical disappointment with the presidency of Jimmy Carter. His 1976 campaign elicited strong allegiance from traditionally Democratic fundamentalists and garnered many votes from Republican evangelicals. As president, however, Carter's actions engendered bitter opposition from many parts of the conservative Protestant community. Religious conservatives increasingly came to view Carter as a traitor because he did not act decisively on behalf of their moral agenda; he did not, for example, advance the prolife cause. He was also sharply attacked for his failure to appoint conservative evangelicals to high-ranking government posts. Soon Carter's enemies painted him as just another disappointing sign of a secular corruption of American elites. This corruption, they surmised, had now infected one of their own.

Much effort has been spent exploring the dynamics that led to the most important single event of the first phase of the Christian Right: the birth of the Moral Majority in 1979. There is no doubt that impetus came from conservatives from outside the evangelical world and Republicans such as Richard Viguerie and Paul Weyrich, both of whom wanted to mobilize Christian conservatives for their own causes. But they worked in fertile soil, finding plenty of disillusioned and sometimes angry people ready for organized protest.

There were plenty of incidents besides *Roe* v. *Wade* in the 1970s that prepared the soil for the growth of the Christian Right. There was, for example, the fight in West Virginia over public school textbooks labeled by parents as antireligious and determinedly liberal. There was the censoring of Rev. James Robison's antigay sermon by Dallas television. Above all, there was the fight over the Equal Rights Amendment, which was defeated in part because of the efforts of Concerned Women for America founder Phyllis Schlafly.

There is no doubt, moreover, that opponents of the Christian Right gave it a great boost in the late 1970s and early 1980s. The elite media showered the Christian Right with tremendous publicity, which made it into a phenomenon that appeared to be far larger in numbers, organization, and influence than it actually was. The media may not have "made" the Moral Majority, but they certainly helped it enormously.

On the other hand, the Christian Right's spurt into popular awareness in the 1980s had its price—one that eventually became costly. It quickly became an inviting target and attracted many enemies. It increasingly met with vigorous opposition from an attentive liberal culture and received extensive—and highly negative—coverage in such national magazines as *Time* and *Newsweek*.[9] It also generated counterorganization (spawning groups such as People for the American Way) and countermobilization by already existing groups (for example, the National Council of Churches). This was, in short, the moment when the cultural battles with which Americans are now so familiar first emerged. Conservative religious groups came to clash with liberal media, intellectual, and artistic forces.

The first phase of Christian Right activism ended with the 1988 election, which was something of a defeat for the Christian Right.[10] This was true for two reasons. First, Rev. Pat Robertson lost his fight for the Republican presidential nomination (though his campaign did make some waves). Second, George Bush, once he won the 1988 general election, proved to be lukewarm at best toward the Christian Right and its agenda.

Well before 1988, however, other troubles had bedeviled the Christian Right. Its original organizations stumbled after early enthusiasm cooled and determined opponents appeared on the field. The Moral Majority, the flagship organization of the Christian Right, had collapsed entirely by 1988. It ran out of money and lost its leadership; it ultimately closed up shop with few supporters and a great many enemies. Jerry Falwell quit full-time politics, and there were few who could fill his shoes. Christian Right organizations were becoming increasingly obsessed with fund-raising, but they had less and less to show for it.

Inexperience on the national political scene, and sometimes with lobbying in particular, proved to be damaging. So did divisive splits within the evangelical and fundamentalist communities over the effort's appropriateness, importance, leadership, and agenda. As Pat Robertson learned in 1988, this lack of unity among religiously conservative Christians was frustrating. In the end, great hopes were tempered and plans for national victories disappeared.

The somewhat sour conclusion of the first phase of the Christian Right in 1988 was speeded by a series of scandals and controversies that led to the downfall of several televangelists, some of whom, like Jim and Tammy Faye Bakker, had been allied with the Christian Right; others, like Oral Roberts, had not been affiliated with the movement. As a result, the media tightly linked all televangelists and the Christian Right together, which proved a heavy burden for the Christian Right.

There was, however, a certain logic here. During its first phase the Christian Right and televangelism had in fact often been deeply intertwined. Jerry Falwell, for example, reached a wider audience because of his television show, *The Old Time Gospel Hour*. The use of modern broadcasting and mailing techniques to build the Christian Right movement, moreover, derived from televangelists' experience with such modern technology. How political televangelists were, how many people watched them, and how many people they actually influenced are matters of dispute. Still, the Christian Right and the televangelists were inseparable. The fall of televangelists (except for Pat Robertson) from grace struck a major blow and provided the media and other opponents with a field day of criticism.[11]

There were ironies in the end of the first phase of the Christian Right in 1988. From one perspective, Pat Robertson's 1988 presidential race was a sign of Christian Right vitality. After all, Robertson was their first official candidate for president and he attracted quite a bit of attention. The fact is, however, that Robertson ultimately did not do very well in his campaign for the Republican nomination. His campaign revealed the Christian Right's inability to mobilize religiously conservative Christians—even in support of one of their own. Robertson was also hobbled by the fact that he is a Pentecostal; as a result of his own religious background, he did not do well among non-Pentecostal evangelicals (and even less well among fundamentalists) for whom his politics were often less objectionable than his religion. Moreover, Robertson had rivals within the conservative Protestant community who did not hesitate to oppose his effort. Jerry Falwell, for example, publicly endorsed George Bush.[12]

Though Robertson's campaign faltered because of divisions among conservative Christians as well as the strength of Bush's candidacy, his own political inexperience showed through his employment of some staffers who were themselves political neophytes, stumbling into amateurish mistakes that a hostile press reported one after another. The reality is that Pat Robertson and his staff did not know much about running a national presidential campaign. What they did accomplish came in spite of their inexperience and naïveté.

Still, Robertson's candidacy was an historic event, if for no other reason than that he entered the presidential sweepstakes as a conservative Protestant religious leader (though he sought to downplay his status as such). Though he failed, Robertson's candidacy demonstrated some of the potential strength of a grassroots Christian Right effort. Robertson raised $41 million for his campaign. He won victories in a number of caucus states where numbers matter less than the vocal dedication of followers. He galvanized a new corps of evangelical activists who stayed in politics long after the campaign was over. Equally important, the grassroots organizational work of Robertson's campaign set the stage for the emergence in the 1990s of his more sophisticated and successful Christian Coalition.[13]

The 1988 presidential race between Bush and Michael Dukakis showed the continuing and solidifying strength of the religious Right. Bush swept about 80 percent of the white evangelical vote. Dedicated supporters of the Christian Right backed Bush even more overwhelmingly. For example, 99 percent of those who had donated to the Robertson campaign voted for Bush in the general election, and members of the conservative, religious Concerned Women for America voted for Bush at least as one-sidedly.[14] Though the religious Right hardly "delivered" this vote, it worked hard on Bush's behalf.

Current Directions

From a contemporary view, the Christian Right would seem to have recovered from its deep slump of the middle to later 1980s. It underwent a serious organizational shake-up and has learned a great deal from its sometimes trying adventures in politics during the 1980s. It has emerged as a more experienced and more locally based movement that is now a force to be reckoned with in U.S. politics.

Perhaps the most significant activist group within the Christian Right since the late 1980s has been the Christian Coalition.[15] It grew in part from the organizational energies of Robertson's 1988 presidential campaign and became a serious national organization with many local chapters. By 1994, it claimed more than 1 million members (half regular donors, half "activists"), whereas the Moral Majority's "members" had mostly been one-time contributors who were not otherwise connected with the organization. By 1998, the Coalition had active organizations in forty-eight states and nearly 1,000 local chapters.[16] The organization links its chapters by computer communications and fax machines, sponsors frequent regional training workshops for local activists on precinct organization, and hosts a national "Road to Victory Conference" each year.

The Christian Coalition garnered significant public notice during the 1992 election when it pushed hard for the reelection of George Bush, though it did not formally endorse him. The organization distributed millions of brochures comparing the three major presidential candidates, through which it conveyed an unsubtly pro-Bush message. It has also issued "report cards" on the voting records of members of Congress for congressional elections since the early 1990s. In the wake of Bush's defeat, Ralph Reed, then executive director of the Christian Coalition, claimed he had good reason to be pleased with the Coalition's effort. After all, Bush had carried the votes of a majority of white evangelicals and fundamentalists. Moreover, the election gave the Christian Coalition and its allies more time and opportunity to organize. It taught them a great deal that they could (and did) use later.[17]

As a result of the efforts by the Christian Coalition and groups allied with it, the Christian Right became a real force in the Republican party in the 1990s. The push to get adherents trained and actively involved in Republican party politics was successful enough that by 1994 political pundits were taking notice. According to *Campaigns and Elections*, a magazine for campaign insiders and consultants, the Christian Right had major influence in the Republican party in eighteen states and had significant influence in another thirteen.[18] This influence in the party was complemented by a large turnout of conservative evangelical voters in the 1994 congressional elections—by some estimates they accounted for close to one-third of all voters—spurred on by the assertive efforts of the Christian Coalition. These evangelical voters mostly backed Republican candidates, which contributed to the GOP takeover of Congress and other gains in some states. The Christian Coalition was particularly influential in southern states, such as South Carolina and Oklahoma.[19] This strong support for Republican congressional candidates continued in 1996.

The prominence of the Christian Right began to cause queasiness in some Republican circles. Republican moderates such as Senator Arlen Specter (R–Pennsylvania) have warned against the influence of the antiabortion Christian Right movement in the party. And prominent prochoice Republican governors, such as Pete Wilson of California and Christine Todd Whitman of New Jersey, have distanced themselves from the Christian Right movement. The face of the Christian Right, however, is in flux today. The Christian Coalition has come upon some hard times since the June 1997 resignation of its popular and successful executive director Ralph Reed (Box 6.2). Reed was replaced by president Donald Hodel and executive director Randy Tate, but since Reed left the fortunes of the Christian Coalition have declined somewhat.[20] The current direction of the Christian Right, therefore, should not be measured only in terms of the activities of the Christian Coalition. There is much else going on that warrants attention

There are many other "profamily" organizations. Concerned Women for America (CWA), now led by Carmen Pate but founded by Beverly LaHaye,

---

BOX 6.2   RALPH REED: CHRISTIAN RIGHT ICON

When the Moral Majority burst onto the scene in the early 1980s, Ralph Reed was an undergraduate at the University of Georgia, immersed in campus politics. He reveled in the role of iconoclast, mounting demonstrations and petition drives for conservative causes. In his senior year, 1982, he was elected national executive director of the College Republicans, partly by portraying his opponent as a "preppie."

Though raised a Methodist, Reed has described how, in the summer after graduation, his thirst for a deeper spiritual life led him to begin attending a church he chose randomly from the telephone book. Eventually he became a born-again charismatic. After working in a number of campaigns, Reed earned a Ph.D. in history from Emory University.

In 1989, at the age of 29, he met Pat Robertson, who saw in Reed the perfect person to implement his vision of a new Christian political organization. As executive director of the Christian Coalition, Reed emerged as one of the most significant leaders of the Christian Right movement. Some observers worried that Reed was dangerous because of his political savvy.

In 1997, Reed stepped down as executive director of the Christian Coalition to form his own political consulting firm, Century Strategies. His exit from the Christian Coalition left the organization in disarray; it has recently faced significant financial and legal challenges. Reed's new career as a political consultant has drawn a great deal of attention, and many candidates are seeking his advice. Even Ralph Reed cannot guarantee victory, however, as Mike Fair of Greenville, South Carolina, learned in June 1998. Fair employed Reed's firm in a failed attempt to secure the Republican nomination in the race for an open House seat in South Carolina's Fourth Congressional District. Nonetheless, Reed will remain an important political player in the years ahead.

SOURCES: http://www.cc.org/publications/ccnews/rr_state.html; Laurence I. Barrett, "Fighting for God and the Right Wing," *Time* (September 13, 1993), 58–61; Ralph Reed, *Politically Incorrect: The Emerging Faith Factor in American Politics* (Dallas: Word Publishing, 1994); David Von Drehle and Thomas B. Edsall, "The Religious Right Returns," *Washington Post National Weekly Edition* (August 29–September 4, 1994), 6; Dan Hoover, "DeMint Upsets Fair in GOP Runoff," *Greenville News* (June 24, 1998), 1A; Ralph Reed, interviewed by Allen D. Hertzke, August 1991, Chesapaeke, VA.

---

focuses in particular on local issues. CWA is among the largest women's political organizations in the United States. Its stated purpose is to "protect and preserve biblical values" and to reverse what its members see as a decline in American moral values.[21] The increasingly visible Family Research Council (FRC), headed by Gary Bauer, has a larger Washington staff than does the Christian Coalition. Bauer, a former domestic policy adviser to Ronald Reagan, has argued that his organization played a major role in derailing President Clinton's policies regarding gays in the military and in inserting the "profamily" $500-per-child tax credit in the Republican *Contract with America*. While the Christian Coalition has focused on voter mobilization, the FRC has emerged as a premier Christian Right think tank. It provides detailed policy analyses on issues such as the impact of changes in divorce laws, the increasing tax burden on parents, and the societal effects of sex and violence in the media. While FRC is clearly a political organization, it focuses more exclusively than other evangelical political groups on moral and family issues. It encourages people who are sympathetic with its agenda to participate actively in the political process by writing to members of Congress.[22]

Also noteworthy is the Focus on the Family organization and its widely known leader, James Dobson. His radio program is heard weekly on 1,600 stations (only Paul Harvey has wider syndication), and his Colorado Springs–based operation employs 1,000 staff members to produce and distribute a vast array of publications, videos, and tapes.[23] Dobson has played a tremendous role in defining the nature of "proper family life" in evangelical circles and in bringing his opinions to bear in politics. Phones ring off the hook on Capitol Hill and in state legislatures whenever he calls for action (see also Box 6.3).

Chapter 10, on religious politics and the legal system, addresses the host of legal associations that are busy on behalf of the Christian Right. Legal groups are springing up at the state level as well, some affiliated with national organizations, others independent. And there are many more groups that are not necessarily directly affiliated with the Christian Right but are culturally aligned with it. These groups involve themselves in school board races,[24] conflicts over public nativity scenes and gay rights ordinances, and disputes over books in public libraries. Much of their effort is educational, designed to alert citizens of their view that traditional values and institutions are slipping away. These groups' larger goal is to goad others into action. In their view, America is in the midst of a culture war over values, which can be won only by the alert and committed. Dedicated foot soldiers for this war are thus at a premium.[25]

Assessments of the Christian Right's Success

No one knows the limits of the Christian Right's long-term political influence at either the local or national level. It is clear, however, that the Christian Right is far from dead today.[26] In any case, it is important to consider different explanations for the origins and current strengths of the Christian Right.[27] One theory suggests that the key to understanding the movement is to see it as a group of people with authoritarian personalities who simply cannot deal with the realities of life in a free and somewhat

---

BOX 6.3   THE PROMISE KEEPERS AND
POLITICAL POTENTIAL

Sometimes the most interesting stories about politics are those that *might* play out, rather than those that actually do transpire. In 1997, such a story became popular fodder for debate among pundits when former University of Colorado football coach Bill McCartney led throngs of men calling themselves "Promise Keepers" on a march on Washington. The October 4 rally was modeled on McCartney's smaller-scale Promise Keepers stadium rallies, of which he held twenty-two in 1996. The 1.1 million men who attended the stadium rallies were drawn together out of a common concern for the moral fabric of America and a shared desire to foster a return to their biblical vision of manhood and male leadership.

Political observers of all stripes watched the Promise Keepers rally with fascination, but they reacted in a variety of ways. Women's groups expressed alarm at the exclusion of an entire gender from the movement and worried about the implications of the "male headship" message that was central to the rally. Some African American groups were pleased at the interracial nature of the movement and its vocal calls for racial reconciliation. Most common, however, was speculation about whether this grassroots network of religious men had political aspirations. Many observers noted that the Promise Keepers' political potential was quite substantial, and that it had clear ties with the religious Right. All that is certain is that the entire story of the Promise Keepers has not yet been written.

SOURCES: Ron Stodghill II, "Sins of Our Fathers," *Time* (October 6, 1997), 10–14; Katha Pollitt, "The Promised Land," *The Nation* (October 27, 1997), 10; "Promise Keepers Survive Attacks," *Daily Oklahoman* (November 4, 1997), 4; http://www.promisekeepers.org.

---

disorderly nation. Proponents of this analysis are invariably hostile to the Christian Right. How plausible is their view? Scholars have discredited this hypothesis since discovering that members of the Christian Right are not any more or less authoritarian than other Americans. Moreover, if members of the Christian Right were authoritarian, that fact would not explain why the movement appeared in the late twentieth century.[28]

A second view involves the classic "alienation thesis," which has often been used to explain the actions of people who do not follow conventional patterns in religion or in politics. Alienation theorists argue that the Christian Right is a movement of people who feel distant from or hostile to the United States, its culture, and its institutions. Once again, however, scholars have not found much evidence that Christian Right sympathizers are highly alienated from society at large. To be sure, members of the Christian Right often criticize American society, but they are also usually quite patriotic.

Another explanation stresses social status (or people's own perceptions thereof). It is sometimes argued that declining social status leads people toward conservative religious politics. At other times, though, the suggestion is that increasing social status actually draws people to the Christian Right. Either way, the claim is that status pressures in people's lives create turmoil and a desire to preserve what they have; this is said to lead them into the Christian Right. The problem with this thesis is (again) a lack of evidence. It is impossible to generalize easily about the social status of Christian Right supporters or about changes in their social status. Nor has it been possible to ascertain any clear relationships between social status or changes in social status and support for the religious Right.

Clyde Wilcox argues that all of these hypotheses reflect a long-standing social-scientific tradition determined to explain (but not respect) all varieties of conservative movements. Wilcox contends that the best way to understand the Christian Right is to see it straightforwardly, as a broad-based expression of the beliefs of its supporters. There is no deep psychological or sociological mystery about it. The Christian Right simply represents the views of people who believe that the American political and cultural order often violates their values and want to change the situation as a result. Wilcox's thoughtful argument makes sense, but we still need to explore *why* adherents of the religious Right believe what they do. We also need to understand why some have been politically mobilized by their values while others have not. Of course, people who disagree with our assertion here should not simply be dismissed as irrational believers in social or psychological pathologies.

Cultural analysis is another approach to understanding the Christian Right. One version posits that the United States has a long history of populist protests. These protests have been undertaken by Americans who maintain—sometimes quite correctly—that the country is controlled by selfish elites who do not care about the needs and desires of ordinary citizens. Sometimes populist upheavals have revolved around economic issues. This was true of the famous Populist revolt of the late nineteenth century. Sometimes, though, such protests have focused on moral and religious dissatisfaction. Perhaps this describes what the Christian Right (and a good deal of Jesse Jackson's parallel movement on the Left) have been about.[29]

By this view, the Christian Right is nothing new. It is an old manifestation of a constant tension in American culture about the responsiveness of the political system and which views it takes seriously. Thus the Christian Right may be as much about representation as it is about anything else, a cry from evangelicals that they too should be heard. If this is so, then the Christian Right's ultimate legacy may turn out to be meaningful political representation for a large segment of the population that has felt left out.

Another facet of cultural analysis is the "unconventional partners" thesis, which focuses on the many ways in which religion and American society cooperate with each other. Religion offers some of the meaning, morality, and community that are often otherwise missing in American society. American society sustains organized religion by guaranteeing broad freedom of belief and religious association. Thus in an interesting way religion and American society support one another, despite the existence of certain surface tensions between them. The unconventional partners thesis argues that Americans do not come to religion for the purpose of politics. Instead, religion provides them with temporary refuge from the larger society. For most people, religion does not need to have anything to do with politics.[30]

The unconventional partners analysis helps us understand the emergence of the very political Christian Right. The Christian Right's dissent stems from a belief that today's society denies Christians the opportunity to nurture their versions of meaning, morality, and community. As the Christian Right sees it, society is attacking the traditional Christian refuge. So the Christian Right emerged to insist that society must be changed. At the same time, however, the unconventional partners thesis predicts that the Christian Right will have limited impact. Few of its members will be interested in politics over the long term, since few come to conservative churches specifically to hear sermons about the necessity of political action.

The Future of the Christian Right

As best we can tell, the Christian Right will have a long future. Whether it will be a politically successful future is much less clear. One question of great interest is what the Christian Right's future will be within the Republican party (Box 6.4).

Although Christian Right leaders made a choice in the 1980s and 1990s to associate with the Republican party in order to maximize their political influence, we do not know how wise that choice will prove to be in the long run. The Christian Right has done well within the Republican party, but it has plenty of enemies there also. Some Republicans have argued that the Christian Right is already too powerful in the party, especially in some southern states. They see that influence as damaging the party's prospects with the larger electorate and they predict—and sometimes even favor—confrontation to weaken the Christian Right in the party. This has been the situation in Minnesota, where the Christian Coalition gained a foothold but then found itself engaged in open confrontation with state Republican leaders.[31]

One should not, however, assume that conflict is inevitable within the Republican party. The Clinton presidency, for example, united various Republican activists and led them to compromise in the face of their com-

---

BOX 6.4   CHRISTIAN RIGHT RUMBLINGS
WITHIN THE REPUBLICAN PARTY

Simmering frustration among Christian Right leaders, who felt they had little to show for their two decades of support for the Republican party, erupted in a public venting in 1998. Charging that Republican congressional leaders had "betrayed" social conservatives, James Dobson, head of Focus on the Family, threatened to bolt from the party and "take as many people with me as possible." His sentiment was echoed by Richard Land of the Southern Baptist Convention, who declared the end of what he called evangelicals' "go-along, get-along" strategy.

A more quiet but no less potent threat came from Gary Bauer, head of the Family Research Council, who began signaling that he might run for president in the Republican primaries in order to hold the party's feet to the fire. Republican party officials, meanwhile, were upset that Bauer had backed conservative candidates in Republican primaries against more "electable" moderates. The Republican party responded to this saber rattling in May 1998 by promising to form a "values action team" in Congress and demanding that President Bill Clinton discipline aide Sidney Blumenthal for calling a deputy of independent prosecutor Kenneth Starr a "religious fanatic."

SOURCES: Laurie Goodstein, "Conservative Leader Takes on GOP," *New York Times* (February 12, 1998), A21; Patrick B. McGuigan, "Bauer Calls Race a Possibility," *Daily Oklahoman* (February 19, 1998), 4; Laurie Goodstein, "Frustrated Christian Leaders Trying New Tactic on GOP," *New York Times* (March 23, 1998), A1, A12; Thomas B. Edsall and Ceci Connolly, "The GOP is Coming Apart at the Seams," *Washington Post National Weekly Edition* (April 6, 1998), 13; Fredreka Schouten and Chuck Raasch, "GOP, Religious Right Renew Commitments," *Greenville News* (May 9, 1998), 4A.

---

mon enemies. It will be fascinating to see what happens in future presidential and congressional elections.[32]

Another crucial question for the Christian Right involves identifying strategies other than working through the Republican party. The Christian Right has recently chosen to pursue a significant expansion of its emphasis on largely nonpartisan local politics, issues, and organizing. Skeptics argue that this is a strategy born of defeat at the federal level, whereas its advocates say that it is only realistic when the presidency and the national bureaucracy are in unfriendly hands.

Yet the turn toward local politics is also a declaration of hope. Because many of the moral issues at stake in realms such as education policy, pornography, and gay rights are fought over in local settings, time and money spent elsewhere are a waste. Moreover, the local level provides the perfect setting for educating people and the ideal training ground for future leaders (Box 6.5).

BOX 6.5   THE CHRISTIAN RIGHT IN LOCAL
POLITICS: THE CASE OF BOB JONES UNIVERSITY

Greenville, South Carolina, is home to one of the paragons of Christian fundamentalism in the United States: Bob Jones University. The university, which was founded in 1927 and relocated to Greenville in 1947, enrolls about 5,000 students. Traditionally, fundamentalists have eschewed politics more than any other group of evangelicals. Bob Jones University, however, has come to play an important role in local politics.

It was in the 1960s that some members of the Bob Jones community were first attracted to politics because of the presidential campaign of Barry Goldwater. The 1970s brought further political engagement. In 1976 two individuals affiliated with the university masterminded a takeover of the Greenville County Republican party—even before the "Solid South" had switched its dominant party affiliation. In 1981, the university lost its battle to retain its tax exemption with the Internal Revenue Service, which had objected to its racially discriminatory admissions practices *(Bob Jones University v. United States)*.

The political clout of Bob Jones University in South Carolina grew in the 1980s and 1990s. This was so despite the fact that the university administration itself stepped away from organized political efforts. Nonetheless, its network of alumni, some of whom emerged as key fundamentalist Republican activists, continued to advance a morally conservative agenda and ultimately came to enjoy disproportionate influence in state and local politics. The Moral Majority never attracted much notice in South Carolina, largely because of personal disagreement and animosity between Jerry Falwell and Bob Jones II. The Christian Coalition faced an even rockier road because Pat Robertson is a Pentecostal. By the late 1990s, various elements of the Republican party in South Carolina—including the Bob Jones faction—were working in concert, but the university and the activists it graduates will continue to exercise substantial influence in state and local politics.

SOURCES: James L. Guth and Oran P. Smith, "South Carolina Christian Right: Just Part of the Family Now?" in Mark J. Rozell and Clyde Wilcox, eds., *God at the Grass Roots, 1996: The Christian Right in the 1996 Elections* (Lanham, MD: Rowman and Littlefield, 1997); Oran P. Smith, *The Rise of Baptist Republicanism* (New York: New York University Press, 1997); Mark Dalhouse, *An Island in the Lake of Fire: Bob Jones University, Fundamentalism, and the Separatist Movement* (Athens: University of Georgia Press, 1996); http://www.bju.edu.

Some social scientists argue that religiously conservative Protestants, especially their most well-educated proponents, are becoming more liberal in their religion, politics, and social attitudes. Such observers conclude that in the long run the Christian Right may find that it is less warmly welcomed in its traditional evangelical circles. The evidence for this thesis is partial and intensely controversial, but without conservative Protestants, the reli-

gious Right could continue only in a shadow form. Thus the evolution of
the political and social attitudes of evangelical and fundamentalist
Protestantism will be of great importance in the years ahead.[33]

Even if attitudes do not change, issues may—and with huge consequences.
Shifting agendas could either strengthen or weaken the Christian Right.
Abortion may be one example. If modern technology makes abortion easier
and public opinion makes it more acceptable, would this undercut the
Christian Right? We doubt it. It would be unwise to underrate the Christian
Right's ability to adjust its focus with the times. It has already shown that it
has the flexibility to debate whatever issues are sensitive at any given time.
Moreover, the Christian Right is not focused on any one specific issue. Its fo-
cus instead is on broad dissatisfaction with the culture in general.

Another theory is that if increasing numbers of conservative Christians
continue to select religious schools or home-schooling for their children, issues arising from dissatisfaction with the public schools, which have fueled
so much of the movement, will fade from the Christian Right agenda. The
consequence, some argue, would be a loss of political steam for the
Christian Right. This is possible, but there would have to be a drastic
change in intensity of conservative Christians' connections with the public
schools. Despite much discussion of Christian schools and the home-
schooling movement, the vast majority of conservative Christians do send
their children to public schools. There is little indication of a sharp trend
away from this pattern. Until any such trend surfaces, encounters with secularism and liberalism in some public schools will continue to be an acti-
vating force for the Christian Right.[34]

Implications for Religion and Politics

Perhaps the most important lesson to be learned from the experience of the
Christian Right is about the dynamic nature of politics in the United States.
After all, who predicted fifteen or twenty years ago that a vigorous, organized Christian Right movement would become well established on the
American political scene? Who predicted what its dynamic, complex, and
volatile history through the 1980s and 1990s would be like? American politics remains open and changing, and the history of the Christian Right
demonstrates that reality.

Of course, the same point applies to religion and politics in the United
States in general. Americans today are worlds away from the "settled" universe of religion and politics that characterized the United States twenty
years ago. The religious Right changed all of that. We should expect other
changes, perhaps of equal power and sweep, in the years ahead. Religion
and politics in the United States, like much else, cannot for a moment be
put in a bottle and set securely on a dusty shelf.

The experience of the Christian Right underlines the political importance of nurturing unity—and the costs of failing to achieve such unity. Religious divisions among evangelicals, fundamentalists, Pentecostals, and among assorted leaders, denominations, and subcultures within conservative Protestantism have hurt its potential as a political force. So too has its failure to forge alliances with African Americans and Jewish and Catholic conservatives. The Christian Right's record is improving on this count, but it has a long way to go in its efforts to reach out to Americans who often agree with it on moral matters but are nervous about its religious and political assertiveness.

A final painful lesson for the Christian Right has been the discovery of the importance of elite access. One of the greatest impediments to Christian Right success has been the hostility of the elite media. There is no question that leading print and television news sources have been decidedly negative toward the religious Right. Once they discovered its existence in 1980, they began to attack it—and they continue to do so today.[35]

Elite access is in short supply elsewhere, too. The Christian Right largely lacks access to top bureaucrats, members of Congress, the judiciary (Presidents Reagan and Bush appointed many conservatives to the federal courts, but few were affiliates of the Christian Right), and the White House. The same situation exists in intellectual and artistic circles, where there is little sympathy—much less support—for the Christian Right.

How does the Christian Right overcome such a problem? Going toe-to-toe with such elites in the 1980s and 1990s just did not work as well as some had hoped. Quietly building bases on the local level, often in places where such elites are not so important, would seem to be a more viable strategy. This may make sense for now, but it only postpones the larger problem of how to wring legitimacy from a hostile elite culture in the United States.

Further Reading

Bromley, David G., and Anson Shupe, eds. *New Christian Politics*. Macon, GA: Mercer University Press, 1984. An important set of studies of the first phase of Christian Right activism.

Cromartie, Michael, ed. *The Religious New Right in American Politics*. Washington, DC: Ethics and Public Policy Center, 1993. A wide-ranging series of essays on the religious Right, its history, and its future.

Hertzke, Allen D. *Echoes of Discontent: Jesse Jackson, Pat Robertson, and the Resurgence of Populism*. Washington, DC: CQ Press, 1993. Consideration of the 1988 candidacies of Rev. Jesse Jackson and Rev. Pat Robertson for president.

Liebman, Robert C., and Robert Wuthnow, eds. *The New Christian Right*. New York: Aldine, 1984. A valuable study of the first phase of Christian Right activism.

Martin, William. *With God on Our Side: The Rise of the Religious Right in America*. New York: Broadway Books, 1996. A comprehensive history of the rise of the religious Right.

Marty, Martin E., and R. Scott Appleby. *The Glory and the Power: The Fundamentalist Challenge to the Modern World*. Boston: Beacon Press, 1992. Part of a huge scholarly effort, directed by Martin Marty at the University of Chicago, to understand the impact of religious fundamentalism in the United States and around the globe.

Moen, Matthew C. *The Transformation of the Christian Right*. Tuscaloosa: University of Alabama Press, 1992. Insightful discussion of the religious Right's movement from phase one to phase two.

Oldfield, Duane M. *The Right and the Righteous: The Christian Right Confronts the Republican Party*. Lanham, MD: Rowman and Littlefield, 1996. An excellent discussion of the past and present relationship between the Christian Right and the GOP.

Reed, Ralph. *Politically Incorrect: The Emerging Faith Factor in American Politics*. Dallas: Word Publishing, 1994. The former leader of the Christian Coalition speaks out.

Wilcox, Clyde. *God's Warriors: The Christian Right in Twentieth-Century America*. Baltimore, MD: John Hopkins University Press, 1992. Fascinating contemporary and historical data on the religious Right.

Wilcox, Clyde. *Onward Christian Soldiers? The Religious Right in American Politics*. Boulder, CO: Westview, 1996. A useful discussion of the identity of the Christian Right and its prospects for future success.

7

African American
Religion and Politics

$\mathcal{R}$eligion has always been a central element in the African American community. In no other major racial or ethnic group, in fact, does religion play a more crucial role. Moreover, politics and religion are tightly woven together in the African American community. Religion often takes on an overtly political dimension, which is untrue of other sectors of American religion where, as we have seen, there is much uneasiness about connections between religion and politics and church and state.

Every survey of African Americans confirms a high level of religious involvement. Eighty-two percent of black Americans say that religion is a very significant force in their lives; 80 percent maintain that they belong to a church; nearly 50 percent state that they attended church within a given week. Moreover, the proportion of African Americans who say they espouse no religion is only about 6 percent. By each of these measures, African Americans are far more religious than the rest of the population.

The vast majority of African Americans—over 80 percent—are Christians, despite extensive media publicity about the rise of Islam in the African American community. Fifty percent are Baptists, around 10 percent are Methodists, and the rest belong to a wide variety of other denominations and churches. The Pentecostal movement is also growing rapidly in the African American community. It is organized in several major denominations, especially the Church of God in Christ (COGIC), and numerous independent churches. Finally, about 2 percent of African Americans are Muslims.[1]

There are a number of large black denominations. The largest is the National Baptist Convention, USA, Inc., with 8.5 million members.[2] Since 1994 its leader has been Rev. Henry Lyons, who has become a controversial figure in American religion today.[3] Two other large Baptist denominations include the National Baptist Convention of America and the Progressive National Baptist Convention. Among the Methodists are the African Methodist Episcopal (AME) Church (which is the oldest African American denomination), the African Methodist Episcopal Zion (AMEZ) Church, and the Christian Methodist Episcopal (CME) Church. The fastest growing African American denomination today is the Pentecostal COGIC. There is also an active national ecumenical organization of nine African American denominations called the Congress of National Black Churches, which was founded in 1978 and has its headquarters in Washington, D.C.

Toward a Broader View

In his fascinating and sometimes eccentric *American Religion*, Harold Bloom argues convincingly that to understand black manifestations of Christianity in the United States one must appreciate both their evangelical side and their distinctly African American side.[4] Black Christianity is rooted in American evangelicalism, but it has also been profoundly shaped by the historical experience of African Americans in the United States. It is important to remember that African American religion is overwhelmingly Protestant—and evangelical—in nature. African American Christians are keenly focused on scripture, and many affirm the Bible as literally true. In fact, about 70 percent claim that it is true in all aspects or nearly so. Moreover, like their white counterparts, about half of all African Americans report reading the Bible weekly.

Another indication of the evangelicalism of African American Christianity involves the basic format of worship services. African American services emphasize preaching and music, and often considerable expressiveness, as is the case in some white evangelical services. There is little of the liturgy that one might find in Roman Catholic, Lutheran, or Episcopal services, whose roots are more clearly Catholic in origin. This is not to say that the typical African American worship service is indistinguishable from a white evangelical service. In African American churches, there is significantly more interaction between the congregation and the pastor during worship. Music plays a central role; there is a clear connection between the "call and response" musical motif and the typical flow of an African American service. In fact, some of the roots of jazz lie in black spirituals of the eighteenth and nineteenth centuries.

A third similarity involves church organization. African American and white evangelical denominations share a loose organizational structure that tends to uphold the sovereignty of the individual church. Such "conventions" bring together many individual churches, but they usually support neither firm hierarchical direction from the top, nor big headquarters, large staffs, or formidable budgets. As the names of some of these organizations imply, Christianity in the black community, as in the white community, has experienced numerous and sometimes very contentious conflicts that produced permanent schisms, sometimes over doctrine and sometimes over personalities. The evangelical tendency—regardless of race—is toward decentralization and division. This tendency is a testimony to the fierce evangelical determination to pursue the truth and bow before no organization or leader. As is the case in the white evangelical world, there are also hundreds of other independent African American churches, from simple storefront operations to large, sophisticated institutions, which function independently of denominational structures.

In evangelical churches, whether they have white, black, or multiracial congregations, the laity normally hire the pastor directly. In many black churches the pastor (who is usually a man) is a powerful and generally dominant figure. The pastor is almost always the center of his church. He makes the important decisions about community and political activities. His church often rises and falls with him. Recruiting a good pastor is therefore essential for every African American church.[5]

A recent study of African American clergy found that many have not completed college or advanced theological training, though a number of black pastors hold doctorates. It is also very important to note that a significant number of African American clergy must find employment outside of their churches for financial reasons. There are plenty of exceptions, but often black pastors must confront economic struggles in their families as well as in their churches, especially when they serve small or rural congregations. The situation is often complicated by the serious challenges faced by African American laity in the South and in the central cities of the North. African American clergy who serve in central city neighborhoods must deal with issues of drug abuse, violence, and abject poverty on a regular basis. Sometimes black pastors have to take personal action just to keep members of their congregations and residents of their church neighborhoods alive.[6] Samuel G. Freedman's powerful *Upon This Rock: The Miracle of a Black Church* further describes some of these challenges in unmistakable terms.[7]

Attracting young people is a universal challenge faced by modern American religious groups. Some black clergy say that they have a particularly hard time attracting young black men to church. Many African American congregations have a large majority of female members, a fact that sometimes discourages male attendance. There is a feeling in some African American circles that church, if not religion, is a woman's business. Moreover, there are religious alternatives that seem to appeal more to men than women in the African American community. Among these alternatives is Islam; a vast majority of African American Muslims are men.[8]

Of course, African American Christianity is not exclusively evangelical and Protestant. It is crucial to remember that African American Christianity is inseparable from the history and shared experiences of black people in the United States. Religion has served as a crucial refuge for African Americans for several hundred years. During slavery and beyond, the church was the one place where African Americans were usually able to be safe and free. The church remains today as the central institution of the black community and is integral to the identities of many African American citizens.[9]

The historic role of African American churches is explored carefully in one of the best studies of black religion in recent decades, Eric Lincoln and Lawrence Mamiya's *The Black Church in the African American Experience*. For them, to know the history of African American Christianity is to understand its traditions of both resistance and accommodation; to appreciate its communal side and its individualism; and to recognize its prophetic dimension and its priestly focus.[10]

But the distinctly African American side of black Christianity goes quite beyond history and values, and includes such things as popular music. African American spirituals are now widely copied and sung by Christians of all racial and ethnic backgrounds.[11] This fact is both ironic and inspiring, because these spirituals emerged from the dim days of slavery. African slaves, stripped of all freedom, invented the spirituals to bring themselves a modicum of hope during long days of forced labor in places such as the cotton fields of the South. One spiritual, for example, contains the lyric "Before I'll be a slave, I'll be buried in my grave, and go home to my Father and be free." Slavery ended, but among its legacies is the black spiritual. The content of these spirituals clearly establishes the connection between African American Christianity and the theme of liberation.

African American Christianity has always stressed the image of God as an avenging liberator of the oppressed. This should come as no surprise in light of the historical treatment of black people in the United States. Religion provides a vehicle of hope for the weary and the downtrodden; this function continues to be as important for African Americans today as it was in the days of slavery. To this day, many African Americans find some comfort in the face of discrimination and inequality, assured of heavenly peace and salvation by a fervent and celebratory belief in a benevolent God.

There has been a self-conscious effort within some black theological circles to develop a black liberation ideology. James Cone and Cornel West have been the leading black liberation theologians. Cone played a crucial role in the late 1960s as elements of the civil rights movement turned toward more radical expressions of discontent. His seminal work, *Black Theology and Black Power*,[12] justified the black power movement in religious terms. It also solidified the position of the recently formed National Conference of Black Churchmen, which ultimately rejected the willingness of other civil rights movement organizations (such as the influential Southern Christian Leadership Conference) to work hand in hand with white Christian groups (such as the National Council of Churches).[13]

History and Black Political Attitudes

What is most striking about black religion and politics in the United States is how closely they are linked. Black Christianity has a major political component, and African American churches are often openly involved in politics in a variety of ways. There is simply no sharp division between religion and politics in the African American community today, which embraces the Old Testament image of the crossing and sometimes converging paths of religion and politics.

Religion and politics mix for African Americans despite a long historical experience for blacks before the civil rights revolution in the South that taught that involvement in politics could be dangerous and sometimes deadly for African Americans. To be sure, African American churches have long taught that the Gospel speaks of a just and equitable society. And even before the civil rights movement began in the 1950s, there were plenty of African American citizens fighting for social change—though often behind the scenes. Nonetheless, before the 1950s there was substantial agreement among African Americans that the public arena was a dangerous place that ought to be avoided.[14]

The early years of African American Christianity clearly exemplified this apolitical model. In two hundred years of slavery, many black people converted to Christianity—but theirs was still a distinctly white religion and church. Few allowances were made for black adaptations of white Christianity, though a black manifestation of Christianity developed anyway, out of the range of white vision. Its practices and expressions differed from those of traditionally white Christianity, but the result was no less robust or deep. Slaves took what they were learning about Christianity and molded it to their own circumstances—as had many other groups of Christians before them. The first black Baptist congregations were organized in the South at the end of the eighteenth century. But many slaves were not allowed to attend services at these or other churches. Therefore clandestine worship groups formed on plantations, coming to be known collectively as "the invisible institution."[15]

The early African American Methodist churches were organized not by slaves but by free people living in the North. White churches were seen as complicit in the perpetuation of the institution of slavery, and segregation was enforced in white churches even in the North. Northern black

Christians felt that by creating their own separate churches, they would be able to assert their collective power more forcefully. The beginnings of organized, separate African American Protestant expression date to 1787, when several African Americans withdrew from St. George's Methodist Episcopal Church in Philadelphia. They met and prayed together informally for years with other African Americans. Finally in 1794, the white Methodist Bishop Francis Asbury dedicated Bethel Church of Philadelphia, the first African Methodist Episcopal church, which survives to this day and is known as Mother Bethel.[16]

The second phase of African American religion began after the Civil War. Black Christianity became more formally organized, and it no longer operated under the tutelage of whites. This period saw major expansion of black Baptists and Methodist denominations. It was also in this era that the African American Pentecostal movement was born. African American Pentecostal leaders today are proud of the fact that their religious movement does not trace its roots explicitly to European Protestantism. The result was a lively religious world, but after Reconstruction African Americans shied away from open political engagement. The vast majority of African Americans lived in the South, where the political freedom of Reconstruction proved fleeting.

During World War I, African Americans began moving north in search of jobs and a better life outside of the segregated South. This process accelerated during World War II and in the years afterward, when the mechanization of southern agriculture spurred even more northward migration. Eventually about half of all African Americans settled outside the South.

The quotient of fear among black religious people who had moved north began to diminish. Big northern cities soon developed large African American communities; this bred a comfort level that moved many African Americans to express their opinions freely and without substantial fear in and out of church. These changes did not, however, lead very much of the African American religious community toward political engagement. Old suspicions remained, and evangelical theology continued to teach what previous black experience had underlined: that politics was corrupt and dangerous. So African American churches continued to shun official political involvement. They urged their members to follow suit.[17]

Despite this legacy, everything changed in the 1950s. African American churches shifted dramatically toward politics, and this choice changed history. The civil rights movement that began in the 1950s was led in its earliest and most productive years by African American Christians. Black pastors played a crucial role in this effort. Rev. Martin Luther King Jr. was certainly the most visible, but he worked in coalition with others, such as Rev. Ralph Abernathy and Rev. Fred Shuttlesworth, through the Southern Christian Leadership Conference (SCLC).

For these pastors, the time had come to claim civil rights for all African Americans. They had few doubts that God supported this prophetic decision, and African American churches—particularly Baptist churches—throughout the South were quickly transformed into organizational centers for the nascent movement. Though African American clergy were not the only forces arrayed on behalf of the civil rights revolution, without the crucial support of black churches it would never have happened.[18] It was in church that African Americans heard the message that called them into the politics of protest. It was in church that they planned strategy. And it was in church that they found the moral inspiration to risk a great deal individually for the collective benefit of all.

The movement for civil rights did not, however, win quick support from all African American churches. Such an involvement—and confrontation—with the world did not sit well with dominant theologies, nor with the painful and sometimes terrible past experiences of those African Americans who had dared to get involved. There was a strong and active resistance to the civil rights movement from within organized black Christianity. Perhaps the most visible opponent was Rev. Joseph H. Jackson, longtime head of the National Baptist Convention, USA, Inc., and a major figure in the African American Christian community. In his retrospective account, he portrayed himself and others like him as deeply committed to traditional "Christian activism" on behalf of African Americans. But he— and many other voices of African American religion—opposed Dr. King and his form of religious politics.[19]

One of the civil rights crusade's most obvious victories actually came within African American religion. The movement changed long-standing attitudes toward political involvement. This revolution produced the political church that is common—though not universal—in the African American community today. To be sure, a certain ambivalence remains. African Americans accept and often welcome political involvement by their churches and especially by their pastors. Many, but by no means all, African American pastors are deeply involved in politics. Some preach regularly about political issues. Some invite candidates for public office to address their congregations from the pulpit. Some run local political organizations and lead marches. Some speak out frequently about politics in the local media. And some even wear two hats by serving simultaneously as clergy and as elected or appointed public officials.

At the same time, African American laity expect that political activity by their clergy will not come at the expense of visiting sick members, preaching effectively, or being available to counsel those with personal crises.[20] While it is important to keep in mind that there are plenty of African American pastors who shun politics, those who engage in political activity to the exclusion of other responsibilities are often viewed with displeasure by their congregations. Furthermore, some African American religious traditions are generally less accepting of political activism than others. Particularly skeptical are African American Pentecostals. At a 1997 summit of African American church leaders, for example, representatives of the Church of God in Christ expressed reservations about the appropriateness of sustained political activism. Nonetheless, it is important to keep in mind that politicized black churches produce members who are themselves quite likely to participate in politics.[21]

The civil rights movement put black churches—as they slowly mobilized behind the cause—on the liberal side of American politics. In the process, civil rights liberalism strengthened economic liberalism among African Americans. At that time, both forms of liberalism were firmly and increasingly coming to be associated with allegiance to the Democratic party. Indeed, by the end of the 1960s, the Democratic presidential nominee could count on receiving about 85 percent of the vote of the expanding African American electorate.

The political attitudes of African Americans today are closely linked to perceptions of their collective treatment in American society and the conclusion that they need assistance from the government to achieve equal political and civil rights and real economic opportunities. This has led many African Americans to embrace a strongly favorable view of government and what it might do for them. Such attitudes have reinforced support for the Democratic party, which is far more sympathetic to government action than the GOP. Nonetheless, there is a distinct but small minority, both in black intellectual circles and in the larger electorate, who are much less impressed with big government. Still, many African Americans continue to embrace the government as the best hope for their improvement.

Connections Between Religion and Politics

As we have already suggested, the most visible connections between black religion and American politics have come through the actions of various African American clergy. Especially since the 1960s, many black pastors have been deeply involved in politics. One important pioneer was Rev. Adam Clayton Powell, pastor of the large and influential Abyssinian Baptist Church in New York City. He served as a member of Congress for years after World War II and provided a vigorous and controversial voice for African American civil rights.

Rev. Martin Luther King Jr. became the most famous model of the black pastor as political activist during his career as a civil rights crusader in the late 1950s and 1960s. King's activism attracted a host of other African American pastors to politics. From our contemporary perspective, one of the most important black clergy has been Rev. Jesse Jackson, who is the current symbol of African American clerical activism. Today black clergy are engaged at all levels of politics, addressing local issues, serving in state legislatures, and contributing as members of Congress (one recent example was Rep. Floyd Flake [D–New York], a pastor from Brooklyn). But it is Jackson who most visibly represents the model of the contemporary African American pastor in government and politics.

Jackson is involved in politics every day, in both the United States and abroad. His activity touches virtually every imaginable issue, and he gets involved at every level, from the most local to campaigns for president. The activities of his Chicago-based Operation PUSH, as well as his efforts to register millions of voters, have gained considerable notice. It was his 1984 and 1988 races for the Democratic party's presidential nomination, however, that brought him the most fame. His candidacies also increased other African American pastors' comfort with political engagement.

By no means have all African Americans rallied around Jackson—and a few have based their criticism partly on his deep affinity with religion.[22] But their voices form only a small ripple in a larger tide of sympathy and support for Jackson among African Americans. Most have not been bothered by Jackson's religious commitment nor by his status as a pastor. Indeed, such matters are perfectly routine in a politicized black community that has strongly supported political involvement by clergy in the decades since the emergence of Dr. King.

Jackson's presidential campaigns, especially the 1988 run, have been studied at length. The findings have confirmed that Jackson won massive support from African American Christians. Though racial pride was the most important single factor in rallying support to Jackson, the religious dimension was also significant. This was particularly true for African American women, who we know are more likely than men to be religious. They were absolutely central to both Jackson campaigns, from his campaign organization to the voting booth. Jackson's support network also included such established African American religious figures as Rev. T. J. Jemison, the former leader of the National Baptist Convention, USA, Inc. Much of Jackson's campaign rhetoric was distinctly Christian in its overtones and orientation. He emphasized sympathy for the suffering and a determination to build community despite the terrible wounds caused by poverty, drugs, and crime.[23]

The Jackson campaigns also illustrated another dimension of black religious politics: The tremendous importance of local churches. African American churches and their pastors were the "precincts" of his campaigns. Here rallies were held, publicity produced, and organizations formed to ensure that Jackson would receive significant support from the black community.[24]

Though the Jackson campaigns garnered great publicity and displayed the connection between black churches and national politics, we should

---

BOX 7.1 AFRICAN AMERICAN CLERGY
IN LOCAL POLITICS

African American clergy have a long tradition of political involvement, particularly at the local level. In cities across the United States, African American clergy are involved in a variety of political activities, many of which lead them to work in concert with white clergy.

In Milwaukee, Wisconsin, for example, there is an ecumenical political group called the Milwaukee Innercity Congregations Allied for Hope (MICAH). MICAH was founded in 1985 as an interracial and interfaith coalition of clergy and laity dedicated to addressing the challenges of life in Milwaukee's central city through political means. It focuses its attention specifically on education, crime, drugs, housing, and economic development.

The most striking fact about MICAH is that it is an interfaith and interracial effort. Even though Milwaukee is one of the most racially divided of all American cities, black and white pastors work side by side in MICAH for what they see as the benefit of all Milwaukeeans. And they are extremely dedicated to their cause. In the words of one pastor, "MICAH meets all the time, at all hours, . . . but when they call, I come running!"

SOURCE: Laura R. Olson, *Filled with Spirit and Power: Protestant Clergy in Politics* (Albany: State University of New York Press, forthcoming).

---

not be distracted from the politics in which many African American churches and pastors engage every day on local, county, and state levels. Such involvement has little or nothing to do with Jesse Jackson. The bulk of African American church politics focuses on local issues and problems involving education, civil rights, and economic opportunity (Box 7.1).[25]

In many cases, there is a tight congruence between what black leaders and churches propose politically and what the African American community will support. This is definitely the case with regard to the key issue of improving economic opportunities for African American citizens. Many African Americans rally around the issue of economic improvement not only out of pragmatism but also because of the heavy emphasis placed in black churches on the message of liberation.

But there are other issues about which it is clear that religious African Americans hold somewhat different views than their more secular counterparts. African American Christians are often very conservative on issues such as abortion and women's roles. Yet it is noteworthy at the same time that African Americans as a group are more sympathetic to gay rights and economic parity for women than are white evangelicals. Evidently some African Americans perceive gays and women as kindred beleaguered spirits in some meaningful sense. The picture is mixed and complicated, but noneconomic issues have not affected African

American politics much because the economic agenda has been paramount; moreover, black religious leaders continually reinforce this priority.[26]

Most major African American interest groups, such as the National Association for the Advancement of Colored People (NAACP) and the Urban League, are not religious in form or focus. To be sure, they welcome religious leaders and laity as members and afford them equal participatory opportunities. As it is elsewhere in the black community, there is no clear dividing line between religion and politics. The lack of a religious orientation on the part of these groups is an artifact of their creation in the first two decades of the twentieth century. Groups like the NAACP were often intended as an alternative to black churches, which were sometimes perceived as overly concerned with the next world—and thus not sufficiently devoted to assisting African Americans in this world. We know, however, that there is usually regular contact between African American pastors and churches and branches of the NAACP and the Urban League. This is inevitable, since these organizations are as intertwined with the black middle class as are the large African American denominations.

An aspect of religious politics that is increasingly on the African American agenda today is the matter of black empowerment. What the term "black empowerment" exactly means is frequently debated, but the central idea is that *African American* power is crucial to changing black lives. It is also a significant affirmation of African Americans as worthy creations of God.[27]

The empowering theme of African American politics is closely related to the liberation theme in black churches. Since the 1960s, theologians such as James Cone have spearheaded a movement to commit black Christianity to a liberation model of politics and society. This view, also articulated by some evangelical black activists, holds that the United States is a racist nation and that white Christianity is a racist religion. Jesus Christ, who some liberation theologians portray as black, was a liberator, and his message was about human liberation here on Earth.

Though the African American voices of evangelical Christianity did not conceptualize God as black, other African Americans did, including James Cone. Rev. Albert B. Cleage Jr. of the Shrine of the Black Madonna in Detroit was another person who took this approach, but he added an element of black separatism.[28] Cleage was among the most controversial theologians of the 1960s. He argued that Jesus Christ was the *black* messiah and that he had preached racial separatism and liberation. Black people, to Cleage, were chosen by God and called to undo the damage done by whites. He taught that white-centered manifestations of Christianity were lies and that universal love was not among Christ's messages. Drawing on the rhetoric of the black power movement, Cleage attempted to mobilize African Americans "to stand against their white oppressors."[29]

The formal liberation theology of Cleage, Cone, and Cornel West, however, has not made many inroads with most black clergy. Still, African American pastors and churches are convinced that political activity is a legitimate and necessary means of improving the African American lot on Earth. Ninety percent of African American clergy approve of political action, according to one study.[30]

African American Christianity in the United States today is self-consciously political and increasingly comfortable with that fact. In this way it is unlike most of the rest of religion in the United States. Though organized American religion in general has become more openly political today than it was twenty-five years ago, many people have not made peace with this development. Politics has only one comfortable home in American religion, and that is in African American churches.

The Muslim Challenge

Today a modest but growing number of African Americans are Muslims, many of them rather recent converts to the faith of the seventh-century Arabic prophet Muhammad.[31] Most Americans are aware of this population because of popular Muslim figures such as boxer Muhammad Ali and basketball star Hakeem Olajuwon. The story of the Muslim dimension of the African American experience illustrates clearly the fluid nature of American religious culture and the unpredictable political consequences that arise from religious movements.

Though a number of Africans were followers of Islam before they were enslaved in America, only traces of that heritage survived. Modest interest in Islam existed among some nineteenth-century African Americans; certain black intellectuals saw it as an authentic African legacy that had been erased by the slave master. By the early part of the twentieth century, however, unorthodox, "proto-Islamic" movements emerged among growing African American populations in some northern cities.[32] These were tiny, isolated groups with teachings that seemed bizarre to outsiders.

Most notable among these groups was the Nation of Islam, led by Elijah Muhammad from 1934 until his death in 1975 (Box 7.2). Centered in Detroit, the Nation of Islam was a religion of the urban dispossessed, and it remained small and largely unrecognized until its most gifted disciple, Malcolm X, burst onto the scene in the 1960s.[33] In the 1990s, Malcolm X became a cultural icon, with the ubiquitous merchandising of "X" hats and sweatshirts, after the release of filmmaker Spike Lee's movie about Malcolm's life, *X*. Even those with only a vague understanding of his life and legacy have come to admire Malcolm's reputation for uncompromising militancy in

BOX 7.2   ELIJAH MUHAMMAD

Born Robert Poole, Elijah Muhammad claimed to have received a fantastic theological revelation from his predecessor as head of the Nation of Islam, a mysterious Detroit silk merchant named Mr. Farad. At the heart of this revelation was the idea that whites were a race of devils and an aberration. Blacks, on the other hand, were descendants of an ancient master race whose wizards had ruled for millions of years over an empire that even included Mars. Whites were genetically created by a malcontented mad scientist. They gained ascendancy through "Tricknology," and enslaved the remnant of the "Original People," the "Tribe of Shabazz."

Elijah Muhammad was quite critical of African American Christians, particularly clergy. He called black Christian clergy fools for following and perpetuating the religion of slave masters. During the 1960s Muhammad made inroads among African Americans, and the Nation of Islam grew. However, the rift between Muhammad and Malcolm X halted the movement's growth. Elijah Muhammad died in 1975. The Nation of Islam was ultimately taken over by the controversial Louis Farrakhan, who continues to preach Muhammad's message of racial separatism.

SOURCE: Gayraud S. Wilmore, *Black Religion and Black Radicalism: An Interpretation of the Religious History of Afro-American People*, 2d ed. (Maryknoll, NY: Orbis, 1983).

the face of white American racism. During the early 1960s he helped inspire the black power movement. A popular speaker, he offered an early challenge to Dr. King's nonviolent resistance campaign. In many respects King and Malcolm represented opposite poles of African American experience. King was born to middle-class respectability; his highly educated father was a minister. Malcolm, by contrast, was a street hustler turned leader of the outcast black Muslims. While King preached nonviolent action, Malcolm threatened violence, though he was moving away from this stance at the time of his death (Box 7.3).

The appeal of the black Muslim movement in the 1950s and 1960s was twofold. On the one hand, it preached an appealing message to alienated urban blacks, especially men and prisoners, that placed their plight on the shoulders of a race of white devils destined by Allah to be eradicated. The faith also emphasized education, sexual discipline, hard work, cleanliness, conservative dress, economic self-sufficiency, and rejection of the white man's welfare.

Malcolm X expressed deep concern over the growing numbers of young African Americans who lived the kind of self-destructive street life from which Islam had freed him. The patriarchal aspect of the faith appealed to black men emasculated by racist society; as a result, the membership of the Nation of Islam remained heavily male. In contrast to the matriarchal cul-

---

BOX 7.3   MALCOLM X

Born in Omaha, Nebraska, Malcolm Little was a gifted youth whose father, an admirer of Marcus Garvey's pan-American movement, was murdered
when Malcolm was just six years old. His impoverished mother migrated
from city to city. By his early teens Malcolm had become a street hustler involved in theft, drugs, and prostitution. Arrested for burglary, he was sent to
jail in 1946, when he was twenty-one years old. It was there that Malcolm
was introduced to the teachings of the Nation of Islam, which profoundly altered his life.

Inspired by the idea that the white person was the devil, Malcolm transformed himself by reading voraciously and developing a steely discipline that
would become his trademark. When he was released from prison in 1952, he
took the name Malcolm X, with the X signifying his lost African name. He
quickly became the most effective spokesperson for black Muslims and Elijah
Muhammad's right hand.

Malcolm and Muhammad parted ways in 1964, however. At that time
Malcolm founded the Muslim Mosque, Inc., which he wished to be more in-
clusive than Muhammad's Nation of Islam. In particular, he welcomed
African American Christians, who were shunned by Muhammad. Malcolm
X's assassination in 1965, which silenced one of the most influential voices of
the later stage of the civil rights movement, was ultimately linked to Elijah
Muhammad.

SOURCES: Malcolm X, with Alex Haley, *The Autobiography of Malcolm X* (New
York: Grove, 1964); Gayraud S. Wilmore, *Black Religion and Black Radicalism: An
Interpretation of the Religious History of Afro-American People*, 2d ed. (Maryknoll,
NY: Orbis, 1983).

---

ture of the broader African American community, black Muslims taught
that the man was the head of the family and the woman was to be his help-
mate and homemaker. Black Muslims attained a certain stature in many
cities—even among some non-Muslims—for being proud, disciplined, and
militantly separatist from the white world. They had charismatic leaders,
were organized around beliefs that were seen as "peculiar" by the broader
society, and placed stringent demands on their members.

By 1960, the movement still had only a small membership,[34] but it was
making a serious effort to create a separate society of temple-run schools,
businesses, and radio stations, as well as a well-armed militia (the Fruit of
Islam) that operated in a number of cities. The political importance of the
movement was magnified by Malcolm's high level of visibility. He combined Elijah Muhammad's theology with a call for black consciousness, assertion, and pride. Malcolm told angry African Americans that they had
every right to use "any means necessary" to defend themselves against violence by whites, and he challenged the very premises of Dr. King's nonvio-

lent push for integration and civil rights. Like the black liberation theologians, Malcolm proposed separation from whites instead of integration. He declared: "We, the black man of the world, created the white man and we will also kill him." This rhetoric, of course, was explosive in the atmosphere of the mid-1960s.[35]

The most remarkable part of Malcolm's story, however, came toward the end of his life. Disciplined and puritanical in his behavior, Malcolm X was shocked to learn that his leader Elijah Muhammad lived a lavish and lascivious life. A rift quickly developed between them, as did political divisions. When Malcolm remarked that John Kennedy's assassination marked "the chickens coming home to roost," Elijah ostracized him. Malcolm had become too visible, too controversial, and too much of a threat to Elijah's leadership.

One of Malcolm's responses was to make the traditional pilgrimage to Mecca, an event that transformed his understanding of Islam and led him to reject the teachings of the Nation of Islam. He was dazzled by the vision of a multiracial, Islamic society. In his autobiography he describes seeing people of all colors and nationalities coming together at Mecca. Upon returning to America he renounced the white devil theology and announced that he had taken a new name, El-Hajj Malik El-Shabazz, an indication of his embrace of Orthodox Islam.[36] Cut off from the Nation of Islam, he formed his own Orthodox (Sunni) Islamic mosque and created the Organization of Afro-American Unity. His new vision was still incomplete when he was gunned down by Nation of Islam assassins in 1965.

Malcolm's legacy is a complex one. To the end he remained pessimistic about the possibility of eradicating white racism in America. He was also suspicious of white liberals who wanted to "help" the cause, and he continued to preach a kind of separatist doctrine that emphasized African American self-sufficiency. Thus he symbolizes black pride and assertion for those for whom integration proved less than salutary. Nearly three decades after his death, the problems of the underclass seem to reflect the glaring failure of integration among a segment of the African American population. Moreover, Martin Luther King's dream of a truly integrated society remains elusive, with social segregation on college campuses on the rise and racial tensions in cities continuing to erupt. Some black youths today are especially receptive to the Malcolm X image that has filtered through the culture—an image of a strong, angry, and uncompromising advocate of black assertion.

But there is another legacy that is less well appreciated. When Elijah Muhammad died in 1975, his son Wallace (who took the name Warith Deen Muhammad), assumed the leadership of the Nation of Islam and quietly and assiduously began to lead the movement toward a merger with Orthodox Islam—the very direction Malcolm X had envisioned. Like Malcolm, he rejected the racist teachings of his father. He dismantled some of the black Muslim institutions and integrated them into the mosques, which were being fed by the growing immigrant population of Muslims from the Middle East and Southeast Asia. Thus, today, the vast majority of African American Muslims worship alongside immigrants in Sunni mosques around the country.[37]

This merger has probably facilitated the conversion of more African Americans to Islam by providing them with the structure of a highly developed world religion as an alternative to the "white man's" Christianity. Conversions to Islam among African Americans have increased, and African Americans now make up more than 40 percent of the nation's Muslim population. However, neither the exact overall size of the Muslim population nor the size of its African American component is known with great certainty. Of 30 million African Americans, estimates of the Muslim population range as high as 2.5 million.[38].

We are only beginning to discern the consequences of the growth of Islam in the United States. It is obviously an important expansion of religious pluralism. Organizers and activists in some cities now routinely view Muslims as key political constituencies. During his presidential campaign in 1988, Jesse Jackson championed the cause of Arab Americans and campaigned actively in mosques in cities such as Detroit. Muslims of all racial and ethnic backgrounds have often joined forces to criticize U.S. support for Israel, much to the disappointment of American Jews.

And there are other developments. Muslims are decidedly conservative on family issues and education. Like conservative Catholics and evangelicals, many Muslims strongly object to abortion, sexual permissiveness, and gay rights, and these diverse religious groups may coalesce in battles over such issues. Moreover, Muslims have no tradition of secular schools and believe that religion must be taught to children along with math, language, and science. With the sprouting of Islamic parochial schools in the United States, we may see Muslims of all backgrounds joining with Catholics and evangelicals to lobby for educational vouchers and the accommodation of religion in the public schools.[39]

A small group of African Americans remain loyal to the Nation of Islam and Elijah Muhammad's vision, including his doctrines about the origin of the races and the white devil.[40] The Nation of Islam today is led by the fiery Louis Farrakhan, who continues to preach black superiority and separation. Farrakhan has achieved an influence well beyond his core religious following (which numbers no more than 10,000) because he articulates the same kind of rage as did the young Malcolm X. His critics are uneasy, however, about what they see as Farrakhan's anti-Semitism.

Farrakhan gained prominence in 1984 when his association with Jesse Jackson (to whom he provided bodyguards) became an issue in the presidential campaign. At that time Farrakhan referred to Jews as members of a "gutter religion," and Jackson was chastised for not renouncing such talk and severing his ties with Farrakhan. The issue dogged Jackson's presidential quest in both 1984 and 1988.

Farrakhan's politics represents a mixture of militant racial separatism, self-reliance, and traditional moral values. On abortion, gay rights, and welfare his message is pointedly conservative. His actual political impact, however, is hard to measure. His organization has gotten nowhere when it has fielded candidates for local and national offices, but it has attracted broad support for its antidrug activities.[41] Farrakhan also organized the widely publicized Million Man March in 1995. There is no doubt that Farrakhan has some followers in many of America's central cities, and as a result he has been courted in the 1990s by some mainstream African American groups such as the Congressional Black Caucus and the NAACP.

Conclusion

Islamic influence in the United States may go in a number of directions in the future, from militancy to conservatism. Where it will ultimately lead we do not profess to know. But the growing Muslim presence in the United States will likely make an increasingly important mark on American culture and politics. If it does, it will be following in the established tradition of African American Christianity. For in the much larger world of black Christianity, as we have seen, religion and politics are now pervasively intertwined.

Further Reading

Baer, Hans A., and Merrill Singer. *African-American Religion in the Twentieth Century: Varieties of Protest and Accommodation.* Knoxville, TN: University of Tennessee Press, 1992. A fine history of African American religion and its diversity in a key century of change.

Cone, James. *A Black Theology of Liberation.* Philadelphia: Lippincott, 1970. The classic on black liberation theology.

Garrow, David J. *Bearing the Cross: Martin Luther King Jr. and the Southern Leadership Conference.* New York: Morrow, 1986. The story of King's political and religious activism.

Haley, Alex, ed. *The Autobiography of Malcolm X.* New York: Grove Press, 1965. Malcolm X's account of his life.

Hertzke, Allen D. *Echoes of Discontent: Jesse Jackson, Pat Robertson, and the Resurgence of Populism.* Washington, DC: CQ Press, 1993. Discussion of the 1988 Jesse Jackson campaign.

Lincoln, C. Eric, and Lawrence H. Mamiya. *The Black Church in the African American Experience.* Durham, NC: Duke University Press, 1990. Superb work on African American religion.

8

Women, Religion,
and Politics

*I*n any consideration of religion and politics in the United States today
women merit special attention. Of course all women do not share the same
religion or politics, but at present women in the United States are more religious as a group than men. Many women also spearhead or are otherwise
deeply involved in religious and political causes and controversies.

In this chapter we first consider the facts about women's involvement in
religion in the United States. Next we discuss some of the ways in which activist religious women involve themselves in political life through their actions and thoughts. Third, we explore the religious and political attitudes
of women in the pews, who are not the same as the religious activists.
Finally, we come back to the subject of women, religion, and politics in a
general way and reflect on the future of this dynamic aspect of American
religious life.

Women and Religion in American Life

There is no doubt that American women as a group are religious, definitely
more so than men. Public opinion polls have noted this consistently for
years. Consider the following findings: Women say that religion is important to them much more frequently than men (69 to 51 percent); the majority of women (55 percent) say they find a great deal of consolation in religion, compared with 38 percent of men; women also overwhelmingly
believe that God works miracles and that God is often with them. And they
believe that religion is relevant to most of life's challenges and difficulties.

Many women are also quite traditional in their religious beliefs compared with men. In the United States, this means that women are largely

Christian. Two-thirds of American women hold that Christ is the only way to eternal life, as do only half of all men. Similarly, most women respect the Bible as a source of truth; only 11 percent of women judge it to be little more than fable, whereas more than 20 percent of males hold this view.

These attitudes extend even to women who came to adulthood in the 1960s and early 1970s, the so-called baby boom generation, which is sometimes characterized as the least religious group of women in American history. In fact, boomer women have not brought about a break in the long tradition of religiosity among American women. Even in this generation of alleged rebels, a sizable majority of women rate religion as very important in their lives. Most of the rest say it is fairly important in their lives. About two-thirds expect that religion will become even more important to them in the future. More than two-thirds of all American women claim to be church members, and about 40 percent who are not now church members expect to join in the near future. Also, the baby boom generation has furnished more women clergy than any previous generation. In some mainline denominations, such as the United Church of Christ and the Presbyterian Church (U.S.A.), women now compose more than 10 percent of all clergy, and their numbers are growing.[1]

Women of all generations are more likely than men to be actively connected to and active in religious institutions. Though the statistics vary, perhaps three-quarters of all women belong to a church or other religious group. This is an astounding proportion of the female population, especially in light of the fact that less than two-thirds of all American men have a similar affiliation.

The proportions of men and women who belong to the Roman Catholic Church and to evangelical Protestant churches are about equal. But in mainline Protestant denominations, such as the United Methodist Church and the Episcopal Church, the picture is different: There women predominate. For example, some estimates place the proportion of women members in the Presbyterian Church at 70 percent. In any given week almost half of all women in the United States say they attend a religious service, whereas less than 40 percent of men say the same. Similarly, women are considerably more likely than men to watch religious television.

African American women tend to be more religious than white women; some surveys portray them as considerably more religious. Black churches in the United States attract and retain the support of the vast majority of black women—despite some discussion in the media of Islam's appeal in the African American community. Black churches are filled largely by women and children and much less by men, a fact that is of serious concern in the black community.[2]

At the same time, as we saw in Chapter 7, African American clergy are almost always men. This is not to say that women are not respected in

African American churches; they are, and some elder women bear the formal honorary title of "Mother." Still, less than 5 percent of all black pastors are women. Most of these women clergy actually serve in largely white denominations or churches, though there are some women preachers in Pentecostal African American churches. How long this tradition of female parishioners and male clergy will endure is one of the most intriguing questions facing black Christianity in the United States. It is particularly interesting given that African American women are often quite sympathetic to some aspects of feminism, including greater economic opportunities for women. At present, however, even though women are clearly the heart of African American religion, they rarely serve as clergy.

Women also play a central role in the operation of most white churches in the United States. This is particularly important in the Roman Catholic Church—despite its all-male priesthood. Today the majority of parish leaders and Church employees are women, many of whom enjoy significant influence. Moreover, the declining number of priests promises to increase the role of women within American Catholicism even more. As the priest shortage has reached crisis proportions, more women have shouldered an increasing share of the responsibility for day-to-day parish functioning.[3] The influence of women is also pervasive within mainline Protestant churches.

Women also exert substantial influence within American Judaism. Many Jewish women of the baby boom generation have displayed renewed interest in some of the traditions of Judaism. There has been fierce debate and concern within the Jewish community about the continued vitality of Judaism—and the Jewish people themselves—in the United States. These debates flow from perceptions of a decline in religious commitment among American Jews, an issue that has been pushed to the fore as the size of the Jewish population in the United States has dropped to less than 2 percent[4] (and Jewish intermarriage rates have skyrocketed to over 50 percent). Yet there are clear signs that many Jewish women have chosen to preserve Jewish traditions, sometimes religious, sometimes cultural, that their parents often did not stress.

In the distinctively American manner, some Jewish women tailor their religious practices to their own personal desires. They choose what they wish to do on an individual basis, some keeping kosher kitchens, others observing the weekly *Shabbat* (Sabbath) in the synagogue or at home, some emphasizing Jewish holidays such as *Pesach* (Passover), others working to ensure that their children receive training in Hebrew and the Torah. When Jewish women are able to tailor their own set of customs in this way, it enables them to keep the Jewish faith and culture alive.[5] Also, a number of women have turned to strict Jewish religious orthodoxy; some of these women come from rather unlikely backgrounds, including secular ones.

Orthodox Judaism continues to hold its own among both women and men, accounting for about 10 percent of all American Jews.[6]

The gender dynamics in American church life are not restricted to the increasing role of women. In recent years two highly publicized men's events occurred: the Million Man March in 1995 and the Promise Keepers' rally in 1997. Both displayed clear religious overtones: the Million Man March was organized and led by controversial Nation of Islam leader Louis Farrakhan; the Promise Keepers purvey a distinctly evangelical Protestant message. Each of these events brought hundreds of thousands of men—exclusively—to Washington to demonstrate for what they saw as a need for male family responsibility and spiritual leadership.

Thus men of a variety of walks of life—black and white, Protestant and Muslim—are reasserting their place in organized religion, the family, and society precisely at the time when women are becoming more prominent in these realms. Perhaps the feminization of organized religion has sparked this reaction among men. Or perhaps men are striving to reassert their patriarchal role in American society. In any case, both these movements illustrate the importance of understanding the intersections between religion, politics, and gender in the United States.

Women, Religion, and American Politics

There are a great many connections between religious women and politics in the United States today. This is not surprising in this age of engagement between religion and politics, because many women are both religious and political. The *political* orientations of religious women today defy easy generalization. Women are organized for social change in liberal groups such as womenchurch and in conservative groups such as Concerned Women for America. They are often at the center of election campaigns, as was the case in the presidential campaigns of Jesse Jackson and Pat Robertson.

Clearly women cannot be categorized in any orderly fashion. They do appear to be voting somewhat differently than men in recent years, however; in 1996, the majority of women (54 percent) voted for Bill Clinton, whereas a slight plurality of men (44 percent) voted for Bob Dole. Among all Protestants, Dole received 51 percent of the male vote versus only 44 percent of the female vote. The same pattern characterized the white Catholic vote: Dole got 46 percent of the male vote but only 37 percent of the female vote.[7]

Women also lead the way theologically; they are active within Christianity and Judaism in both challenging and defending existing beliefs and structures. More radical women have been involved in developing new (or reborn) spiritualities such as ecofeminism, witchcraft, and goddess religions that are designed to transform not only religion but every aspect of

---

BOX 8.1   KAY COLES JAMES: CONSERVATIVE
AFRICAN AMERICAN CHRISTIAN

A woman who defies all stereotypes is Kay Coles James, an African American woman and conservative Christian leader. The daughter of a welfare mother, she lived in a public housing project in Richmond, Virginia, before moving in with relatives nearby. As an African American growing up in the segregated South, she endured racial slurs, taunts, and (as one of the first group of students to integrate a Richmond junior high school in 1960) physical abuse. She credits her extended family, her faith, and her church with sustaining her during those years. Kay Coles James attended Hampton University, an historically black college, where she became involved in the evangelical InterVarsity Christian Fellowship.

After college she began a career in management with the Virginia telephone company, which she left to raise a family. Her evangelical faith intensified and she became actively involved in the antiabortion movement. She headed Black Americans for Life and served as public affairs director for National Right to Life. Though she was a major figure in the movement, she thinks the mainstream press ignored her because she contradicted its image of a prolife activist.

As a prominent black conservative, Kay Coles James has served on several presidential commissions and was tapped to serve in the Department of Health and Human Services during the Bush administration. With Bush's 1992 defeat, she returned to political advocacy as vice president of the Family Research Council. In 1994, she was selected by the newly elected Republican governor of Virginia to be cabinet secretary for Health and Human Resources. Kay Coles James is now dean of the Robertson School of Government at the evangelical Regent University.

SOURCES: Kay Coles James, with Jacqueline Cobb Fuller, *Never Forget: The Riveting Story of One Woman's Journey from Public Housing to the Corridors of Power* (Grand Rapids, MI: Zondervan, 1992); Barbara Woerner, "James Credits God's Influence," *Christian American* (January 1995); Kay Coles James, interviewed by Allen D. Hertzke, Republican National Convention, New Orleans, 1988.

---

social and political life. Meanwhile, some women organize in opposition to such new religions and their controversial social agendas.

Conservative Intersections

Today it is commonplace in American religion to find women committed to conservative political causes (Box 8.1). Consider as an example the role of an organization called Concerned Women for America (CWA). It is a decidedly conservative political group with a large national membership; it claims to have over 700,000 members, so that it is "the nation's largest profamily women's organization."[8] Its members are overwhelmingly evangelical Protestant women who affirm the literal truth of the Bible, hold conservative political beliefs, and vote Republican.

Beverly LaHaye founded Concerned Women for America in 1989 and remained as its leader until Carmen Pate replaced her in 1998. LaHaye has written many books, including *I Am a Woman by God's Design,* in which she addresses a wide range of political issues.[9] Her writings tightly interweave political conservatism and Christianity. LaHaye and CWA have been particularly interested and involved in "family" issues and lobbying on behalf of the prolife cause. CWA operates largely through local chapters connected to the national headquarters and its "Prayer/Action Network."[10]

Other conservative organizations also combine religion and politics. Phyllis Schlafly's Eagle Forum has been involved in fighting for conservative moral concerns for several decades. It led the movement that defeated the Equal Rights Amendment in the 1970s. Eagle Forum is explicitly Christian, though it is interdenominational within that context. Despite a common assumption that she is an evangelical Protestant, Schlafly is actually a Roman Catholic; many members of Eagle Forum, though, are evangelical and fundamentalist Protestants.

Eagle Forum is, however, less explicitly religious in its focus than Concerned Women for America. It is also less consumed with questions of family and personal morality. Phyllis Schlafly first appeared on the national political scene in 1964, as a supporter of Barry Goldwater and his campaign for a smaller federal government, long before the modern Christian Right was born. Thus Eagle Forum's newsletter typically addresses economic and foreign policy issues at least as much as personal and religious issues.[11]

Organizations like Concerned Women for America and Eagle Forum are important, but they do not even begin to tell the entire story of religious women and conservative politics. Everywhere one looks in conservative politics today, in fact, there are religious women involved—especially where moral issues are at stake. This was famously true, for example, of Pat Robertson's 1988 presidential campaign. Women served as key staffers at every level of his campaign organization, including the very top. And 70 percent of his voters in Republican primaries were women. These Robertson supporters were overwhelmingly religious and conservative women. Only 26 percent of them favored full equality of the sexes.[12]

Women are the soul of conservative religious struggles at the local level over school curricula, library books, public religious ceremonies, and similar issues. Today we know that these local disputes are really the center of religious politics in the United States. It is there that conservative women are both the generals and foot soldiers in religio-political battles.[13]

In both local and national conflicts, there is no doubt that conservative religious women lack elite access compared with more liberal religious women. This is perhaps the single most important problem conservative women have in politics. They are the insurgents, whereas feminist voices, including religious ones, dominate. Liberal women have a voice in the media, the leading nonsectarian and mainline Protestant theological seminaries, such as the divinity schools of Harvard University and the University of Chicago, and also in numerous orders of Roman Catholic nuns. Many women in these settings are well connected and able to make a lasting impression in the public sphere. Conservative religious women have had a much harder time matching up.

Yet there are some fascinating journeys waiting to be discovered by a larger audience. Consider Kay Coles James, a conservative African American woman who propelled herself, as she says, "from public housing to the corridors of power."[14] James has moved into a life of political activism that has taken her from business to prolife campaigns, to Washington service as an Assistant Secretary in the Department of Health and Human Services, and now to her current position as dean of the Robertson School of Government at Regent University. James argues firmly that the prolife and profamily causes must be committed to racial equality and human compassion (for example, availability of support services for pregnant women might eliminate many abortions). What she always makes clear, however, is that her religion is her proverbial rock of support. She is a religious woman impelled by her religion into politics.

Liberal Intersections

By no means, however, should anyone assume that religious women are necessarily conservative. This is far from the case (Box 8.2). Tremendous diversity characterizes the many religious organizations that connect women to politics. Liberal women's groups normally concentrate on the status of women in church, society, religion, and politics.

This is true of groups like Catholics for a Free Choice and Church Women United (whose members are mainline Protestants). Catholics for a Free Choice concerns itself primarily with "policy analysis, education, and advocacy on issues of gender equality and reproductive health."[15] Such liberal groups have encountered some problems, however, as the case of Church Women United illustrates. Church Women United was founded in 1941 and became active politically in the 1950s and 1960s on behalf of civil rights causes. It moved on in the later 1960s toward issues concerned specifically with women, their rights, and their development as people. Yet the organization has seen better days, as have many religious women's groups at the local and the national levels. There are fewer middle-class women available today who have the time to devote to such organizations than there were thirty years ago.[16]

BOX 8.2   HILLARY RODHAM CLINTON: LIBERAL METHODIST

Hillary Rodham was born into a Methodist family with lineal roots back to England, where Methodism was born. She attended First United Methodist Church in Park Ridge, Illinois. A pious young woman, she volunteered in the 1964 campaign of Republican presidential candidate Barry Goldwater. Like many of her generation, though, she was swept up in the antiwar movement and became a McGovern Democrat. Still, she remained active in religious circles.

As a Wellesley student Hillary Rodham Clinton attended church, joined an interdenominational chapel society, and read widely among the liberal religious thinkers of the times. She took naturally to the intensifying "social gospel" activism of the United Methodist Church, which epitomized the liberal Protestant emphasis on using government to promote economic and social justice for the poor.

Throughout her adult life Hillary Rodham Clinton has remained a churchgoing Methodist who believes in the Trinity and the atoning death and resurrection of Christ. As the wife of Arkansas Governor Bill Clinton she often attended his Baptist church, then her own Methodist congregation, where she taught Sunday school. In Washington the Clinton family attends Foundry United Methodist Church. Its pastor, Rev. J. Philip Wogaman, is a noted ethicist who embraces the social gospel agenda. Castigated as left wing and New Age for her speeches on the "politics of meaning," Hillary Rodham Clinton contends she is actually an old-fashioned Methodist striving to build the Kingdom of God on Earth.

SOURCES: Kenneth Woodward, "Soulful Matters," *Newsweek* (October 31, 1994), 22; Laurie Goodstein, "Pastor to the President Says Morality Includes One's Courage and Caring," *New York Times* (March 1, 1998), A16.

In recent years a more prominent liberal group has been womenchurch, a loosely structured organization founded by Catholic women and strongly promoted by Rosemary Radford Ruether, an activist feminist Catholic theologian. Womenchurch has been at the forefront of the attempt to develop a feminist religion with a suitable political agenda. Womenchurch's religious politics stress a vaguely Christian God, creed, and church, all of which must be strongly egalitarian and communitarian. The group is committed to converting the larger society to the same goals.

Ruether in particular has encouraged women to form feminist communities of egalitarian worship outside the Catholic Church and the rest of Christianity, which she deems too hierarchical and male-oriented. There are a host of other ideas and conceptions within womenchurch, but all share the premise of women's equality with men and sometimes with

God—as well as the belief that political action must be taken to reorient society to these ends.[17]

To this point, womenchurch is merely one expression of the feminist movement within American religion. It has been most active, especially in the Roman Catholic Church, on such issues as abortion rights and ordination for women. Its larger effort, however, has really been aimed toward changing consciousness among the faithful to advance an egalitarian and communal social and religious order.

Those connected with womenchurch are generally white, well-educated, middle- and upper-middle-class women whose views are not representative of most women in the pews of Roman Catholic churches or elsewhere. Womenchurch is not yet a political force of serious strength. It is more given to holding conferences than to lobbying. But it could emerge as a force of considerable significance over time. From within the ranks of womenchurch, as well as from the much broader ranks of liberal religious women, there are many women who have already become deeply involved in politics and are now on the front lines of a variety of battles as activists for change.

A good illustration is provided by the considerable numbers of African American women who were central to Jesse Jackson's presidential campaigns and who today provide most of the time and energy behind dozens of local African American political causes. Again and again, religious black women in action provide the muscle for many of the day-to-day African American political efforts.

Another example of liberal politics among religious women is evident in the emergence of explicitly feminist theologies. Quick generalizations about the complex subject of Christian or Jewish feminist theology are not a good idea. But the rise of feminist theology represents both an intellectual and political movement of some importance. The goal of feminist theologians is to attack past and present male domination in religion and in churches. In the process they sometimes raise fundamental questions about images of God as Father and the male hierarchies of some faiths and religious institutions. Some feminist theologians seek to undermine and then abolish male (and all other) hierarchies in every part of society, including the political order.[18]

Most feminist theologians propose as their alternatives the values of holism and interrelationship, caring communities, radical egalitarianism, and the worth of the physical body. In this context, some feminist thinkers view traditional Western religions (mostly Christianity) as redeemable, whereas others have concluded that feminism requires a complete break with Christianity (and Judaism) and the Western societies with which they are associated. This is not the only dividing line among these very political religious feminists, but it is an essential and illuminating one.[19]

Feminist Arguments on the Redeemability of Religion. There is no doubt that tremendous intellectual energy has gone into the development of feminist theology, nor that it has taken a number of different directions beyond the common attack on patriarchy. A great deal of feminist theology proceeds through a historical lens and involves investigation of the Bible, early Christianity, and the struggles surrounding its early growth. The intention is to indict the patriarchal aspects of the Bible and early Christianity; or, in a more optimistic mindset, to recast the record in the light of a lost, nonpatriarchal, early Christianity.

Often the effort is less about history and more about current situations. Anne Carr is a leading feminist theologian who self-consciously locates herself within the Christian tradition. For Carr, Christianity and feminism can and should go together, so by no means should all of Christianity be discarded as hopelessly antifeminist. Of course, she argues, Christianity is not about a God who is fundamentally male. For Carr, God is not essentially male, but a deeply relational being who exists in association with human beings. Nor is Carr sympathetic to traditional interpretations of Jesus as a passive sufferer or servant forced into those roles against his will. Jesus made the choice to serve and to suffer, and this act of choosing is crucial to understanding the specific choices he made.

As Carr sees it, women should draw on this model of God for their own lives, just as they must also draw heavily on their own experiences. As people of God, they must insist that women be welcome in all roles in church and society. Women must be able to be active participants in lives of choice, human growth, and vigorous participation in relationships with God and all God's people.[20]

A somewhat more radical view has been developed by Sallie McFague. She has been a leader in seeking new "models" of God to replace what she calls "God-he," though there are now many other participants in this enterprise. Often these theorists exist self-consciously within the Christian tradition. Some propose to view God as an androgynous being. Others see God as mother, some as friend, some as lover. The thinking is often boldly unconventional, and numerous alternatives have been proposed. The objective is a reconceptualization of God that paves the way to political and social change.[21]

Most feminist Christian theology (including its change-oriented politics) emanates from within liberal Protestant and Catholic circles and definitely reflects feminist strength in American society among well-educated, middle-class women. Yet it has faced plenty of criticism and has not found its way easily. For example, a huge controversy broke out in mainline denominations over a 1994 conference in Minneapolis on "Re-Imaging" God, where, critics charged, religious feminists affirmed every imaginable image of God—except God the Father and God the Son. From within Roman Catholicism the sharpest critique of feminist religion has come from Donna Streichen in her biting book *Ungodly Rage: The Hidden Face of Catholic Feminism*. She suggests that most Catholic feminist thinkers and leaders are neither Catholic nor Christian. For Streichen, feminism is their real faith and they mean to make Christianity, politics, and all society bend to it.[22]

Despite such critics, feminism has moved steadily into other precincts of American religion besides the obvious centers of liberal religion and politics. For example, a fierce and continuing controversy over the religion and politics of feminism has recently developed within white evangelical Protestantism. By the early 1970s a group of evangelical women had begun publishing the feminist journal *Daughters of Sarah*. Another early voice of dissent was that of evangelical Virginia Ramey Mollenkott, who contended that the Bible was supportive of feminist ideas. She has now declared herself a lesbian and shifted her attention to other, more radical matters, but she continues to defend her understanding of evangelical feminism.

A more recent development has been the emergence of an organization called Christians for Biblical Equality. Speaking from within an evangelical/fundamentalist perspective, this group maintains that equality between the genders is set forth in the Bible. They focus their efforts on publishing and holding workshops on "biblical equality." They distance themselves, however, from the disrespect for the biblical interpretations they see as characteristic of many religiously liberal feminists. They also reject any edging away from the evangelical tradition, which is something they believe many evangelical feminists have done.[23]

To be sure, most conservative Protestants of both genders are not sympathetic to feminism: neither the term nor the movement, nor feminist-oriented religion or feminist models for the family, society, or political life. Yet enthusiasm has waned also for those such as Marabel Morgan (see her book *Total Woman*),[24] who argues that pleasing her man is the main earthly function of a godly woman. Moreover, evangelical and fundamentalist writings today take for granted the concept of equal rights for men and women in political and economic life.[25]

The same does not apply, however, with regard to religion. In nearly all conservative Protestant settings, men alone are pastors, and that is accepted policy. Though there are women pastors in a few Southern Baptist churches and some Pentecostal churches, they are definitely exceptions. It is also understood that the man is to be the earthly head of the family, as St. Paul stipulated in First Corinthians, even as both husband and wife are to acknowledge God as the true head of the entire family. At the same time it is agreed among conservative Christians that women are vital to the preservation of Christian family and religious and moral training for children. Overall, themes of moral and religious conservatism are pervasive, which in turn encourages a politics of conservatism.[26]

Feminist currents have had a far greater impact on Judaism. Many Jewish feminists have concluded that Judaism as they understand it is redeemable as a religion or at least as a spiritual tradition. The effects of feminism in Judaism are most obvious in the dramatic breakthroughs of the past twenty years for women who wish to serve as rabbis. Though the first woman rabbi was ordained in 1972, that now seems ancient history. At first only the liberal, nontraditional, and small Reconstruction branch of Judaism allowed women rabbis, but then Reform Judaism and now Conservative Judaism abolished age-old prohibitions against women rabbis. Since every study in existence demonstrates that Jewish women as a group are more liberal—often far more liberal—than other Americans on so-called women's issues and almost all other political questions, change in the structure of Judaism proved irresistible.[27]

Feminist Arguments on the Irredeemability of Religion. To get a full sense of the ferment in feminist religious thinking and the political implications that accompany it today, it is important to realize that there are a good many feminist religious thinkers who have given up entirely on the Christian and Jewish religions. To these women, Western faiths may have a few positive qualities, but they are at root sexist and supportive of the repression of women. These theorists insist that Americans must rethink spirituality and society in a radical way because the traditional Jewish and Christian religions are inadequate in their (male-centered) understandings of God. They believe that if religion is drastically altered, male images of God will fade, as will any sense of hierarchy or division in the universe. Radical feminist theologians prize the ideals of equality, community, and holism and believe that these ideals may be realized by developing a new religion, a new politics, and a new society.

Mary Daly is perhaps the most important advocate of the argument that Western religions were irredeemable and that radical shifts in both religion and politics were necessary. Ironically, she remains today as a theologian at a Catholic institution, Boston College. In 1973, she published the first of her many books, which she titled *Beyond God the Father*. In the 1970s, Daly was still accepting of some of the Christian tradition, though she was already complaining that the religion was too male-dominated in both theory and practice. She has long since left Christianity behind. Today she is a radical lesbian feminist whose example is admired by some religious women.[28]

Goddess religion is an influential example of the spiritual directions taken by those who repudiate Christianity and Judaism altogether. The standard argument of goddess worshippers is that in ancient times, goddesses were the most common form of deity. In such a world, life was better for women—and for men as well—since society was more egalitarian, communal, and peaceful. In the eyes of goddess worshippers, such worlds sadly fell under the repression of male-dominated social orders. Defenders of goddess religion insist that old goddess models need to be rediscovered to replace the antifemale, hierarchical, and dualistic kinds of religion that have oppressed women for centuries. This perspective has limited appeal today, but there are signs of some interest among women of the baby boom generation, who often see such spirituality as empowering. Moreover, it is now routine to encounter arguments for goddess religion on the edge of a wide variety of feminist religious groups.[29]

Some celebrate goddess religion more as a kind of feminist statement about patriarchal religion or as a weapon of change for women than as an historical or metaphysical reality. Nonetheless, there are some true believers who make no apologies for their faith. Some critics of goddess religion are skeptical of the often sketchy claims about the extent of past civilizations' allegiance to goddesses. Others protest casual generalizations about past goddess religions that sweep across cultures and millennia. Still others note that ancient goddesses were fertility deities, a rather dubious model for modern feminists.

Rosemary Radford Ruether approaches these dilemmas from a sympathetic radical feminist perspective that nonetheless spurns claims that Christianity is irredeemable. She appreciates the idea of a female deity. For her it provides an alternative conception of God that many women may understandably find attractive—even as she points to problems inherent in goddess religion. Ruether also understands that for adherents of Western religious traditions, interest in goddess religion could only create fissures. As radical as Ruether is, she is not prepared to give up Christianity for images of goddesses from another time and place.[30]

Another current direction in feminist spirituality is witchcraft religion. Its adherents consider the mainstream Western religions hopeless due to their historic oppression of women. Though witchcraft religion has long had an underground life in American society, it has recently emerged more openly, especially through its most organized and noted version, the wicca religion. It is no longer unusual to find an ad for wicca Sunday services in the newspaper along with other ads for more conventional services. Nor is it unusual to encounter voices of the witchcraft religion such as Starhawk or Margot Adler in public forums or on TV talk shows.

People are divided over what witchcraft involves. Practitioners themselves do not agree, except about their view that human consciousness can be altered through rituals and practices and that the power of the natural and spiritual worlds have definite effects on people and events. By this view, there are spiritual powers and forces with which people can connect if they know how. Practitioners of witchcraft use all sorts of rituals from the past, though some also embrace newer traditions. This is because witchcraft is a relatively open, pluralistic, and malleable kind of spirituality. Some forms of witchcraft are exclusively lesbian; others are self-consciously feminist; still others have no such boundaries. The lines between one version and another may be great at times, but overall the movement has been inclusive.

Though practitioners of witchcraft over the years have rarely been political, in recent years a more explicitly feminist and radical side of witchcraft religion has emerged. There is no unitary attitude toward either feminism or politics, but more and more witchcraft has become an explicitly feminist religion, attracting people who are militantly opposed to the patriarchal aspects of American society.[31]

Ecofeminist spirituality is a third feminist approach that treats Western religion as largely irredeemable. Though the term "ecofeminism" dates only from 1974, the ecofeminist movement has ancient roots. Many devotees of ecofeminist spirituality explicitly repudiate the Christian and Jewish religious traditions as male-centered. Under these religions, ecofeminists argue, both nature and women have been mistreated. "Reforms" can never be enough to eliminate the patriarchal structures of thought and organization that have facilitated this oppression. Thus ecofeminism involves a widespread search for alternative religions that may provide spiritual sustenance. Above all, ecofeminists search for holistic spiritualities. Sometimes they direct favorable attention to goddess and nature religions, witchcraft, Native American faiths, and Buddhism, among others. Ecofeminists who are unwilling to abandon Christianity strive to recast its traditional vocabularies and conceptions.[32]

Ecofeminism's basic premise is that both nature and women have been oppressed throughout Western history by men; male hierarchies (men over women, men over nature); male dualisms (mind versus body, men versus nature and women); and male-centered religions, especially Christianity and Judaism. This domination has proceeded in direct disregard for the holism that ecofeminists maintain is characteristic of both women and nature. Ecofeminists say that it is obvious that both nature and women have suffered terribly under male domination. They note that women who have not cooperated with the male-dominated society have paid a high price (as did witches, for example, in the early years of American history).[33]

The political side of ecofeminism treasures the goal of the liberation of both nature and women. To accomplish this goal, ecofeminists advocate transcending hierarchy and dualism (that is, male rule in all areas of life), particularly in the realms of religion and politics. Women must lead the way to some kind of revolution to create an egalitarian community where holism, care, and healing will flourish among human beings.

The ecofeminist expectation is that in this ideal community spiritualism will also be nourished. Many, perhaps most, ecofeminists are self-consciously spiritual in their outlook; nature provides the common source of grounding and moral standard. Though ecofeminists are clear in defining their goals, it is unclear exactly how these goals will be achieved. Ecofeminists are, however, committed to educating people toward a new consciousness, and they accept the need for practical political action when necessary.

Though ecofeminism speaks much of unity and community, its proponents often celebrate women as being especially close to nature due to menstruation and childbirth. There are more than a few hints of female triumphalism inherent in this view that mix poorly with the ecofeminist ideal of terminating male domination. Equally debatable has been the ecofeminist invocation of nature as the standard of value and the claim that most societies once worked better because they were closer to nature. Women critics in particular have attacked the idea that nature is the proper moral foundation for everything.[34]

Women in the Pews

Though political debates over feminist theology and the value of Christian and Jewish religions dominate a good deal of the intellectual discourse surrounding women, religion, and politics, these matters do not appear to have engaged many women in the pews of churches and synagogues. Indeed, the fact is that aside from women clergy, the more a woman is involved in organized religion, the more likely she is to be relatively conservative on political and religious questions as compared with women who are relatively uninvolved.

Studies of the baby boom generation of women confirm this scenario. The more a woman socialized in the 1960s and early 1970s is connected with a church or other religious group, the more conservative she will be on issues such as women's ordination. On the other hand, women who are attracted to less conventional spiritual journeys—often outside of organized religion—are much more likely to have liberal religious and political attitudes, including a strong attachment to feminism.[35]

Yet the situation is complicated. Consider women of the baby boom generation who claim to be "born again," who are mostly evangelical Protestants. These women are distinctly conservative in their religious and political attitudes. Many of them believe that mothers of preschool children must not work outside of the home, but the majority do favor the ordination of women. Moreover, evangelical women are divided over how much authority the husband should enjoy in the family.[36]

It is instructive to consider Catholic women of all generations. They tend to favor women's rights strongly, and as a group they are considerably more feminist on a wide array of issues than Protestant women. Whereas many Catholic women feel that their church meets women's needs, others consider the Church's record only fair, and about one-fourth rate it as poor. Women's assessments of the Church improve when the question is whether it adequately addresses the individual needs of individual women themselves—as opposed to their perceptions of the Church's success with women as a group. And attitudes are most positive when women assess their own particular parish's treatment of women.

The undertone of uneasiness does not mean that Catholic women favor drastic changes in the Roman Catholic Church. This is definitely not the case. Thus, even as most Catholic women now support the idea of a married priesthood, the idea of female priests still provokes very divided opinions. How long this division will last, however, is uncertain. Among Catholic women there is a distinct age factor at work. The generation of women who reached adulthood in the 1960s and early 1970s tends to form the line of demarcation. Younger Catholic women are much more liberal on matters involving the priesthood, and they express a greater overall degree of discomfort with the Church.[37]

Other students of Catholic women paint a similar picture. Jane Redmont, in her book *Generous Lives: American Catholic Women Today*, found that Catholic women, activist or not, are strong in their religious faith but divided about the institution of the Catholic Church. There was considerable agreement among many, though, that the status of women in the local church was a matter of serious concern—and that the Catholic Church needed to be more respectful of women in general. In Redmont's study, opinions differed somewhat by age, as we would expect, and by marital status.[38]

The irony here is that some antifeminist elements in the Roman Catholic Church are also growing dissatisfied and beginning to raise questions about the increasing role played by women in the Church. Critics raise the specter of what they call the "feminization of the church," expressing their fears that fewer men will be interested in Roman Catholicism if it responds to every desire of feminist women. There is also some apprehension that the male leaders who remain will become "feminized."[39]

The attitudes in the pews are illuminated by opinions about abortion, a crucial issue that lies at the intersection of women, religion, and politics. As we know, much of the battle over abortion is fought by combatants whose base lies in organized religion. This is true both of some prochoice *and* prolife activist women for whom religion matters—and in fact forms the underpinning of moral and political commitments.[40]

The split among women on abortion is real. The more a woman is involved in religion and the more traditional her religious views, the more likely she is to be conservative on abortion questions. This does not mean that all active Catholic or Lutheran women are prolife. This is far from the case. But it is true that religious intensity is the best single factor predicting conservative abortion attitudes.[41]

TABLE 8.1   Presidential Votes, Congressional Votes, and Party Identification of White Protestants and White Catholics by Gender, 1996

	Dole	Clinton	Perot	Democratic House Vote	Republican Party ID	Democratic Party ID
White Protestants						
Women	47	46	7	44	43	35
Men	54	34	10	35	47	25
White Catholics						
Women	35	56	9	57	36	35
Men	44	43	12	46	30	47

SOURCE: Voter Research Survey and Exit Poll, November 1996 (N=16,627).

Religious (and secular) women on both sides of the abortion debate often have more in common with each other than many think. They usually share a strong belief in the value of women, motherhood, and caring. They frequently share a certain suspicion of men and a sense that women must ultimately rely on themselves.[42] Yet the abortion debate does divide women, including religious women, despite the fact that in the most liberal and prochoice religious settings, such as the Episcopal Church, the more involved a woman is in the church, the more likely she is to be uncomfortable with abortion.

In 1992, 37 percent of women voters felt abortion should be legal in all cases; 28 percent, legal in most cases; 22 percent, illegal in most cases; and 10 percent, illegal in all cases. Among born-again voters—usually evangelical Protestants—the figures were very different: 13 percent believed abortion should be legal in all cases; 19 percent, legal in most; 41 percent, illegal in most; and 24 percent, illegal in all. Church attendance also matters. Among weekly worshippers, 19 percent felt abortion should be legal in all cases; 25 percent, in most; 35 percent, in few; and 17 percent, in none. The point is that opinions differ, but religious involvement correlates clearly with conservative attitudes on abortion.[43]

Gender differences in voting behavior are also quite apparent now. Women of all faiths are more likely to claim that they identify with the Democratic party and vote for Democratic presidential and congressional candidates (see Table 8.1). Gender even appears to have a more significant effect on partisanship and voting behavior than religion itself; Protestant women were more likely than Catholic men to vote for Bill Clinton in

1996, for example. Another interesting fact is that the Republican party has a slight edge with Catholic men, but it clearly has a long way to go with Catholic women. In part these gender differences in 1996 may be attributed to the fact that Clinton's "M2E2" message (emphasizing Medicare, Medicaid, education, and the environment) has been shown to have resonated more with American women than with men. Nonetheless, gender differences within religious groups cannot be ignored, and they may grow even more pronounced in the years to come.

Conclusion

Though there are plenty of crosscurrents, women play a central role in American religion, and the importance of their role is growing. The future of women, religion, and politics is not obvious, but we can expect that the politics of religion will continue to involve women—and may ultimately be led by women. Among the areas to watch most closely in the future are feminist movements in American religion—and the reactions to them. Feminists will tackle the theologies and practices of American religion, including ordination issues, the proper place of religious hierarchy, and much more. Women will not just stir the political pot within churches and religions; they will affect the stance and involvement of organized religion on issues of gender and family in the politics of the larger society.

Also important to observe will be the continuing conflict over abortion and developments regarding other moral issues on the conservative religious agenda in America. The role of conservative religious women in promoting and defending a "family agenda" may turn out to have a major impact, no matter how many books on feminist theology are published.

Relations among women in American religion will also be important in the future. We have noted that religious women are often divided in their orientations toward feminism and liberal politics, just like the population at large. Though many female religious leaders are liberal, this is far less true of women in the pews. Whether this gap closes or becomes wider in the years ahead will have major implications for the effectiveness of religious women in politics.

Finally, it will be fascinating to observe national political developments, including presidential campaigns, to see what connections they make with religious women. The more American politics focuses on issues that are important to religious women, or on candidates' positions on such issues, the more likely religious women are to be mobilized. We know that many religious women were mobilized during the 1988 presidential campaigns of Jesse Jackson and Pat Robertson, and during various state and local campaigns since then. We know it did not happen during the 1992 presidential election, but we also know that President Clinton received more support from women in the American electorate than he did from men. Which of these indicates the path of the future for women, religion, and politics remains open.

Further Reading

Daly, Mary. *Beyond God the Father: Toward a Philosophy of Women's Liberation.* Boston: Beacon, 1973. Radical feminist attack on traditional religion.

Davidman, Lynn. *Tradition in a Rootless World: Women Turn to Orthodox Judaism.* Berkeley: University of California Press, 1991. Interesting exploration of women and traditional Judaism.

Diamond, Irene, and Gloria Feman Orenstein, eds. *Reweaving the World: The Emergence of Ecofeminism.* San Francisco: Sierra Club, 1990. Thorough considerations of ecofeminism.

Loades, Ann, ed. *Feminist Theology.* Louisville, KY: Westminster, 1990. An excellent array of essays on the subject.

McFague, Sallie. *Models of God: Theology for an Ecological, Nuclear Age.* Philadelphia: Fortress, 1987. Reflections of an influential feminist liberal Protestant theologian.

Piper, John, and Wayne Grunden, eds. *Recovering Biblical Manhood and Womanhood: A Response to Evangelical Feminism.* Wheaton, IL: Crossway, 1992. Conservative Protestant views on women.

Ruether, Rosemary Radford. *Gaia and God: An Ecofeminist Theology of Earth Healing.* San Francisco: HarperCollins, 1992. The perspective of a leading feminist theologian.

Streichen, Donna. *Ungodly Rage: The Hidden Face of Catholic Feminism.* San Francisco: St. Ignatius, 1991. Sharp criticism of religious feminists in action.

9

The Politics of Small Religious Movements

$\mathcal{M}$ost of the discussion of religion and politics in the United States concentrates on the political activity of large, familiar, and well-established religious groups: Catholics, Jews, and various Protestant denominations and outlooks. This focus makes sense, since these groups are the most important and visible elements of the complex and pluralistic politics of religion in the United States. But these major religious groups hardly constitute the entire story of religion—or religion and politics—in the United States.

After all, the United States is a nation in which there are literally hundreds of religions and thousands of religious communities and churches. Every one of them is a part of the larger nation, and that simple fact affects each of them of necessity. Of course, each American religious group has political objectives—even if it simply wishes to be left alone. And each exercises political influence, however small, indirect, or unintended. Smaller, less popular religions have important lessons to teach about what they do, how they protect themselves, and how they advance their values. Such tales will be ever more relevant as the pluralism of American religion continues to grow.

It is not obvious how to study the political dimensions of smaller religious groups in the United States. Few have done so, and as we proceed we are acutely aware that our approach represents only one possible method. We approach smaller religions with respect—not as strange phenomena. Small religious movements deserve to be taken seriously.

In this chapter we divide small religious movements into two groups: those that are separatist and those that reach out to the mainstream. In both instances we give attention to their attitudes toward, and involvement in, political life. It is our argument that the kinds of politics these two types of groups practice—and that they can practice—usually differ.

Small, Separatist Religions and Politics

A good many religions in the United States have relatively few members and adopt a distinctly separatist orientation toward the broader culture. By the term "separatist" we mean that these religious communities set stricter moral boundaries for their members than do mainstream religions, and that these boundaries necessarily separate their members from the larger society to some degree. Most of these groups are deeply critical of the larger society, which they portray as immoral, evil, or wrongheaded. Some have an interest in reaching out to the larger society to gain converts, but many enjoy only limited success in such efforts, due to the heavy demands required of group members.

It is also helpful to subdivide small, separatist religions into two types. Some have a membership who share a common history or ethnic origin. Such characteristics provide a powerful basis for community, but also limit growth. Other groups have no such basis for unity, so they substitute some other foundation for their tightly bounded community.

The Amish are a good example of a religious group whose community is based in a shared history. Most Amish originally came from the sixteenth-century Anabaptist movements that began during the Protestant Reformation in Switzerland. The Amish broke away from one Anabaptist branch over issues that are now dusty with time. They began their formal existence as a separate religious group in 1693, though it was not until the eighteenth century that Amish people began migrating to the United States. Today Amish people reside in many states, but their most well-known communities are located in southern Pennsylvania.[1]

The Christian Protestant religious beliefs of the Amish are reasonably familiar in the American context. After all, the Amish constitute a fragment of the larger Protestant Reformation, the descendants of which now form the Protestant majority of the United States. At the same time, however, the Amish are not a part of mainstream American religion or culture. Their focus on maintaining a tightly knit and separatist religious community, as well as their buggies, plain clothes, and rejection of electricity in the home, make this obvious. This separatism is particularly clear to the Amish themselves as they struggle to maintain their way of life against an indifferent and occasionally hostile American culture.

The Amish have traditionally displayed little interest or faith in politics or government. Their numbers are tiny and their chances of having much political influence are extremely modest. In the United States the Amish have usually had only the most minimal contact with the government. Some Amish citizens vote, and there have been some Amish efforts to lobby state legislatures over issues of urgent importance to them. In 1972, they were involved in a noted U.S. Supreme Court case in which they won the right not to send their teenagers to high school *(Wisconsin* v. *Yoder)*. Mostly, though, the Amish have turned away from politics. Their politics is really the politics of noninvolvement and withdrawal.

Because it is dictated by a sense of religious and cultural separatism, political disengagement has worked well for the Amish. They have acquired a reputation as a quaint and inoffensive people that should be left in peace. This is why they have escaped significant persecution and interference. The broader U.S. culture seems to accept the Amish as a charming expression of a past and a people who pose no threat (with perhaps the small exception of some local drivers who find slow-moving Amish buggies an annoyance). Amish separatism has turned out to be a form of politics that has provided protection from the broader society.

Another much discussed example of a small, separatist religious group with its own distinctive historical tradition is the Hasidim, or Hasidic Jews. Adherents of Orthodox Judaism represent 10 percent of all Jews in the United States. The largest single group within the Orthodox community are Hasidic Jews, who are concentrated in New York City and the surrounding areas.[2] It is important to note that the Hasidim are not a thoroughly unified group; they are in fact divided into several subgroups.

Hasidic Judaism claims to represent ancient Jewish traditions and beliefs and stands against modernist forces that it contends have overwhelmed most Jews and Jewish culture. The Ba'al Shem Tov (Israel ben Eliezer; c. 1700–1760) founded the Hasidim in Poland in the eighteenth century. He was determined to revive Judaism through the creation of tight Hasidic communities, each organized under a *rebbe* (master) and devoted to the laws and teachings (the 613 Mitzvahs) of ancient scripture. Unlike many other Orthodox Jews, however, the Hasidim do not single-mindedly study the scriptures. For the Hasidim, this approach is much too formal and scholarly; it downplays the essential importance of emotion in their worship of God.

The political tradition of the Hasidim has been mostly one of political withdrawal from larger, usually Christian societies. Hasidic Jews are similar to many fundamentalist Protestant groups in that they seek distance from societies they judge as corrupting or otherwise dangerous to the faithful. At the same time, however, the Hasidim do sometimes participate in politics. In the United States this has included regular voting. Because the Hasidim are usually socially conservative, it has also meant voting Republican in many instances. Moreover, the Hasidim have on occasion tried to elect their own candidates in local and state contests where they perceive crucial issues to be at stake and where they have a chance to win (as in parts of New York City).

The Hasidim are generally no more interested in politics than the Amish, but the realities of Hasidic life have sometimes forced them to become involved. Close and crowded quarters in New York City in particular have led to racial and religious quarrels with other groups that have sometimes become ugly. In some such instances, Hasidic Jews have turned to political involvement simply as a means of survival. On the whole, however, the Hasidim have not favored political involvement nor considered it particularly fruitful. They have usually gone their separatist way.

Other small, separatist religions define themselves by shared racial or ethnic characteristics. The Native American religions are good cases in point. Native American spiritual life has long been a highly complex and diverse phenomenon. It includes a great many Christians who no longer adhere to their past traditions. Most Native American religious groups today are fairly loosely organized. Some, however, are institutionalized in familiar senses. Thus Native American religion is the organized expression of one faith, influenced to some extent by Christianity, focused at times on worship of Jesus, and perhaps best known for the use of the drug peyote as a part of worship.

Despite their diversity, Native American religious groups frequently share certain commonalities. These include beliefs in a supreme being; the reality and power of spirits, visions, and ghosts; life after death; and the omnipresence of a spiritual aspect, usually unseen but of great significance in the empirical world. Along with these well-established beliefs come a variety of rituals and practices. Native American religions also feature clergy and other signs of organization. Yet in most instances formal religious organization and institutionalization are modest in comparison with other American religions.[3]

And this fact matters. Despite the occasional court case about the use of peyote, Native American spiritual communities play no visible role in the politics of religion in the United States today. To be sure, there are a few organized Native American groups involved in American politics, and the political perspectives of individual believers may be influenced greatly by their spirituality. But unorganized and numerically modest religious groups such as those represented by Native American religions have little political sway. Thus Native American religions do not constitute a political movement in any collective sense.

On the one hand, the lesson here is that organization is necessary for influence. On the other hand, like the Amish, Native American religions illustrate the point that most religious groups choosing separatism are not usually attacked by the larger culture. They are instead simply ignored.

The Fellowship of Metropolitan Community Churches represents another small and (though against its will) separatist religious community, defined in this instance by sexual orientation. The Metropolitan Churches are surrounded by controversy in Christian circles because they have a largely gay membership. As a result the Metropolitan Churches have been and remain isolated. For example, they have sought and failed to receive even observer status in the liberal National Council of Churches.

The Fellowship includes nearly three hundred affiliated churches and approximately 30,000 members.[4] Yet it has not progressed beyond the outsider role it plays as a gay church, because it approves of gay sexual activity (as do few other religious groups). Though the church itself has not been particularly politically active or influential, some of its members have become involved in various gay rights campaigns. Again we see an example of the difficulties faced by small religious movements in the political realm. Even if the Fellowship of Metropolitan Community Churches wished to exert collective political clout, it would be hard-pressed to succeed because of its small numbers. Individual members may make a difference politically, but not directly on account of the religious group itself.

Markedly different small and separatist religions are those that are not based on any specific tradition or human characteristic. Though these religions seek to exclude no one, they remain very small. They are usually intensely cohesive, and they exist in major tension with the society around them. This is why many of their efforts to recruit members fail. These groups often conflict more with the broader society than most other religions, in part because of the assertiveness with which they recruit members. Their members are rarely seen as quaint; instead, they are often seen as an annoyance and occasionally as dangerous. A classic illustration is the Jehovah's Witnesses. We will consider them in some detail later, in contrast with the Mormons. It must be noted now, though, that the Witnesses have clashed with the government and society over the years. Though they are not interested in or approving of politics, they have learned to participate, when necessary, for their own protection.

"Cults" are the prime illustration today of small, separatist religions that reach into the society for converts but more often receive opprobrium. Every year or two, TV, radio news, and newspapers are full of reports of one "cult" religion or another and the seemingly strange, dangerous, or fanatical activities of its members.[5] Most recently cults made the news when, in March 1997, thirty-nine members of the Heaven's Gate religious group committed mass suicide in a rented San Diego mansion. They believed and followed the teachings of their leader, Marshall Herff Applewhite, who taught that humans had to shed their bodies (which he called "earthly containers") in order to reach "the next level." The group committed suicide, believing that they would go on to rendezvous with a UFO following the Comet Hale-Bopp, which was passing Earth at that time.[6]

In recent years few cults have had much political influence, but a few have locked horns with the government. The fiery April 1993 demise of David Koresh and the Branch Davidian community outside Waco, Texas, demonstrated this fact. The Branch Davidian community was a breakaway group of another breakaway group of the Seventh-Day Adventists. Under Koresh, the Branch Davidians soon became a classic illustration of a strictly separatist community led by a charismatic leader. Its eventual destruction had a definite political impact, especially on the Bureau of Alcohol, Tobacco, and Firearms and the FBI, while dramatically demonstrating the Branch Davidians' own lack of political influence.[7]

The term "cult" has always seemed to us to be a prejudicial one, since in American society its meaning is always negative. The terms "alternative religion" or "unconventional religion" might be better, but they are not precise enough. As we have argued, there are many kinds of alternative or unconventional religions. This is why we reluctantly continue to use the term "cult" for a specific type of highly dissident alternative religion organized into a tight community and existing in great tension with the broader culture. Often such religious groups are headed by a single charismatic leader whom the community members are willing to follow—sometimes to death, as was the case with Marshall Applewhite and his Heaven's Gate followers.

There are estimated to be as many as 5,000 or as few as 700 cults in the United States, depending on how strictly one interprets the definition. Few are, or have been, as well known as Heaven's Gate, the Branch Davidians, or the equally deadly People's Temple cult, which was led to mass death in Guyana in 1978 by their leader, Jim Jones. Most cults are nonviolent and shun the public eye—and the political realm. Perhaps the largest cult in America today is the Los Angeles–based Church of Christ, which is said to have about 100,000 members. It is known for its very close guidance (called shepherding) of its adherents, though it understandably resists the label "cult."

On the extreme fringe of American religious life is the tiny but noteworthy Christian Identity movement, which is made up of small separatist organizations whose leaders preach hate through religion. Most Christian Identity groups espouse negative attitudes toward racial and ethnic minorities, people who practice faiths other than Christianity, and gays and lesbians. They embrace the "Israel message," which means that white people are chosen by God and that Jews and persons of color are subhuman. In the view of Christian Identity followers, an apocalyptic holy war will destroy all people except white Christians. As postmillennialists, Christian Identity followers see this battle as imminent, so they often arm themselves heavily and live together in remote compounds. The Christian Identity movement's political approach is intensely reactionary and sometimes violent; convicted Oklahoma City–bomber Timothy McVeigh is said to have had links to the movement.[8]

Ironically, there may be as many self-consciously anticult organizations as there are cults. The largest of these is the Cult Awareness Network. Many anticult groups are connected with government and politics so they can call on government agencies to challenge cults or "recover" individual family members who have joined cults. Sometimes they have received substantial legal (and not-so-legal) assistance from government in their efforts.

There is little doubt that the extent of the cult phenomenon gets exaggerated when sporadic outbursts of media attention flare up. This is doubly true if we think about cults as political actors, since most stay out of politics as much as they possibly can. They know society does not like them and that the public eye can only be cruel to them. Though they seek converts, they also seek withdrawal. They may not want to let society alone, but they certainly want society to leave them alone.

The Unification Church of Rev. Sun Myung Moon presents an exception to cults' standard strategy of political avoidance. This movement—its followers are universally known, often derisively, as "Moonies"—is committed to politics. How influential the Unification Church is, however, is another matter. Though the membership, financial resources, and political influence of the Unification Church are not well understood, we do know that the church in the United States is part of a larger movement, based in South Korea, that has substantial financial resources. It has been willing to commit these resources, for example, to funding the politically conservative *Washington Times,* a newspaper that is the major alternative to the liberal *Washington Post.*[9]

Small Religions Reaching for the Mainstream

Two significant examples of large—and growing—religions that are reaching for the mainstream in America today are the Mormon faith and Islam. Later in this chapter we consider Mormons in detail by contrasting them with the Jehovah's Witnesses. Here we point out that Mormons and adherents of other minority religions of relatively large size are far more willing to involve themselves politically than are people who belong to smaller, separatist religions. Even so, Mormons are cautious and aware of the potential dangers of political engagement. And only sometimes are they effectively organized for politics.

Islam today receives a fair amount of media attention, a sign that observers are finally discovering its sizable presence in the United States. Though the precise number of Muslims living in the United States is unknown, standard estimates are around 6 million.[10] This counting problem is complicated because surveys must be adjusted for the fact that many American Muslims are immigrants who sometimes do not speak English well or at all. A reasonable estimate is that more than 1 percent of the U.S. population is now Muslim. The number of Muslims is growing; as recently as fifty years ago there were no more than 20,000 Muslims in the United States. The numbers of Muslim places of worship have also risen rapidly.

There was only one mosque in the United States in the early 1930s, but now there are at least 1,000 Islamic religious centers. By every measure this growth is very real and there is no reason to think it will not continue.[11]

Though many American Muslims are first- or second-generation immigrants, a sizable proportion (some would estimate as many as half) are African Americans. Most African American Muslims adhere to mainstream Islam and do so proudly, though there are assorted splinter groups, including the much discussed Nation of Islam led by Louis Farrakhan (see Chapter 7). Perhaps the most popular and influential black Muslim leader is Warith Deen Muhammad, the son of Elijah Muhammad, who was the famed leader of the Nation of Islam in the time of Malcolm X. As Malcolm X had wished, Warith Deen Muhammad has led his followers toward mainstream Islam and away from Farrakhan's racially separatist theories.

The ethnic diversity that characterizes other American Muslims is remarkable. Muslim immigrants have come to the United States in considerable numbers, especially from Pakistan, Iran, Bangladesh, Nigeria, Egypt, and other Middle Eastern countries, as well as the Philippines, Indonesia, and other places. Ethnic diversity also means that immigrant Muslims represent both major traditions of Islam, Sunni and Shi'ite, though Sunni Muslims predominate both in the U.S. and in Islam as a whole.

Today there are signs of organization that one day could result in some political influence for American Muslims. The basic federation of Islamic groups in the United States is called the Islamic Society of North America. It supports a political action committee, though this fact is not well known. There is also a Muslim League of Voters, but it too has not held much clout even within Islamic communities. Perhaps the most potent Islamic organizations are the ethnic ones that give voice to some groups of immigrant or ethnic Muslims. A number of these ethnic groups have sprung up, but they usually choose to underline the importance of ethnicity rather than Muslims' common religion.

Given the large number of immigrant Muslims in the United States (many of whom are not citizens) and the racial and ethnic divisions inherent in American Islam, collective Muslim political muscle is unlikely to develop.[12] Moreover, Muslims do not yet agree on what would be—or will be—the appropriate political agenda for the Islamic community in the United States. Though there are Muslims of every political persuasion, there is no question that they and their organizations tend to be quite conservative on social and moral issues such as abortion, women's rights, and sexual behavior. Indeed, many people who convert to Islam from other religions are attracted to its confident discipline and clear boundaries. It is possible that as adherence to Islam in the United States grows and as it becomes more organized, it may become something of a partner in the conservative movement in American religion, which today includes evangelical

Protestants and Orthodox Jews. Still, it is interesting to note that in the 1996 presidential election, Bill Clinton garnered three times as many Muslim votes as did his opponent, Bob Dole.[13]

Organized Islam may also become more active in apologetics in the United States. Some of its spokespersons already spend much time confronting and debunking the false perception that most Muslims are anti-American political extremists, an impression that was reinforced by the bombing of the World Trade Center in 1993 and memories of the American hostages held in Shi'ite Iran from 1979 to 1981. The media have a tendency to jump to the worst possible conclusions when it comes to terrorism and Muslims. For example, when TWA flight 800 exploded over Long Island in July 1996, there was a rush to implicate Muslim extremists. As it turned out, the investigation of the crash found no evidence of a bomb on the airplane. Such false perceptions are painful and harmful to Muslim Americans, and Islamic leaders understand that such stereotypes must be dismantled if Muslims are to gain political influence in the United States. Perhaps the best way for these myths to be debunked is through the growing visibility of young Muslims, who are assimilating into corporate America with relative ease.[14]

A third possibility, of course, is that policy concerns affecting Islamic countries will become a political agenda for Muslims in the United States, at least in the near future. Such an agenda would mirror American Jews' concern for Israel. To some extent this is true already, though it has not necessarily led to a single set of policies, given the diversity both of Islamic nations and of Muslims in America. The exception is strong, universal support for the Palestinian cause. And when in 1998 it appeared that the United States might again go to war with Iraq, the American Muslim Council organized a lobbying campaign against military action.[15]

It is distinctly possible that Islam will never have substantial political leverage in the United States regardless of what agenda(s) it may pursue. Perhaps it will remain divided and subdivided along ethnic and racial lines, which may undercut the development of any serious Islamic political agenda in the United States. In the short run we suspect that this is what will happen. But in time ethnicity may become less important in defining Muslims' identity, as has been the case with American Catholics due to assimilation. In that event, a politics of a more unified Islam could well emerge. It is interesting to consider how Islam might proceed if its believers do move toward greater engagement in American politics. Focus on a single political agenda must be a top priority, and a serious effort must be made to fashion a more positive image of Islam in America. Improved relations with American Jews would also be beneficial.

Features of Islam that clash with mainstream American culture, however, pose difficulties. This is true, for example, of Islam's conservative attitudes toward women. More broadly, there is the fact that Islam is not well understood in most parts of the United States, a reality that must be met and overcome. But these difficulties can be addressed. Other groups have done so in American history, including both Roman Catholics and Jews. After all, they too were once religions without political influence in the United States.

The New Age movement is another example of a large spiritual movement (it is not a single religion) that is reaching for the mainstream. New Age religion or New Age spirituality is, by its nature, not very institutional. It is not about churches, much less a single church, and its varied practitioners often are positively resistant to any development of such institutions. Instead, adherents of New Age spiritualities are often highly individualistic. Among the many types of New Age spirituality are dream analysis, astrology, channeling (and other techniques of contacting spirits), consultation with psychics, goddess affirmation, and assorted forms of nature worship.[16]

Because these spiritual practices proceed largely in a noninstitutional context, or operate through small, local gatherings, we have no real idea how many people are involved. It is no secret that New Age approaches have proved highly attractive to some baby boomers. However, no one knows the exact degree of popularity New Age religion enjoys. Part of the reason for this lack of data is that many people who embrace New Age sentiments also belong to more conventional religious groups.[17]

Scattered evidence suggests that New Agers tend to be very liberal politically, but it is not clear whether New Age spiritualities themselves play a role in shaping these attitudes. Nor is there any sign of an overtly organized relationship between the New Age movement and liberal politics. Indeed, there is little sign of any organized political effort within the diverse New Age movement. Much harder to assess is what role New Age sensibilities, which are somewhat countercultural—oriented to the soul, yet sympathetic to the communal life—may play in the personal politics of individual citizens.

Political Assessments

The overall political strength of unconventional religious groups in the United States is modest at best. Few of them have much political influence. Some have made a political impact in the courts by seeking to protect themselves, as has been the case with the Jehovah's Witnesses. The few exceptions, such as the Mormons, are large groups composed of members who are well integrated into American life and willing to undertake political action.

Of course numbers are a factor that can hardly be ignored in explaining why some groups count for so little in American politics. We know that most alternative religions are small, comprising a tiny fraction of a country with nearly 300 million people. Many of these faith groups are not growing, either. Only a few are growing fast enough to increase their share of the nation's population. To be sure, numbers are not everything, but they matter in politics. They furnish activists, supporters, and much more. A group begins at a serious disadvantage without those numbers, even if the politics it practices is almost entirely defensive, as is the case with the Witnesses or the Amish.

The issue of isolation is also important. Many smaller religious communities choose withdrawal or isolation, as we know, because they fear the corrupting power of the larger culture (the Amish and Hasidim are examples). Sometimes this decision also reflects a realistic analysis of the slim chances these groups have to affect the broader culture. Often, however, disengagement is rooted in theological belief. The Jehovah's Witnesses hold that the true believer should not be concerned with governments and nations, so political engagement becomes almost sacrilege.

The reasons for avoiding politics vary. But whatever these reasons, groups that are not willing to engage in politics have only a small chance of enjoying influence. This is simply the way of the world of politics, and it is a price, for better or for worse, that most of these religions end up paying.

Islam may be at an advantage, since its religious principles encourage political involvement. Islam holds that religion should pervade every aspect of life. Thus Muslim leaders have argued that politics and government are legitimate and important realms. This tenet should provide hospitable theological and ideological support for Muslims as they enter American politics.

Geography can also influence isolation. This has been true throughout Mormon history. It is still true today, at least to some extent, since the majority of American Mormons still reside in Utah and surrounding western states. Today Mormons are mostly integrated into the larger culture, but this is much less true of many Native Americans on reservations. For them, geography has played a major role in fostering separation. Though such geographical isolation or concentration is often treasured by separatist religions, it can pose major problems for political influence.

Socioeconomic isolation also has an effect. Many smaller religions have a high number of adherents who are poor, sometimes because of restrictions imposed by their faiths. This situation limits their potential political influence. They have fewer resources, from money to highly educated members, to bring to bear on politics than do religious communities with affluent and well-educated memberships. A small religion of the poor faces daunting odds if it seeks to make a political impact. This has been the case for many Native American groups and the Jehovah's Witnesses.

Something that also matters a great deal is what we call "respectability." Many alternative religions are unknown and lack the automatic respectability of mainstream religions. In some cases they acquire a reputation as less than respectable groups, and for this they pay a considerable political price. Such has been the fate of cults. Fashion, though, can make unheralded groups and their religions popular, which benefits them. This is increasingly true of Native Americans in the United States—and thus of Native American religions. As a host of Hollywood movies illustrate, Native Americans and Native American spirituality are increasingly being celebrated. This is bound to increase their political clout in the long run.

A Case Study: Mormons and Jehovah's Witnesses

The example of the Church of Jesus Christ of Latter-day Saints, or the Mormons, seems to belie much of our argument about unconventional religions and political effectiveness. The Mormons constitute a serious political force in American politics. In contrast, the Jehovah's Witnesses would seem to be the perfect case to illustrate our argument that smaller religions have little political sway. Comparing and contrasting these two religious communities sheds light on the problems and challenges politics presents for minority religions today in the United States.

Because of a unique combination of factors that have come together for them, Mormons are serious players in modern American religion and politics. Two of these factors are their size and steady growth. Mormons may now constitute up to 2 percent of the U.S. population, and their numbers continue to grow steadily.[18] But this growth in numbers and political influence has not come easily. The story of Mormonism presents a remarkable case study of an unconventional religion overcoming tremendous disadvantage. In their early days, the Mormons had no influence. Indeed, it can accurately be argued that no religious group in the United States has suffered more discrimination—indeed, often severe persecution—than the Mormons did in the nineteenth century.

Yet today the Mormons' situation has changed dramatically. Headquartered in Salt Lake City, the Church of Jesus Christ of Latter-day Saints (LDS Church) is highly organized. Its members are engaged in local, state, and national politics all across the country, but especially in western states. The church itself is also involved in politics, but mostly behind the scenes.

Whether Mormonism is a form of Christianity or not is a hotly contested matter. The church itself says it is; many traditional Protestant and Roman Catholic groups disagree. It was, however, Christianity and Judaism that inspired Joseph Smith in 1830, when he founded the LDS Church in western New York.[19] Smith contended that the angel Moroni directed him to golden plates that translated into the Book of Mormon. The plates explained the history of a tribal branch of Israelites who came to the Americas after about 600 B.C. This tribe was visited by Jesus Christ and was eventually destroyed because its members failed to follow God's will. Mormons believe that in his earthly life, Moroni was the son of a prophet, Mormon, who repeatedly warned the tribe of its impending doom. They also hold that Mormon himself recorded most of the history recounted on the golden plates and that he buried them several thousand years before they were revealed to Joseph Smith.

The story of the Mormon religious community in the nineteenth century is an often heroic and always controversial account. From the founding of the church in 1830 to the murder of Joseph Smith in 1844 to the settlement of Utah a few years later, Mormons clashed with the broader Christian culture. The result was a great deal of pain and suffering for the Mormons—which intensified when the broader culture became aware of the Mormon practice of polygamy (now officially abandoned).

Mormonism's belief system affirms the three persons of the Christian Trinity—the Father, Son, and Holy Spirit—but maintains that they are separate entities, not three persons in one. Mormons also believe that all people were with God before creation and that they move on after death to live with God. In the Mormon view, people who lived before Smith's revelation, and thus did not know the Mormon truth, may be saved by present-day Mormons. This is why Mormons have such a great interest in genealogy: They are seeking past relatives to help toward salvation.

The socioeconomic profile of Mormons is fairly consistent with that of the U.S. population at large. There are some differences, however. Mormons are overwhelmingly white (94 percent) and have a higher than average marriage rate. Mormons are unusually likely to vote, and they tend to be sharply more conservative than the population as a whole on almost every policy issue. They are also distinctly Republican in their party affiliation and voting behavior.[20] In the 1996 presidential election, 74 percent of all Mormon voters preferred Bob Dole over Bill Clinton and Ross Perot. Moreover, 79 percent of all votes cast by Mormons in congressional elections went to Republican candidates.[21] This is not to say, however, that Mormons are politically homogeneous (Box 9.1).

Part of the explanation for these facts has to do with Mormon commitment to family life, individual responsibility, and moral conservatism. Another reason lies in their deep suspicion of government, which is rooted in Mormon history. This attitude can lead some Mormons to adopt more liberal political causes, such as the widespread Mormon opposition to mobile MX missile bases in Utah and Nevada in the 1970s. In alliance with Native American groups and others, Mormons helped defeat this scheme.[22]

The LDS Church contends that it is not really political. Like most religious associations in the United States, it does not endorse candidates for

---

**BOX 9.1   ARE MORMONS
NATURAL CONSERVATIVES?**

Not necessarily. That is the conclusion of a new study by Jeffrey Fox, who finds far greater political diversity among Mormons than their image suggests. Previous studies hold that Mormonism encourages conservatism on social and economic issues and interventionism in foreign policy; surveys report that Mormons are also heavily Republican. However, these findings are drawn principally from samples of white members of the LDS Church in Utah, who now represent less than 15 percent of the entire church membership. The majority of Mormons now live outside of the United States, and a growing number of Mormons inside the United States are members of racial or ethnic minority groups. Fox finds considerable diversity of views on economic and foreign policy issues when these Mormons are taken into consideration. Nonwhite Mormons, for example, are significantly more progressive on most issues, and Canadian and Mexican Mormons differ systematically from their American counterparts in ways that reflect their political cultures (Canadian Mormons support socialized medical care, for example).

Nonetheless, Fox's study confirms the existence of a core set of Mormon values. Mormonism instills strong family ties and traditional moral values, a personal desire for economic self-sufficiency, and a strong sense of civic responsibility. By studying Mormons from different cultural contexts, Fox has been able to isolate what is distinctive about the LDS Church.

SOURCE: Jeffrey C. Fox, "Religion, Culture, and Public Opinion: A Cross-National and Cross-Cultural Exploration Using Multiple Methodologies" (Ph.D. diss., University of Oklahoma, 1998).

---

office, nor does it contribute directly to candidate campaigns. Evident in this reticence is the fact that Mormons have obviously learned from their tumultuous experiences in the nineteenth century, when popular and governmental hostility forced them to try to fashion a political theocracy—a nation of Zion. That effort brought Mormons only grief in the end. Though the LDS Church lost this political struggle, it learned how to have an effective political voice in the process.

The fact is that the LDS Church is very political—but it works carefully within the American political system. The LDS Church is political in several senses: It encourages involvement in politics; it has created a setting where conservative values and politics are a way of life; and from time to time it quietly advances specific public policies. This is why in Utah, and other heavily Mormon areas, clashing with the LDS Church can be a serious political mistake.

The Jehovah's Witnesses are quite another story. Though the Witnesses achieved some notable political victories through their use of the courts, at least in the 1940s, they have no political impact today. They are correctly cited as a prime example of the more normal pattern of small religious groups having no political power.[23]

The Jehovah's Witnesses emerged in the United States in the 1870s under the leadership of their founder, Charles Russell. The Witnesses declare that they are true followers of the Bible. They affirm Jehovah (God the Father) and acknowledge Jesus Christ as the son of God—indeed, God's first creation. However, Witness theology contends that though Christ is the son of God, Christ is not God. This marks a crucial difference from Christian belief. Witnesses also believe that at the end of the world there will be 144,000 disciples who will be glorified with God. The rest of the dead will live again on an Earth that will have become a wonderful land of peace and happiness.

Their view is that the end of the world is near, so no one ought to waste time trying to help others via politics or government. Helping individuals to discover religious truth is the only answer now. Witnesses distance themselves from government, politics, and even the nation itself. They refuse to salute the flag, serve in the military, or otherwise do anything that might violate their beliefs or indicate that they value the nation. For them, loyalty must be to God, so they have opted for strict separatism.

Still, it would be inaccurate to say that the Witnesses have had no political impact. Over the years their involvement in court cases to defend their religious freedom has expanded religious liberty for all kinds of small religious groups, especially against the government. Realistically, minority religions may not be able to have any greater political impact. In terms of day-to-day politics and policymaking in the United States, however, the Witnesses do not count, nor do they want to count. Although not all small religious groups share this goal of noninvolvement, most encounter the same political fate whether they like it or not.

Conclusion

Pluralism defines religion in the United States, but all religious groups are not politically equal. Instead, religious influence in politics is wielded largely by conventional Christian and Jewish groups. There are exceptions, though, like the Mormons. Such groups are relatively large, actively seek influence, and possess the right balance of strengths. There are other religious faiths (such as Islam) with the potential for influence, though it is as yet unrealized. Most smaller religions, though, lack the motivation and the combination of other necessary factors to be part of the world of religion and politics. This may change with one or another religion over time, but in most cases this situation is just what these religions desire. For them, politics is part of the larger, corrupt world about which they are uneasy at best. They correctly understand that their chances to be major players in it are slight.

Further Reading

Bromley, David G., and Anson Shupe. *Strange Gods: The Great American Cult Scare*. Boston: Beacon, 1981. Cults in the United States.

Conklin, Paul K. *American Originals: Homemade Varieties of Christianity*. Chapel Hill, NC: University of North Carolina Press, 1997. Excellent account of Mormons, Jehovah's Witnesses, and Pentecostals, among others.

Haddad, Yvonne Yazbeck, and Jane Idelman Smith, eds. *Muslim Communities in North America*. Albany, NY: State University of New York Press, 1994. The best book on American believers in Islam.

Heilman, Samuel C., and Steven M. Cohen. *Cosmopolitans and Parochials: Modern Orthodox Jews in America*. Chicago: University of Chicago Press, 1989. Very interesting discussion of Orthodox Jews.

Kephart, William M., and William W. Zellner. *Extraordinary Groups*, 5th ed. New York: St. Martin's, 1994. Good study that considers a number of the same groups as does this chapter.

Sullivan, Lawrence E., ed. *Native American Religions: North America*. New York: Macmillan, 1987. Thoughtful introduction to its subject.

10

Religious Politics and
the Legal System

*I*n this chapter and the next we enter the realm of law and the courts. We also consider policy decisions that are affected by the legal system of the United States. Legal decisions made by state and federal courts have an enormous influence on public policy in areas from aid to private religious schools to prayer in public schools. Groups from all sides have become increasingly involved in legal struggles to promote their points of view. Besides being the arenas for struggles over specific policies, American courtrooms have come to be the setting for the airing of cultural disagreements about the general role of organized religion and the interaction between religion and politics. The stakes are high, and the legal conflict between religion and politics is often intense.

No one should make the mistake of thinking that the American legal system, from the humble living room of the most rural justice of the peace to the magnificent U.S. Supreme Court building in Washington, exists independently of politics. Instead, commonplace political pushing and shoving are very much a part of the American legal system at all levels. This is neither shocking nor lamentable; it is simply reality. This is not to say that politics entirely defines the American legal system. It has its own internal norms, such as the principle of *stare decisis* and concern for due process. Moreover, many judges are eminently fair and strive not to allow political judgments to color their rulings.

In this chapter we examine the efforts of religio-political forces to affect legal outcomes. We consider some of the reasons for this development and the specific resources that help to make groups effective in the legal arena. In the process we will introduce some of the most significant organizations involved in the legal struggle over religion and politics. After reflecting on some of the implications of this struggle, we will consider broader theories of how organized religion ought to relate to government, which together form the context of various legal arguments. In Chapter 11, we examine the specific religio-political disputes that have occupied the courts—and how these disputes have been resolved.

Judicial Politics

Though historically most religious groups in the United States have ignored the courts, many are now deeply involved with the legal system. It has become routine for such groups to work through the courts in order to try to achieve—or protect—objectives that they cannot accomplish in any other way. A variety of religious legal organizations help to shepherd cases through the courts, and some bring their own suits. By far the most common approach to judicial politics today for such groups, however, is the filing of *amicus curiae* (friend of the court) briefs. *Amicus* briefs allow third parties (in this instance religious legal organizations) to register their views on pending cases. Even if the court does not take heed of the views of a particular group filing as *amicus curiae*, the group's views will nonetheless become a matter of public record.

Why has this turn to the courts taken place? In good part, it reflects broad-based developments in the American political system as a whole. Over the last fifty years the United states has embraced a more centralized national political system. This trend began in the 1930s and 1940s with the emergence and success of a single leader, Franklin Delano Roosevelt, who was comfortable addressing crises such as the Great Depression from the national level. From Roosevelt the American people learned that at least in some instances the federal government can resolve issues of great significance. One result of the federal government's growth has been considerable activism on the part of the federal judiciary, most notably the U.S. Supreme Court. In turn, interest groups, including religious groups, have stepped up their efforts to affect legal outcomes. This is because they realize that the federal courts have come to exercise tremendous influence over national policy.

The First Amendment holds that "Congress shall make no law respecting an establishment of religion, or prohibiting the free exercise thereof." Before the 1940s almost all church-state controversies were aired in state courts. This was because until 1940 the U.S. Supreme Court interpreted the First Amendment to apply only to actions of the *federal* government. In short, prior to 1940 the states were not forced to comply with the religion clauses of the First Amendment. Most cases involving religious disputes, then, were not thought to be part of the Supreme Court's domain. In the 1940s, however, the Court changed its mind about this long-standing interpretation of the First Amendment's meaning and began ruling on a wide range of religious issues. They insisted that national standards were necessary and acceptable—and should supersede state and local standards.

The Court accomplished this by interpreting parts of the Fourteenth Amendment to mean that state and local laws and practices must meet with the standard of the First Amendment. The Fourteenth Amendment holds that: "No State shall make or enforce any law which shall abridge the privileges or immunities of citizens of the United States; nor shall any State deprive any person of life, liberty, or property, without due process of law; nor deny to any person within its jurisdiction the equal protection of the laws." According to the Court, this means that no state should be able to abridge the religious freedoms protected by the First Amendment. This is despite the fact that the words of that amendment state that "*Congress* shall make no law," not "*Congress and the state legislatures* shall make no law." Since 1940, the latter has been taken to be the basis of the true constitutional meaning of the First Amendment's religion clauses. In asserting this interpretation, the Court extended the "doctrine of incorporation," its overall argument that the *states* are bound by the Fourteenth Amendment to guarantee their citizens the civil liberties set forth in the Bill of Rights.[1]

The Court first decided to incorporate the Free Exercise Clause of the First Amendment in *Cantwell* v. *Connecticut* (1940). In that case the Court held that the provisions of the First Amendment regarding religious freedom should constrain the actions of state and local governments as well as those of the federal government. The state of Connecticut could not prevent Jehovah's Witnesses from proselytizing, because doing so violated their free exercise rights. According to the Court, "The Fourteenth Amendment has rendered the legislatures of the states as incompetent as Congress to enact laws which violate the provisions of the first amendment."[2] With its judgment in *Cantwell*, the Supreme Court claimed for itself a great deal of decisionmaking power and thus provided an incentive for religious groups, and many others, to turn to the federal courts for the resolution of their problems with any and all governmental institutions and policies.

Other factors were also at work. As religious pluralism increased in twentieth-century America, an increasing number of religious groups found themselves in conflict with the government or the society around them. Some of them entered the federal courts to seek redress. This was particularly true of small religious groups, which often felt they had no other way to exert influence. During the 1940s, the Jehovah's Witnesses, a small religious group, pioneered this process by seeking relief in the federal courts from assorted local and state regulations and ordinances limiting door-to-door proselytizing or requiring salutes to the American flag. Such regulations severely limited Jehovah's Witnesses' freedom to practice their religion, which demands active proselytizing and prohibits the salute of any flag. In most of these instances they succeeded in securing their free exercise rights.[3]

The success of the Jehovah's Witnesses encouraged other groups to believe that the federal courts presented both a possible and a proper realm for addressing the problems faced by minority religions. Such groups, in effect, encouraged the federal courts to take an active role in shaping the politics of religion in the United States. Since the 1940s, what was once a trickle of cases has become a flood as the conflict between religion and politics in America is increasingly played out in its courts. It has been a busy half-century for the federal courts since *Cantwell* was decided in 1940. Some of the reason for this broader engagement is the judiciary's own preference for involvement in disputes between organized religion and the political system. Neither the lower federal courts nor the U.S. Supreme Court have been shrinking violets in this arena. This extends to the federal courts' willingness to intervene in abortion policy. For better or for worse, the Supreme Court's decision in *Roe v. Wade* (1973) that abortion was constitutional has generated an enormous amount of controversy—and legal action.

The nature of the courts' rulings, especially those of the Supreme Court, has magnified legal conflicts that are rooted in church-state disputes and other religious matters. As we will note in Chapter 11, the Supreme Court's pronouncements in these areas have too often been unclear—some say contradictory—and thus resolve little. This uncertainty ensures that there will be further litigation and more dispute. Moreover, as the federal courts have taken on a more visible role since the 1940s, an incredible variety of interest groups have been drawn in. Even religious groups that are successful in legislative and executive arenas realize that they must be participants in *every* major playing field, including the courts, if they are going to count in American politics.[4]

Every group makes calculations about who might succeed in the courts. In the 1980s conservative religious groups concluded that their odds in the courts had improved because Presidents Ronald Reagan and George Bush had appointed more than 50 percent of all sitting federal judges. Moreover, Reagan and Bush had pursued a much publicized plan to place conservative judges on the federal bench. This encouraged conservative religious groups to enter the courts more aggressively. Groups favoring strict separation between church and state judged that their odds had dropped, but felt they had to battle in the courts anyway. As the Reagan-Bush appointees gradually leave the courts, there will undoubtedly be new calculations about which groups are likely to win in the courts. The necessity for using the courts to achieve political ends, however, will endure as an imperative for all sides.[5]

Another factor that has increased the role of the courts is the simple reality of the steady pace of expanding religious pluralism in the United States.

The strength of minority religions can easily be exaggerated, but there is no doubt that every year there are ever more alternative religions emerging and gathering strength in the United States. The growth of this pluralism began in earnest with the expansion of Roman Catholicism in the nineteenth and twentieth centuries. Around 25 percent of the American people now identify themselves as Catholics. While they have assimilated neatly, some tensions continue around such issues as state aid to parochial schools.

There has also been steady growth of small, non-Christian religious groups, from the Jehovah's Witnesses to the Church of Scientology, that are highly diverse in their beliefs and programs. These expressions of religious pluralism have often been seen in American courts despite their small memberships. Sometimes they are there using the courts because of conflicts with the government in order to defend their existence and rights as a group. At other times, they turn to the courts to achieve changes that favor them. Leaders of small religious groups often recognize that, whereas neither Congress nor the executive branch is likely to be responsive to a small religious minority, the federal courts sometimes prove more hospitable.

Perhaps the most important dimension of expanding religious pluralism in the United States has been the rise of groups that characterize themselves as scarcely religious or completely secular. As we will see, some organizations that represent this sector of the population have become quite involved with the legal system in recent years, especially in church-state disputes. They are frequently found asking the courts to eliminate public expressions of religion. Their role in the judicial politics of religion can only be expected to increase.[6]

Key Players

In short, the legal system today bursts with activity as religious associations attempt to influence court rulings. None of these groups represents a majority of the American public. Still, many have had a significant impact on judicial politics at the federal, state, and local levels. Many of the key players are connected with what may be termed the "separationist coalition." Recently, however, such groups have been challenged by an emerging set of groups affiliated with evangelical and fundamentalist Protestantism.

Separationist organizations come in three varieties. There are those that trace their roots to a separationist Protestant tradition that goes back to Roger Williams in colonial Rhode Island.[7] Its members are often quite religious. Their goal is to nurture free exercise rights by keeping religion separate from government. As Roger Williams himself envisioned it in 1744, separationists believe there should be a "wall of Separation between the Garden of the Church and the Wilderness of the World."[8] One separa-

---

BOX 10.1   PEOPLE FOR THE AMERICAN WAY

People for the American Way (PFAW) was founded in 1980 by Hollywood producer Norman Lear "to monitor and counter the divisive agenda of the religious Right." It is not attached to any branch of Christianity or to any religion at all, though it steadfastly maintains that it is sympathetic to religion. Among its most central characteristics is the fact that it presents itself as a clear alternative to the religious Right. Though PFAW has not expended much legal energy to oppose the public policy goals of religious groups, it has been extremely active in taking legal action to promote separationism in church-state affairs, especially by trying to frustrate or defeat the religious Right. Indeed, PFAW, which now claims over 300,000 members, was initially formed to combat the now-defunct Moral Majority. It is in the name of separationism that it continues to combat the religious Right in the courts and elsewhere.

SOURCE: http://www.pfaw.org.

---

tionist organization of note is the Baptist Joint Committee. Long committed to separation of church and state, the Baptist Joint Committee is one of the most active groups in American judicial politics today. It draws support from a variety of Baptist organizations, though of late it has lost the support of the largest Baptist denomination, the increasingly fundamentalist Southern Baptist Convention.

Another major separationist organization is Americans United for Separation of Church and State. Its major outlet is the *Journal of Church and State*, a publication that is distinctly sympathetic to the separation of church and state. Though Americans United has a long history and has enjoyed considerable publicity since the 1940s for its zealous opposition to state aid for Catholic schools (if not Catholicism itself), it now is part of the broader separationist coalition that includes other associations that have not historically been aligned with a separatist Protestantism. One example is People for the American Way (PFAW), created by Hollywood producer Norman Lear, who is famous for *All in the Family* and other television comedies (Box 10.1).

Also integral to the separationist coalition are a number of Jewish organizations and their legal arms.[9] This is most prominently true of the American Jewish Committee, but it is not alone. Most of these Jewish groups have been involved in legal battles to promote separation of church and state as a way of protecting Jews (and other minorities) from the official establishment of any form of Christianity. Whenever a crèche (manger scene) appears on public property, or prayers are being said in public schools, or other potential violations of the separation of church and state occur, it is common to find the American Jewish Committee and its allies going to court to halt these practices.

Indeed, for some years, especially in the 1960s and 1970s, Leo Pfeffer of the American Jewish Committee was one of the most visible figures in America, fighting for the separation of church and state in both the courts and in the battle for public opinion. Though no single figure of Pfeffer's stature has emerged in recent years, the work of the American Jewish Committee, the American Jewish Congress, the Anti-Defamation League, and similar organizations has continued unabated in this area. Eternal vigilance is their motto, and they live up to its demands.

A third, and perhaps more uneasy, partner in the separationist coalition today represents the truly secularist part of the movement. The American Civil Liberties Union (ACLU) is the most famous and assertive member of this wing. Indeed, the ACLU gets more involved than any other organization in church-state controversies and other legal disputes involving religion. It is committed to full separation of church and state, and often to free exercise rights for small religious minorities that have been affected negatively by the state.

Though the ACLU's lack of connection with religion has not prevented it from rallying to help selected religious groups that have been oppressed by the government, other secular organizations exist to advance secular values and institutions only. This is a fair description of the objective of the Society of Separationists and a group called simply American Atheists, both of which were founded by Madalyn Murray O'Hair. American Atheists claim to be "a nationwide movement for the advancement of atheism, and the total, absolute separation of government and religion."[10] These groups have challenged all abridgments of separation of church and state, including the printing of "In God We Trust" on U.S. currency and the saying of prayers before public legislative bodies.

This same principle underlies the efforts of the Freedom from Religion Foundation, whose title leaves no doubt about its objectives. Founded in Madison, Wisconsin, by Anne Nicol Gaylor and her daughter, Annie Laurie Gaylor, but now operating nationally, the Freedom from Religion Foundation has assertively sought to make a difference in the church-state controversy by fighting in the courts to dismantle all linkages between church and state.[11] The fact that such organizations are more numerous and active today may be part of the reason that the courts have increasingly limited the presence of religion in public life.[12]

The activity of the separationist lobby (and its frequent ally, the antireligious lobby) in the courts, and public perceptions of success on their part, has provoked a counterreaction. Today, religious groups that are determined to fight back in court are a growth industry. Most of these are associated with evangelical Protestantism, but they often have contributors who are sympathetic with their efforts regardless of religious background.[13]

Some religious legal organizations have existed for decades. The Christian Legal Society was founded in 1962, for example. Most, however, were born in the 1980s, and they represent another step for conservative groups in the process of learning how American politics works. That is, they are a manifestation of the discovery by the Christian Right that the courts matter in the United States and that whatever one's influence with legislatures, executives, or the people in general (or lack thereof), the courts matter. Moreover, during the Reagan and Bush administrations, many religious conservatives felt that the courts remained far less sympathetic to their concerns than did Congress or the president. In part this was because many "conservative" appointments to the judiciary were not the sort of conservatives that the religious Right preferred. "Conservative" Supreme Court Justices Anthony Kennedy, Sandra Day O'Connor, and David Souter all proved to be disappointments for the religious Right. This sense heightened the religious Right's concern with the judicial selection process and strengthened its resolve to be involved in the politics of court decisions.

One well-known conservative religious legal organization is the Rutherford Institute, which has been involved in many high-profile cases and maintains a large and systematic national fund-raising effort. It is particularly interested in protecting the religious freedoms of evangelicals and fundamentalists and in defending traditional practices such as prayer at high school graduations and crèches on public grounds. The Rutherford Institute argues that its mere presence in many of these disputes has a positive effect (from its point of view) and that it often prevents its opponents from taking legal action in the first place (Box 10.2).

Another important religious legal organization is the American Center for Law and Justice (ACLJ), a creation of Rev. Pat Robertson and his associates. The ACLJ has entered a number of legal disputes, and even when it has lost cases it has sometimes actively sought to thwart the implementation of their results. Its aggressive letter-writing campaign to discourage school districts from banning all prayers at graduation ceremonies despite the Supreme Court's 1992 decision in *Lee* v. *Weisman* constituted one highly visible example. The ACLJ's argument was that if clergy-led prayers had to be dropped, student-led prayers ought to replace them.

Not all religious legal groups represent evangelical Protestants and their interests. The Office of the General Counsel of the National Conference of Catholic Bishops (NCCB) and the United States Catholic Conference plays a significant role in church-state disputes. It represents the American Catholic Church in litigation both directly as a party and indirectly by filing *amicus curiae* briefs.[14] Many specific denominations also undertake their own legal efforts, particularly as *amicus curiae*. The prolife Lutheran Church–Missouri Synod, for example, frequently files *amicus* briefs with the Supreme Court in abortion cases.

BOX 10.2   THE RUTHERFORD INSTITUTE

The Rutherford Institute takes its name from a seventeenth-century Scottish intellectual named Samuel Rutherford, who was among the first to reject the idea of the divine right of kings. Founded in 1982 by John Whitehead as a legal foundation dedicated to protecting Americans' religious freedoms, the Rutherford Institute has broadened its agenda over the years. It is a conservative legal and educational organization with clear ties to the religious Right, but it claims only to be the defender of people "whose constitutional rights have been violated." The Rutherford Institute has assembled a nationwide network of attorneys who defend individuals free of charge. The organization's most visible recent endeavor has been the defense of Paula Corbin Jones, who accused President Bill Clinton of sexually harassing her when he was governor of Arkansas. This stance against sexual harassment marks a further broadening of the Rutherford Institute's legal agenda. They may be expected to be important players in American jurisprudence for years to come.

SOURCE: http://www.rutherford.org.

Some organizations are extremely specialized in their endeavors. Don Wildman's American Family Association Law Center has been particularly active in disputes over family issues and television. The Home School Legal Defense Association pursues legal issues that relate to preserving the rights of its members, who do not send their children to school outside the home. But there is rarely any neat dividing line among issues—or groups. Money and opportunity play significant roles in groups' decisions about when to go to court. What is clear is that the use of the courts is on the rise, and the increasing legal efforts by separationists have met with a parallel response from those who oppose the separationist agenda.

Factors for Success

What contributes to the success or failure of religious organizations as they enter the courts? Of course, sympathetic judges and propitious times always help, but what else matters? What are the dynamics that contribute to legal success? One crucial factor is money. This painful but real fact has sometimes proven to be an awkward matter, as there can be substantial competition for limited dollars among various legal action organizations. Moreover, fund-raising efforts require both time and money and leave less of both for the legal causes at hand.

Equally important, of course, are experience and expertise, both of which take time to fashion. We have already noted that in building lobbying organizations, especially effective ones, people who know their way around Congress or the statehouses are indispensable. So are those who understand the concerns of the religious groups they represent, how their members think, and how they want their story told. The same applies to religious associations in the legal arena. After all, they are really just interest groups involved in the legal process, campaigning in the courts for their self-defined interests. The lawyers who spearhead these efforts must know both the legal and religious terrain. New groups, including those from the conservative Christian perspective, have sometimes stumbled. They have had to learn things the hard way, and they have now come to nurture savvy legal activists. Such people cost money.

A third factor for success is support for legal activism among group members. If a group's members do not want their contributions to fund legal efforts, the group will find itself seriously stifled. Government support has also been of great assistance at times. This was true for many conservative Christian legal organizations during the 1980s that found themselves in the often favorable position of working with Republican-appointed Justice Department lawyers on the same cases, toward the same ends. During the Clinton administration other organizations came to enjoy this advantage, so Christian Right organizations experienced what their liberal counterparts had endured during the 1980s. Finally, support from the larger public can help, too. Public support generates funds and favorable publicity, both of which may affect the legal contests in a myriad of ways.

The embrace of legal strategy by many religio-political groups appears to be growing, and this makes sense in light of the increasing religious pluralism of American society. Today the United States is less and less a Protestant nation; less than 60 percent of the population now claim to be Protestants.[15] Moreover, the fault lines within Protestantism over moral and political issues have now become as deep as any between Protestantism and other religious persuasions. In short, American society now faces an expanding religious pluralism that is accompanied by moral pluralism. Such a context is hardly a congenial one for any religious group that tries to affect politics by working only through legislatures, governors, or the president.

This reality is sharpened in light of the fact that American religion is increasingly politically organized. Every religious interest understands that it may face opposition—and that such opposition will undoubtedly be organized. In religion, as elsewhere, the truth today is as James Madison suggested it should be in *Federalist No. 51*: Interest checks interest and ambition checks ambition. Such a situation almost impels those who seek social change into the courts, for it is often the case that judges alone can make authoritative decisions that can break the organized pluralist impasse that so often holds sway. The courts can render clear decisions; they can break impasses; and they can side with even the smallest religious interest if they feel that the law or the Constitution directs such a decision.

It often makes sense for religious organizations to take legal action in the current political arena. Yet we need to be clear that such a step, especially for many small religions, usually amounts to a largely defensive move designed to protect against domination by more powerful groups and perspectives. Indeed, in an increasingly pluralistic society, there is little else that small religious groups can do when they perceive themselves to be threatened. When they act to make positive changes—and when they have sufficient lead time—they often form coalitions that can enable them to enjoy some significant political clout, even in Washington. But in times of crisis, they have only one serious recourse: the law and the courts.

Religious groups are increasingly using the courts for publicity, as well. When a group is involved in litigation, its members know that their goals are being pursued in a concrete manner. And even if the group has little actual influence over the judges' decision, it can still claim credit if the case is decided in line with its stated agenda. Litigation can also attract the attention of people outside of the group, which brings new members and lays the foundation for coalition-building with other (potentially larger and more powerful) groups. Coalition-building is particularly valuable because it can facilitate a division of labor. The ACLJ, for example, hires many of its lawyers from the evangelical Regent University School of Law. It also receives financial and research support from the Christian Coalition. All of this would not be possible if the ACLJ were shy about its engagement in judicial politics. Coalition-building can also allow religious legal organizations to pursue a wider variety of goals. Some groups may focus on education, others on abortion, and still others on pornography, but they may also mutually support each other.

It is important to keep the historical context of the courts themselves in mind. A useful contrast may be drawn between the U.S. Supreme Court under Chief Justices Earl Warren and William Rehnquist. The Warren Court of the 1950s and 1960s was generally open to the complaints of small groups who contended that assorted government laws and practices violated their free exercise rights. It was equally open to the arguments of the separationist lobby, which was interested in striking down what it saw as violations of the Establishment Clause, such as prayer or Bible reading in public schools. The decisions of the Warren Court demonstrated a clear embrace of the separation of church and state and naturally encouraged groups sympathetic to that view to embrace legal strategies.

By contrast, the Rehnquist Court of the 1980s and 1990s has shown no particular eagerness to advance the free exercise rights of small, dissenting religious groups at the expense of legislation passed by state legislatures or Congress. The Rehnquist Court has a mixed record in cases in which official establishment has come under fire, so the legal efforts of antiestablishment forces continue unabated. Perhaps only a Supreme Court determined to get out of the religion business, by resisting the impulse to be the arbiter in the realm of church-state politics, could stop the now almost automatic decision by religious groups to seek justice in the courts. Meanwhile, the intense litigiousness of American society has combined with a desire to circumvent ordinary political channels, which has brought legal action by religious groups to an all-time high.

For many religious groups, the politics of legal action presents pronounced advantages. Taking politics to the courts does not require a large membership, elite access in the powerful worlds of official Washington and the national media, or even vast financial resources. Thus legal strategies make sense for small and otherwise powerless groups. For more well-endowed and well-placed interests, such as the separationist groups, going to court is definitely the best strategic choice, since they would usually lose if popularly elected legislatures had the last word on their concerns.

For some religions, legal strategies present an additional advantage of fostering the illusion that they avoid politics, a world that many groups (such as the Jehovah's Witnesses and the Amish) dislike, fear, or oppose. Somehow, conventional wisdom suggests that the courts are a pure, nonpolitical realm, uninvolved in the grubby world of clashing interest groups. This sometimes treasured—but inaccurate—belief attracts many religious groups to the courts to accomplish what are ultimately political ends.

For the United States as a whole, the strategy of fighting battles between religion and politics in the legal system presents mixed blessings. The federal court system is highly elitist, composed of people who are appointed to serve for life and deliberately shielded from the larger public. The federal courts are hardly a monument to democracy, and few of their defenders claim the contrary. This portion of the political system is designed in part to protect the minority against the follies of the majority. The same logic attended the drafting of the Bill of Rights.

There is much dispute about whether religio-political controversies ought to be resolved in a democratic arena or a federal courtroom. Should religious freedom be subject to definition by the majority? Should the limits of government establishment of religion be outlined by the majority? Indeed, some participants in the church-state debates of today wonder whether democracy is an important value to begin with. Those who point out that democracy is not enshrined in the Bible or any other sacred text refuse to worry about whether the courts contribute to or hinder democracy.

For such individuals, the real issue is the need to protect rights, whether they are the rights of the Amish, strict separationists, or Mormons. By this view, if the courts serve as a setting where such questions can be addressed—and addressed without too greatly inflaming hatreds that often accompany religious diversity, free exercise, and official establishment—then they contribute immeasurably to a healthy society. And, one may argue, sometimes the result is a flowering of democracy, because freedom and democracy belong together. After all, it is only through the courts that unpopular outlooks can be represented fairly.

The Politics of Church and State

In the midst of the legal struggle for advantage in the wars of religion and politics today there lie broader considerations of the relationship between church and state. We have already noted that some religious interest groups are consistently identified with specific positions. Thus, in a broader sense, what is at stake in many legal conflicts is the definition of religion's role in society—specifically in terms of church and state. How should the courts and those who appeal to them for recourse establish relationships between church and state, and between religion and politics? Chapter 11 will examine some of the church-state matters that have engaged the courts. Here, however, we introduce several classic perspectives on church-state relations and the extent to which the courts have embraced them.[16]

The Separationist Approach

We have already considered the separationist view and its energetic approach to judicial politics. For its advocates, the First Amendment's religion clauses—"Congress shall make no law respecting an establishment of religion, or prohibiting the free exercise thereof"—mean that government cannot be involved with religion *in any way*. Separationists insist that they merely walk in the footsteps of the authors of the Constitution, whom they believe to have had no respect for England's state-established church or the established churches of many of the American colonies.[17]

Separationists look with pride to those chapters in colonial history that were part of the journey toward separation of church and state. They honor Roger Williams, founder of Rhode Island, for his determination to separate church and state, and William Penn, founder of Pennsylvania, for his commitment to Quaker tolerance of other religious faiths. They respect the histories of colonies like New York and Pennsylvania, which pioneered the tradition of separationism. Such colonies were sure that true free exercise was possible only when the state and the law were kept far removed from organized religion.

Though church-state relations during the colonial era were complicated, there is no doubt that the separationist point of view united many people. Separationism formed an umbrella under which those who feared state religions and those who were skeptical of religion in any form could gather. It also accommodated those whose ardent commitment to minority and dissenting religions made them worry about how they—and thus true religion—would fare if the government were to become involved in religious matters. From these diffuse roots, ranging from the skeptical Thomas Jefferson to the earnest New England Baptists, the separationist tradition grew.[18] Sophisticated separationists, however, were and are well aware that even after the adoption of the Constitution and the Bill of Rights, the American record hardly showed commitment to separationism. Religion (especially Christianity) has always been deeply connected with, and often supported by, the state.

Thus there has been much for separationists to litigate. Separationists have been concerned about the saying of prayers at the opening of sessions of state legislatures and Congress, the president's inauguration, and even the opening session of the U.S. Supreme Court itself. They worry about government-sponsored chaplains in the military, aid for religious hospitals, religious social service agencies, and religious colleges. They note with displeasure the references to God on American currency and in the Pledge of Allegiance. They dislike seeing crèches on public land in December and hearing government officials speak of God on Thanksgiving. In short, separationists argue that American culture is schizophrenic in that it is theoretically committed to the principle of separationism and yet far from separationist in practice.

Perhaps it is not surprising that public attitudes are equally mixed. Studies consistently demonstrate that people in the United States reflexively endorse "separation of church and state" and oppose the mixing of religion and politics. But there is often considerable support for specific actions that hardly fit with such a view. Thus more than 80 percent of the population support government funding for military chaplains; 70 percent favor prayer in the public schools; more than half agree that government should take action to restrict assorted unpopular religious groups such as Satanists or Hare Krishnas.[19]

As with anything else, there are degrees of separation, but the toughest test for a strict separationist is the matter of taxing nonprofit religious enterprises and institutions. For many separationists, to tax religious institutions (that is, to make them pay property taxes) is to go from separationism to hostility toward religion. Other separationists disagree, insisting instead that separationism must mean the removal of what is today the greatest benefit religion receives from the U.S. government: freedom from taxation.

Separationists hold that separationism (the absence of official sanctioning of religion by government) and free exercise of religion go together. They believe that the more government remains separate from religion, the more citizens will be able to enjoy religious freedom. Separationists argue that this belief was held by many of the framers of the American Constitution, including James Madison, who was the author of the Bill of Rights. The idea is that an activist government cannot possibly promote religious freedom—and that it in fact presents a real threat when it becomes involved with religious institutions.

Neutrality

Neutrality is a second perspective that has often enjoyed strong support from the Supreme Court. According to this perspective, the courts should be neutral on all religious conflicts that clog the courts. By this view the courts should neither promote nor impede religion; they should just ignore it.

The Supreme Court's version of the neutrality doctrine was formulated in the classic case *Lemon v. Kurtzman* (1971). It held that if a law has a secular purpose and a secular effect, neither advances nor inhibits religion, and does not result in excessive entanglement between religion and government, then it is constitutional. By this view, it is acceptable for there to be incidental government support for religion, but only as a byproduct of some law that is secular both in intent and effect. Similarly, it is acceptable to impair religious freedom, but only as a byproduct of a law with a secular purpose and a secular effect. The goal is for the state to be neutral, and neutralists have assumed that the way to do this is to ignore religion in any analysis as much as possible.[20]

This understanding often angers separationists. Separationists appreciate that neutrality eliminates flagrant, overt aid to organized religion and forbids any formal establishment of religion. But they want the Court to take religion into account in order to ensure that no matter what a law's main purpose or principal effect, religion does not obtain any government benefits. For separationists, neutrality can be (and has been) used by the courts as a way to turn a blind eye toward the clever ways government hides laws that aid and support religious purposes under seemingly secular objectives and language. For radical separationists, state laws that allow nonprofit groups freedom from taxation constitute a prime example. Under the neutralist approach, such laws would be constitutional because they have a secular purpose and mainly secular effects (since they are for nonprofit groups of all types). But in practice such rules grant an enormous privilege to religious nonprofit organizations. They meet the nonprofit test and may thus receive substantial state benefits.

A softer version of the neutrality stance regarding religion is "benevolent neutrality."[21] Supporters of this approach approve of neutrality as the proper stance for the courts to assume, because they are confident that it will prevent religion and churches from becoming a larger factor in government decisions. At the same time, however, benevolent neutrality tries to have it both ways. Its advocates argue that there should be sympathetic acceptance from time to time of the religious effects of "secular" government actions and laws.

Supporters of the benevolent neutrality position maintain that application of the secular purpose and secular effect test avoids government sponsorship of religion, but at the same time they insist that this test must not be followed in such a rigid fashion that religion will lose its freedom. Government must not sponsor religion, but it must not destroy it either. Though government should generally stay neutral, it must do so in a benevolent mood, and no fixed formula can make that happen. Judgment is therefore needed on a case-by-case basis according to the benevolent neutrality view.

The Accommodationist Approach

A third understanding stresses the pragmatic politics of accommodation. According to this view, the courts should accept the reality that religion and religious groups are major parts of American society and politics, so the courts should play the role of a pragmatic reconciler. Toward this end, the courts should let stand traditional connections between religious practices and the state, such as tax breaks for churches and synagogues or prayers at the beginning of congressional sessions. Meanwhile, they should also accommodate separationist sentiments by discouraging the development of any additional connections between church and state, such as massive state aid to religious schools. Above all, accommodationists believe that the courts must move to accommodate interests in this contested area as gently and as generously as possible.

Proponents of the accommodationist view insist that the courts are political institutions and must be so in matters of church and state and religion and politics. They can help achieve compromises that respect the past and yet acknowledge the more diverse present. The results may often be messy and short on neat logic, but few things in politics are neat and logical and, given the nature of the human being, perhaps that is just as well.

Equal Treatment

A fourth view is known as "equal treatment." Its supporters maintain that the courts should sanction government assistance to churches and other religious groups *if this is done for all of them equally* (equal treatment) and *if it would encourage free exercise of religion.* Those in favor of equal treatment declare that religion sometimes needs the state to help free exercise become a reality. Thus separationists may not necessarily be correct when they assert that free exercise expands when the separation between church and state grows.[22]

In American history this was, in effect, part of the case made by those (primarily Roman Catholics) who felt that state aid for religious schools was a good idea. From time to time they succeeded. For example, in the years after the Civil War, President Ulysses S. Grant undertook an effort to promote peace between whites and Native Americans by encouraging the assimilation of Native Americans through education. To provide such education, he turned to churches and granted them the privilege of establishing schools on reservations. For the last three decades of the nineteenth century, Congress funded a number of denominations as part of this effort, including the Catholic Church. In 1899, however, the entire program came to an end, in part because Protestant groups objected to the funding of Catholic schools.

This education program was very much the exception rather than the rule. A portion of the traditional argument in favor of state aid for Catholic schools was practical: Catholics wanted and needed the money to keep their schools going. Another part, though, is the argument some Catholics make that access to religious school education is vital for real free exercise of religion and the only way to achieve this goal for many Catholics is through government assistance. This view came to be shared in the 1980s and 1990s by some (but by no means all) evangelical Protestant "Christian school" supporters.

In other areas, equal treatment has many supporters, even though they are not always fully aware of the underlying implications of this position. For example, to justify tax deductions for all nonprofit religious organizations is to support the principle of equal treatment. There is no doubt that such policies help organized religion in quite a material sense and may therefore encourage their existence.

Opponents of equal treatment, of course, see all of this very differently. They contend that nontraditional forms of equal treatment (such as substantial state aid for religious schools) and in some cases all forms (including property tax forgiveness) are unconstitutional and threaten religious freedom. For such opponents, to have the state involved with religion, and certainly with religious schools, raises the very real specter of state control. That, they believe, would be a disaster.

The argument goes back and forth (Box 10.3). Those who favor positive accommodation, as they might put it, sometimes suggest a case-by-case approach. They often turn back to history to make part of their case. As they read it, the historical record reveals a complex and diverse pattern in which there was once a great deal of official establishment and accommodation of religion that did not involve the sacrifice of free exercise or the establishment of a single church.

For proponents of equal treatment, sweeping historical claims about separationism and the framers simply do not work. They point out that when the First Amendment was adopted, a number of states continued to maintain official religions. Massachusetts, the last to give up its established church, did not do so until 1833. Moreover, while Congress operated in

---

BOX 10.3   RELIGIOUS NONPROFIT ORGANIZATIONS
AND PUBLIC MONEY

A paradox of American politics is that, although fierce legal battles are fought over state aid to parochial schools, billions of dollars of government funds flow annually through other religiously based nonprofit organizations. Normally this occurs without fanfare or legal challenge.

Since colonial days, all levels of American government have sought to achieve public purposes by working through nonprofit charities, hospitals, educational institutions, and relief agencies. Many of these nonprofits are faith-based and receive a substantial portion of their budgets from government contracts, grants, or patron vouchers. This system works well from the standpoint of governments because nonprofit organizations are closer to the communities they serve, less bureaucratic, and more flexible. In turn, religious communities are left relatively free to provide faith-inspired services, such as succor to the needy, adoption services, refugee resettlement, and health care.

The dilemma, according to Pepperdine University professor Stephen Monsma, is that the doctrine of strict separation of church and state, which has been invoked by courts to strike down parochial aid, puts this partnership in legal jeopardy. As a result, Monsma believes that refinements in church-state doctrine are in order.

SOURCE: Stephen V. Monsma, *When Sacred & Secular Mix: Religious Nonprofit Organizations & Public Money* (Lanham, MD: Rowman and Littlefield, 1996).

---

the early years as though the First Amendment prohibited all government connection with religion or churches, at other times it gave a contrary signal. The very year Congress approved the First Amendment, for example, it also reenacted the Northwest Ordinance, the document governing much of the western U.S. territory (now the Midwest). Section III of the Northwest Ordinance observed that "religion, morality, and knowledge being necessary to good government and the happiness of mankind, schools and the means of learning shall forever be encouraged."[23]

Advocates of further state aid to religion also take issue with the image of such crucial constitutional framers as Thomas Jefferson and James Madison as radical separationists. They argue that neither Jefferson nor Madison believed that there needed to be dogmatic lines separating church and state, and moreover that normatively speaking there should not be such lines in a complex, diverse political order. It is no simple matter; free exercise has sometimes been harmed by the state's assistance to religious groups, but it has also sometimes required such aid.[24]

Some proponents of equal treatment openly declare that what they favor amounts to multiple establishment—the official (or semiofficial) establishment of all faiths in the United States—because of its enormous religious pluralism. Advocates of this approach embrace as reality exactly what their opponents believe—and fear—is the essential truth about equal treatment. For advocates of multiple establishment, the logic of equal treatment can derive from a postmodern world in which there are no shared truths, and where the necessity of pluralist tolerance is absolutely essential.[25]

Conclusion

More than 150 years ago Alexis de Tocqueville discussed the inclination of Americans to try to resolve policy disputes in the courts. He saw the legal system as a way for people in the United States to avoid messy and contentious political fights. Instead, they used "neutral" judges and courtrooms to work out resolutions. Today there are many more factors impelling people to turn to the legal system to address policy conflicts, including the presence in the United States of nearly 1 million lawyers.

In any case, Tocqueville would probably be astounded today at how often policy conflicts are met and sometimes "resolved" in the courts. This is certainly true in the area of religion and politics and church and state. The legal system is, in fact, perhaps the favorite avenue for religious politics, and its terrain is contested with all the resources and political skills that can be mustered by the interested parties. Thus it is essential for any religious group entering the political realm in the United States to know how judicial politics works.

Further Reading

Cord, Robert L. *Separation of Church and State: Historical Fact and Current Fiction.* Cambridge, MA: Lambeth, 1982. Interesting discussion of the religious and political views of the framers.

Epstein, Lee. *Conservatives in Court.* Knoxville: University of Tennessee Press, 1985. A consideration of conservatives at work in the courts.

Kramnick, Isaac, and R. Laurence Moore. *The Godless Constitution: The Case Against Religious Correctness.* New York: Norton, 1996. A fascinating separationist interpretation of the founding period.

Malbin, Michael. *Religion and Politics: The Intentions of the Authors of the First Amendment.* Washington, DC: American Enterprise Institute, 1978. Another able argument about the religious and political views of the framers.

Miller, Robert T., and Ronald B. Flowers, eds. *Toward Benevolent Neutrality: Church, State, and the Supreme Court.* Waco, TX: Baylor University Press, 1987. A defense of the neutrality doctrine.

Monsma, Stephen V. *When Sacred and Secular Mix: Religious Nonprofit Organizations and Public Money.* Lanham, MD: Rowman and Littlefield, 1996. Important work on one of the most important areas of contemporary religious jurisprudence.

Monsma, Stephen V., and J. Christopher Soper, eds. *Equal Treatment of Religion in a Pluralistic Society*. Grand Rapids, MI: Eerdmans, 1997. Probing analyses of the notion of equal protection.

Pfeffer, Leo. *Religion, State and the Burger Court*. Buffalo, NY: Prometheus, 1984. The classic defense of separationism.

Segers, Mary C., and Ted G. Jelen. *A Wall of Separation? Debating the Public Role of Religion*. Lanham, MD: Rowman and Littlefield, 1996. A discussion of various perspectives of the role of religion in democratic society.

Weber, Paul J. *Equal Separation: Understanding the Religious Clauses of the First Amendment*. Westport, CT: Greenwood, 1990. Thoughtful reflections on church and state.

11

Church and State in the Courts

$\mathcal{M}$ost legal struggles involving religion and politics focus on policy issues that flow from church-state relations. Such issues often necessitate clarification of the meaning of the First Amendment's religion clauses—"Congress shall make no law respecting an establishment of religion, or prohibiting the free exercise thereof."

The First Amendment and its religion clauses were adopted by the first Congress of the United States, under the leadership of James Madison. Congress began its work on this task in the spring of 1789 because of agitation for the inclusion of a list of guaranteed civil liberties in the Constitution during the debates leading up to adoption. Chief among the agitators for the Bill of Rights were the Antifederalists, who feared that the expansion of the federal government would curtail personal liberty. Records of the congressional debate indicate that bargaining and compromise were vital to the eventual agreement on the content and wording of the First Amendment. James Madison introduced the proposed amendment in its first form in June 1789. It subsequently went through several revisions, in both the House of Representatives and the Senate, before a conference committee agreed on a bill that passed Congress in September 1789; it was later sent to the states, who duly ratified it.

Madison knew he had to fashion an amendment that would satisfy critics who feared that the Constitution was hostile to religion (and suspected the same of him). Madison wanted to include what he called "rights of conscience" in the First Amendment, but some critics thought that the provision of such rights might result in government neutrality between religion and atheism, so it was dropped. Madison also failed in his attempt to eliminate the official establishment of religion within some states. The final version of the First Amendment applied only to the federal government ("*Congress* shall make no law . . . ").

From the beginning, the issues of church-state policy that have arisen from disagreements over the meaning of the First Amendment have included (1) how to balance free exercise of religion with laws that are otherwise clearly constitutional, and (2) how to decide when government activities that somehow involve or benefit religion mark an unconstitutional establishment of religion. In this chapter we will explore these two concerns. These two concerns, however, represent only one part of a larger domain that finds religion, politics, the courts, and public policy profoundly intermixed.

The classic example involves abortion politics, which has mobilized religious groups of all types and with a wide variety of opinions. Little of the courts' handling of the abortion dispute, however, has turned squarely on church-state issues, as the decisions in *Roe* v. *Wade* (1973), *Harris* v. *McRae* (1980), and *Planned Parenthood* v. *Casey* (1992) illustrate. Since 1973, the Supreme Court's treatment of the abortion issue has hinged, of course, on an implied constitutional right to privacy. Ironically, the language and logic of the First Amendment (including the religion clauses) contributed to the Court's assertion that the right to privacy exists under the constitutional rubric, much to the chagrin of many prolife religious groups.

Prochoice advocates have insisted that the prolife position on abortion by definition implies official establishment of religion, since they see the prolife position as a byproduct of a distinctly Western religious tradition. They have also noted that much of the drive for restrictions on abortion has been led by religious groups and individuals, especially Roman Catholics, evangelical Protestants, and (less visibly) some Muslims and Orthodox Jews. At the same time, prolife critics have contended that the *prochoice* position constitutes an official establishment of religion: the religion of secular humanism or atheism.

Religious Free Exercise

The framers of the Constitution thought governments posed a constant threat to the free exercise of religion. They based this view on their experience with the British government during the colonial period and even sometimes with their own colonial governments. Thus the framers were eager to protect the free exercise of religion from government interference. For them, protecting free exercise meant curtailing or eliminating government establishment of, and interference with, religion.

Thomas Jefferson, who wrote the Declaration of Independence, and James Madison, the principal author of the Constitution and the First

Amendment, were among the strongest proponents of religious free exercise. Both had been active in opposing the establishment of religion in colonial Virginia. They also helped to bring about the disestablishment of the Anglican (now Episcopal) Church there. Neither Jefferson nor Madison advocated complete separation of church and state during their subsequent presidencies, but they definitely tried to move in that direction. Reality, however, forced them to accept some compromises to accommodate organized religion at the federal level, and they did nothing to interfere with the states, where there was sometimes very little separation between church and state. Still, they both made important contributions to the development of American free exercise rights.[1]

Historically, Americans have enjoyed a great deal of free exercise latitude. The majority of Americans over the years have been Christian and Protestant, and free exercise rights have abounded for most of them. Though Protestantism has historically been dominant, free exercise rights were slowly extended to Roman Catholics, Jews, and others. Of course such groups could not constitutionally be denied free exercise rights. Still, they faced varying degrees of discrimination, which slowly gave way to a broad-based acceptance of the pluralist reality of American religious life. There has been plenty of argument along the way, but free exercise has steadily expanded in the United States. Today, the existence of an enormous degree of religious freedom—which encompasses many religious persuasions, groups, and practices—is something of which Americans may justifiably be proud. This does not deny the history of conflict that paved the American road to free exercise, nor that there are still religions struggling today against American culture for their free exercise rights. There will always be religious groups that push against the margins of American society and its unwritten rules about the limits of acceptable religious practices.

In attempting to interpret the framers' mandate that citizens should have the freedom to practice whatever religion they choose, the Supreme Court has distinguished between religious beliefs themselves and actions taken as a result of those beliefs. Beliefs are absolutely protected, but actions that the Court deems questionable may be restricted. For more than a century and a half, courts ducked religious issues as much as possible. They also tried to make sure that the other branches of government followed suit. For example, courts have been loathe to adjudicate arguments among members of disbanded religious groups. They have understood that to get involved in these often bitter fights may be to interfere improperly with a religion and by extension deter free exercise. This standard remains today. Religious groups are allowed to resolve their own disputes, under their own rules, as much as possible. This is especially so when the basic doctrines of a religion itself are at issue.[2]

If the courts have generally avoided becoming involved in arguments within religious organizations, they have also steered away from attempting to settle disagreements over what constitutes a "religion." Judges realize that this is treacherous ground. But this policy of avoidance has, in fact, proven to be supportive of free exercise. After all, if the definition of religion were left to the government rather than to believers themselves, free exercise would undoubtedly be threatened.

It is not easy to resolve these sorts of disputes, which lure government into such dangerous waters, but the courts' standard policy has been to avoid defining religion or making pronouncements about whether the claims of a religion are true. For example, in *United States* v. *Ballard* (1944), the Supreme Court was asked to decide whether a man who was using the U.S. mail to solicit funds for his "I Am Movement" was guilty of mail fraud. Ballard, who said he was a divine messenger who could communicate with Jesus Christ, had his conviction overturned. The Court stated that "Men may believe what they cannot prove. Religious experiences which are as real as life to some may be incomprehensible to others. . . . If one could be sent to jail because a jury in a hostile environment found his or her religious teachings false, little indeed would be left of religious freedom."[3]

A large number of free exercise controversies arise over taxes. In a recent case, *Hernandez* v. *Commissioner* (1989), which involved the Church of Scientology, the Supreme Court ruled that fees for specific services such as training in Scientology could not be counted as nontaxable gifts. Critics of the Court's decision in this case complained that it implicitly stated that Scientology was not a serious religion, thereby setting a dangerous precedent. If Scientology is not a religion, then what are the parameters of the religious and the secular—and who sets them?

Thus there is a continuing controversy over what exactly constitutes a religion—and what services an organized religion may provide. For example, the nonprofit activities of organized religions are free from taxation, a policy that has long been in place. But just what is a "religion" and what is a "nonprofit activity"? The traditional approach has been that minimizing government interference in such matters maximizes religious freedom. On the other hand, it may also leave room for abuse by groups that some consider dubious religions, sham activities, or rituals, as may have been the case in *Ballard*.

Some religious practices make today's headlines as sources of controversy. Often the courts have decided the resulting cases in ways that affirm religious freedom. One example surrounds the issue of clergy "malpractice" (Box 11.1).[4] Another issue of great importance concerns the level of confidentiality clergy should be allowed to maintain. This is especially difficult when clergy learn, through pastoral counseling, that a member of the

---

BOX 11.1   THE NALLY CASE: "CLERGY MALPRACTICE"

Consider the case of Californian Ken Nally, a mentally troubled individual who repeatedly sought help from clergy but eventually committed suicide. Family and friends sued his church, charging clergy malpractice. They claimed the clergy had misadvised Nally on how to manage his mental condition, thereby not only failing to help him but also contributing to his suicide. Eventually the California state courts decreed in *Nally v. Grace Community Church of the Valley* (1988) that there was no basis for charges of clergy malpractice. And in 1989, the U.S. Supreme Court declined to review the decision. As a result, religious freedom and religious free exercise (including the right of clergy to make mistakes) won out, but the issue of whether there is such a thing as clergy malpractice remains very much alive.

SOURCE: Margaret P. Battin, *Ethics in the Sanctuary: Examining the Practices of Organized Religion* (New Haven, CT: Yale University Press, 1990).

---

congregation has committed a serious crime, such as child abuse or even murder. State policies differ, but the current trend is toward requiring clergy to report violations of the law when they learn of them, though some clergy argue that this represents an erosion of their pastor-penitent privilege. Information gleaned through the seal of private confession in Roman Catholicism, however, remains sacrosanct. The confidentiality of pastoral counseling is far more controversial.

A third sensitive question is the extent to which personal risk taking should be allowed within a church. Almost always, the issues arise as a result of health risks incurred because of religious practices. Examples include the refusal of Jehovah's Witnesses to accept blood transfusions, Christian Scientists' belief in faith healing (and their consequent rejection of modern medicine), and the practice of serpent handling in a handful of Pentecostal churches. Such issues may be approached from many directions, and of course it matters whether church groups are honest with their members about the possible consequences of any risky behaviors they practice and encourage. The limits of religious freedom become especially important when the lives or fundamental health of children are at stake.

Disputes also swirl around the question of whether there are limits to some religious groups' perpetual search for converts. Almost all religions assert that they only seek followers who knowingly choose their faith, so they renounce the use of fraud or manipulation to trick people into embracing their faith. But what constitutes a "trick" or a "fraud"? For an atheist, to use the extreme example, every religion is in the business of fraud. How much can government regulate what it—or society—determines to be fraudulent behavior without infringing on free exercise?

There have been some exceptions, such as the Court's decision to outlaw the Mormon practice of polygamy in *Reynolds* v. *United States* (1879), but broad free exercise rights have generally been permitted in the United States. The law is often murky, and even contradictory, but there are many rulings that testify to the American commitment to free exercise, especially for mainstream religions. Of course, rarely does this reality involve any sacrifice of secular national policies that the government and the courts have deemed essential to the general welfare.

Perhaps the classic Supreme Court case in which a generous range of free exercise rights were affirmed is *Cantwell* v. *Connecticut* (1940). In *Cantwell*, the Court invoked both of the religion clauses and other parts of the First Amendment to strike down local ordinances that interfered with Jehovah's Witnesses' desire to distribute literature to and request contributions from the general public. The Court's decision in *Cantwell* to allow religious groups the right to proselytize pursuant to their freedom of religion has often been reaffirmed, subject to restrictions on the setting.[5] Likewise, attempts by states to penalize fund-raising by unpopular religions have been rejected.[6] The Court has also ruled that neither clergy nor religious organizations may be prevented from becoming involved in politics.[7] Similarly, the Court has granted some religious freedom in federal institutions (prisons are the most controversial arena), but only so long as religious practices do not disrupt standard operating procedures.[8]

In public schools, the courts have created a rather narrow zone of free exercise. Still, in *Wisconsin* v. *Yoder* (1982), the Court defended the decision of Amish people not to attend high school, as Amish doctrine does not require or respect that sort of schooling. It also declared in *West Virginia State Board of Education* v. *Barnette* (1988) that Jehovah's Witnesses have the right to refuse to say the Pledge of Allegiance in school, as their religion forbids commitment to any nation-state, and in *Pierce* v. *Society of Sisters* (1928) it supported the right of Roman Catholic schools (and thus other private and religious schools) to exist alongside public ones. All of these cases were momentous because they demonstrated that public education must be aware that it operates in an environment of religious free exercise and must therefore take the Supreme Court's definition of that reality into account.

The Limits of Free Exercise

In principle there is no debate about the government's ultimate authority to restrict the free exercise of religion. In the United States nothing is superior to the powers of the government—except the people from whom the state's authority derives. Even rights granted in the Constitution and the Bill of Rights are not absolute and may be limited by other constitutional provisions and

---

BOX 11.2   RELIGIOUS SOLICITATION IN AIRPORTS

The U.S. Supreme Court has struggled to fashion a consistent stance on solicitations by religious groups in airports that respects their right to proselytize while not abridging state authority to regulate activities for the public good. How assertive may a religious group be in an airport? Airports are public places, but they are different from other public forums such as parks. Airports, after all, are busy commercial centers through which many people must pass. They are places where one cannot easily choose to avoid assertive representatives of religious groups. In a case involving Hare Krishnas proselytizing in the LaGuardia, John F. Kennedy, and Newark Airports, the Court ultimately ruled that groups may hand out literature in airports, but they may not try to raise funds.

SOURCE: *International Society for Krishna Consciousness v. Lee* (1992).

---

by the government. Thus it is always conceivable that the free exercise of religion may be restricted (Box 11.2).

The Supreme Court has made some controversial decisions in recent years that have limited free exercise. In *Goldman* v. *Weinberger* (1988) it decided to uphold military regulations providing that no Jewish person could wear a yarmulke (skullcap) while on duty in the U.S. military. At issue was not the wisdom of the regulation but whether or not the Court should defer to military rules and the reasons behind them: the need to maintain military order and regularity. The Court concluded that it should defer to the military. Congress later passed a law allowing Jews to wear yarmulkes in the military, but it did so without challenging the authority of the federal government to decide such matters. A similar issue arose in a New Jersey case, *O'Lone* v. *Estate of Shabazz* (1988), in which Muslims in state prisons claimed that prison work rules interfered with their practice of Islam. The Court held that deference to prison rules and the administrators who make them (that is, the government) must take precedence over free exercise.

In practical policy terms, there have been two significant areas in which limits to free exercise of religion have been allowed to exist. One is the realm of *traditional* welfare policies, which the courts have sometimes upheld even in the face of claims that free exercise had been violated. The second is *modern* "common good" policies: laws passed for the "common good" in pursuit of goals such as ensuring equal rights or eliminating drugs.

The view that some government provisions designed to protect the general welfare have priority over the First Amendment guarantee of free exercise rights has been endorsed in the courts for some time. A long line of cases has held that such things as required vaccinations to protect public health or laws forbidding child labor must take precedence over free exercise rights, even though some groups' religious freedoms may thereby be violated. For example, in *Braunfeld* v. *Brown* (1981), the Court ruled against a group of Orthodox Jews who felt that their ability to earn a living was being compromised by Pennsylvania's Sunday closing laws. Their religion forbids them to work on Saturday, and the state forbids them to work on Sunday. The Court recognized that the Pennsylvania law made Orthodox Judaism "more expensive" than Christianity, but because the law did not prevent anyone from the actual practice of religion—"the Sunday law simply regulates a secular activity"—it did not violate the Free Exercise Clause.[9]

In areas such as these the crucial question centers on where to draw the line between the pursuit of government goals and the protection of religious free exercise. The fact is, the U.S. Supreme Court has never sent a clear message about where that line ought to be drawn. It has usually appeared to be more impressed with upholding government policy than with protecting some small, dissenting religious group. But there has been no obvious and consistent pattern. From the late 1930s until the 1960s, however, it was a safe bet that most free exercise appeals would meet with defeat in court. The Supreme Court usually sided with the federal and state governments and their laws in such conflicts. Since the 1960s, however, these matters have been less clear, as the pendulum began to swing toward the expansion of free exercise rights.

In the landmark free exercise case of *Sherbert* v. *Verner* (1963), the Court stated that the standard of "strict scrutiny" (the most exacting level of judicial review) must apply to any law that conflicted with the free exercise of religion. By imposing this standard the justices meant to underline the importance of free exercise, though they did not mean that any laws clashing with free exercise would automatically fail the strict scrutiny test. In *Sherbert*, a Seventh-Day Adventist won her claim against South Carolina for denying her unemployment benefits after she was fired from her job for refusing to work on Saturday (the Adventist Sabbath). The Court stated clearly that "the burden on the free exercise of appellant's religion must be justified by *a compelling state interest.*"[10] Thus the *Sherbert* case set a high standard, which the Court continued to use for many years in deciding a variety of free exercise disputes.

More recently, however, the Rehnquist Court has been less congenial to free exercise claims—which usually involve the practice of minority religions. In the much discussed 1990 case of *Employment Division* v. *Smith*, the Court specifically reversed the strict scrutiny doctrine that it had set forth in *Sherbert*. No longer would states be forced to demonstrate a compelling interest if their laws had the effect of restricting free exercise rights. Though the picture is complicated and the results mixed, the Court has been increasingly willing to uphold "common good" legislation despite protests of particular religious groups and individuals who have contended that such laws infringe upon their religious practices.

In the *Smith* case, the Supreme Court affirmed Oregon's drug policy. In that state, two Native American drug counselors had been fired and prevented from collecting unemployment compensation. They had been fired for violating terms of their employment that prohibited the use of peyote, a practice that plays a significant spiritual role in their religion as members of the Native American Church. Though the Court's ruling in *Smith* came as something of a surprise, it was the legal doctrine upon which the ruling was based that caused a real uproar. The Court declared that it was no longer committed to automatic "strict scrutiny" of laws that restrict free exercise of religion, thereby undoing the decades-old *Sherbert* precedent. In *Sherbert*, of course, the Court had not said laws restricting free exercise would automatically be ruled unconstitutional, but it did suggest they would find the going tough. Therefore, the reversal of this precedent seemed to bring to a close an era in which the Court provided a specially protected role for religious exercise in the United States.

Meanwhile, at the state level, some government regulators became quite zealous in challenging alternative religious schools and home schools, which raised similar conflicts.[11] The Supreme Court's 1993 decision in *Church of the Lukumi Babalu Aye* v. *City of Hialeah* came as a relief to some critics. In this case the Court struck down an ordinance passed by the city of Hialeah, Florida, that prohibited the ritual sacrifice of animals. The court ruled that this ordinance had been designed specifically to forbid the animal-killing rituals practiced as part of the Santeria religion. The Court agreed with the Santeria Church of the Lukumi that the ordinance in question was extremely selective, since it did not forbid other forms of animal-killing such as hunting or Jewish ritual preparation of kosher food. It was aimed at one group alone: practitioners of Santeria. What distinguishes the *Smith* case from the *Lukumi* case is that laws designed to interfere with the free exercise of particular faiths that do not further a major state policy may be ruled unconstitutional. Laws pursuant to the common good that are not intended to oppress a particular religious group, however, are likely to be upheld.

Some critics complain that Court rulings that uphold "common good" legislation actually do promote particular moral positions at the expense of religious free exercise of others. They are correct, of course, but the reverse is just as true when free exercise claims do win out. In each instance moral choices are clearly implied. The question becomes one of where religious free exercise ought to rank in comparison with other moral values. In the American legal system, for better or for worse, free exercise is not always at the top of the list. As a nation Americans have not fully advanced beyond nineteenth-century norms that allowed the Supreme Court to force

Mormons to abandon the practice of polygamy in *Reynolds* v. *United States* (1879).

Though the Supreme Court would no longer defend decisions in the language of Christian morality, as was the case in *Reynolds*, it often accedes to the decisions of Congress and the state legislatures, even at the expense of religious free exercise. Much of the Rehnquist Court's energy for such decisions has not come from sympathy with such laws themselves, but instead from a commitment to the proposition that courts ought not to interfere with the decisions of democratically elected legislatures.

In response to the Rehnquist Court's actions, religious groups united to push the Religious Freedom Restoration Act (RFRA) through Congress. This law, which President Clinton signed in 1994, required the federal courts to return to the doctrine of strict scrutiny when reviewing any law that abridges religious free exercise rights. In essence, Congress forced the Court to return to the *Sherbert* precedent, which effectively undercut the Court's logic in the *Smith* case. In 1997, however, the Supreme Court retaliated and struck RFRA down. Congress's initial passage of RFRA actually constituted an interesting example of the raw power American religious groups can exercise when they unite. But its days were numbered.

The Supreme Court declared RFRA unconstitutional in *City of Boerne* v. *Flores* (1997). A Roman Catholic congregation in Boerne, Texas, wished to expand its church sanctuary but was denied a building permit. The city's policies on the protection of the historic district in which the church was located prevented any further development. Buoyed by RFRA, the church argued that the city did not have a compelling interest in preventing it from expanding. The Court supported the city's counterargument, simultaneously striking down the provision of RFRA, which called for the existence of a compelling state interest when laws restrict free exercise rights.[12]

And the debate continues over the proper limits of free exercise. In August 1997, the Clinton administration outlined a plan to protect religious expression in federal government offices. The guidelines allow bureaucrats to wear religious jewelry, hold prayer meetings during lunch breaks, distribute religious literature to coworkers, and keep scriptures on their desks. In formulating the plan, the administration was assisted by a wide array of interest groups, from the conservative Christian Legal Society, to the liberal National Council of Churches, to the separationist People for the American Way.[13]

The Politics of Religious Establishment

Whether there really is separation of church and state in the United States, in theory or in practice, is a very controversial matter. Perhaps the best strategy is to say that everything depends on what the term "establish-

---

BOX 11.3 ESTABLISHMENT IN THE COURTROOM: JUDGE ROY MOORE AND THE TEN COMMANDMENTS

One of the more well-publicized debates over religious establishment in recent years has involved, ironically, a courtroom itself. Judge Roy Moore, who presides over Etowah County, Alabama's Circuit Court, has been involved since 1995 in a legal battle with the American Civil Liberties Union (ACLU) over two matters. First, Moore opens his court each day with an explicitly Christian prayer; second, he has a handmade plaque bearing the Ten Commandments hanging on the wall behind his bench. The ACLU has argued that Moore's actions represent an egregious violation of the Establishment Clause, but in 1997 Moore defied an order by State District Judge Charles Price to remove the plaque. Alabama Governor Fob James rushed to Moore's aid, as did 25,000 citizens who attended a rally for him on the steps of the state capitol on April 12, 1997. Numerous web sites have also appeared to urge support for Moore. This is a matter that has the potential to become the subject of a landmark decision by the United States Supreme Court, and will continue to be a judicial cause célèbre of the religious Right.

SOURCES: Jay Grelen, "Ten Commandments Judge Looking for Federal Fight," *Christianity Today* (December 8, 1997), 60; http://www.aclu.org.

---

ment" means. There is no doubt that there has been plenty of official religious establishment by one definition or another throughout American history. Most of the colonies officially established one Protestant church or another and expected all taxpayers to help finance that single church. Though the First Amendment of the U.S. Constitution outlawed the establishment of any single religion at *the national level*, some states continued to support their own establishments. This practice came to an end when Massachusetts became the last state to do away with officially established religion in 1833. That marked the end of *legal* establishment (Box 11.3), but it was hardly the end of the notion of establishment. After all, throughout much of the nineteenth century the United States had implicitly established Christianity—and Protestant Christianity in particular. This was most obvious in the widespread reading of the Protestant King James Bible in public schools.

The fact is that there remains plenty of establishment in various forms. Separationist and antireligion lobbies have had only mixed success in attempting to dismantle these more subtle forms of establishment. For example, the atheist leader Madalyn Murray O'Hair failed in her 1979 attempt to convince the United State Court of Appeals (Fifth Circuit) to banish "In God We Trust" from the currency *(O'Hair v. Blumenthal)*. Efforts in 1983 to get the Supreme Court to eliminate prayer at the beginning of sessions by legislative bodies also proved unsuccessful *(Marsh v. Chambers)*. The weight of the

---

BOX 11.4   RELIGIOUS ESTABLISHMENT AND CITY SEALS

Symbolic establishments of religion in general and of Christianity in particular are quite different. This is well illustrated by the legal dispute over city seals. The courts forced Zion, Illinois, to drop its municipal seal, which proclaimed "God Reigns" and prominently featured a cross. Its new seal, affirming "In God We Trust," represents establishment of religion in general rather than the symbolic establishment of Christianity in the earlier seal.

In 1996, the Supreme Court refused to intervene in the issue of establishment and city seals by refusing to hear the case of *City of Edmund* v. *Robinson*. The Court let stand a lower court's ruling that a cross on the seal of Edmund, Oklahoma, was an unconstitutional establishment of Christianity, affirming again that single establishment does not pass Supreme Court muster.

---

traditional establishment of what may be called *religion in general* has been substantial throughout American history. Nonetheless, pressures against the symbolic establishment of *Christianity* have grown stronger over the years—and have been increasingly successful. The coalition against official endorsements of Christianity is often broad and frequently includes the legal arms of prominent Jewish groups (for further discussion, see Box 11.4).

On the other hand, the technique most often used by those who wish to defend symbolic establishment has been to repackage establishment and present it—at least for the benefit of the courts—as something that is not religious at all. In instances when these efforts succeed, courts often appear to wink and go on to what they judge to be more important matters. This has been evident in arguments over public crèches (manger scenes depicting Jesus' birth). In both *Lynch* v. *Donnelly* (1984) and *Allegheny County* v. *Greater Pittsburgh ACLU* (1989), the Supreme Court allowed crèches to stand on public land or in connection with public buildings only if they are merely one element of what the Court has chosen to describe as a "winter display." When crèches exist alone as a Christian symbol, however, as was the case in a Pittsburgh courthouse at stake in *Allegheny County* v. *Greater Pittsburgh ACLU*, the Court has deemed them unconstitutional. Hairsplitting of this sort has not won the Court many plaudits, and to some critics it just seems absurd.

Governments in the United States—local, state, and federal—funnel tremendous amounts of financial aid to various religions. Insofar as they do so, they are sustaining an establishment of religion and undermining the principle of separation. Government aid to nonprofit organizations (which includes religious groups) for assorted public purposes constitutes the most obvious illustration. Examples of this practice, affirmed by the courts since 1899 in *Bradfield* v. *Roberts*, include assistance to religious hospitals and clinics, orphanages, halfway houses, retirement homes, refugee resettlement projects, and other social service endeavors and programs. The exact amounts of aid and the specific rules governing its use vary from federal to state governments, from state to state, and from one policy area to another, but the practice itself is widespread.

The governing principle in establishment cases today is the so-called *Lemon* test. Formulated in *Lemon* v. *Kurtzman* (1971), the *Lemon* test holds that laws are constitutional when they serve a secular legislative purpose, neither advance nor inhibit religion, and do not foster an excessive entanglement between government and religion.[14] It matters not whether the law also happens to aid or hurt some particular religious group. In establishment cases the *Lemon* test has been used in a variety of ways, and its implementation has been a controversial undertaking even within the Supreme Court. Justice Antonin Scalia, for example, has bemoaned "the strange Establishment clause geometry of crooked lines and wavering shapes its intermittent use has produced."[15]

The *Lemon* test allows the constitutional provision of substantial government aid to religious organizations of all sorts. Thus if governments decide that aid to nonprofit hospitals is in the public interest, then it is constitutional because the legislation from which the hospitals would benefit may be said to have a secular purpose, neither advance nor inhibit religion, and fail to foster any excessive entanglements between church and state. It is still true, however, that in such a situation government is undeniably aiding religious groups and thus promoting some form of religious establishment. Granted, this sort of implicit establishment is by no means the same as the official establishments of the colonial era. In that age, government support was enjoyed exclusively by one church. Instead, the modern arrangement normally takes the form of "multiple establishment." Government provides aid in a particular policy area to all qualified applicants. For example, both secular and religious hospitals may receive government funds.

Contemporary establishment also occurs in the common practice of granting all nonprofit groups (again, including religious institutions) freedom from property taxes. Since churches, synagogues, and mosques often occupy extensive properties, this arrangement is a tremendous financial boon for them. Again the principle is familiar: This benefit has been defended not as a grant to religious groups *per se*, but as a neutral law with the secular purpose of helping nonprofit (and only nonprofit) groups that benefit society. Though some separationists have argued strenuously against this arrangement as a flagrant example of establishment, they have not succeeded in the courts. Establishment in the United States is often legal if it is indirect and accomplished through "neutral" laws that stand up to the *Lemon* test.

Education policy is another arena in which many conflicts have emerged over religious establishment. The battle over religion in the schools has

been waged throughout American history, and it continues unabated today. The American culture's faith in schooling demonstrates a deep concern for youth and a belief that schools shape young people's futures.
Struggles over education policy will continue, for Americans believe that a
great deal is at stake.

All sorts of religious practices in schools, some of which have reflected
the beliefs of a particular religious group, have been common throughout
the history of American public education. Public prayers and Bible reading
in class have been the most widespread of these practices. However, such
policies began to face serious criticism after World War II. Religious release-time education became a widespread fashion after the war. Such programs allowed religious teachers to come into public schools during regular hours and teach religious lessons to students who had the permission of
a parent or guardian. In the late 1940s and early 1950s the Supreme Court
was indecisive about the constitutionality of this practice. In *McCollum* v.
Board of Education (1948), release-time classes held on school grounds
were ruled unconstitutional. In 1952, the Court seemed to reverse itself in
Zorach v. *Clauson*, but the release-time classes at stake in that case took
place off of school property.

Release-time programs are now ancient history in most places, but the
disputes surrounding them were an early sign of the courts' willingness to
tackle establishment issues that related to public education. Steadily since
the 1960s, courts have brought about a sweeping disestablishment of
conventional religion in public schools. This is seen as a great victory by
separationist and antireligious groups that argue religion has no place in
the classroom.

The Court's first step was to banish prayer from the schools in the mon-
umental 1962 case of *Engel* v. *Vitale*. One year later, the Court also put a
stop to Bible reading in public schools in *Abington School District* v.
Schempp (1963). In 1980, the posting of the ten commandments in classrooms was ruled unconstitutional *(Stone* v. *Graham)*. For some critics the
last straw came in *Wallace* v. *Jaffree* (1985), in which the Court struck
down an Alabama law requiring public school teachers to open each day
with a moment of silence. The Court interpreted the law as Alabama's "effort to return voluntary prayer to our public schools."[16] The Court did not
accept Alabama's argument that the moment of silence served the secular
purpose of encouraging good student behavior. The latest issue of this nature to come before the Court has involved the constitutionality of prayer
at public school graduation ceremonies. The Supreme Court rejected
clergy-led prayers in *Lee* v. *Weisman* (1992), but in the same year the
United States Court of Appeals (Fifth Circuit) ruled that student-led
prayers were acceptable in *Jones* v. *Clear Creek Independent School
District* (1992).

Critics have sometimes lamented the exit of nondenominational religion from public schools, charging that religion has been replaced by secular humanism (a very small organized "religion" that places humans above all else). But in the 1987 case of *Smith* v. *Board of Commissioners,* the United States Court of Appeals (Eleventh Circuit) disagreed, apparently believing instead that it is possible to foster neutrality. Some religious groups have welcomed the Supreme Court's effort to force religion out of the public schools. They believe religion belongs at home and in church; they often have no use for vague nondenominational religion in the first place. Other observers, however, are uneasy about the need for many public schools to take great lengths to avoid the presentation or teaching of anything religious.

Despite a long history of religious establishment in American public schools, this policy has now ceased in most school districts. This fact is reflected in the failure of efforts by conservative Protestants to force school districts in several southern states to provide instruction in creationism. Such efforts have invariably been deemed a manifest establishment of religion. Teachers in the early twentieth century could face serious trouble for teaching Charles Darwin's theory of evolution, as Tennessee teacher John Scopes learned. His 1925 trial for violating Tennessee's policy of prohibiting the teaching of Darwinism, which came to be known as the Scopes Monkey Trial, gained wide publicity in part because of the involvement of two high-profile attorneys, William Jennings Bryan and Clarence Darrow. More recently, though, the Supreme Court has protected the teaching of evolution. In 1968, the Court struck down an Arkansas law forbidding the teaching of evolutionary theory in *Epperson* v. *Arkansas.* It is also unconstitutional for a state to require the teaching of both creationism and Darwinism, according to the Court's ruling in *Edwards* v. *Aguillard* (1987). In both instances the Court felt that the states in question were specifically attempting to establish Christianity.

Disputes over the judiciary's view of establishment have also raged in the context of financial aid to religious schools. Historically this meant that aid to Roman Catholic schools was denied on establishment grounds because to give such aid would be to establish a branch of Christianity, Roman Catholicism. Since public schools were once permeated by practices such as group readings from the Protestant King James Bible, skeptics have suggested that the real problem was not with establishment *per se*; it was rather a question of which religion would be given preference in most public schools. Though modern courts have removed much of the old Protestant establishment from public schools, they have been inconsistent on the matter of financial aid to religious schools. Aid for teacher salaries, which is by far the greatest portion of school budgets, has repeatedly failed on establishment grounds, as was the case in *Lemon* v. *Kurtzman* (1971).

At the same time, the Supreme Court has upheld state laws allowing several significant forms of assistance to religious schools. According to the Court's 1947 decision in *Everson* v. *Board of Education*, public school buses may be used to transport children to and from religious schools. Transportation to religious schools was not perceived to be a substantial violation of the Establishment Clause. A similar logic drove the Court's 1968 decision in *Board of Education* v. *Allen*, in which it upheld New York's policy of allowing religious schools to borrow secular textbooks from public school districts. In *Meek* v. *Pittenger* (1975), however, the Court ruled that neither state-paid staff nor instructional materials other than books could be loaned to religious schools. In *Wolman* v. *Walter* (1977), the Court affirmed *Meek* and further rejected state aid by declaring that public school buses could not be used to transport children from religious schools on field trips. Finally, in *Aguilar* v. *Felton* (1985), the Court struck down a New York law providing state-financed remedial courses and guidance services in religious schools.

More recently the Court ruled in *Zobrest* v. *Catalina Foothills School District* (1993) that government funds could be used to pay an interpreter to accompany a deaf student attending a religious school. Proponents could see no problem since insignificant establishment, at most, was at issue. Opponents, however, said the policy was a serious breach of the no-establishment principle, since taxpayers would be financing translation by the interpreter of such sectarian events as mass in the school. In *Kiryas Joel Village School District* v. *Grumet* (1994), however, the Court held that New York could not set up a special school district for disabled children in an Orthodox Jewish town in suburban New York City. Whereas only one student was being assisted in *Zobrest*, the Court saw the creation of an entire school district for disabled Orthodox Jewish children as another matter altogether. Finally, in *Agostini* v. *Felton* (1997), the Court specifically overturned *Aguilar* v. *Felton* in holding that public school teachers may provide state-mandated special services in religious schools.

Taken as a whole, Establishment Clause jurisprudence in the twentieth century has for many observers amounted to nothing more than a confusing mess. As one remarks:

> Bus trips from home to religious schools are constitutional, but bus trips from religious schools to local museums are unconstitutional. . . . Standardized tests are o.k., but teacher-prepared tests are not. Government can provide parochial schools with books but not maps, provoking Senator Daniel Moynihan's quip: "What about atlases?" The Court has invoked *Lemon* to strike down a nativity scene surrounded by poinsettias and to uphold a nativity scene surrounded by elephants, teddy bears, Santa's workshop, and a talking wishing well.[17]

The Court's logic has been based in its attempt to balance two goals: ensuring no establishment and benefiting children. On the one hand, the Court's reasoning has been that establishment is especially dangerous in the schools because children are much more vulnerable to inculcation than are adults; on the other hand, that very vulnerability has led the Court to avoid disadvantaging children in any fundamental way if they happen to attend religious schools. Thus the Court has been understanding if states decide that all children need textbooks and transportation to school. State-paid religious school teachers, however, would move too far toward establishment.

Obviously there is room for argument at every point. Advocates contend that if religious schools can receive only a certain amount of aid for specific services from the government, then families of religious school students ought also to receive some compensation for the costs they incur in sending their children to these schools. Families that send children to religious schools commonly complain that they are forced to pay twice to educate their children—once through taxes to support public schools they do not use and again in tuition to the religious school. Opponents reply that no one is forced to send their children to a religious school. They question why taxpayers should have to pay for the choices of one small portion of the population, especially when those choices may involve an establishment of religion.

However, some Catholics, evangelical Protestants, Muslims, and Orthodox Jews believe today that they must send their children to religious schools in order to practice their religion freely—especially in light of what they perceive to be growing secularism in public schools. For them, state support for religious schools, if it is made available to all, does not involve much establishment. Nor, they insist, does it hinder free exercise. Critics reply that such support constitutes unacceptable religious establishment. They argue that it makes all citizens contribute to the education of children in religious schools. Such critics find allies among some supporters of religious schools who fear that the heavy hand of government regulation might come along with aid.

In the past, the courts have sided with citizens who oppose any form of financial relief for families sending children to private schools. State tuition grants, for example, have been held unconstitutional. The governing rule now, however, is not quite the same. In 1983, the Supreme Court decided in *Mueller* v. *Allen* that Minnesota's policy of allowing tax deductions for tuition, textbooks, and transportation to private schools, including religious ones, was permissible. The Court cast aside charges of establishment because Minnesota made such expenses deductible only if they were provided to all state-approved private schools. Minnesota has now expanded its program to allow tax deductions for *any* expense (within prescribed financial limits) for private education and has introduced a $1,000 tax credit for lower-income citizens who incur expenses other than tuition costs in sending their children to private schools.

It is not obvious what the Court's reaction would be to widespread tuition grants to students if many states or localities adopt school choice plans, which permit families and students to choose among public and private schools at state expense. Several cities, including Milwaukee, Wisconsin, and Cleveland, Ohio, now have school choice plans in operation that allow families to choose certain religious schools. Both cities' programs now face legal challenges and are making their way through the court system. On June 10, 1998, the Wisconsin Supreme Court upheld Milwaukee's school choice program in the case of *Jackson* v. *Benson*. This decision marked the most significant legal victory yet for school choice advocates. The decision cleared the way for 15,000 low-income students to select any school from a list including over eighty religious schools for the 1998–1999 academic year.[18] This decision will certainly be appealed to the U.S. Supreme Court.

The courts have consistently ruled that aid directed to religious colleges and universities raises considerably less concern about establishment. The assumption is that college students, as adults, are a good deal less vulnerable to religious propaganda than are children and young adults in elementary, middle, and high schools. Thus aid may be provided to religious colleges for buildings as long as they are not used for worship or sectarian education, according to the Court's decisions in *Tilton* v. *Richardson* (1971) and *Roemer* v. *Board of Public Works* (1976).

Conclusion

One of the most interesting issues today in modern church-state politics is the relationship between free exercise and establishment. The framers of the Constitution took for granted that establishment of religion by definition meant restriction of free exercise rights. And they were correct when establishment means state sponsorship of a single religion. At least for practitioners of minority religions, free exercise was bound to be burdened (at best) in the face of a single established religion. At worst, they would face drastic curtailment of their free exercise rights.

Much of current church-state jurisprudence proceeds under the same assumption, namely that no official establishment can possibly enhance the free exercise of religion. But this assumption is not always self-evidently true; sometimes, in fact, establishment may make free exercise more of a reality for many citizens. The classic illustration is provided by the benefits that flow from state aid to religious schools. If state aid is given to all religious schools, religious free exercise may be expanded for families that desire a religious education for their children but cannot afford it. Some critics point out that implicit in this view is the idea that somehow government has an obligation to promote the free exercise of religion, an assumption at which they insist the First Amendment does not even hint. They read the First Amendment to mean that government should not interfere with religious free exercise, which is far different from providing active support for religion.

Such an interpretation of the First Amendment is only one possible understanding of its protection of free exercise rights, and it is no longer consonant with the Supreme Court's approach to free exercise. The Court has defined free exercise of religion as a constitutional right that must be affirmatively protected. But does this mean that the government must promote free exercise? Even if one concludes that government must promote free exercise, it does not follow that it should also offer state aid to religious schools. The point is that it is not always obvious that an increase in establishment (of all religions) leads necessarily to a decrease in free exercise rights. In some instances, the opposite may be true. Some argue that, as a result, sweeping formulas should be replaced by more case-by-case analysis and discussion. The courts have argued for decades that expressions of religion in public schools constitute unacceptable establishment. To say the least, these decisions have offended many critics who contend that the resulting absence of religious expression in the public schools amounts to an establishment of secularism.

Some critics have proceeded to try to create opportunities in public schools for extracurricular student-led religious groups to meet. The Supreme Court upheld such a policy on college campuses in 1981 by arguing that if a university offers the use of facilities to one extracurricular group, it must do so for all *(Widmar v. Vincent)*. In 1984, Congress passed the Equal Access Law, which applied the same principle to public high schools. It provided that high schools had to allow student-led religious groups to meet after school if other extracurricular clubs were also permitted to do so. Many schools have resisted, but the Supreme Court affirmed the law in *Board of Education v. Mergens* (1990) by contending that granting space to an after-school Bible club did not amount to establishment of religion—as long as club meetings were not led by a teacher.

The impact of the Court's decision to allow high school Bible clubs to form has already been felt, as an increasing number of schools have developed such clubs. Close to 20 percent of all American high schools now have at least one extracurricular religious club. High school ministries such as Young Life, the Fellowship of Christian Athletes, Youth for Christ, and Student Venture (the high school ministry of Campus Crusade for Christ) have also been joined by an energetic new group called First Priority. This group, which has established itself in more than 3,000 high schools in nearly 200 cities, says it is designed "to encourage, equip, and empower students to reach their campus with the Good News of Jesus Christ."[19]

Battles over such clubs and organizations continue, however. In 1993, the Court ruled that if a school district allows other community groups to use its buildings when classes are not in session, then religious groups must also be offered the same privilege *(Lamb's Chapel v. Center Moriches Union Free School District)*. The Court also held in *Rosenberger v. Rector* (1995) that because the University of Virginia provides support to a wide variety of student publications, it must as a matter of equal access do the same for a campus Christian publication. The university at first had not assisted the Christian publication for fear of violating the Establishment Clause. And a recent controversy has involved not only prayer in schools but also the wearing of cloth bracelets and other jewelry and clothing with the letters "W. W. J. D." for "What would Jesus do?"[20]

When faced with a choice between sustaining free exercise or allowing establishment in public schools, the Supreme Court has usually chosen to protect free exercise rights. It has not, however, always chosen free exercise. Religious cases often involve other constitutional protections, such as freedom of speech, freedom of assembly, and equal protection of the laws. The Court considered all of these protections, of course, in judging the constitutionality of the Equal Access Law. In the end the Court chose to uphold equal access—even if it could imply (multiple) establishment of religion in the schools.

It is, however, quite possible to disagree with the Court and insist that the Equal Access Law facilitates establishment. It may be a rather weak version of establishment, of course. Though school teachers may not run Bible clubs and other religious groups that meet after school, meetings do take place on public school grounds. Recent developments also constitute a form of multiple establishment because any religious group may take advantage of the policy. But establishment it remains, legally justified by the principles of free speech, free exercise of religion, and equal protection of the laws. Behind the legal principles, however, are two implicit principles. First, compromise is probably the best policy when it comes to the politics of church and state in the United States, as opposed to rigid insistence on one principle or another. Second, all-out efforts to prevent establishment of religion in public schools may already have narrowed free exercise of religion. In the final analysis it is important to return to the thorny matter of wondering exactly when, if ever, multiple establishment might encourage free exercise of religion.

It is also crucial to ask whether the political issues of the day should be fought out in the courts in the first place.[21] And the issue is not only one of how elitist or democratic the courts may be, though that is certainly a subject that deserves reflection. Nor is the question as straightforward as deciding on the wisdom of removing controversial religio-political issues from the public arena. The fact is that the legal remedy, given its focus on adversarial conflict, often exacerbates tensions and thus frequently fails to encourage the compromise that is essential for the increasingly multicultural and multireligious character of American society.

The reality of the politics of church and state today is that all sides turn to the courts when they believe they will win, and to the legislatures when they seem to need a more sympathetic hearing. This is well illustrated by the recent efforts of some 150 members of Congress who believe that the federal courts, especially the Supreme Court, do not care enough about freedom of religious expression in public settings. Led by Rep. Ernest Istook (R–Oklahoma), these congressional activists unsuccessfully sought the adoption of a constitutional amendment designed "to secure the people's right to acknowledge God according to the dictates of conscience." The amendment would also have provided that "the people's right to pray and to recognize their religious beliefs, heritage or traditions on public property, including schools, shall not be infringed." The Religious Freedom Amendment (RFA) was endorsed by over thirty religious organizations, most of them conservative, including the Christian Coalition, the Family Research Council, and Focus on the Family. Several denominational groups, such as the Southern Baptist Convention and the National Baptist Convention USA, Inc., also supported the amendment. The House rejected the RFA after heated debate, however, on June 4, 1998.[22]

Certainly there is a need for a perspective on church-state politics that is much more sophisticated than that which often dominates the headlines. There are more than just two positions. There are many kinds of establishment and separationism, many degrees of free exercise and limits on free exercise. Everything is dependent upon specific circumstance. The concrete issues that shape the politics of church and state are complicated, fascinating, and always evolving.

Further Reading

Battin, Margaret P. *Ethics in the Sanctuary: Examining the Practices of Organized Religion.* New Haven, CT: Yale University Press, 1990. An interesting consideration of the ethical and constitutional issues regarding controversial religious practices.

Malbin, Michael. *Religion and Politics: The Intentions of the Authors of the First Amendment.* Washington, DC: American Enterprise Institute, 1978. A study of the church-state ideas of the framers.

Miller, Robert T., and Ronald B. Flowers, eds. *Toward Benevolent Neutrality: Church, State, and the Supreme Court.* Waco, TX: Baylor University Press, 1987. A defense of the neutrality doctrine.

Miller, William L. *The First Liberty and the American Republic.* New York: Knopf, 1986. A wide-ranging, interesting discussion of church and state and the founding of the American nation.

12

Theories of Religion, Culture, and American Politics

$\mathcal{N}$ow that we have studied religion in American politics in its many forms, we need to step back and obtain a broader perspective. In this concluding chapter we explore some broad interpretations that paint an overall picture of the relationships among religion, politics, and culture. These broader theories should help us put much of the previous discussion into a more meaningful context. All theories are simplifications of reality, but the best make comprehensible a world of sometimes bewildering complexity. Some consider worldwide forces; others restrict themselves to the United States. Each has its own emphases and makes its own case—and offers illumination in the search to understand religion and political culture in the United States.

Culture Wars

No theory that addresses religion, politics, and culture in the United States today gets more attention than the "culture wars" thesis. It argues that we can understand the contours of religion and politics in America today by recognizing the existence of deep social divisions over values and lifestyles. On the one hand, conservatives stress the importance of traditional values: religion, marriage and family, discipline, and opposition to abortion and gay sexuality. On the other hand, liberals stress the importance of choice and diversity in every area of life, including religion, family, and sexual behavior. Supporters of each perspective are sharply critical of—and feel threatened by—the other point of view. Each is struggling for dominance in American culture.

This division cuts across all sorts of lines in American life, including traditional religious lines. Thus some Catholics today have found themselves aligned with conservative evangelicals on social and political issues. Both groups oppose abortion, support public expressions of faith, criticize secular public schools, and decry the effects of the sexual revolution. Theological and cultural differences remain between orthodox Catholics and evangelical Protestants, to be sure, but many in each group unite in rejecting what they see as a secular assault on traditional values. Similarly, liberal Protestants find they often have more in common with liberal Catholics, Jews, and secular elites than they do with conservatives within their own denominations. They speak a common language of peace and justice, and they identify the great issues of the day as racism, sexism, injustice, and war, rather than themes that resonate on the Right.

A kind of cultural alliance has formed between conservative evangelicals and fundamentalists, some Catholics, and a few ultraorthodox Jews. Activists call this alliance "an ecumenism of orthodoxy." On the other side are liberal Protestants from the old-line denominations, liberal Catholics, most Jews, and a small but highly influential secular segment of the culture who have come together as a "progressive" coalition.

African American denominations often join the liberal alliance, but the fit is not always snug. For example, some leaders of African American Christian denominations helped block the gay-oriented Fellowship of Metropolitan Community Churches from obtaining membership in the National Council of Churches. Similarly, black Muslims join with liberal Protestants on U.S. policy toward Israel, but on abortion, drugs, alcohol, and gay rights they line up with conservative evangelicals and many Catholics. Of course it is important to remember that, although Muslims may agree with Christians on some issues, it would be difficult at best for them to form a strategic alliance.

A similar fault line also separates genders. Conservative evangelical and prolife Catholic women often see themselves deeply at odds with their liberal sisters in mainline churches or Jewish temples. Many female prolife activists judge feminists as adversaries, despite sharing with them a style of political assertiveness that feminists generally applaud. In churches and outside them, feminists believe just as strongly that their conservative sisters are a negative force at best and traitors at worst. Everywhere there is a sense of deep cultural division.

Several scholars advance evidence of a culture war. James Guth and his colleagues have found strong evidence that something akin to a culture wars split does, in fact, exist among many Protestant clergy.[1] Sociologist Robert Wuthnow concludes that a massive restructuring of American religion has occurred that has polarized religious Americans into hostile camps of conservatives and liberals. Not too long ago, he suggests, denominations meant something. To be a Methodist, Presbyterian, Catholic, Lutheran, or Baptist implied that there was a shared religious and ethnic heritage with distinctive customs and beliefs. Today a theological and cultural divide cuts across denominations. It matters more, in terms of political attitudes and behaviors, whether one is a liberal Catholic or a conservative Catholic, or a liberal Methodist or an evangelical Methodist, than whether one is a Methodist or a Catholic. Thus a liberal Methodist will probably feel more comfortable with secular liberals than with fellow Christians who call themselves evangelicals.[2]

This same case is made by James Davison Hunter. In two books, *Culture Wars* and *Before the Shooting Begins,* Hunter articulates the culture wars thesis clearly and then explains how it plays out in a number of areas of American life, including religion and politics.[3] Hunter notes various divisions as they manifest themselves in specific skirmishes—over school curricula, ordinances to recognize gay rights, abortion battles in the states, and the like, especially at the state and local levels.

In popular versions of the culture war thesis, especially those filtered through the media, the clash pits such polar opposites as, say, a fundamentalist preacher with many children and a stay-at-home wife against a pro-choice lesbian member of the National Organization for Women. The fault lines are sometimes that stark, but this analysis is too stereotypical to provide a meaningful analysis.

Imagine instead two women who have some things in common. Both are married, both are college graduates, both are church members, and both are economically comfortable. One woman attends an independent evangelical church, views abortion as morally offensive, and is an avid reader of the conservative religious and political literature found in some Christian bookstores. Deeply alienated from public schools, which she sees as having low academic standards and promoting secular and hedonistic values, she has chosen to home school her children. She is an active member of a home school association, which provides her with information about Christian curricula and ways to avoid being harassed by state education authorities. She sees that she is engaged in a conflict with the "dominant" culture, which includes the movie and television industries, public education, antifamily feminists, gay activists, and the government. She votes Republican.

The other woman, who came of age in the sixties, sees the defining experience of her life as her participation in the civil rights and Vietnam War protests. She is now an active member of a United Methodist congregation known for its "peace and justice" activism. A strong feminist and a supporter of abortion rights, she belongs to several feminist organizations and donates to PACs that support women candidates. She dislikes television preachers such as Jerry Falwell and Pat Robertson, and she fears fundamentalist influence in school board elections. She deplores what she sees as religious attempts to censor books and art. She has gay friends and sympathizes with their struggle for equal rights. To her, the idea of a "dominant culture" means white male businessmen who belong to country clubs. She is a liberal Democrat.

Moreover, there are a variety of prominent figures who take the culture wars seriously but do not confirm the idea of a clear, irreconcilable conflict. Consider Senator Daniel Patrick Moynihan (D–New York). Christian conservatives often praise his arguments in favor of stable families and committed fathers, but Moynihan is no friend of the religious Right on other issues. Or consider Robert Casey, recent Democratic governor of Pennsylvania; his prolife stance puts him firmly on the conservative side of that issue, but he generally stands with liberals on other issues. The division is deep, but it is not always simple.

As Robert Wuthnow notes, despite all the talk of polarization, few people are comfortable with either side of the culture wars. Many are in fact unaware of any culture war. To be sure, many parents—from moderate Catholics to conservative Protestants—view television as unhealthy and get angry when public schools uncritically embrace the latest curriculum fad. They take their children to church and otherwise attempt to counteract the messages purveyed by the pop culture. But they do not necessarily view these actions as battles in some cosmic conflict over the very soul of America. Whether more Americans will embrace the culture wars perspective in the future remains to be seen.[4]

There is also a self-fulfilling quality about discussion of the culture wars. Mutual stereotyping, polarization, and inflamed passions may help create culture wars where none previously existed. Talk of culture wars also undermines the possibility that adversaries may discover common ground. Compromise, that staple of American politics, is hard if one's opponents are enemies bent on destroying one's very way of life. The two hypothetical women described above might agree, in fact, that television is largely trash, that public schools are too lax, or that pornography has an unhealthy influence, but they miss the chance to work together to address such feelings because of the blinding rhetoric of cultural conflict.

Yet it is also true that signs of culture wars in the United States are unmistakable. At root the question is one of the appropriate character of American society. Religion and churches are deeply involved in the struggle over this question. Thus the culture wars theory is essential to any understanding of religion and politics in the United States today. By itself it is not a sufficient guide, but it is without question important.

The Secularization Thesis

While the culture war thesis focuses on today's struggles, the "secularization" thesis takes a somewhat longer view. It suggests that we look away from the events directly before us to connect with broader developments that have served to condition culture, religion, and politics.

Proponents of the secularization thesis argue that religion has declined as secularism has advanced. They contend that this development is an inescapable result of modernity, which has already greatly influenced Western Europe and, to a lesser degree, the United States. As modernity spreads, secularism spreads in its wake—sweeping the influence of religion away. With religion's gradual decline, they conclude, we can expect to see religious involvement with politics decrease in the long run, both in the United States and elsewhere.[5]

The short-run picture may be different. There may be temporary surges in religio-political involvement. Losing out to secularism, some religious groups might try to use politics to stem the tide. If so, such efforts would represent a sort of dying gasp on the part of religious forces. For some secularization analysts, this describes the current situation in the United States. Assorted religious groups with different—even opposing—agendas have hurled themselves into American political life relatively recently. But this may not be a sign of the strength of religion in politics or in any other forum. Instead, for some secularization theorists it is a sign of weakness, a sign of desperate efforts to halt a decline that threatens American religion.

Some classic advocates of the secularization thesis were giants of nineteenth-century European thought. Karl Marx was among them. He was sure that class struggle and the triumph of communism would be the tale of modern life—a tale in which religion would soon be a mercifully finished chapter. Max Weber, the great German sociologist, was another classic secularization theorist. He believed that with modernity would come mighty forces of rationalism and bureaucratization that would defeat organized religion, if not entirely eliminate religious people. Sigmund Freud, the founder of psychoanalysis, also spoke of secularization. Freud was quite interested in religion and religious traditions, especially those of his fellow Jews. Though Freud knew that there was no guarantee religion would fade, he hoped that "the future of an illusion" would prove poor as people came to see that the modern world gave them a chance to be free of religion.[6]

Since secularization theorists take modernization to be the key to the decline of religion, we need to have some sense of what they mean by the term "modernization." Analysts usually include many factors in definitions of this concept, including the scientific way of thinking; modern technological advances; complex economic life; contemporary forms of mass communication and entertainment; and the growth of government bureaucracies and public education. Secularization theorists suggest that in modern societies, rational, scientific approaches dominate, whereas in traditional societies, religious worldviews govern life. In modern societies public policy is dominated by clashes of self-interested individuals and groups pursuing their "rational" interests. Education becomes an engine of secularization as it teaches science and denigrates supernatural explanations. The capitalist marketplace also mutes religious enthusiasms as it captures people in a consumer culture and the workaday corporate world.

There is ample support for the secularization worldview. Religion governs the United States today much less than it does, say, a traditional African or Native American tribe (or than it did in earlier eras of American history). There is no doubt that many Americans today compartmentalize their faith and do not manifest it in many areas of their lives. Many of the major institutions of the United States—giant corporations, public schools and universities, governmental bureaucracies, television networks—now operate on the basis of secular concerns and logic. Often they either ignore religion and the spiritual dimensions or are positively hostile toward them.

Yet in recent years the secularization thesis has come under fire. It has lost some of its luster, in large part because of the amazing resilience of religious faith in the face of secular forces. In the past two decades there has been a notable growth of evangelical commitment in the United States, a resurgence of religious practice in Russia and Eastern Europe, and a major increase in religious energy in many Islamic countries. Religion's demise, once so confidently predicted, has just not taken place in most parts of the world. Nor is there evidence that it is going to vanish anytime soon.

Moreover, in recent years religion has not always been content to remain in a narrow private realm. Religion has been very busy in the larger, public world, challenging secular authorities in places such as the United States, the former East Germany, Iran, Poland, Egypt, and the Philippines. In many places, including the United States, religion may not be as tightly interwoven into most people's lives as it once was, but it has clearly not withered away. Indeed, it may be that the secularization thesis has the situation reversed. Perhaps the "unsecularization"—or even sacralization—of the world is one of the characteristics of the modern age.[7]

The response of those who have been impressed with the secularization view is that religion's current health is temporary. To them, religious vitality is really further proof of secularization's progress through the world, no more than a temporary reaction to the inevitable. Perhaps secularization will proceed, but there are many reasons for doubt, including the fact that the death of religion is now very much overdue. Modernity has infused many corners of the world, but people have often chosen to retain their religions.

There are also variants of the secularization thesis, often as interesting as the theory itself. One is the "elite secularization thesis." In this view, even though religion continues to speak to most human beings, elites and elite institutions have become highly secular. The idea is that the larger secularization thesis applies, but only for one crucial sector of the population:

elites. In the United States a number of theorists advance this analysis. Richard John Neuhaus, for example, uses the metaphor of the "naked public square" to describe how elites have largely banished faith-based, moral arguments from American politics. According to Neuhaus, the language of rights, efficiency, and practicality have crowded out considerations of moral obligation and timeless spiritual truths.[8] This view is echoed in Stephen Carter's influential book *The Culture of Disbelief*, in which he takes American media, law, and education to task for trivializing faith.[9]

This complaint has become part of popular political discourse, especially on the conservative side. Observers from William Bennett to Pat Buchanan to Rush Limbaugh routinely castigate "cultural elites" who denigrate the enduring faith and traditional values of common citizens. They know that there is some evidence that such an elite-mass split exists. For example, though the majority of Americans profess a religious faith, members of the elite press tend to be secular in their outlooks.[10]

The gap between the "secular" elites and "religious" masses, of course, becomes especially pronounced when the popular religion of ordinary people is traditional or fundamentalist. Here the gap becomes a major chasm. Many academics, reporters, media elites, political leaders, and government bureaucrats profess a religious faith, but few are comfortable with born-again evangelicalism, traditional Catholicism, Orthodox Judaism, or revivalist Islam. As the argument goes, Americans with orthodox religious beliefs must now confront hostile elites with the power to shape the schools their children attend, the television and movies they and their children watch, and the government edicts with which they must comply.

One problem with the elite secularization thesis rests, however, in the unevenness of the phenomenon. To be sure, elites in the national news media are highly secular. So are those who dominate the entertainment media, such as television, movies, and most popular music. But elected officials— members of Congress and state legislators, not to mention presidents—do a better job of reflecting the diversity of the population at large.[11] Moreover, the remarkable growth of scholarship and intellectual discourse on religion and society belies the notion of totally hostile elites. There are now several widely cited "elite" journals publishing criticism of other "elites" for their hostility to faith.[12]

Another variant is sociologist David Yamane's neosecularization thesis. Yamane argues that it is erroneous to claim that religion is disappearing from American life. In this sense, the secularization thesis is simply incorrect as a description of the contemporary United States. Yet Yamane insists that tremendous secularization is occurring, as measured by the role religion now plays in individual lives, in American institutions, and in the culture as a whole. The key is to understand that religion, even as it continues to be very much present, nonetheless recedes increasingly to private compartments of American life and culture. For Yamane, the true test of secularization, then, is not the disappearance of religion but its diminishing influence in ordinary lives and institutions, as well as in the broader culture. Observing the United States over its history, such neosecularization becomes clear.[13]

Culture Shift Analysis

Ronald Inglehart has pioneered another approach to understanding secularization today that has gained substantial notice from a variety of scholars. His culture shift analysis dovetails with the secularization thesis in holding that old-time religious understandings are dying. Inglehart explains this slow death by arguing that cultures, especially those of the Western world, are undergoing dramatic changes in response to modernization. Old institutions, old modes of thinking, and the old politics of class and economics are receding (despite occasional revivals). In this modern age of relative plenty, what is now common is a politics concerned with values more than material gain.[14]

The result, however, is not what the standard secularization thesis would predict. Spiritual concerns have not disappeared, nor will they disappear. If anything, spiritual concerns may grow among individuals, but this concern will be made manifest less through formal institutions than through individual journeys of the spirit. It follows for the culture shift analysis that formal religious involvement in politics will decline over time, but that does not mean that the spiritual concerns of individual citizens will decline in their impact on politics and elsewhere. Thus, according to this view, what looks like secularization around us may actually be a shift in the nature of spiritual life from the organized and public to the individual and private. It is not the end of the influence of spiritual concerns but rather a change in how they work.[15]

There is no doubt that students of the generation that came of age during the 1960s and 1970s in the United States find plenty of evidence that something like a culture shift has taken place within their ranks. Wade Clark Roof has portrayed this cohort poignantly as "a generation of seekers."[16] Sociologist Phillip Hammond argues that American religion is actually undergoing a major "disestablishment" that demonstrates how widespread the culture shift has been. As Hammond describes it, American culture now honors choice, expressivism, and individualism in religion as elsewhere. Traditional religions in the United States that focus on duty, institutions, and collective practices face a tremendous challenge and are slowly losing out. Mainline Protestantism in particular is suffering, though it is far from alone in its predicament. All established churches and synagogues are threatened by the movement toward individualistic spirituality.[17]

Many of Wade Clark Roof's "seekers" remain within the realm of traditional organized religions, where they are helping to bring about major changes. For example, one excellent recent study of evangelical Protestant churches that reflect this "new paradigm" (and are booming as a result) notes that members of such churches insist on expressive and contemporary music and other means of worship that allow them to move beyond what they see as rather staid, traditional experiences in order to achieve a deeply felt, individualistic spirituality. They also stress the importance of a personal relationship with Jesus Christ, support the institution of the nuclear family, encourage participation in small groups at church, and radiate a decidedly unstuffy aura. The overall result is very different from traditional mainline churches, which rarely experience such growth any more.[18]

It remains to be seen what the long-term consequences of the experiences of the "seeker" generation will be for religion and politics. As American religion is transformed into an increasingly individualistic spirituality, one might expect a less focused, organized, and unified impact on political life. Thus the politics of religion may become less important over time, just as the secularization thesis suggests (though for quite different reasons). On the other hand, this is not self-evident. After all, if spirituality becomes more important and more deeply valued among more Americans, it is bound to affect their political outlooks and behavior, possibly more intensely—and more widely—than ever before.

Civil Religion

Another perspective that seeks to illuminate the relationship between religion and politics in America is the civil religion thesis. This view contends that the one important religion in the United States is the political religion, the religion of America, of its culture, and of the nation—the civil religion. Those attracted to this thesis agree that the civil religion exists right along with the other religions in the country without challenging them. Civil religion is nonsectarian in its belief that God has blessed the United States, endowed it with special opportunities, and assigned it special responsibilities to do good. It is important, analysts suggest, because it aids in providing stability for the nation. Every nation has a faith of sorts, a belief in itself, a civil religion—and in the United States this is linked to God.

The civil religion thesis downplays the importance of various (perhaps passing) events such as culture wars or evidence of one type of secularization or another. It points us instead toward the existence of enduring connections between government and religion and warns us that the religions that count most in political terms may not be practiced in conventional churches. The idea that there may be a civil religion first received extensive attention because of a 1967 essay by sociologist Robert Bellah. In it, he compares the inaugural addresses of Abraham Lincoln and John F. Kennedy and notes that these two seminal American leaders from different eras both affirmed that the nation had a divine purpose and called upon God to bless the country.[19] Others have since observed how presidential inauguration ceremonies are steeped in religious imagery and how often incoming presidents make reference to God. True to this tradition, and despite their political dissimilarity, both Bill Clinton and Ronald Reagan ended speeches to the nation with the phrase "God bless you and God bless America."[20]

Historian Sidney Mead approaches the idea of civil religion by documenting how a "national religion" grew steadily through the early years of the United States until it was firmly established by the Civil War. As he observes, there are really two kinds of religion in the United States—that of specific religious denominations and what he terms "the American faith" or the civil religion. Both forms, he realizes, are intertwined and mutually supportive. Patriotism in many churches is real, as anyone who has seen the American flag in houses of worship or heard a spirited singing of "God Bless America" can attest. In turn, religious Americans gain affirmation of the importance of their faith when they hear political leaders publicly call on God, when they use currency that affirms "In God We Trust," and when they repeat the Pledge of Allegiance, which proclaims the existence of one nation "under God."[21]

In the end the ultimate question is how to evaluate such analysis. Does the United States have a civil religion? We think there is some real evidence to support the assertion. From Lincoln's sublime vision of the nation as the last best hope on Earth to Reagan's invocation of the Puritan notion of a "city on a hill," civil religious images that suggest America is an agent of the divine with special duties on Earth are evident. And this is a view that many religious leaders like to echo. For decades evangelist Billy Graham has invoked God's blessing on the nation's leaders, institutions, and purposes. Many other religious leaders continue to do so.

There are also signs of civil religious rituals everywhere, such as Fourth of July ceremonies, Memorial Day observances, and that most distinctly civil religious holiday, Thanksgiving. Each marks the calendar with its own blend of religion and patriotism, faith and political history. American civil religion has its own sacred places too, such as the majestic Lincoln Memorial or the hallowed ground of Gettysburg. There are also sacred documents, such as the original copies of the Declaration of Independence and the Constitution. At the National Archives in Washington, pilgrims enter a churchlike atmosphere, which is softly lit and so amazingly quiet that people start whispering upon entering. They walk in a narrow, semicircular corridor until they enter the room containing indestructible glass cases holding these documents for the faithful to venerate.

Finally, there are the prophets and saviors in the American civil religion. In Washington, D.C., one can read prophetic words carved in stone at the Jefferson Memorial or stare in awe at the soaring monument to George Washington. At the very center of the civil religion is Abraham Lincoln, "the martyred Christ of Democracy's passion play."[22] The story of his presidency, of his remarkable maturation and tragic assassination, invokes religious images of Christlike sacrifice and death for the nation's rebirth.

In short, we feel that the United States does have something of a civil religion, though this conclusion is far from universally shared.[23] It is there in the culture, however thinly it may be worn in these increasingly multicultural and fractious times. Perhaps the larger question is whether the civil religion thesis helps us understand religion and politics in the United States. Civil religion does tell us a part of the story. It does tell us something about what may still bind many Americans together politically, but this insight may be decreasing in value as civil religion declines in the face of cultural pluralism and political cynicism. It does not, however, tell us much about—or help us understand—religious voting, religious interest groups, church-state conflicts, or much else in the boiling pot of religion and politics in America.

The Unconventional Partners Thesis

Another perspective on the relationships among culture, religion, and politics is the unconventional partners thesis. This analysis says that religion provides great assistance to the American culture and that the culture in turn greatly assists religion. While it takes some inspiration from the civil religion thesis, the unconventional partners framework is larger and it looks beyond the periodic rituals of civil religion to the deeper, day-to-day cultural patterns of the nation. It posits that religion helps to sustain America's individualistic political culture and its governmental institutions. Religion accomplishes this task not through active engagement in politics but by offering a source of meaning, morality, and community that the culture and government cannot provide. In turn, the government and the culture promote broad religious freedom. But this symbiotic relationship is largely unintentional; hence the "unconventional partners" label.[24]

A very early variant of this theory was put forward by the French statesman-author Alexis de Tocqueville. Observing conditions in America in the early nineteenth century, Tocqueville noted that in his native France the "spirits of religion and of freedom" always marched in opposite directions. Not so in America, where the spirit of liberty and the spirit of religion marched together, supporting and reinforcing each other. Tocqueville became impressed with the extent of political freedom enjoyed by full American citizens (white males). But his European experience taught him that such freedom could easily degenerate into anarchy and then despotism. Moreover, even if such perils were avoided, maximum individual freedom, when left to itself, could promote a materialistic society of individual strivers isolated from their fellow citizens. To his amazement, though, this was not what Tocqueville found in the United States.

The explanation, he concluded, was the crucial role that religion played in instilling moral self-restraint combined with the way churches helped people overcome their isolation. When political freedom implied that a nineteenth-century man could do as he pleased, religion taught him he should not do things that were destructive to his family or the community. Thus religion made liberal democracy possible by instilling the inner mores that prevented the society from plunging into chaos. In turn, religion and churches thrived in the United States because they were relatively free from persecution and unencumbered by the debilitating government paternalism found in Europe.[25] Thus an unintentional symbiosis developed between government and religion.

Of course, the contemporary United States is a far cry from the still-developing republic Tocqueville observed in the 1830s. In many ways American culture is now far more materialistic, skeptical, and focused on individuals. But that has only sharpened the continuing partnership between religion and culture in America. In its modern form, religion helps to sustain a liberal, individualistic society in a paradoxical way: by offering a temporary refuge from the culture. Indeed, there is plenty of evidence that people who turn to organized religion do so because they want it to be—as it sometimes is—different from the world they live in ordinarily. They want a refuge from the enormous burden that is the struggle to live in a society where meaning, morality, and community are often confusing or missing.

It is crucial to understand, however, that the unconventional partners thesis sees people getting involved in organized religion for temporary refuge only, not as a permanent, radical alternative to the broader society, which is something that most participants in organized religion do not desire. Most people want religion to give them just enough communal sharing and spiritual sustenance to enable them to persist in the competitive, individualistic broader culture. Without this kind of refuge, the unconventional partners thesis argues, society might find itself wracked by radical challenges from the Right and the Left. Thus religion sustains the liberal social order by providing what that very order lacks.

To flesh out this theory, let us consider the ways in which religion aids American culture. First, for many citizens, religion provides meaning, a grounding for values in a culture in which such meaning is far from automatically available. Second, it helps provide moral values for a culture in which skepticism and cynicism are pervasive. Finally, it encourages community in a culture that often lacks it. Study after study demonstrates the extent to which people understand religion in precisely these ways, as a place to go in search of meaning, morality, or community. When a religion or a church can offer these things, it flourishes; when it cannot, people drift away. Community and meaning may come in a variety of forms within the capacious realm of American religion. There is no single voice, to say the least, but this very fact is an immense plus for the culture. It means that American religion can and does serve many more people in this pluralistic age than it would were there only one religion in the land.

The other side of the partnership is, of course, how American culture and government assist religion. There are many ways in which they do so, despite illusions that church and state are somehow separate in America. Perhaps the most important form of assistance comes in the generous protection of free exercise that the major American religions enjoy. The First Amendment is alive and well. The fact that both government and culture have some sympathy for religion makes a tremendous difference for the viability of organized religious life in the United States.

Moreover, the courts have sometimes shown a proclivity to extend the government's protective role to minority religions (some of which are controversial). Though the courts' attitudes vary from case to case and from time to time, religious pluralism is a fact in the United States. This pluralism is possible in good part only because the state and the culture have both tacitly accepted it and allowed broad (if not limitless) religious freedom to flourish. This is a tremendous gift not only to specific religions but to religion in general throughout the nation. It is confirmation that religion is important, no matter what form it takes.

At another level organized religion has reaped extraordinary financial advantages from government and the culture on which government rests. As we discussed in Chapter 11, the United States demonstrates a great deal of "multiple establishment," which results in all sorts of concrete financial benefits from aid to church hospitals to freedom from property taxes for churches. There are no definite figures for how much direct or indirect aid religious institutions receive, but it is certainly many billions of dollars. This sort of help matters, but so too does the climate of broad religious freedom. It constitutes the other side of the partnership from which both religion and culture benefit.

This kind of partnership has existed for a long time in the United States. Government may provide more aid today, but that is mainly a reflection of the overall growth of government through American history. Today there is a broader range of religious freedom than was the case in previous eras, but it is an extension of over two centuries of determination, as expressed in the First Amendment, to guarantee religious freedom.

The unconventional partners thesis offers some perspective on conflicts between church and state in the courts and on the activities of religious interest groups. The occasional sound and fury of conflict should not drown out the reality of a continuing partnership among religion, government, and culture. This is not to say that the ordinary aspects of religion and politics—interest groups, voting, reform efforts, and court cases—are meaningless; far from it. They are an important part of the religion and politics story. But the unconventional partners thesis reminds us that their significance must be tempered in light of the deep affinity between religion and culture in the United States. That relationship will remain secure, for better or for worse, just as long as organized religion does not transform itself from a temporary refuge into a permanent enemy of American culture, and as long as those who seek a total separation of religion and government do not fully succeed.

Populism

The unconventional partners thesis tends to discount the importance of religious participation in politics, but this view is not shared by those who are impressed with the frequency and power of religiously based populist movements in American politics. There has been a great deal of religious energy in American politics in the past—as there is today—and some observers stress the role of populist movements in generating much of the resulting political activism.[26]

The link between populism and religion flows in part from the nature of church life in America. Because churches operate in a highly competitive religious marketplace, they live or die on the basis of their popular support. Only churches that tap into the deepest needs, frustrations, or anxieties of their members will thrive. Moreover, unlike the elite membership of most interest groups, church membership is decidedly broader. There is no comparable collective institution in which Americans of all socioeconomic strata participate in such large numbers. Especially in a highly individualistic and mobile society, churches represent one of the few settings in which many people meet—and sometimes discover their common grievances. In spite of some skittishness about political engagement, church-based political movements have allowed segments of the population that are otherwise unable to find a political voice to register their discontent. Local churches become the focal point of community responses to all sorts of threats. They are a place to organize, to develop leadership, and to call upon members for sacrifice.

At the national level, the existence of the religious Right and the political mobilization of African Americans in their churches are the most prominent recent examples of this populist-religious intersection. Both are undeniably expressions of populism that have achieved a far-reaching impact on political party platforms, voter alignment, and presidential politics. That the same theory can accommodate such different movements illuminates its broad utility.

From the civil rights movement of the 1950s and 1960s to the two presidential campaigns of Jesse Jackson in 1984 and 1988, black churches have provided most of the organizational base, leadership cadre, money, and moral support for African American political mobilization. In doing so, various congregations channeled aspirations for equal rights in the 1960s and discontent with economic disparities in the 1980s. Similarly, some conservative white evangelical churches have captured the growing discontent of their members with the "decaying" state of American culture, family breakup, loss of discipline in schools, acceptance of abortion, and the like—and turned these members toward politics as a result. In both instances criticism of the power of "elites" abounds.

By 1988, these two populist movements had gained enough steam to propel the presidential candidacies of Jesse Jackson and Pat Robertson, two ministers who had never held elective office but who enjoyed a strong church base and a loyal following. Despite their ideological differences, both candidates shared much of the traditional populist view of the world. Jackson expressed prophetic outrage at what he viewed as the economic abandonment of working class and poor Americans; Robertson vented his anger against cultural elites, who, he argued, undermined traditional values. Both candidates used their religious charisma to champion "the people" and castigate elites. Moreover, both emphasized to some degree the historic populist blend of economic progressivism and social conservatism.

Jackson's liberal economic and civil rights platform draws on a strong dose of religious fervor and moral traditionalism. He admonishes his followers to heed the Ten Commandments and to shun drugs, sexual promiscuity, and laziness. Robertson's moral conservatism, on the other hand, is mixed with a populist distrust of large banks, economic conglomerates, and elite foreign policy makers. Jackson and Robertson both evoke a populist style in their politics and a characteristic populist mix of ideological perspectives.[27]

As we can see, the populist thesis emphasizes not only the ways churches can vent their discontent but the ways they can infuse the political system with a politics that does not fit neatly into a left-right political spectrum. Moreover, events in other nations suggest that this link between religion and populist uprisings may be a global phenomenon. As such, the theory of populist religion helps us to understand the ways in which religion sometimes taps sentiments that elites do not notice or acknowledge.

Two cautions are in order. First, given the importance of charismatic leadership in mobilizing populist discontent, one must question whether such leaders reflect—or in fact create—popular concerns. Critics assert that both Jackson and Robertson exhibit a tendency to conflate their own ego needs with the aspirations of the communities they claim to represent, a tendency that limits their ability to work within the system. Perhaps the populist style in general expresses discontent better than it fashions realistic remedies.

Second, one must resist taking the populist thesis too far. Many churches are not strategically positioned or inclined to sustain major political efforts; so even if their members experience frustration with current politics, they may not be able to vent that frustration through their churches. Finally, and perhaps most important, it is not clear how often populist sentiments constitute the link between religion and politics in American life. Put another way, how important was the election of 1988 for understanding the dynamics of religion and politics in American life?

Market Theory, Religious Pluralism, and Politics

The most important and most controversial new theory regarding religion and society that matters for the study of religion and politics in the United States is market theory. Its proponents argue that religion's relative strength in every society is largely a function of how much competition there is among religions in a society, and the degree to which that competition is unfettered. According to market theory, which obviously draws on an economic model, religion in the United States should be expected to remain very strong.

This prediction has implications for the continuing political importance of American religion. First, we know that there is intense competition among various religions in the United States. This competition draws people in and provides them with an almost unbelievable variety of religious niches among which to choose. This diversity suits Americans' pluralist tastes. Market model analysts believe that aspects of American religion that are faring poorly, such as Catholicism among Hispanics and mainline Protestantism in general, are just not competing hard enough. Second, religion in the United States is characterized by almost unlimited free competition. While there is plenty of traditional "establishment" religion in the United States, the fact that there is no single official American religion means that government's relationship with it is mostly supportive—and that religious freedom must be extended to all groups. Meanwhile, of course, free exercise of religion, while not limitless in the United States, is broad and deep.

Market theorists compare and contrast the enduring strength of religion in general in the United States with the situation in other nations to illustrate their thesis more fully. The implication for us, of course, is that American religion is therefore clearly able to exert a continuing political force. For example, market theorists note that the intense religious competition that exists today in Latin America and much of Africa is resulting in tremendous growth among a variety of religious groups. They observe, however, that this growth has been possible only when governments have abandoned old alliances with particular religious groups; such arrangements inevitably restricted or even forbade competition.

Market analysts note that outside of the United States, such as in much of Western Europe, religion is weak and in serious decline; consequently, its political impact has also diminished. They explain these developments partly as the result of limited competition fostered by the existence of long-standing government-established churches. This is the case in Scandinavian countries. Whenever religious groups that lack the fire to compete aggressively for souls dominate the scene, all religions pay a steep and inevitable price. Competitive evangelicalism is the essential ingredient for the success of any religious group, according to market theorists. Tired, insular religions, often propped up by government, face serious decline and an attending loss of political influence.[28]

Toward the Future

Which of these theories, alone or in combination with others, will best serve to illuminate the relationship between religion and politics in the United States in the next century remains to be discovered. Perhaps none of them will prove very useful. They cannot explain everything, nor can they even begin to do so, though they are useful in that they give us perspective. Moreover, what the future will produce in terms of the theory and practice of religion and politics in the United States may surprise all of us. After all, who predicted the rise of the religious Right in the 1980s? Who expected that an African American minister named Jesse Jackson would play a major role in electoral politics in 1984 and 1988? Who could have known in 1960 that Catholics and evangelical Protestants would one day be forming political alliances? And who thought that the religious Right, after its collapse in the late 1980s, would reemerge in a new and more impressive form? The subject of religion and politics in America, because it is so dynamic, defies any theoretical attempt to capture it fully. But that should not deter us from trying to understand its contribution to the life and culture of the United States.

Further Reading

Bruce, Steve. *Religion and Modernization.* New York: Oxford University Press, 1992. A helpful introduction to secularization theory.

Finke, Roger, and Rodney Stark. *The Churching of America, 1776–1990: Winners and Losers in Our Religious Economy.* New Brunswick, NJ: Rutgers University Press, 1992. The central articulation of the market model.

Fowler, Robert Booth. *Unconventional Partners: Religion and Liberal Culture in the United States*. Grand Rapids, MI: Eerdmans, 1989. Contemporary account of unconventional partners thesis.

Hertzke, Allen. *Echoes of Discontent: Jesse Jackson, Pat Robertson, and the Resurgence of Populism*. Washington, DC: CQ Press, 1993. Contemporary account of populist thesis.

Hunter, James Davison. *Culture Wars: The Struggle to Define America*. New York: Basic Books, 1991. Leading version of culture wars argument.

Inglehart, Ronald. *Culture Shift in Advanced Industrial Society*. Princeton, NJ: Princeton University Press, 1990. Best account of culture shift theory.

Richey, Russell, and Donald Jones, eds. *American Civil Religion*. New York: Harper and Row, 1974. A set of interesting views on civil religion theory.

Wuthnow, Robert. *The Restructuring of American Religion: Society and Faith Since World War Two*. Princeton, NJ: Princeton University Press, 1988. Valuable reflections on religion in the United States.

Notes

Chapter 1

1. See Perry Miller, *Errand into the Wilderness* (Cambridge, MA: The Belknap Press of Harvard University Press, 1956); and Edmund Morgan, *The Puritan Dilemma: The Story of John Winthrop* (Boston: Little, Brown, 1958).

2. A. James Reichley, *Religion in American Public Life* (Washington, DC: Brookings Institution, 1985).

3. Sydney Ahlstrom, *A Religious History of the American People* (New Haven, CT: Yale University Press, 1972); and Reichley, *Religion in American Public Life.*

4. This point is made by Barry Allen Shain, *The Myth of American Individualism: The Protestant Origins of American Political Thought* (Princeton, NJ: Princeton University Press, 1994).

5. Alexis de Tocqueville, *Democracy in America,* trans. George Lawrence and ed. J. P. Mayer and A. P. Kerr (Garden City, NY: Doubleday/Anchor, 1969).

6. Shain, *The Myth of American Individualism.*

7. See Allen D. Hertzke, *Echoes of Discontent: Jesse Jackson, Pat Robertson, and the Resurgence of Populism* (Washington, DC: CQ Press, 1993), chap. 3.

8. Robert Booth Fowler, *Unconventional Partners: Religion and Liberal Culture in the United States* (Grand Rapids, MI: Eerdmans, 1989).

9. Mark Noll, ed., *One Nation Under God? Christian Faith and Political Action in America* (San Francisco: Harper, 1988).

10. Ahlstrom, *A Religious History of the American People.*

11. Leonard Levy, *The Establishment Clause: Religion and the First Amendment* (New York: Macmillan, 1986).

12. Jon Butler, *Awash in a Sea of Faith: Christianizing the American People* (Cambridge, MA: Harvard University Press, 1990).

13. Andrew Greeley, *The Denominational Society: A Sociological Approach to Religion in America* (Glenview, IL: Scott, Foresman, 1972); Ahlstrom, *A Religious History of the American People*; Will Herberg, *Protestant-Catholic-Jew* (New York: Doubleday, 1955).

14. Sydney Mead, *The Lively Experiment: The Shaping of Christianity in America* (New York: Harper and Row, 1963), 35.

15. Michael Malbin, *Religion and Politics: The Intentions of the Authors of the First Amendment* (Washington, DC: American Enterprise Institute, 1978); Gary Glenn, "Forgotten Purposes of the First Amendment Religion Clause," *Review of Politics* 49 (1987), 340–366.

16. Steve Rabey, "Pensacola Outpouring Keeps Gushing," *Christianity Today* (March 3, 1997), 54–57; Leo Sandon, "Pentecost in Pensacola: The Brownsville Revival," *Christian Century* (August 27, 1997), 748–749; Kenneth L. Woodward, "Living in the Holy Spirit," *Newsweek* (April 13, 1998), 54–60.

17. Ahlstrom, *A Religious History of the American People*, 501–509.

18. Ibid.

19. Anson Phelps Stokes, *Church and State in the United States*, vol. 2 (New York: Harper, 1950), 275–285.

20. *The World Almanac and Book of Facts* (Mahwah, NJ: K-III Communications, 1997), 651.

21. Phillip Hammond, *The Protestant Presence in Twentieth Century America: Religion and Political Culture* (Albany: State University of New York Press, 1992).

22. Stokes, *Church and State in the United States*, 285–292.

23. Roger Finke and Rodney Stark, *The Churching of America, 1776–1990: Winners and Losers in Our Religious Economy* (New Brunswick, NJ: Rutgers University Press, 1992).

24. Donald E. Miller, *Reinventing Protestantism: Christianity in the New Millennium* (Berkeley: University of California Press, 1997).

25. Robert N. Bellah, Richard Madsen, William M. Sullivan, Ann Swidler, and Steven M. Tipton, *Habits of the Heart: Individualism and Commitment in American Life* (New York: Harper and Row, 1985); Jack Miles, "Religion Makes a Comeback (Belief to Follow)," *New York Times Magazine* (December 7, 1997), 56–59.

26. Dean M. Kelley, *Why Conservative Churches Are Growing: A Study in Sociology of Religion* (San Francisco: Harper, 1972).

27. Finke and Stark, *The Churching of America*, 115.

28. William D'Antonio, ed., *Laity, American and Catholic: Transforming the Church* (Kansas City, MO: Sheed and Ward, 1996).

29. Andrew Greeley, "Defection Among Hispanics (Updated)," *America* (September 27, 1997), 12–14.

30. See Ahlstrom, *A Religious History of the American People*; Reichley, *Religion in American Public Life*; William McLoughlin, *Revivals, Awakening, and Reform: An Essay on Religion and Social Change in America, 1607–1977* (Chicago: University of Chicago Press, 1978).

31. Reichley, *Religion in American Public Life*, 74.

32. Luke Eugene Ebersole, *Church Lobbying in the Nation's Capital* (New York: Macmillan, 1951).

33. Ahlstrom, *A Religious History of the American People*, 657.

34. Ibid., 653–654.

35. Norman H. Clark, *Deliver Us from Evil: An Interpretation of American Prohibition* (New York: Norton, 1976).

36. Ibid.

37. Ibid.

38. Ibid.

39. This claim is supported by Reichley, *Religion in American Public Life*; McLoughlin, *Revivals, Awakening, and Reform*; Robert Shalhope, *The Roots of Democracy: American Thought and Culture, 1760–1800* (Boston: Twayne, 1990); and Shain, *The Myth of American Individualism*.

40. Nathan O. Hatch, *The Democratization of American Christianity* (New Haven, CT: Yale University Press, 1989).

41. As quoted in Finke and Stark, *The Churching of America*, 86.

42. The literature on the populist movement, including its religious dimensions, is extensive and growing. It is summarized by Hertzke, *Echoes of Discontent*, chap. 2.

43. As quoted in John D. Hicks, *The Populist Revolt: A History of the Farmers' Alliance and the People's Party* (Lincoln: University of Nebraska Press, 1961).

44. This point is developed more fully in Hertzke, *Echoes of Discontent*, chap. 2.

45. Paul Kleppner, *The Cross of Culture: A Social Analysis of Midwestern Politics, 1850–1900* (New York: Free Press, 1970).

46. Hertzke, *Echoes of Discontent*.

Chapter 2

1. Robert Bezilla, ed., *Religion in America: 1992–1993* (Princeton, NJ: Princeton Religion Research Center, 1993).

2. Larry Witham, "America's Faith in God Surged During Past Decade," *Washington Times* (January 4, 1998), 1.

3. George Gallup Jr., *The Gallup Poll: Public Opinion 1995* (Wilmington, DE: Scholarly Resources, 1996), 260.

4. George Gallup Jr., *The Gallup Poll: Public Opinion 1996* (Wilmington, DE: Scholarly Resources, 1997), 260.

5. Bezilla, *Religion in America: 1992–1993*.

6. James Davison Hunter, *Culture Wars: The Struggle to Define America* (New York: Basic Books, 1991); John C. Green, James L. Guth, Corwin E. Smidt, and Lyman A. Kellstedt, *Religion and the Culture Wars: Dispatches from the Front* (Lanham, MD: Rowman and Littlefield, 1996).

7. George Gallup Jr., *Religion in America, 50 Years: 1935–1985*, The Gallup Report No. 236 (May 1985).

8. National Opinion Research Center (NORC) data, as presented in *American Enterprise* (November–December 1992), 93–97.

9. George Bishop, "The Religious Worldview and American Beliefs About Human Origins," *The Public Perspective* (August/September 1998).

10. Gallup, *Religion in America, 50 Years*.

11. Bezilla, *Religion in America: 1992–1993*.

12. Gallup, *Religion in America, 50 Years*.

13. Gallup, *The Gallup Poll: Public Opinion 1995*, 261.

14. Bezilla, *Religion in America: 1992–1993*.

15. *Emerging Trends* (Princeton, NJ: Princeton Religion Research Center, June 1988).

16. *Religion in America: Approaching the Year 2000*, Princeton Religion Research Center 1990 Report (Princeton, NJ: Princeton Religion Research Center, 1990).

17. Bezilla, *Religion in America: 1992–1993*.

18. See Philip Johnson, *Darwin on Trial* (Lanham, MD: Regnery Gateway, 1991).

19. Gallup, *The Gallup Poll: Public Opinion 1996*, 260.

20. Andrew Greeley, *The Denominational Society: A Sociological Approach to Religion in America* (Glenview, IL: Scott, Foresman, 1972).

21. NORC data, in *American Enterprise*.

22. Gallup, *The Gallup Poll: Public Opinion 1996*, 260.

23. Gallup figures on church attendance are disputed by C. Kirk Hadaway, Penny Long Marler, and Mark Chaves, "What the Polls Don't Show: A Closer Look at U.S. Church Attendance," *American Sociological Review* 58 (1993), 741–752. See also C. Kirk Hadaway and Penny Long, "Did You Really Go to Church This Week? Behind the Poll Data," *Christian Century* (May 6, 1998), 472–475.

24. See George Gallup Jr. and Jim Castelli, *The People's Religion: American Faith in the 90's* (New York: Macmillan, 1989).

25. This argument is made by Allen D. Hertzke, *Echoes of Discontent: Jesse Jackson, Pat Robertson, and the Resurgence of Populism* (Washington, DC: CQ Press, 1993). See also Benjamin Cheever, "God or BMW," *New York Times Magazine* (December 7, 1997), 42–44.

26. Hampton Sides, "The Calibration of Belief," *New York Times Magazine* (December 7, 1997), 92–95.

27. David Larson and S. Larson, *The Forgotten Factor in Physical and Mental Health: What Does the Research Show?* (Arlington, VA: National Institute for Healthcare Research, 1992).

28. Barbara Dafoe Whitehead, "Dan Quayle Was Right," *Atlantic Monthly* (April 1993), 47–68.

29. NORC data, in *American Enterprise*.

30. Sidney Verba, Kay Lehman Schlozman, and Henry E. Brady, *Voice and Equality: Civic Voluntarism in American Politics* (Cambridge, MA: Harvard University Press, 1995).

31. Robert D. Putnam, *Making Democracy Work: Civic Traditions in Modern Italy* (Princeton, NJ: Princeton University Press, 1993).

32. Kenneth D. Wald, Dennis E. Owen, and Samuel S. Hill Jr., "Churches as Political Communities," *American Political Science Review* 82 (June 1988), 531–548; Kenneth D. Wald, Dennis E. Owen, and Samuel S. Hill Jr., "Political Cohesion in Churches," *Journal of Politics* 52 (March 1990), 197–215; Christopher P. Gilbert, *The Impact of Churches on Political Behavior: An Empirical Study* (Westport, CT: Greenwood Press, 1993).

33. *Religion Watch* (June 1997), 4.

34. *The World Almanac and Book of Facts* (Mahwah, NJ: K-III Communications, 1997), 651.

35. Stephen Monsma, "Public Money and Religiously Based Nonprofit Organizations: The Church-State Dance" (paper presented at the annual meeting of the American Political Science Association, New York, 1994).

36. Ibid.

37. For an extensive discussion of the choices clergy make about political participation in one American city, see Laura R. Olson, *Filled with Spirit and Power: Protestant Clergy in Politics* (Albany: State University of New York Press, forthcoming).

38. Aldon D. Morris, *The Origins of the Civil Rights Movement* (New York: Free Press, 1984).

39. On the religious experiences of gay men, see Brian Bouldrey, ed., *Wrestling with the Angel: Faith and Religion in the Lives of Gay Men* (New York: Free Press, 1995).

40. Gallup, *The Gallup Poll: Public Opinion 1995*, 261, puts the Catholic population at 23 percent, and other surveys put it as high as 27 percent, so elsewhere in the text we sometimes use a figure of 25 percent for the Catholic population. The Gallup figure for total Protestants may also contain a number of only nominally religious individuals, as we suggest in Chapter 4.

41. This electoral breakdown is provided by Lyman Kellstedt, John C. Green, James L. Guth, and Corwin Smidt, "It's the Culture, Stupid! 1992 and Our Political Future," *First Things* (April 1994), 28–33; David Leege, "The Decomposition of the Religious Vote: A Comparison of White, Non-Hispanic Catholics with other Ethnoreligious Groups, 1960–1992" (paper presented at the annual meeting of the American Political Science Association, Washington, DC, 1993); and John C. Green, "Religion, Social Issues, and the Christian Right: Assessing the 1992 Presidential Election" (paper presented at the Ethics and Public Policy Center, Washington, DC, 1993).

42. Gallup, *The Gallup Poll: Public Opinion 1996*, 260.

43. On InterVarsity, see http://www.gospelcom.net/iv; on Campus Crusade, see http://www.uscm.org. Religion on college campuses also reflects the tremendous pluralism of American religion in general. See Diane Winston, "Campuses Are a Bellwether for Society's Religious Revival," *The Chronicle of Higher Education* (January 16, 1998), A60.

44. Laura R. Olson, "Bill Clinton's Strategic Use of Religious and Family Rhetoric: The Co-Optation of Partisan Symbolism" (paper presented at the annual meeting of the Midwest Political Science Association, Chicago, 1997).

45. William Martin, *With God on Our Side: The Rise of the Religious Right in America* (New York: Broadway Books, 1996).

46. Gallup, *The Gallup Poll: Public Opinion 1996*, 260.

47. Ibid.

48. Duane M. Oldfield, "The Christian Right in Civil Rights Clothing: The Racial Rhetoric of the Christian Right" (paper presented at the annual meeting of the American Political Science Association, Washington, DC, 1997).

49. Joel A. Carpenter, *Revive Us Again: The Reawakening of American Fundamentalism* (New York: Oxford University Press, 1997); Mark Dalhouse, *An Island in the Lake of Fire: Bob Jones University, Fundamentalism, and the Separatist Movement* (Athens: University of Georgia Press, 1996).

50. For a detailed discussion of Pentecostalism in one context, see Margaret M. Poloma, *The Assemblies of God at the Crossroads* (Knoxville: University of Tennessee Press, 1989). See also Kenneth L. Woodward, "Living in the Holy Spirit," *Newsweek* (April 13, 1998).

51. For a fine historical discussion of fundamentalism in the United States in the 1930s and 1940s, see Carpenter, *Revive Us Again*.

52. See Woodward, 1998.

53. On this topic, see James F. Findlay Jr., *Church People in the Struggle: The National Council of Churches and the Black Freedom Movement, 1950–1970* (New York: Oxford University Press, 1993).

54. http://www.esa-online.org; see also Ronald J. Sider, *Rich Christians in an Age of Hunger: Moving from Affluence to Generosity* (Dallas, TX: Word Publishing, 1997).

55. For a fine discussion of the Christian Right, see Clyde Wilcox, *Onward Christian Soldiers? The Religious Right in American Politics* (Boulder, CO: Westview, 1996).

56. Harold E. Quinley, *The Prophetic Clergy: Social Activism Among Protestant Ministers* (New York: Wiley, 1974).

57. Laura R. Olson, "The Impact of Neighborhood Socioeconomic Status on the Political Participation of Protestant Clergy" (paper presented at the annual meeting of the Midwest Political Science Association, Chicago, 1997); Sue E. S. Crawford and Laura R. Olson, "Clergy as Political Actors in Urban Contexts" (paper presented at the annual meeting of the Midwest Political Science Association, Chicago, 1998).

58. Kenneth D. Wald, *Religion and Politics in the United States*, 3d ed. (Washington, DC: CQ Press, 1997), chap. 4.

59. Jeffrey Hadden, *The Gathering Storm in the Churches* (Garden City, NY: Doubleday, 1969); A. James Reichley, *Religion in American Public Life* (Washington, DC: Brookings Institution, 1985); James L. Adams, *The Growing Church Lobby in Washington* (Grand Rapids, MI: Eerdmans, 1970); Quinley, *The Prophetic Clergy*.

60. Hadden, *The Gathering Storm in the Churches*.

61. Phillip Hammond, *The Protestant Presence in Twentieth-Century America: Religion and Political Culture* (Albany: State University Press of New York, 1992).

62. Dean M. Kelley, *Why Conservative Churches Are Growing: A Study in Sociology of Religion* (San Francisco: Harper, 1977); Roger Finke and Rodney Stark, *The Churching of America, 1776–1990: Winners and Losers in Our Religious Economy* (New Brunswick, NJ: Rutgers University Press, 1992); Robert Wuthnow, *The Crisis in the Churches* (New York: Oxford University Press, 1996).

63. Laurie Goodstein, "Pastor to the President Says Morality Includes One's Courage and Caring," *New York Times* (March 1, 1998), A16; Jay Nordlinger, "Clinton's Man in the Pulpit," *Weekly Standard* (March 16, 1998), 19–20.

64. See Wuthnow, *The Crisis in the Churches*. Some observers do see hope for the mainline. Consider as an example Milton Coalter, *Vital Signs: The Promise of Modern Protestantism* (Grand Rapids, MI: Eerdmans, 1996).

65. Richard John Neuhaus, *The Catholic Moment: The Paradox of the Church in the Postmodern World* (San Francisco: Harper and Row, 1987).

66. See John Courtney Murray, *We Hold These Truths: Catholic Reflections on the American Proposition* (New York: Sheed and Ward, 1960). Murray concluded that the American experiment, properly understood, was compatible with Church teachings.

67. Samuel Huntington, *The Third Wave: Democratization in the Late Twentieth Century* (Norman: University of Oklahoma Press, 1991).

68. Peter Steinfels, "When is a Catholic Not a Catholic?" *New York Times Magazine* (December 7, 1997), 63–65.

69. Finke and Stark, *The Churching of America*.

70. Andrew Greeley, "Defection Among Hispanics (Updated)," *America* (September 27, 1997), 12–14. See also William D'Antonio, ed., *Laity, American and Catholic: Transforming the Church* (Kansas City, MO: Sheed and Ward, 1996).

71. J. J. Goldberg, *Jewish Power: Inside the American Jewish Establishment* (Reading, MA: Addison-Wesley, 1996); Bernard M. Lazerwitz, *Jewish Choices: American Jewish Denominationalism* (Albany: State University of New York Press, 1988).

72. Gallup, *The Gallup Poll: Public Opinion 1995*, 261.

73. Rodger Kamenetz, "Unorthodox Jews Rummage Through the Orthodox Tradition," *New York Times* (December 7, 1997), 84–86.

74. On this point see Lazerwitz et al., *Jewish Choices*.

75. Robert Wuthnow, *The Restructuring of American Religion: Society and Faith Since World War Two* (Princeton, NJ: Princeton University Press, 1998); Hunter, *Culture Wars*; Green et al., *Religion and the Culture Wars*.

76. Wuthnow, *The Restructuring of American Religion*.

Chapter 3

1. For an account of the formative years, see Luke Eugene Ebersole, *Church Lobbying in the Nation's Capital* (New York: Macmillan, 1951).

2. Daniel J. B. Hofrenning, *In Washington but Not of It: The Prophetic Politics of Religious Lobbyists* (Philadelphia: Temple University Press, 1995).

3. A fuller development of strategies may be found in Allen D. Hertzke, *Representing God in Washington: The Role of Religious Lobbies in the American Polity* (Knoxville: University of Tennessee Press, 1988).

4. Michael Farris, president of the Home School Legal Defense Association, sounded the alarm on February 21, 1994, when a provision was added to H.R. 6 (The Improving America's Schools Act of 1994) that would have required private and home school teachers to be state-certified in every subject they teach. Fearing this would put most home schoolers out of business, Farris's group, allied with Focus on the Family, the Christian Coalition, Concerned Women for America, and the Family Research Council, blanketed Congress with mail. The House responded by voting 424–1 to strip the provision. See Scott DeNicola, "Ouch: Capitol Hill's Meddling with Home Schoolers Provokes a Stinging Rebuke It Won't Soon Forget," *Focus on the Family Citizen* (May 16, 1994).

5. See, for example, http://www.cc.org.

6. S. Robert Lichter, Stanley Rothman, and Linda S. Lichter, *The Media Elite* (Bethesda, MD: Adler, 1986). In this controversial work the authors argue that elite journalists are in fact highly secular in their behavior and attitudes.

7. Lydia Saad, "Issues Referendum Reveals Populist Leanings," *The Gallup Poll Monthly* (May 1996), 2–6.

8. See Hertzke, *Representing God in Washington*.

9. http://ncccusa.org.

10. Allen D. Hertzke, "An Assessment of the Mainline Churches Since 1945," in James E. Wood Jr. and Derek Davis, eds., *The Role of Religion in the Making of Public Policy* (Waco, TX: Dawson Institute of Church-State Studies, 1991).

11. *Sherbert* v. *Verner* 374 US 398 (1963).

12. "Remarks on Signing the Religious Freedom Restoration Act of 1993," November 16, 1993, *Presidential Documents*, Administration of William J. Clinton, 2377–2378.

13. This model is a revised version of one developed by Robert Booth Fowler, *Religion and Politics in America* (Metuchen, NJ: Scarecrow Press, 1985).

14. Lawrence Kersten, *The Lutheran Ethic: The Impact of Religion on Laymen and Clergy* (Detroit, MI: Wayne State University Press, 1970).

15. James L. Guth, John C. Green, Corwin E. Smidt, Lyman A. Kellstedt, and Margaret M. Poloma, *The Bully Pulpit: The Politics of Protestant Clergy* (Lawrence: University Press of Kansas, 1997).

16. This is a charge made frequently about liberal Protestant churches. See Jeffrey Hadden, *The Gathering Storm in the Churches* (Garden City, NY: Doubleday, 1969); Hertzke, "An Assessment of the Mainline Churches Since 1945," in Wood and Davis, *The Role of Religion*.

17. Sidney Verba, Kay Lehman Schlozman, and Henry E. Brady, *Voice and Equality: Civic Voluntarism in American Society* (Cambridge, MA: Harvard University Press, 1995).

18. James M. Wall, "Setting an Antipoverty Agenda," *Christian Century* (April 15, 1998), 387–388.

19. James F. Findlay Jr., "Religion and Politics in the Sixties: The Churches and the Civil Rights Act of 1964," *Journal of American History* 77 (June 1990), 66–92.

20. James F. Findlay Jr., *Church People in the Struggle: The National Council of Churches and the Black Freedom Movement, 1950–1970* (New York: Oxford University Press, 1993).

21. James Adams, *The Growing Church Lobby in Washington* (Grand Rapids, MI: Eerdmans, 1970), 10.

22. Findlay, "Religion and Politics in the Sixties."

23. Hertzke, "An Assessment of the Mainline Churches Since 1945," in Wood and Davis, *The Role of Religion*.

24. See Hadden, *The Gathering Storm in the Churches*; Hertzke, "An Assessment of the Mainline Churches Since 1945," in Wood and Davis, *The Role of Religion*.

25. See Hertzke, *Representing God in Washington*.

26. Laura R. Olson, *Filled with Spirit and Power: Protestant Clergy in Politics* (Albany: State University of New York Press, forthcoming); Laura R. Olson, "The Impact of Neighborhood Socioeconomic Status on the Political Participation of Protestant Clergy" (paper presented at the annual meeting of the Midwest Political Science Association, Chicago, 1997); Sue E. S. Crawford, *Clergy at Work in the Secular City* (Ph.D. diss., Indiana University, 1995); Sue E. S. Crawford and Laura R. Olson, "Clergy as Political Actors in Urban Contexts" (paper presented at the annual meeting of the Midwest Political Science Association, Chicago, 1998).

27. http://www.tialliance.org.

28. Liberation theology, which originated in Latin America, teaches that churches must work to liberate those who are oppressed by economic and political inequality. See Paul E. Sigmund, *Liberation Theology at the Crossroads* (New York: Oxford University Press, 1990).

29. William D'Antonio, ed., *Laity, American and Catholic: Transforming the Church* (Kansas City, MO: Sheed and Ward, 1996).

30. See Timothy A. Byrnes and Mary Segers, *The Catholic Church and Abortion Politics: A View from the States* (Boulder, CO: Westview, 1991).

31. See Mary Ann Glendon, *Abortion and Divorce in Western Law* (Cambridge, MA: Harvard University Press, 1987).

32. For a good history of this case, see Edward M. Gaffney Jr., "The Abortion Rights Mobilization Case: Political Advocacy and Tax Exemption of Churches," in Wood and Davis, *The Role of Religion*.

33. This point is made on the basis of national survey data as analyzed in Hertzke, *Representing God in Washington*, chap. 5.

34. See Byrnes and Segers, *The Catholic Church and Abortion Politics*.

35. Todd S. Purdum, "President Vetoes Measure Banning Type of Abortion," *New York Times* (April 11, 1996), A1; James Bennet, "Clinton Again Vetoes Measure to Ban a Method of Abortion," *New York Times* (October 11, 1997), A9.

36. For an excellent overview of various aspects of just war theory, see Terry Nardin, ed., *The Ethics of War and Peace: Religious and Secular Perspectives* (Princeton, NJ: Princeton University Press, 1996).

37. Kenneth Wald notes that most Catholics had not read the document. Still, the extensive discussion surrounding it in parishes and the news media, along with the distribution of summary pamphlets, apparently succeeded in shifting Catholic opinion in a more dovish direction (if only temporarily). See Kenneth Wald, "Religious Elites and Public Opinion," *Review of Politics* 54 (Winter 1992), 112–143.

38. James McCormick, "Congressional Voting on the Nuclear Freeze Resolutions," *American Politics Quarterly* 13 (January 1985), 122–134.

39. Hertzke, *Representing God in Washington*, 178.

40. For an excellent discussion of the churches and the Gulf War, see Andrew R. Murphy, "The Mainline Churches and Political Activism," *Soundings* (Winter 1993), 525–549; James Turner Johnson and George Weigel, *Just War and the Gulf War* (Washington, DC: Ethics and Public Policy Center, 1991). Johnson and Weigel argue that the Gulf War did meet just war criteria, much along the lines that Bush did in his speech to religious broadcasters. What weakened the Catholic Conference's influence, in part, was the natural ambiguity inherent in deciding whether criteria are met or not.

41. Ruth Wallace, *They Call Her Pastor: A New Role for Catholic Women* (Albany: State University of New York Press, 1992).

42. This is how their lobbyist put it. See Hertzke, *Representing God in Washington*.

43. http://www.aipac.org; Thomas Friedman, "Jewish Lobbyist Ousted for Slurs," *New York Times* (June 29, 1993), A6.

44. Ronald R. Stockton, "Christian Zionism: Prophecy and Public Opinion," *Middle East Journal* 41 (Spring 1987), 234–253.

45. AIPAC President David Steiner, for example, was forced to resign in November 1992 after he bragged about the organization's influence over the selection of President-elect Clinton's cabinet. Not long afterward, the vice president of AIPAC was censured for his criticism of Israeli Prime Minister Yitzhak

Rabin's consideration of trading land for peace with Syria. Finally and most dramatically, the organization's powerful executive director, Thomas Dine, was forced to resign in 1993 amid charges that he slandered fellow Jews. Basking in his reputation as one of the most feared lobbyists in Washington, Dine may have simply gotten careless when he referred in an interview to the perception that Orthodox Jews were "smelly" and "low class" (a reflection of a religious and class schism within Jewish circles). This revelation came on the heels of reports that AIPAC had assembled an enemies list of domestic politicians, such as Jesse Jackson, deemed hostile to Israel. See Friedman, "Jewish Lobbyist Ousted for Slurs."

46. See Matthew C. Moen, *The Christian Right and Congress* (Tuscaloosa: University of Alabama Press, 1989); and Matthew C. Moen, *The Transformation of the Christian Right* (Tuscaloosa: University of Alabama Press, 1992).

47. Robert P. Dugan Jr., *Winning the New Civil War* (Portland, OR: Multnomah Press, 1991).

48. For a good historical account of the Christian Coalition, see Justin Watson, *The Christian Coalition: Dreams of Restoration, Demands for Recognition* (New York: St. Martin's, 1997).

49. John B. Judis, "Unchristian: Partisan and Political Christian Coalition," *New Republic* (July 1, 1996), 8–10; Ceci Connolly and Dan Balz, "The Christian Coalition, Born Again," *Washington Post National Weekly Edition* (January 5, 1998), 15; Michael J. Gerson, "Christian Coalition in Unprecedented Crisis," *U.S. News & World Report* (February 16, 1998), 33–36.

50. Mark J. Rozell and Clyde Wilcox, eds., *God at the Grass Roots: The Christian Right in the 1994 Elections* (Lanham, MD: Rowman and Littlefield, 1995); Mark J. Rozell and Clyde Wilcox, eds., *God at the Grass Roots, 1996: The Christian Right in the 1996 Elections* (Lanham, MD: Rowman and Littlefield, 1997).

51. Connolly and Balz, "The Christian Coalition, Born Again," 15.

52. Laurie Goodstein, "Conservative Leader Takes on G.O.P.," *New York Times* (February 12, 1998), A21.

53. Fred Barnes, "Bauer Power," *Weekly Standard* (December 22, 1997), 18–22; Connolly and Balz, "The Christian Coalition, Born Again"; Gerson, "Christian Coalition in Unprecedented Crisis"; Patrick B. McGuigan, "Bauer Calls Race a Possibility," *Daily Oklahoman* (February 19, 1998), 4; Bob Jones IV, "Focus on a Family Feud," *World* (February 28, 1998), 12–15.

Chapter 4

1. See Allen D. Hertzke, *Echoes of Discontent: Jesse Jackson, Pat Robertson, and the Resurgence of Populism* (Washington, DC: CQ Press, 1993). Pat Robertson was not popular with Southern Baptists and remains highly controversial among many other born-again Christians.

2. Ibid., 3.

3. See A. James Reichley, *Religion in American Public Life* (Washington, DC: Brookings Institution, 1985).

4. See Paul Kleppner, *Continuity and Change in Electoral Politics, 1893–1928* (Westport, CT: Greenwood, 1987), and *The Cross of Culture: A Social Analysis of Midwestern Politics, 1850–1900* (New York: Free Press, 1970).

5. Robert Booth Fowler, *Religion and Politics in America* (Metuchen, NJ: Scarecrow Press, 1985), chap. 3.

6. For an illuminating discussion of these trends, see John Green, Lyman Kellstedt, James Guth, and Corwin Smidt, "Who Elected Clinton: A Collision of Values," *First Things* (August/September 1997), 35–40.

7. For an excellent summary of the New Deal coalition, see Everett Ladd Jr. with Charles D. Hadley, *Transforming the American Party System: Political Coalitions from the New Deal to the 1970s,* 2d ed. (New York: W. W. Norton, 1975).

8. Lyman A. Kellstedt, John C. Green, James L. Guth, and Corwin E. Smidt, "Has Godot Finally Arrived? Religion and Realignment," in John C. Green, James L. Guth, Corwin E. Smidt, and Lyman A. Kellstedt, eds., *Religion and the Culture Wars: Dispatches from the Front* (Lanham, MD: Rowman and Littlefield, 1996), 291–299; Green et al., "Who Elected Clinton."

9. Ladd and Hadley, *Transforming the American Party System.*

10. Ibid., chap. 1.

11. Ronald Inglehart, *The Silent Revolution: Changing Values and Political Styles Among Western Publics* (Princeton, NJ: Princeton University Press, 1977).

12. Lyman A. Kellstedt, John C. Green, James L. Guth, and Corwin E. Smidt, "Religious Voting Blocs in the 1992 Election: The Year of the Evangelical?" in Green et al., eds., *Religion and the Culture Wars,* 267–290; Green et al., "Who Elected Clinton." See also Robert Wuthnow, *The Restructuring of American Religion: Society and Faith Since World War Two* (Princeton, NJ: Princeton University Press, 1988); James Davison Hunter, *Culture Wars: The Struggle to Define America* (New York: Basic Books, 1991).

13. These estimates of the electorate are from Voter Research Survey (VRS) exit polls, as reported in the *New York Times* (November 5, 1992), B6.

14. John Green, "Religion, Social Issues, and the Christian Right," in Michael Cromartie, ed., *Disciples and Democracy: Religious Conservatives and the Future of American Politics* (Grand Rapids, MI: Eerdmans, 1994).

15. Robert Axelrod, "Presidential Election Coalitions in 1984," *American Political Science Review* 80 (1986), 281–284.

16. Albert Menendez, *Religion at the Polls* (Philadelphia: Westminster, 1977).

17. Ibid., chap. 7.

18. Phillip E. Converse, *Religion and Politics: The 1960 Elections* (Ann Arbor: University of Michigan Survey Research Center, 1961).

19. John Kenneth White and William D'Antonio, "The Catholic Vote in Election '96," *Public Perspective* (June/July 1997), 45. See also David C. Leege, "The Catholic Vote in '96: Can It Be Found in the Church?" *Commonweal* (September 27, 1996), 11–18.

20. Kevin Phillips, *The Emerging Republican Majority* (New Rochelle, NY: Arlington House, 1969).

21. The CBS News–*New York Times* exit poll had Catholics giving 52 percent of their votes to Bush, whereas the ABC News exit poll reported 51 percent for Dukakis. These results suggest the need for caution in interpreting close margins.

Though news organizations often note that their surveys should be accurate within certain confidence limits—usually plus or minus three percentage points—commentators are tempted to treat the results of surveys as hard, cold facts.

22. Green et al., "Who Elected Clinton"; White and D'Antonio, "The Catholic Vote in Election '96," 45–48.

23. White and D'Antonio, "The Catholic Vote in Election '96"; Leege, "The Catholic Vote in '96," 15.

24. Kellstedt et al., "Has Godot Finally Arrived?"

25. White and D'Antonio, "The Catholic Vote in Election '96," 46.

26. These figures are taken from the 1992 VRS Exit Poll, as reported by Everett Ladd, "The 1992 Vote for President Clinton: Another Brittle Mandate?" *Political Science Quarterly* 108 (1993), 1–28.

27. Leege, "The Catholic Vote in '96," 11.

28. David Leege, "The Decomposition of the Religious Vote: A Comparison of White, Non-Hispanic Catholics with other Ethnoreligious Groups, 1960–1992" (paper presented at the annual meeting of the American Political Science Association, Washington, DC, 1993); John C. Green, "Religion, Social Issues, and the Christian Right: Assessing the 1992 Presidential Election" (paper presented at the Ethics and Public Policy Center, Washington, DC, 1993).

29. This argument is developed in Lyman Kellstedt, John C. Green, James L. Guth, and Corwin Smidt, "It's the Culture, Stupid! 1992 and Our Political Future," *First Things* (April 1994), 28–33; and by James L. Guth, John C. Green, and Lyman A. Kellstedt, "God's Own Party: Evangelicals and Republicans in the '92 Elections," *Christian Century* (February 17, 1993), 172–176.

30. See Guth, Green, and Kellstedt, "God's Own Party"; Kellstedt et al., "It's the Culture, Stupid!"

31. For a fine overview of the voting behavior of evangelicals, see Albert J. Menendez, *Evangelicals at the Ballot Box* (New York: Prometheus, 1995).

32. Paul Lopatto, *Religion and the Presidential Election* (New York: Praeger, 1985). Lopatto concluded that Carter split the theologically conservative (or evangelical) vote with Ford, but lost among Protestants more generally. See also Albert Menendez, *Religion at the Polls* (Philadelphia: Westminster, 1977). Menendez gave the evangelical edge to Ford, but also concluded that Carter did better with evangelicals than mainline Protestants (who backed Ford by a wide margin).

33. Kellstedt et al., "Religious Voting Blocs in the 1992 Election."

34. Kellstedt et al., "Has Godot Finally Arrived?"

35. Green, "Religion, Social Issues, and the Christian Right," in Cromartie, *Disciples and Democracy.*

36. http://www.senate.gov/~ashcroft.

37. Dan Hoover, "Ashcroft Wins Poll with Appeal to 'Family Values,'" *Greenville News* (May 17, 1998), 1B.

38. Jason Zengerle, "The Gospel According to John," *New Republic* (December 22, 1997), 18–20.

39. This pattern is better illustrated by surveys from the 1992 National Election Study, Inter-university Consortium for Social and Political Research (University of Michigan), which are not reported here. These studies group Protestants by denomination, unlike the VRS.

40. Green, "Religion, Social Issues, and the Christian Right," in Cromartie, *Disciples and Democracy.* The same phenomenon characterizes Catholics as well. See Green et al., "Who Elected Clinton," 37.

41. Green et al., "Who Elected Clinton."

42. Norman Ornstein, Andrew Kohut, and Larry McCarthy, eds., *The People, Press & Politics: A Times Mirror Study of the American Electorate Conducted by the Gallup Organization* (Reading, MA: Addison-Wesley, 1988).

43. Green, "Religion, Social Issues, and the Christian Right," in Cromartie, *Disciples and Democracy.*

44. Green et al., "Who Elected Clinton."

45. Lee Sigelman, "Jews and the 1988 Election: More of the Same?" in James L. Guth and John C. Green, eds., *The Bible and the Ballot Box: Religion and Politics in the 1988 Election* (Boulder, CO: Westview Press, 1991).

46. Ibid.

47. Green et al., "Who Elected Clinton," 37.

48. Sigelman, "Jews and the 1988 Election," in Guth and Green, *The Bible and the Ballot Box,* 193.

49. In the 1992 National Election Study survey respondents are asked, "Do you consider yourself a born-again Christian?" Well over half of all African Americans responded in the affirmative.

50. Much greater detail on the religious commitment and attitudes of African Americans is provided in Hertzke, *Echoes of Discontent,* chap. 6.

51. Steven Peterson, "Church Participation and Political Participation: The Spillover Effect," *American Politics Quarterly* 20 (1992), 123–139.

52. This development is elaborated in Hertzke, *Echoes of Discontent.*

53. Most notable are Hunter, *Culture Wars*; and Robert Wuthnow, *The Struggle for America's Soul: Evangelicals, Liberals, and Secularization* (Grand Rapids, MI: Eerdmans, 1989).

54. The complexities of this value-based dimension are delineated in David C. Leege and Lyman A. Kellstedt, eds., *Rediscovering the Religious Factor in American Politics* (Armonk, NY: M. E. Sharpe, 1993).

55. See especially Kellstedt et al., "It's the Culture, Stupid!"; and Guth, Green, and Kellstedt, "God's Own Party."

Chapter 5

1. Allen D. Hertzke, "Faith and Access: Religious Constituencies and the Washington Elites," in Ted G. Jelen, ed., *Religion and Political Behavior in the United States* (New York: Praeger, 1989).

2. Charles Colson, *Kingdoms in Conflict* (Grand Rapids, MI: Zondervan, 1987).

3. Barbara Hinckley, *Problems with the Presidency: A Text with Readings* (Glenview, IL: Scott, Foresman, 1985), 29.

4. Robert Booth Fowler, *Religion and Politics in America* (Metuchen, NJ: Scarecrow Press, 1985), 113–118.

5. Ibid. See also Billy Graham, *Just As I Am: The Autobiography of Billy Graham* (New York: Walker, 1997).

6. Jimmy Carter, *Living Faith* (New York: Random House, 1996).

7. See Charles O. Jones, *The Trusteeship Presidency: Jimmy Carter and the United States Congress* (Baton Rouge: Louisiana State University Press, 1988).

8. Doug Weed, then vice-presidential aide, recounted this story to Allen D. Hertzke during an interview in June 1987.

9. This comes from a speech given by George Bush in Garrison, Ohio, December 5, 1987, as recounted in *Bushisms: President George Herbert Walker Bush, in His Own Words,* a compilation by the editors of the *New Republic* (New York: Workman Publishing, 1992).

10. The case involved a Minnesota church, which had received a tithe of $13,450 from a couple who subsequently went bankrupt. Creditors argued that the money should go to them first, and the Justice Department initially backed their claim. President Clinton, however, ordered the Justice Department to withdraw its argument. See *Report from the Capital: Newsletter of the Baptist Joint Committee* (September 20, 1994).

11. http://www.frc.org/frc/letters/march.html.

12. In January 1960, *Congressional Quarterly Weekly Report* began providing a table reflecting the religious affiliations of members of Congress.

13. John C. Green and James L. Guth, "Religion, Representatives, and Roll Calls," *Legislative Studies Quarterly* 16 (November 1991), 571–584.

14. George Gallup Jr., *The Gallup Poll: Public Opinion 1995* (Wilmington, DE: Scholarly Resources, 1996), 261.

15. Ibid.

16. John H. Fenton, *The Catholic Vote* (New Orleans, LA: Hauser Press, 1960).

17. Mary Hanna, *Catholics and American Politics* (Cambridge, MA: Harvard University Press, 1979).

18. This is confirmed by Peter L. Benson and Dorothy L. Williams, *Religion on Capitol Hill: Myths and Realities* (New York: Oxford University Press, 1982).

19. Michele Lindo, "Catholics in Congress: Keepers of the Faith?" (Senior Honors thesis, University of Oklahoma, Spring 1994).

20. Benson and Williams, *Religion on Capitol Hill.*

21. Jason Zengerle, "The Gospel According to John," *New Republic* (December 22, 1997), 20; http://www.senate.gov/~ashcroft.

22. http://www.house.gov/watts.

23. Accounts of Hall's fast may be found in Beth Spring, "The Congressman Who Can't Stomach Hunger," *Christianity Today* (June 20, 1994), 15–17; and *Bread for the World Newsletter* (June 1993). For other background on Hall, see Phil Duncan, ed., *Congressional Quarterly's Politics in America 1992* (Washington, DC: CQ Press, 1991); Michael Barone and Grant Ujifusa, *The Almanac of American Politics 1994* (Washington, DC: National Journal, 1993); Frederica Mathewes-Green, "The Hungry Congressman," *Christianity Today* (September 1, 1997), 44–49.

24. Russell Shorto, "Belief by the Numbers," *New York Times Magazine* (December 7, 1997), 61.

25. Hendrik Hertzberk, "The Narcissus Survey: An Inquiry into Whatever," *New Yorker* (January 5, 1998), 27–30.

26. For an optimistic view, see John Dart and Jimmy Allen, *Bridging the Gap: Religion and the News Media* (Nashville, TN: Freedom Forum, 1993); Mark Silk,

Unsecular Media: Making News of Religion in America (Urbana: University of Illinois Press, 1995).

27. *Sightings*, The Public Religion Project (December 6, 1997).

28. "Has Television Found Religion?" *New York Times* (November 3, 1997), AR37.

29. Shorto, "Belief by the Numbers."

30. Paul Sracic provides evidence of a modest Catholic influence on judicial decisions regarding abortion. He also cites earlier literature that demonstrates a link between Catholicism and liberal judicial behavior. See Paul Sracic, "The Gavel and the Chalice: Catholic Judges and Abortion" (Ph.D. diss., Rutgers University, 1993).

Chapter 6

1. There have been many efforts to measure "membership" in the Christian Right; no one has struggled harder with these issues than Clyde Wilcox. See Clyde Wilcox, *God's Warriors: The Christian Right in Twentieth-Century America* (Baltimore, MD: Johns Hopkins University Press, 1992).

2. James Guth, John Green, Lyman Kellstedt, and Corwin Smidt, "God's Own Party: Evangelicals and Republicans in the 1992 Election," *Christian Century* (February 17, 1993), 172–176; John Green, Lyman Kellstedt, James Guth, and Corwin Smidt, "Who Elected Clinton: A Collision of Values," *First Things* (August/September 1997), 35–40.

3. Duane M. Oldfield, "The Christian Right in Civil Rights Clothing: The Racial Rhetoric of the Christian Right" (paper presented at the annual meeting of the American Political Science Association, Washington, DC, 1997); Ceci Connolly and Dan Balz, "The Christian Coalition, Born Again," *Washington Post National Weekly Edition* (January 5, 1998), 15.

4. Several good works here include George Marsden, *Understanding Fundamentalism and Evangelicalism* (Grand Rapids, MI: Eerdmans, 1991); Ronald H. Nash, *Evangelicals in America: Who They Are, What They Believe* (Nashville, TN: Abingdon, 1987); and Bill Leonard, *God's Last and Only Hope: The Fragmentation of the Southern Baptist Convention* (Grand Rapids, MI: Eerdmans, 1990).

5. Two examples of this argument from rather contrasting perspectives are found in Allen D. Hertzke, *Echoes of Discontent: Jesse Jackson, Pat Robertson, and the Resurgence of Populism* (Washington, DC: CQ Press, 1993); and Michael Lienesch, *Redeeming America: Piety and Politics in the New Christian Right* (Chapel Hill: University of North Carolina Press, 1993).

6. We consider Wilcox, *God's Warriors*, to be the best discussion; see the Introduction and Chapter 4 on the CACC.

7. See Richard J. Neuhaus and Michael J. Cromartie, eds., *Piety and Politics: Evangelicals and Fundamentalists Confront the World* (Washington, DC: Ethics and Public Policy Center, 1987); Corwin Smidt, ed., *Contemporary Evangelical Political Involvement* (Lanham, MD: University Press of America, 1989); Robert C. Liebman and Robert Wuthnow, *The New Christian Right* (New York: Aldine, 1984); Steve Bruce, *The Rise and Fall of the New Christian Right* (New York: Oxford University Press, 1988); David G. Bromley and Anson Shupe, eds., *New*

Christian Politics (Macon, GA: Mercer University Press, 1984); Jerome Himmelstein, *To the Right: The Transformation of American Conservatism* (Berkeley: University of California Press, 1990); and Gary E. McCuen, ed., *The Religious Right* (Hudson, WI: McCuen, 1989).

8. Franky Schaeffer, *Bad News for Modern Man* (Westchester, IL: Crossway Books, 1984).

9. Classic examples include "Born Again at the Ballot Box," *Time* (April 14, 1980), 94; "Born-Again Politics," *Newsweek* (September 15, 1980), 28–36.

10. On the 1988 election campaign and results, see James L. Guth and John C. Green, eds., *The Bible and the Ballot Box: Religion and Politics in the 1988 Election* (Boulder, CO: Westview, 1991); for election data 1976–1992, see "Portrait of the Electorate," *New York Times* (November 5, 1992), B9; Hertzke, *Echoes of Discontent*. See also Robert Booth Fowler, "The Failure of the Religious Right," in Michael Cromartie, ed., *The Religious New Right in American Politics* (Washington, DC: Ethics and Public Policy Center, 1993); Kenneth D. Wald, "Ministering to the Nation: The Campaigns of Jesse Jackson and Pat Robertson," in Emmett H. Buell and Lee S. Sigleman, eds., *Nominating the President 1988* (Knoxville: University of Tennessee Press, 1992).

11. On televangelism, see Jeffrey K. Hadden, "Religious Broadcasting and the Mobilization of the New Christian Right," *Journal for the Scientific Study of Religion* 26 (March 1987), 1–24; Stewart M. Hoover, *Mass Media Religion: The Social Sources of the Electronic Church* (Newbury Park, CA: Sage Publications, 1988).

12. On Robertson and his campaign, see Hertzke, *Echoes of Discontent*; Wilcox, *God's Warriors*; David Harrell, *Pat Robertson* (San Francisco: Harper and Row, 1987); Neil Eshelin, *Pat Robertson: A Biography* (Shreveport, LA: Huntington House, 1987); Hubert Morken, *Pat Robertson: Where He Stands* (Old Tappan, NJ: Revell, 1988); and Pat Robertson, *America's Dates with Destiny* (Nashville, TN: Nelson, 1986).

13. Matthew C. Moen, *The Transformation of the Christian Right* (Tuscaloosa: University of Alabama Press, 1992), 110–116.

14. John C. Green and James L. Guth, "The Christian Right in the Republican Party: The Case of Pat Robertson's Supporters," *Journal of Politics* 50 (February 1988), 150–165.

15. A fine discussion of the history of the Christian Coalition may be found in Justin Watson, *The Christian Coalition: Dreams of Restoration, Demands for Recognition* (New York: St. Martin's, 1997).

16. http://www.cc.org.

17. "Portrait of the Electorate," *New York Times*, B9; Guth et al., "God's Own Party."

18. John F. Persinos, "Has the Christian Right Taken Over the Republican Party?" *Campaigns & Elections* (September 1994), 21–29.

19. James L. Guth, "South Carolina: The Christian Right Wins One," in Mark J. Rozell and Clyde Wilcox, eds., *God at the Grass Roots: The Christian Right in the 1994 Elections*, (Lanham, MD: Rowman and Littlefield, 1995); Nancy L. Bednar and Allen D. Hertzke, "Oklahoma: The Christian Right and Republican Realignment," in Rozell and Wilcox, *God at the Grass Roots*.

20. Connolly and Balz, "The Christian Coalition, Born Again," 15; Michael J. Gershon, "Christian Coalition in Unprecedented Crisis," *U.S. News & World Report* (February 16, 1998), 33–36.

21. http://www.cwfa.org.

22. http://www.frc.org.

23. David Von Drehle and Thomas B. Edsall, "The Religious Right Returns," *Washington Post National Weekly Edition* (August 29–September 4, 1994).

24. Melissa Deckman, "The Christian Right and School Board Elections" (paper presented at the annual meeting of the Southern Political Science Association, Norfolk, VA, 1997).

25. For example, see Robert P. Dugan Jr., *Restoring America's Values: Winning the New Civil War* (Portland, OR: Multnomah Press, 1991).

26. However, there are different opinions on that score. See, for instance, Michael Cromartie, ed., *The Religious New Right in American Politics* (Washington, DC: Ethics and Public Policy Center, 1993); and Michael D'Antonio, *Fall from Grace: The Failed Crusade of the Christian Right* (New York: Farrar, Straus, 1989).

27. Wilcox, *God's Warriors*, chap. 2, presents a good treatment of some of the views. This effort to go beyond the amassing of data to consider theoretical explanations and dimensions deserves strong praise in a field that is generally weak in terms of theoretical understanding. On this point, see Laura R. Olson and Ted G. Jelen, *The Religious Dimension of Political Behavior: A Critical Assessment and Annotated Bibliography* (Westport, CT: Greenwood, 1998). Another interesting discussion, with its own directions, but sometimes more sympathetic to traditional social science explanations applied to the entire Right, is William B. J. Hixon, *Searching for the American Right Wing: An Analysis of the Social Science Record, 1955–1987* (Princeton, NJ: Princeton University Press, 1992).

28. Kenneth D. Wald, "The Problem of Authority in the New Christian Right," in Ted G. Jelen, ed., *Religion and Political Behavior in the United States* (New York: Praeger, 1989).

29. See Hertzke, *Echoes of Discontent,* for development of this thesis.

30. Robert Booth Fowler, *Unconventional Partners: Religion and Liberal Culture in the United States* (Grand Rapids, MI: Eerdmans, 1989).

31. Christopher P. Gilbert and David A. M. Peterson, "Minnesota: Onward Quistian Soldiers? Christian Conservatives Confront Their Limitations," in Mark J. Rozell and Clyde Wilcox, eds., *God at the Grass Roots, 1996: The Christian Right in the 1996 Elections* (Lanham, MD: Rowman and Littlefield, 1997).

32. Much has been written on the question of the Religious Right and the Republicans. See Green and Guth, "The Christian Right in the Republican Party"; Lyman A. Kellstedt, "Religion and Partisan Realignment" (paper presented at the annual meeting of the Midwest Political Science Association, Chicago, 1989); Tod A. Baker, Lawrence W. Moreland, and Robert P. Steed, "Party Activists and the New Religious Right," in Charles W. Dunn, ed., *Religion in American Politics* (Washington, DC: CQ Press, 1989), 161–175.

33. The classic, controversial, and cautious thesis of liberalization may be found in James Davison Hunter, *Evangelicalism: The Coming Generation* (Chicago: University of Chicago Press, 1987).

34. For a fascinating discussion of the Christian Right's involvement in education-related matters, see Stephen Bates, *Battleground: One Mother's Crusade, the Religious Right, and the Struggle to Control Our Classrooms* (New York: Poseidon Press, 1993).

35. Some articles try unsuccessfully to do a better job. See Robert Sullivan, "An Army of the Faithful," *New York Times Magazine* (April 25, 1993), 32–35.

Chapter 7

1. See Arthur Paris, *Black Pentecostalism: Southern Religion in an Urban World* (Amherst: University of Massachusetts Press, 1982).

2. http://www.nbcusa.org.

3. "National Baptists Elect New Leader," *Christian Century* (October 12, 1994), 921.

4. Harold Bloom, *The American Religion* (New York: Simon and Schuster, 1992), chap. 5.

5. The classic work is Charles Hamilton, *The Black Preacher in America* (New York: William Morrow, 1972).

6. Laura R. Olson, *Filled with Spirit and Power: Protestant Clergy in Politics* (Albany: State University of New York Press, forthcoming).

7. Samuel G. Freedman, *Upon this Rock: The Miracle of a Black Church* (New York: HarperCollins, 1993).

8. On this discussion and the entire subject of this chapter, see the wonderfully informative C. Eric Lincoln and Lawrence Mamiya, *The Black Church in the African American Experience* (Durham, NC: Duke University Press, 1990).

9. See such works as E. Franklin Frazier, *The Negro Church in America* (New York: Schocken, 1964); and Clyde Wilcox and Leopoldo Gomez, "Religion, Group Identification, and Politics Among American Blacks," *Sociological Analysis* 51 (January 1990), 271–285.

10. Lincoln and Mamiya, *The Black Church*.

11. See J. Wendell Mapson Jr., *The Ministry of Music in the Black Church* (Valley Forge, PA: Judson, 1984).

12. James Cone, *Black Theology and Black Power* (New York: Seabury, 1969).

13. Gayraud S. Wilmore, *Black Religion and Black Radicalism*, 2d ed. (Maryknoll, NY: Orbis, 1983), chap. 8.

14. See the interesting views in Peter J. Paris, *The Social Teaching of the Black Churches* (Philadelphia: Fortress Press, 1985); James Melvin Washington, *Frustrated Fellowship: The Black Baptist Quest for Social Power* (Macon, GA: Mercer University Press, 1982).

15. Lincoln and Mamiya, *The Black Church*, chap. 2.

16. Ibid., chap. 3.

17. For this four-phase analysis, see Robert Booth Fowler, *Religion and Politics in America* (Metuchen, NJ: Scarecrow Press, 1985), chap. 12.

18. See Aldon D. Morris, *The Origins of the Civil Rights Movement* (New York: Free Press, 1984); Martin Luther King Jr., *Why We Can't Wait* (New York: Mentor, 1964); Hart M. Nelsen and Anne Kusener Nelsen, *The Black Church in the Sixties* (Lexington: University of Kentucky Press, 1975); and David J. Garrow, *Bearing the*

Cross: Martin Luther King, Jr. and the Southern Christian Leadership Conference (New York: Morrow, 1986).

19. Joseph H. Jackson, *A Story of Christian Activism: The History of the National Baptist Convention USA, Inc.* (Nashville, TN: Townsend, 1980).

20. See James H. Harris, *Black Ministers and Laity in the Urban Church* (Lanham, MD: University Press of America, 1987).

21. Allison Calhoun-Brown, "The Politics of African American Churches: The Psychological Impact of Organizational Resources," *Journal of Politics* 58 (November 1996), 935–953.

22. For example, see Adolph L. Reed Jr., *The Jesse Jackson Phenomenon* (New Haven, CT: Yale University Press, 1986).

23. Allen D. Hertzke, *Echoes of Discontent: Jesse Jackson, Pat Robertson, and the Resurgence of Populism* (Washington, DC: CQ Press, 1993), chaps. 3, 4, and 6; Charles P. Henry, *Culture and African-American Politics* (Bloomington: Indiana University Press, 1990).

24. Hertzke, *Echoes of Discontent.*

25. See Hertzke, *Echoes of Discontent,* chap. 4; and Lynda Wright, "Politics and the Pulpit: The Power of America's Black Churches," *Newsweek* (February 15, 1988), 28–31.

26. Tod A. Baker, "Exposure to Religion and Southern Distinctiveness," (paper presented at the annual meeting of the Society for the Scientific Study of Religion, Washington, DC, 1986).

27. Lincoln and Mamiya, *The Black Church*; Freedman, *Upon this Rock*; Will Norton Jr., "John Perkins," *Christianity Today* (January 1, 1982), 18–22.

28. See Gayraud Wilmore and James Cone, eds., *Black Theology: A Documentary History, 1966–1979* (Maryknoll, NY: Orbis, 1979); Lincoln and Mamiya, *The Black Church*; Fowler, *Religion and Politics in America,* chap. 12.

29. Albert B. Cleage Jr., *The Black Messiah* (New York: Sheed and Ward, 1968), 111. Also see Wilmore, *Black Religion and Black Radicalism,* chap. 8.

30. Lincoln and Mamiya, *The Black Church.*

31. The "challenge of Islam" is how one of the major studies of the black church depicts the growth of the Muslim population. See Lincoln and Mamiya, *The Black Church,* 388–391.

32. Lincoln and Mamiya, *The Black Church.*

33. For an excellent analysis of the life and times of Malcolm X, see Marshall Frady, "The Children of Malcolm," *New Yorker* (October 12, 1992). See also David Mills, "Malcolm X: The Messenger and His Message," *Washington Post Weekly Edition* (March 26–April 1, 1990).

34. An indication of how difficult it is to get a handle on small religious groups is the widely varying estimates of the black Muslim membership in the early 1960s. Frady suggests its membership was as small as 10,000; Lincoln and Mamiya suggest it was as sizable as 100,000. Even the higher figure, however, is tiny compared to the black Christian population, which numbers in the millions.

35. See Frady, "The Children of Malcolm."

36. Malcolm X, with Alex Haley, *The Autobiography of Malcolm X* (New York: Grove, 1964).

37. For an excellent look at contemporary American Muslims, see Steven Barboza, *American Jihad: Islam After Malcolm X* (New York: Doubleday, 1993).

38. Carla Power, "The New Islam," *Newsweek* (March 16, 1998), 35.

39. For an analysis of these complexities, see Don Terry, "Black Muslims Enter Islamic Mainstream," *New York Times* (May 3, 1993); Peter Steinfels, "Despite Role on World Stage, Muslims Turn to the Personal," *New York Times* (May 7, 1993), A1, A12; "Islam in America," *U.S. News & World Report* (October 8, 1990); and Ari Goldman, "Reading, Writing, Arithmetic, Arabic and Islam," *New York Times* (October 7, 1992); Heather Ann Forrest, "Maintaining the Five Pillars: In Between Classes" (Unpublished manuscript, Clemson University, 1997).

40. Don Terry, "Minister Farrakhan: Conservative Militant," *New York Times* (March 3, 1994).

41. Shrona Foreman, "Muslims' Tentative Electoral Venture," *National Journal* (September 1, 1990).

Chapter 8

1. Some standard sources for information on women and religion are Robert Bezilla, ed., *Religion in America: 1992–1993* (Princeton, NJ: Princeton Religion Research Center, 1993); Jim Castelli and Joseph Germillion, *The Emerging Parish: The Notre Dame Study of Catholic Life Since Vatican II* (San Francisco: Harper, 1987); George Gallup Jr. and Jim Castelli, *The People's Religion: American Faith in the 90's* (New York: Macmillan, 1989); George Gallup Jr. and Jim Castelli, *The American Catholic People: Their Beliefs, Practices, and Values* (Garden City, NY: Doubleday, 1987).

2. The best discussion is in C. Eric Lincoln and Lawrence H. Mamiya, *The Black Church in the African American Experience* (Durham, NC: Duke University Press, 1990), chap. 10; a wonderful approach from another direction is Samuel G. Freedman, *Upon This Rock: The Miracles of a Black Church* (New York: HarperCollins, 1993).

3. Ruth Wallace, *They Call Her Pastor: A New Role for Catholic Women* (Albany: State University of New York Press, 1992).

4. George Gallup Jr., *The Gallup Poll: Public Opinion 1996* (Wilmington, DE: Scholarly Resources, 1997), 261.

5. Optimists will enjoy Charles E. Silberman, *A Certain People: American Jews and Their Lives Today* (New York: Summit, 1985).

6. Lynn Davidman, *Tradition in a Rootless World: Women Turn to Orthodox Judaism* (Berkeley: University of California Press, 1991).

7. Voter Research Survey and Exit Poll, 1996.

8. http://www.cwfa.org.

9. Beverly LaHaye, *I Am a Woman by God's Design* (Old Tappan, NJ: Revell, 1980).

10. http://www.cwfa.org.

11. For some data on Concerned Women for America, see Lyman Kellstedt, "Religious Interest Groups and Political Behavior," *Evangelical Studies Bulletin* (Fall 1991); for one of Schlafly's most explicit statements, see Phyllis Schlafly, *The Power of the Christian Woman* (Cincinnati, OH: Standard, 1981).

12. Allen D. Hertzke, *Echoes of Discontent: Jesse Jackson, Pat Robertson, and the Resurgence of Populism* (Washington, DC: CQ Press, 1993), 143, 217–219.

13. Stephen Bates, *Battleground: One Mother's Crusade, the Religious Right, and the Struggle for Control of Our Classrooms* (New York: Poseidon Press, 1993).

14. Kay Coles James, with Jacqueline Cobb Fuller, *Never Forget: The Riveting Story of One Woman's Journey from Public Housing to the Corridors of Power* (Grand Rapids, MI: Zondervan, 1992).

15. http://www.cath4choice.org.

16. Barbara Brown Zikmund, "Women's Organizations: Centers of Denominational Loyalty and Expressions of Christian Unity," in Jackson Carroll and Wade Clark Roof, eds., *Beyond Establishment: Protestant Identity in a Post-Protestant Age* (Louisville, KY: Westminster, 1993).

17. Rosemary Radford Ruether, *Gaia and God: An Ecofeminist Theology of Earth Healing* (San Francisco: HarperCollins, 1992); Peter Steinfels, "Catholic Feminists Ask, Can We Remain Catholic?" *New York Times* (April 16, 1993), A9.

18. The classic is Mary Daly, *Beyond God the Father: Toward a Philosophy of Women's Liberation* (Boston: Beacon, 1973); also see Beverly Wildung Harrison, "The Power of Anger in the World of Love," in Ann Loades, ed., *Feminist Theology* (Louisville, KY: Westminster, 1990), 194–213; and Letty M. Russell, "Good Housekeeping," in Loades, *Feminist Theology*, 225–238.

19. For example, see Elaine Pagels, *Adam, Eve, and the Serpent* (New York: Random House, 1988). Also, exploration of many of the essays in Ann Loades, ed., *Feminist Theology*, is a good way to get an idea of the diversity of feminist theology and of where one might want to go to pursue it; also see Sallie McFague, *Models of God: Theology for an Ecological, Nuclear Age* (Philadelphia: Fortress, 1987).

20. Anne E. Carr, *Transforming Grace: Christian Tradition and Women's Experience* (New York: Continuum, 1996).

21. McFague, *Models of God*.

22. Donna Streichen, *Ungodly Rage: The Hidden Face of Catholic Feminism* (San Francisco: Ignatius Press, 1991).

23. http://www.chrbibeq.org.

24. Marabel Morgan, *The Total Woman* (New York: Pocket Books, 1975).

25. For a fascinating series of essays on women and fundamentalism in comparative perspective, see John Stratton Hawley, ed., *Fundamentalism and Gender* (New York: Oxford University Press, 1994).

26. For a lengthy series of affirmations of traditional views, see John Piper and Wayne Grunden, eds., *Recovering Biblical Manhood and Womanhood: A Response to Evangelical Feminism* (Wheaton, IL: Crossway, 1992); and Rebecca E. Klatch, *Women of the New Right* (Philadelphia: Temple University Press, 1987); for her views in her reformist phase, see Virginia Ramey Mollenkott, *Women, Men and the Bible* (Nashville, TN: Abington, 1977); also see the excellent discussion of the situation in Debbie Bendel, "Conservative Evangelical Feminism: The Debate Within the Evangelical Community" (unpublished paper, 1992); and Gretchen Gaebelein Hull, *Call to Serve* (Old Tappan, NJ: Revell, 1993).

27. See Silberman, *A Certain People*; and Davidman, *Tradition in a Rootless World*.

28. Daly, *Beyond God the Father*, is a good place to start.

29. Some relevant works, supportive, ambivalent, and hostile: Carol Christ, *Laughter of Aphrodite: Reflections on a Journey to the Goddess* (San Francisco: Harper, 1987); Susanne Heine, *Matriarchs, Goddesses and Images of God* (Minneapolis: Augsburg, 1988); Janet Biehl, *Rethinking Ecofeminist Politics* (Boston: South End Press, 1991); Mary A. Kassian, *The Feminist Gospel: The Movement to Unite Feminism with the Church* (New York: Crossway, 1992); Ruether, *Gaia and God*; and Wade Clark Roof, *A Generation of Seekers: The Spiritual Journeys of the Baby Boom Generation* (San Francisco: Harper, 1993), 142–143.

30. For example, see Rosemary Radford Ruether, *Sexism and God-Talk: Toward a Feminist Theology* (Boston: Beacon, 1983).

31. On witchcraft religion, two essential sources are Margot Adler, *Drawing Down the Moon: Witches, Druids, Goddess-Worshippers, and Other Pagans in America* (Boston: Beacon, 1981); Starhawk, *Truth or Dare: Encounters with Power, Authority, and Mystery* (San Francisco: Harper, 1990).

32. See Charlene Spretnak, *The Politics of Women's Spirituality: Essays on the Rise of Spiritual Power Within the Feminist Movement* (Garden City, NY: Doubleday, 1982); Ruether, *Gaia and God*.

33. Some key sources include Judith Plant, ed., *Healing the Words: The Promise of Eco-feminism* (Philadelphia: New Society, 1989); Carol Merchant, *The Death of Nature* (San Francisco: Harper, 1980); and Irene Diamond and Gloria Feman Orenstein, eds., *Reweaving the World: The Emergence of Ecofeminism* (San Francisco: Sierra Club, 1990).

34. See such critics as Biehl, *Rethinking Ecofeminist Politics*; Kassian, *The Feminist Gospel*; Heine, *Matriarchs, Goddesses and Images of God*.

35. Roof, *A Generation of Seekers*, 222–223.

36. Ibid., 112–133.

37. Gallup and Castelli, *The American Catholic People*; Roof, *A Generation of Seekers*, 231–232.

38. Jane Redmont, *Generous Lives: American Catholic Women Today* (New York: William Morrow, 1992). Redmont's personal views are hardly kept a secret in this work, but whether one agrees with her or not, it is a revealing and reflective study.

39. For an example of this controversial argument, see Leon J. Podles, "Men Not Wanted: A Controversial Protest Against the Feminization of the Church," *Crisis* (November 1991), 16–20.

40. Kristin Luker, *Abortion and the Politics of Motherhood* (Berkeley: University of California Press, 1984).

41. See here the elaborate study by Elizabeth Adell Cook, Ted. G. Jelen, and Clyde Wilcox, *Between Two Absolutes: Public Opinion and the Politics of Abortion* (Boulder, CO: Westview, 1992), chap. 7.

42. Faye D. Ginsburg, *Contested Lives: The Abortion Debate in an American Community* (Berkeley: University of California Press, 1989).

43. "What Voters Said Election Day," *Public Perspective* (January/February 1993), 103.

Chapter 9

1. Lucian Niemeyer and Donald Kraybill, *Old Order Amish: The Enduring Way of Life* (Baltimore, MD: Johns Hopkins University Press, 1993); William Kephart and William Zellner, *Extraordinary Groups*, 5th ed. (New York: St. Martin's, 1994).

2. See Jack Wertheimer, *A People Divided* (New York: Basic Books, 1993); Samuel C. Heilman and Steven M. Cohen, *Cosmopolitans and Parochials: Modern Orthodox Jews in America* (Chicago: University of Chicago Press, 1989); Kephart and Zellner, *Extraordinary Groups*. See also Samuel C. Heilman and Menachem Friedman, "Religious Fundamentalism and Religious Jews," in Martin Marty and R. Scott Appleby, eds., *Fundamentalism Observed* (Chicago: University of Chicago Press, 1991), 197–264; Robert Eisenberg, *Boychicks in the Hood: Travels in the Hasidic Underground* (San Francisco: HarperCollins, 1995).

3. Lawrence E. Sullivan, ed., *Native American Religions: North America* (New York: Macmillan, 1987).

4. *The World Almanac and Book of Facts* (Mahwah, NJ: K-III Communications, 1997), 651.

5. On cults and topics in the discussion that follows, see Robert Booth Fowler, *The Dance with Community* (Lawrence: University Press of Kansas, 1992), 147–153; "Cultic America: A Tower of Babel," *Newsweek* (March 15, 1993), 60–61; David G. Bromley and Anson Shupe, *Strange Gods: The Great American Cult Scare* (Boston: Beacon, 1981), chap. 2; Willa Appel, *Cults in America: Programmed for Paradise* (New York: Holt, Rinehart and Winston, 1983); Ronald Enroth, ed., *A Guide to Cults and New Religions* (Downers Grove, IL: InterVarsity, 1983); Anthony Hoekema, *The Four Major Cults* (Grand Rapids, MI: Eerdmans, 1963); Walter Martin, *The Kingdom of the Cults* (Minneapolis, MN: Bethany, 1985); and J. Gordon Melton and Robert L. Moore, *The Cult Experience: Responding to the New Religious Pluralism* (New York: Pilgrim, 1982).

6. Evan Thomas, "The Next Level," *Newsweek* (April 7, 1997), 28–35.

7. "The Messiah of Waco," *Newsweek* (March 15, 1993), 56–58; David Gelman, "From Prophets to Losses," *Newsweek* (March 15, 1993), 62; "Adventists Disavow Waco Cult," *Christian Century* (March 17, 1993), 285–286.

8. The Christian Identity movement is monitored closely by the Southern Poverty Law Center. See *False Patriots: The Threat of Antigovernment Extremists* (Montgomery, AL: Southern Poverty Law Center, 1996); http://www. splcenter. org/klanwatch/identity.html.

9. On the Unification Church, see Irving Louis Horowitz, ed., *Science, Sin and Scholarship: The Politics of Rev. Moon and the Unification Church* (Cambridge, MA: MIT Press, 1978); Eileen Barker, *The Making of a Moonie: Choice or Brainwashing* (New York: Basil Blackwell, 1984).

10. Carla Power, "The New Islam," *Newsweek* (March 16, 1998), 35.

11. For a straightforward introduction to Islam, see Edward Mortimer, *Faith and Power: The Politics of Islam* (New York: Random House, 1982); on Muslims in America, Yvonne Yazbeck Haddad and Adair T. Lummis, *Islamic Values in the United States: A Comparative Study* (New York: Oxford University Press, 1987); Yvonne Yazbeck Haddad, *The Muslims in America* (New York: Oxford University

Press, 1991); Yvonne Yazbeck Haddad and Jane I. Smith, eds., *Muslim Communities in North America* (Albany: State University of New York Press, 1994); Steven Barboza, *American Jihad: Islam After Malcolm X* (New York: Doubleday, 1993); Don Terry, "Black Muslims Enter Islamic Mainstream," *New York Times* (May 3, 1993), A1, A9; Richard Bernstein, "A Growing Islamic Presence: Balancing Sacred and Secular," *New York Times* (May 2, 1993), 1, 14–15; Ari Goldman, "Mosque's New Era: Growth and Good Will," *New York Times* (May 4, 1993), A1, A12; Peter Steinfels, "Despite World Stage, Muslims Turn to the Personal," *New York Times* (May 7, 1993), 1, A13; Michael Rezendes, "Wary Times for Muslims in America," *Wisconsin State Journal* (July 1, 1993), 1A; Geraldine Brooks, "What Does the Koran Say About Nasreen's Nose Ring?" *New York Times Magazine* (December 7, 1997), 76–79; Power, "The New Islam."

12. But see Brooks, "What Does the Koran Say?"

13. Power, "The New Islam," 37.

14. Power, "The New Islam"; see also Brooks, "What Does the Koran Say?"

15. Power, "The New Islam."

16. On the New Age movement, see *New Age* magazine for a sense of the rich diversity; for more skeptical views, see Otto Friedrich, "New Age Harmonies," *Time* (December 7, 1987); Douglas R. Groothuis, *Unmasking the New Age* (Downers Grove, IL: InterVarsity, 1986).

17. For a serious and informed discussion of the religion(s) of the generation of the 1960s and 1970s, see Wade Clark Roof, *A Generation of Seekers: The Spiritual Journeys of the Baby Boom Generation* (San Francisco: Harper, 1993).

18. George Gallup Jr., *The Gallup Poll: Public Opinion 1995* (Wilmington, DE: Scholarly Resources, 1996), 261.

19. To begin an exploration of nonmainstream religions, we recommend Kephart and Zellner, *Extraordinary Groups*; and Catherine L. Albanese, *America, Religions and Religion*, 2d ed. (Belmont, CA: Wadsworth, 1992).

20. George Gallup Jr. and Jim Castelli, *The People's Religion* (New York: Macmillan, 1989), 114–116.

21. John Green, Lyman Kellstedt, James Guth, and Corwin Smidt, "Who Elected Clinton: A Collision of Values," *First Things* (August/September, 1997), 37.

22. The story is told in Matthew Glass, *Citizens Against the MX: Public Languages in the Nuclear Age* (Champaign: University of Illinois Press, 1993).

23. On the Jehovah's Witnesses, see James A. Beckford, *The Triumph of Prophecy* (Oxford: Basil Blackwell, 1975); Robert M. Anderson, *Vision of the Disinherited* (New York: Oxford University Press, 1979); Martin, *The Kingdom of the Cults*, chap. 4; Kephart and Zellner, *Extraordinary Groups*, chap. 8.

Chapter 10

1. The doctrine of incorporation traces its roots to the Supreme Court's decision in *Chicago, Burlington, & Quincy Railroad Company* v. *Chicago* 166 US 226 (1897).

2. *Cantwell* v. *Connecticut* 310 US 296 (1940).

3. See Kenneth Wald's thoughtful analysis of this process in *Religion and Politics in the United States*, 3d ed. (Washington, DC: CQ Press, 1997), 105–107.

4. In the realm of strategy, we recommend Lee Epstein's book, *Conservatives in Court* (Knoxville: University of Tennessee, 1985). The particular groups and cases discussed there are not always relevant now, but the strategic discussions have, if anything, been strengthened by subsequent developments.

5. Matthew C. Moen, *The Transformation of the Christian Right* (Tuscaloosa: University of Alabama Press, 1992).

6. Wade Clark Roof and William McKinney, *American Mainline Religion: Its Changing Shape and Future* (New Brunswick, NJ: Rutgers University Press, 1987).

7. For an interesting separationist interpretation of the founding, see Isaac Kramnick and R. Laurence Moore, *The Godless Constitution: The Case Against Religious Correctness* (New York: Norton, 1996).

8. Roger Williams, "Mr. Cotton's Letter Lately Printed, Examined and Answered," in John E. Semonche, ed., *Religion and Constitutional Government in the United States* (Carrboro, NC: Signal Books, 1985), 77.

9. On this topic, see Gregg Ivers, *To Build a Wall: American Jews and the Separation of Church and State* (Charlottesville: University of Virginia Press, 1995).

10. http://www.atheists.org/home.html.

11. http://www.infidels.org/org/ffrf.

12. For an interesting discussion of atheist groups in America, see Marshall Sella, "Godless and Proud of It," *New York Times Magazine* (December 7, 1997), 103–108.

13. Hubert Morken, "The Evangelical Legal Response to the ACLU: Religion, Politics, and the First Amendment" (paper presented at the annual meeting of the American Political Science Association, Chicago, 1992).

14. http://www.nccbuscc.org/ogc.

15. George Gallup Jr., *The Gallup Poll: Public Opinion 1995* (Wilmington, DE: Scholarly Resources, 1996), 261.

16. One interesting typology of positions is presented by Thomas Robbins, "A Typology of American Orientations Toward Church-State Tensions" (paper presented at the annual meeting of Society for the Scientific Study of Religion, Washington, DC, 1986). For a discussion of public opinion regarding these matters, see Ted G. Jelen and Clyde Wilcox, *Public Attitudes Toward Church and State* (Armonk, NY: M. E. Sharpe, 1995).

17. Perhaps the leading writer in support of separationism has been Leo Pfeffer. See Leo Pfeffer, *Religion, State, and the Burger Court* (Buffalo, NY: Prometheus, 1984). On multiple establishment in colonial America, see Leonard Levy, *The Establishment Clause: Religion and the First Amendment* (New York: Macmillan, 1986).

18. Two interesting books on the founding period are Levy, *The Establishment Clause*; and William L. Miller, *The First Liberty and the American Republic* (New York: Knopf, 1986).

19. *The Williamsburg Charter Survey on Religion and Public Life* (Washington, DC: Williamsburg Charter Foundation, 1988).

20. One of the most able and determined neutralist views may be found in Paul J. Weber, *Equal Separation: Understanding the Religious Clauses of the First Amendment* (Westport, CT: Greenwood, 1990).

21. For approaches somewhat sympathetic to "benevolent neutrality," see A. James Reichley, *Religion in American Public Life* (Washington, DC: Brookings Institution, 1985), chap. 3; and Robert T. Miller and Ronald B. Flowers, eds., *Toward Benevolent Neutrality: Church, State, and the Supreme Court* (Waco, TX: Baylor University Press, 1987).

22. For an excellent collection of essays arguing several sides of the equal treatment approach, see Stephen V. Monsma and J. Christopher Soper, *Equal Treatment of Religion in a Pluralistic Society* (Grand Rapids, MI: Eerdmans, 1997).

23. 1 Statute 50, 52, Article III.

24. On the historical record, four interesting discussions are Robert L. Cord, *Separation of Church and State: Historical Fact and Current Fiction* (New York: Lambeth, 1982); Thomas J. Curry, *The First Freedoms* (New York: Oxford University Press, 1986); Reichley, *Religion in American Public Life*, chap. 4; and Michael Malbin, *Religion and Politics: The Intentions of the Authors of the First Amendment* (Washington, DC: American Enterprise Institute, 1978).

25. See Robert Booth Fowler, "A Postmodern Defense of Government Aid to Religious Schools," in Jo Renee Formicola and Hubert Morken, eds., *Everson Revisited: Religion, Education, and Law at the Crossroads* (Lanham, MD: Rowman and Littlefield, 1997).

Chapter 11

1. See, for example, Robert L. Cord, *Historical Fiction and Current Fact* (New York: Lambeth, 1982); Thomas J. Curry, *The First Freedoms* (New York: Oxford University Press, 1986); William L. Miller, *The First Liberty and the American Republic* (New York: Knopf, 1986); and Michael Malbin, *Religion and Politics: The Intentions of the Authors of the First Amendment* (Washington, DC: American Enterprise Institute, 1978).

2. See, for example, *Watson v. Jones* 80 US 679 (1871); and *Jones v. Wolf* 443 US 595 (1979).

3. *United States v. Ballard* 322 US 78 (1944).

4. We draw much of the following discussion on clergy malpractice from Margaret P. Battin, *Ethics in the Sanctuary: Examining the Practices of Organized Religion* (New Haven, CT: Yale University Press, 1990). Though not very sympathetic to organized religion outside of mainline Protestantism, this challenging book is very interesting.

5. See *Airport Commissioners v. Jews for Jesus* 482 US 569 (1987).

6. See *Larsen v. Valente* 456 US 228 (1982).

7. See *McDaniel v. Paty* 435 US 618 (1978); *Catholic Conference v. Abortion Rights Mobilization* 487 US 72 (1988).

8. See *Cruz v. Beto* 405 US 319 (1972); and *O'Lone v. Estate of Shabazz* 482 US 342 (1987).

9. *Braunfeld v. Brown* 366 US 599 (1961). Also see *Jacobson v. Massachusetts* 197 US 11 (1905); *Prince v. Massachusetts* 321 US 158 (1944).

10. *Sherbert v. Verner* 374 US 398 (1963).

11. A thoughtful discussion of this point may be found in National Council of Churches, Dean M. Kelley, ed., *Government Intervention in Religious Affairs* (New York: Pilgrim, 1982).

12. For extensive analysis of the *Boerne* case and its implications, see "Does Religious Freedom Have a Future? The First Amendment After *Boerne*," *Journal of the Chapman Law School* 2 (Fall 1997).

13. Peter Baker, "Workplace Religion Policy Due," *The Washington Post* (August 14, 1997), 1A.

14. On the matter of excessive entanglement, also see *Walz* v. *Tax Commission* 397 US 664 (1970).

15. Justice Scalia made this comment in his opinion in *Lamb's Chapel* v. *Center Moriches Union Free School District* 508 US 385 (1993).

16. *Wallace* v. *Jaffree* 105 S. Ct. 2479 (1985).

17. Jeffrey Rosen, "Lemon Law," *New Republic* (March 29, 1993), 17.

18. Daniel Bice and Richard P. Jones, "Religious Schools Open for up to 15,000 Pupils," *Milwaukee Journal Sentinel* (June 11, 1998), 1A.

19. http://www.1stpriority.org. Also see: on Young Life, http:// falcon.cc.ukans. edu/~bvolk; on Fellowship of Christian Athletes, http://www.fca.org; on Youth for Christ, http://www.gospelcom.net/yfc; on Student Venture, http://www.student-venture.com.

20. "Educator Scorned Over Prayer Case," *Daily Oklahoman* (November 8, 1997), 15.

21. Margaret Battin first got us to take this subject seriously.

22. Katharine Q. Seelye, "House Rejects School Prayer Amendment to Constitution," *New York Times* (June 5, 1998), A13. Also see http://www.house.gov/istook; http://religiousfreedom.house.gov.

Chapter 12

1. James L. Guth, John C. Green, Corwin E. Smidt, Lyman A. Kellstedt, and Margaret M. Poloma, *The Bully Pulpit: The Politics of Protestant Clergy* (Lawrence: University Press of Kansas, 1997).

2. Robert Wuthnow, *The Restructuring of American Religion: Society and Faith Since World War Two* (Princeton, NJ: Princeton University Press, 1988).

3. James Davison Hunter, *Culture Wars: The Struggle to Define America* (New York: Basic Books, 1991); James Davison Hunter, *Before the Shooting Begins: Searching for Democracy in America's Culture War* (New York: Free Press, 1994).

4. Robert Wuthnow, "Divided We Fall: America's Two Civil Religions," *Christian Century* (April 20, 1988), 395–399.

5. For a general discussion of secularization theory, see Steve Bruce, *Religion and Modernization* (New York: Oxford University Press, 1992).

6. See Karl Marx's "Economic and Philosophic Manuscripts," "Critique of Hegel's Philosophy of Right," and "Critique of the Gotha Program," in Robert C. Tucker, *The Marx-Engels Readers*, 2d ed. (New York: Norton, 1978); Max Weber, *The Protestant Ethic and the Spirit of Capitalism* (New York: Scribner's, 1958); Sigmund Freud, *The Future of an Illusion* (Garden City, NY: Doubleday, 1964).

7. For example, see Samuel P. Huntington Jr., "The Coming Clash of Civilizations," *New York Times* (June 6, 1993), 19.

8. Richard John Neuhaus, *The Naked Public Square: Religion and Democracy in America* (Grand Rapids, MI: Eerdmans, 1984).

9. Stephen Carter, *The Culture of Disbelief: How American Law and Politics Trivialize Religious Devotion* (New York: Basic Books, 1993).

10. The major source here is Robert Lichter, Stanley Rothman, and Linda Lichter, *The Media Elite* (Bethesda, MD: Adler and Adler, 1986). Eighty-six percent of elite journalists say they seldom or never go to church, and half listed their religion as "none." A number of other studies have corroborated their finding that top journalists are highly secular compared to the population as a whole.

11. A description of the nature of religion among members of Congress is found in Peter L. Benson and Dorothy L. Williams, *Religion on Capitol Hill: Myths and Realities* (New York: Oxford University Press, 1982).

12. For an example, consider the effective journalism of Richard John Neuhaus, *First Things* senior editor.

13. David Yamane, "Secularization on Trial: In Defense of a Neosecularization Paradigm," *Journal for the Scientific Study of Religion* 36 (January 1997), 109–122.

14. For an interesting new analysis of postmaterialism, see Geoffrey C. Layman and Edward G. Carmines, "Cultural Conflict in American Politics: Religious Traditionalism, Postmaterialism, and U.S. Political Behavior," *Journal of Politics* 59 (August 1997), 751–777.

15. Ronald Inglehart, *Culture Shift in Advanced Industrial Society* (Princeton, NJ: Princeton University Press, 1990).

16. Wade Clark Roof, *A Generation of Seekers: The Spiritual Journeys of the Baby Boom Generation* (San Francisco: Harper, 1993).

17. Phillip Hammond, *Religion and Personal Autonomy: The Third Disestablishment* (Columbia: University of South Carolina Press, 1992).

18. Donald E. Miller, *Reinventing Protestantism: Christianity in the New Millennium* (Berkeley: University of California Press, 1997).

19. Robert Bellah, "Civil Religion in America," in Russell Richey and Donald Jones, eds., *American Civil Religion* (New York: Harper and Row, 1974), 21–44.

20. Laura R. Olson, "Bill Clinton's Strategic Use of Religious and Family Rhetoric: The Co-Optation of Partisan Symbolism" (paper presented at the annual meeting of the Midwest Political Science Association, Chicago, 1997).

21. Sidney Mead, *The Lively Experiment* (New York: Harper and Row, 1975).

22. Clinton L. Rossiter, *The American Presidency*, rev. ed. (Baltimore, MD: Johns Hopkins University Press, 1960), 102.

23. For example, see John Wilson, *Public Religion in American Culture* (Philadelphia: Temple University Press, 1979).

24. For this thesis, see Robert Booth Fowler, *Unconventional Partners: Religion and Liberal Culture in the United States* (Grand Rapids, MI: Eerdmans, 1989).

25. Alexis de Tocqueville, *Democracy in America* (New York: Mentor, 1956).

26. Allen D. Hertzke, *Echoes of Discontent: Jesse Jackson, Pat Robertson, and the Resurgence of Populism* (Washington, DC: CQ Press, 1993).

27. Ibid.

28. For a good introduction to the market approach, see Roger Finke and Rodney Stark, *The Churching of America, 1776–1990: Winners and Losers in Our Religious Economy* (New Brunswick, NJ: Rutgers University Press, 1992); Lawrence A. Young, ed., *Rational Choice Theory and Religion: Summary and Assessment* (New York: Routledge, 1997).

Index

religious affiliation of members of
  Congress, 123
Southern electorate, 89
Revolutionary War, Great Awakening
  and, 17–18
Ritualists, 88–89
Rituals, in civil religion, 259
Roberts, Oral, 144
Robertson, Pat, 39, 40, 153(box)
  American Center for Law and Justice
    and, 216
  Christian Coalition and, 81
  evangelicals and, 102–103
  Jews and, 76, 110
  moral zeal and, 8
  populism and, 263–264
  presidential campaign, 143, 144–145
  Ralph Reed and, 147(box)
  Southern Baptists and, 278(n1)
  women's support and, 179
Robison, James, 143
Roemer v. *Board of Public Works,*
  246
Roe v. *Wade,* 212, 230
Roman Catholics/Roman Catholic
  Church
  in America, growth of, 213
  Anti-Saloon League and, 22
  attendance figures, 106
  cardinals in, political advocacy of,
    48(box)
  Clinton administration and, 122
  conservative-liberal split and, 50
  culture wars thesis and, 250–251
  democracy and, 45, 46
  diversity within, 34
  educational system of, 33
  evangelicalism and, 16–17
  on feminist theology, 183–184
  "feminization" of, 189
  George Bush and, 120
  health-care policy and, 70(box)
  hierarchy in, 44–45
  immigration and, 13
  Kennedy administration and,
    116–117
  legal groups, 216

median household income in,
  51(box)
membership statistics, 34, 35(box),
  36(table)
members of Congress in, 123,
  124(table), 126–127
percent of electorate, 92
percent of general population,
  273(n40)
pluralism within, 44, 45
political groups, 55, 59, 60, 69–75
politics and, 44, 45, 46, 48(box), 62
Protestant culture and, 44
socioeconomic levels of, 47
Supreme Court members and, 134
Vatican II and, 45–46
vitality, loss of, 46–47
voting behavior, 88, 92–99, 190–191
on women's issues, 74–75
See also Catholic-Protestant split;
  Women, Roman Catholic
Roof, Wade Clark, 257, 258
Roosevelt, Franklin D., 89, 90–91,
  101, 210
Roosevelt, Theodore, 89
Rosenberger v. *Rector,* 248
Ruether, Rosemary Radford, 70, 181,
  186
Russell, Howard Hyde, 21
Rutherford, Samuel, 217(box)
Rutherford Institute, 80, 216, 217(box)

Sacred texts, of civil religion, 259. *See
  also* Scripture
Samaritan Project, 38–39, 140
Sandinista government, 73
Santeria religion, 237
Save the Churches Fund, 39, 140
Scalia, Antonin, 61, 134, 241
Schachter, R. Zalman, 49
Schaeffer, Franky, 142
Schlafly, Phyllis, 38, 143, 179
School prayer, 58, 216, 242
Schools. *See* Parochial schools; Public
  schools; Religious schools
Scopes, John, 243
Scopes trial, 243

Am 8/25 – mw
28